I0880012

OCCUPYING OUR SPACE

Occupying Our Space

The Mestiza Rhetorics of Mexican Women Journalists and Activists, 1875–1942

CRISTINA DEVEREAUX RAMÍREZ

Foreword by
JACQUELINE JONES ROYSTER

Translations by
JOEL BOLLINGER POUWELS *and*
NEIL J. DEVEREAUX

THE UNIVERSITY OF
ARIZONA PRESS
TUCSON

The University of Arizona Press
www.uapress.arizona.edu

We respectfully acknowledge the University of Arizona is on the land and territories of Indigenous peoples. Today, Arizona is home to twenty-two federally recognized tribes, with Tucson being home to the O'odham and the Yaqui. Committed to diversity and inclusion, the University strives to build sustainable relationships with sovereign Native Nations and Indigenous communities through education offerings, partnerships, and community service.

First paperback edition 2023

ISBN-13: 978-0-8165-3074-8 (cloth)
ISBN-13: 978-0-8165-5032-6 (paper)

Jacket designed by Nicole Hayward
Jacket and interior images courtesy of Biblioteca Pública Central Esatal José Ignacio Gallegos Caballero in Durango, Durango, Mexico

Publication of this book is made possible in part by the proceeds of a permanent endowment created with the assistance of a Challenge Grant from the National Endowment for the Humanities, a federal agency.

Library of Congress Cataloging-in-Publication Data are available from the Library of Congress

Printed in the United States of America
⊗ This paper meets the requirements of ANSI/NISO Z39.48-1992 (Permanence of Paper).

Contents

List of Illustrations ... vii

Foreword by Jacqueline Jones Royster ... ix

Acknowledgments ... xiii

Introduction—A Feminist Recovery Project: Mexican Women Journalists and Activists at the Forefront of Change ... 3

Chapter 1. Historical and Theoretical Directions in Mestiza Rhetoric ... 33

Chapter 2. Las Hijas del Anáhuac: Laureana Wright de Kleinhans and Other Pioneering Women in Journalism in the Late Nineteenth Century ... 59

INTERLUDE
Saludo y prospecto / Greetings and Prospectus by Laureana Wright de Kleinhans, 1887 ... 89

Chapter 3. "Hear Us!": The Feminist Protests of Las Mujeres de Zitácuaro ... 94

INTERLUDE
Propaganda liberal, Manifiesto / Liberal Propaganda, Manifesto by Las Mujeres de Zitácuaro, 1900 ... 121

Chapter 4. *Rompiendo barreras*: Juana Belén Gutiérrez de Mendoza's Revolutionary Rhetoric ... 132

INTERLUDE
Vésper *siempre ocupará su puesto* / *Vésper* Will Always Occupy Its Space by Juana B. Gutiérrez de Mendoza, 1910 ... 161

Chapter 5. *Mi grano de arena en esa hermosa labor*: Hermila Galindo's Feminationalist Rhetoric 165

INTERLUDE
A la mujer latinoamericana / To the Latin American Woman by Hermila Galindo, 1919 194

Epilogue 204

Notes 213

Bibliography 237

Index 247

Illustrations

Figure 1. An inside page banner of Hermila Galindo's newspaper, *La Mujer Moderna*. 5

Figure 2. Image of Laureana Wright de Kleinhans as it appeared in the 1910 publication of her book *Mujeres notables mexicanas*. 61

Figure 3. Masthead of the independent newspaper *La Bandera Roja*. It first appeared in 1896. 95

Figure 4. The manifesto of women's rights by Las Mujeres de Zitácuaro appeared in the December 7, 1900, edition of *La Bandera Roja*. 122

Figure 5. Masthead of Hermila Galindo's newspaper, *La Mujer Moderna*. 166

Figure 6. October 31, 1915, edition of *La Mujer Moderna*, with female poet Julia D. Febles Cantón vda. de Palomeque on the cover. 176

Foreword

In *Feminist Rhetorical Practices: New Directions in Rhetoric, Composition, and Literacy* (2012), Gesa E. Kirsch and I recognized the increasing numbers of research projects in feminist rhetorical studies that: (1) rescue, recover, and reinscribe histories of rhetorical practice aimed at broadening and deepening our sense of who *rhetors* are; what their contexts, imperatives, and purposes for participation are; and what the impacts and consequences of their rhetorical acts have been; and (2) critique and reconstrue the paradigms by which we envision rhetoric as a human enterprise and articulate measures of excellence. In this volume, *Occupying Our Space: The Mestiza Rhetorics of Mexican Women Journalists and Activists, 1875–1942*, Cristina Devereaux Ramírez demonstrates that she is part of this cohort of scholars by presenting to us a coherent, well-documented, and quite persuasive accounting of a group of rhetors with whom most of us are unfamiliar.

Ramírez brings to scholarly attention the voices of Mexican women who were active from 1875 to 1942, focusing on their participation in the forging of Mexican nationhood and the establishing of woman's "place" in Mexican national discourses. She interrogates what the women had to say and how they constructed spaces for declaring their rightful presence as intellectual beings in the public sphere. She considers the ways in which the women formed a sense of agency, identity, and authority, while noting the different ideological frameworks that they used to do so. She looks closely at the contexts and conditions of their rhetorical activity and draws attention to three genres especially (the plan, *grito*, and manifesto) that they chose to convey their ideas. Most of all, case by case, she tells the stories of these women's lives and work and brings to bolder relief the times and geopolitical particularities of the eras in which they were living. We see a nation in motion and a variously defined segment of the population who perceive themselves as thoroughly vested in these revolutionary/evolutionary processes. In other words, Ramírez offers us a bird's-eye view—through the lenses of these women—of social and political change in the making.

I appreciate particularly two aspects of Ramírez's volume that I find to be very compelling. One is that she permits the women to speak for themselves. Though quite necessarily in translation, since the readers of this volume may not be fluent in Spanish (the language in which the women wrote), still Ramírez chooses with each case a text that serves to exemplify the habits of practice for the writer. What a gift this is! We are not simply told what the women were doing and trying to do. We get to see, in full, open display, samples of how the writers engaged their issues, expressed their viewpoints, and added to the discourse of their nation. We become, potentially, coparticipants in the analysis by being given the opportunity to bring our own tools and frameworks to the task of discovery and knowledge generation, along with the chance to listen, to notice, and to reflect on the possibilities and probabilities.

The second point about her analysis is related to the first. Ramírez provides an accessible template for broadening and deepening the matrices by which we are renewing and revitalizing the standards of practice in our field, given the new and different information that is coming into scope. In this regard, Ramírez's narrative accomplishes three important tasks:

1. From the perspective of rhetorical history, she tacks in to weave a compelling account of how, over several decades of their nation's history, three very distinctive women, along with a group of progressively minded women, found mechanisms for constructing authority, agency, and identity to enable their participation in specific public discourses. She identifies the patterns of their rhetorical choices and performances, the similarities and differences of their imperatives and purposes, the range of genres and styles they employed, and the impacts and consequences of their actions.
2. Ramírez also tacks out to situate these women's practices within the larger sociopolitical scope of the nineteenth and twentieth centuries. We see almost immediately the importance of the social circulation of ideas and strategies. In this case, we bear witness to the implication that women around the globe, including Mexican women, have persistently exhibited deep desires to exercise their own agency, to think about their own place and their own conditions, to speak

their minds, and sometimes to connect their causes to the causes of others across various national and cultural boundaries. In the nineteenth and twentieth centuries especially, these types of "buzz" opportunities were emerging all around the globe, often associated not only with women's movements in terms of gender and social justice but specifically, as Ramírez demonstrates in her case studies, also with revolutionary/evolutionary change at the leading edge of nation-building enterprises.

3. In addition, Ramírez engages in what strikes me as quite a provocative process of recovery and recuperation. She uses the concept of mestizaness as a terministic screen for understanding the intersections of identities and ideological location with the specificity of a Mexican national context. Using a term that runs the risk of jargonization, Ramírez recoups this concept astutely to interrogate transnationalism, transculturalism, and indigeneity, demonstrating that her project is fully anchored, not by mestiza as a convenient metaphor to acknowledge some factors of women's ornamentality, but by mestiza as a site of convergences where Mexican women have played out a matrix of intersections—race, class, gender, sexuality, nation, et cetera—in grappling with various systems of power and performance.

So does *Occupying Our Space* tell us all that we need to know about Mexican women writers? Certainly not, but without a doubt, Ramírez is quite persuasive in convincing her readers that we should know more about Mexican women writers and should develop a more substantive understanding of mestiza rhetorics in motion. The women whom Ramírez presents in this volume write as *mestiza* women, as women who obviously embrace fluid identities within a colonial and then a postcolonial context, exhibiting their capacities to participate with impact in both revolutionary and evolutionary projects of nation building. This volume, then, goes quite far in helping us to know more about this specific group and to stretch the boundaries of our thinking about the continuities and discontinuities of women's rhetorical action around the globe.

Jacqueline Jones Royster
Georgia Institute of Technology
June 26, 2014

Acknowledgments

Occupying Our Space asks you, the reader, to reconsider the traditional voices, languages, and geographical settings of the rhetorical tradition. It challenges and crosses linguistic, cultural, gendered, and political borders. This book project explores Mexican women's voices that have been lost, forgotten, or buried in archives and sidestepped for too long in the pages of history. As with any project, these women's voices appear on these pages because many people first believed in and encouraged me to pursue this venture.

I want to first thank Beth Brunk-Chavez for the faith she had in my ability and knowledge to carry this project to publication. As an excellent teacher and mentor, she taught me about the historical gap these women's voices would fill and how their inclusion could contribute to rhetoric and composition studies' understanding of women's struggles against and strategies to fight the erasure of their identities.

The Mexican women who appear in this study wrote and lived their lives in the Spanish language. While I can easily read and contemplate their writings, I could not have completed this project without the expert translation skills of Joel Bollinger Pouwels and Neil J. Devereaux. With their understanding of Mexican culture, history, and literature, they have captured the essence of the women's writings. My translators also provided important linguistic considerations to further illuminate what the women were doing within their discourse.

I owe a debt of gratitude and appreciation to my colleagues and staff in the English Department at the University of Arizona (UA), who provided support in many ways. With the generous department financial support, I was able to travel to archives in Mexico and Texas on several occasions.

First, a deep thank-you goes to Anne-Marie Hall for her confidence in the validity of my project. Her comments on several early drafts of my introduction and chapter 5 were invaluable. I also want to thank Larry Evers and Meg Lota Brown for providing me with a schedule conducive to completing this project. They encouraged and directed a path for my passions. My immediate colleagues in the RCTE program—Tom Miller, Damián Baca, Adela C. Licona, Amy Kimme-Hea, Ken McAllister, Maritza Cardenas, John Warnock, and Theresa Enos—also deserve a warm thank-you. In a faculty reading response group, they all provided valuable feedback and guidance for my project. A sincere thank-you also goes to Chris Hamel-Brown, writing specialist at the UA Think Tank, for reading many drafts of the manuscript and offering scholarly and unwavering emotional support through this process. Lastly, thank you, Anita August, for your love and endless involvement.

I would like to thank several other institutions and people for their assistance in my research. Thank you to the C. L. Sonnichsen Special Collections at the University of Texas at El Paso, the Nettie Lee Benson Latin American Collection at the University of Texas at Austin, and Biblioteca General de la Universidad Nacional Autónoma de México. A cordial thank-you (*muchísimas gracias*) to Biblioteca Pública Central Estatal José Ignacio Gallegos Caballero in the city of Durango, México. The director of the public archives, Mtro. Oscar Jiménez Luna, gave full and welcoming access to the resources upon each of my visits. Mtro. Luna graciously provided permissions to use various images in the book. Several families in the city of Durango also made my research stays pleasant and memorable. Paloma Rodríguez, Chelly González, Lucy Rodríguez, and her immediate relatives adopted me into their circle. *Mil gracias* for the rides to the library, all the Mexican food after long days of research, tours of the city, and endless laughs.

I am grateful to several other individuals who, whether they are aware of it or not, helped me think about and complete this process. Thank you to Kristen Buckles, the acquisitions editor of UA Press, for listening to the ideas of my manuscript, offering insightful suggestions, and supporting this project. Thank you to Jaime Mejía, Cristina Kirklighter, and the anonymous readers for their careful and thoughtful reviews of the book. Their insights helped me expand upon my concepts and bring further depth to the project. I would like to extend a deep appreciation to Jami McCarty, Leisha Reynolds-Ramos, and Celeste Del Russo for their readings of either all or various parts of the manuscript. A special appreciation goes to Diana

Rico for her sharp eye and gentle voice in the last steps of the book. I am indebted to Jackie Royster for the foreword to the book. She lives and practices her scholarship of coalitions.

Last, but not least, I want to thank my husband and life partner, Alejandro L. Ramírez, for the time, support, love, and certainty he had in me and this project. This book would not have been possible without your steadfast dedication to me and my work.

OCCUPYING OUR SPACE

INTRODUCTION

A Feminist Recovery Project

Mexican Women Journalists and Activists at the Forefront of Change

Women in the last century and the one before that and the one before that, lacked higher education and, when one of them without paying attention to prohibitions and scarcities had the courage to write, she did it in secret or by shielding herself behind a masculine pseudonym. . . . And that was in England! And in Mexico?[1]
—BRIANDA DOMECQ, FROM *MUJER QUE PUBLICA . . . MUJER PÚBLICA*

And where the words of women are crying to be heard, we must each of us recognize our responsibility to seek those words out, to read them and share them and examine them in their pertinence to our lives.
—AUDRE LORDE, FROM "TRANSFORMATION OF SILENCE"

This book's title, *Occupying Our Space*, is a translation of the phrase *ocupando nuestro puesto*, which comes from the Mexican women journalists' early writings. A variation of the phrase appeared in the 1903 writings of Juana Belén Gutiérrez de Mendoza. Invoking female political agency, she used the phrase "occupying their space" in her newspaper *Vésper* on more than one occasion. With "their" referencing the people of Mexico, it signaled that Mexican women journalists, such as her partner Elisa Acuña y Rosette, were claiming a public *puesto* on the journalistic scene in reaction to the lack of public concern for the harassment and silencing of the journalists by the government. She wrote, "Por eso os acusamos y por eso hemos venido a ocupar vuestro puesto" (For this reason we accuse you and for this reason we have come to *take your place [in the fight]*) (emphasis added).[2]

Fearlessly, Gutiérrez de Mendoza accused the Mexican people of being complacent bystanders and declared that she and her colleague Acuña y Rosette would take their place in the discursive battle against governmental tyranny. In conducting the research for this book, I noted that Gutiérrez de Mendoza's expression stands out because it aptly embodies the rhetorical action Mexican women journalists and activists were enacting in the late nineteenth and early twentieth centuries.

In this introduction, I chart the rhetorical terrain that the journalists and activists Laureana Wright de Kleinhans, Las Mujeres de Zitácuaro, Juana Belén Gutiérrez de Mendoza, Hermila Galindo, and others traversed through the interrogation of the Spanish word *puesto*. In Spanish, the word *puesto* encompasses several meanings. One meaning alluded to in Wright de Kleinhans's and Gutiérrez de Mendoza's writings is that of asserting an alternative "space" or "place," which is central to feminist articulations of embodied knowledge. bell hooks articulates the intrinsic knowledge women of color have regarding spaces of resistance. Women who write their stories enter a space of intervention and liberation, "[e]nter that space . . . the space where our words are invoked to serve and support, the space of our absence."[3] My use of the term *puesto* captures the deeper cultural, material, and experiential essence of what the Mexican women were trying to gain. For this reason, throughout the book, I use the word *puesto* instead of the English words *place* or *space*.

In May 1910, just months before the Mexican Revolution erupted, Gutiérrez de Mendoza published a short yet biting article, whose title appeared in bold capital letters, "VESPER SIEMPRE OCUPARA SU PUESTO," meaning, "*Vésper* will always occupy its place." The article's first line announces, "Una vez más *Vésper* viene a ocupar su puesto en el campo del combate" (Again *Vésper* comes to occupy its space in the arena of combat).[4] Gutiérrez de Mendoza's statement challenged numerous historical and modern realities, pushing against the restrictive governmental limitations of freedom of the press promised in the Constitution of 1857 and challenging the masculine monopoly on the practice of protest journalism. The use of all-capital letters in the title phrase "siempre ocupará su puesto," which is a style she frequently used, indicates that Gutiérrez de Mendoza did not speak the statement with calm reassurance. She used the symbolic typographical representation to show that she was shouting this phrase at the top of her lungs. She had a desire to have her sentiments known. In 1901, Gutiérrez de Mendoza arrived in Mexico City, the center of protest against the dictatorial Díaz regime, and she would later call other women to occupy the discursive puesto of protest. They heeded the

¡LA MUJER MODERNA!

POR REFUGIO GARCIA DE ESPEJO

(Concluye. Véase el número anterior)

A la mujer de cuya alma irradia la luz primera por do se guía más tarde el hombre, faltaba la luz intelectual, faltaba en ella la vida grave o plácida del pensamiento; esa luz de la conciencia, esa vida del espíritu que es la vida de la vida! Era pues nuestro sexo, me parece, como materia prima, de excelentes cualidades, pero ¡materia, materia solamente!! Así puede llamarse la inteligencia que, en tan profundo y eternal letargo como estuvo la de la mujer, no da a conocer sus diversas y múltiples manifestaciones. ¡Materia solamente la mujer entonces! ¡materia en gran número todavía! ¡que desventura!!

¿Y quién, quien podrá despertar de ese penoso sueño, que la obliga a pasar en tinieblas el único corto tiempo que en la eternidad se tiene de conciencia?

La libertad, la libertad primero, su esfuerzo personal después.

¡Hosanna, gloria eterna, gratitud infinita brote de nuestro femenino sentimiento, en loor a los hombres dignos de México nuestra amada patria que, aprestando su inteligencia, su energia, su vida, han abatido al siniestro y negro mónstruo del retroceso, que mantener ha querido siempre a la mujer en la ignorancia.

Bendiciones mil reciba de nuestra alma el Constitucionalismo actual, que luchando por la dignidad y honor de la patria ultrajada en sus leyes por la ambición más vil, y traición más inícua, implantar trata en su heróico triunfo, la libertad debida, la justa libertad que sin humillar al hombre en su dignidad y aspiraciones benéficas le mantenga bajo el dominio de la ley, sentimiento que sirve en el pueblo mexicano y que perfeccionará las cualidades despreciadas de la mujer.

A tí, mujer mexicana, inteligente y digna; materia prima en los primeros tiempos, toca ahora en los modernos de libertad y ayuda para el saber, a tí toca por interés y propio decoro, instruirte y aprovechar en bien de todos esta instrucción, demostrando al mundo cuán injusto había sido con la opresión intelectual de la mujer. ¡Qué más loable empeño y actividad más digna de encomio que vencer la inercia de la costumbre e indolencia perniciosa de la preocupación! La ilustración del entendimiento es la vida de la razón, ésta es la verdadera vida de los seres, y la vida cerebral, es la vida de la vida! La inteligencia no se conquista al arbitrio; pero la ignorancia se vence con la voluntad.

¡La ilustración, qué rara es todavía en la mujer de nuestra patria, pero qué esperanza tan risueña, qué plácida alegría me produce la creencia de que después de estas penalidades porque la patria atraviesa, la ilustración más sólida, la educación más radical, serán el verdadero distintivo de la mujer mexicana.

La ilustración con sus límpidos destellos le mostrará la vía porque atraviesa, y entonces, por su bondad inata, sabrá ser mansa con el débil, afable con el cariño y más bondadosa que el mismo bien; pero severa y altiva con el despotismo, respetuosa y digna con la justicia, sabrá, en fin, por su conciencia despejada por la ilustración, merecer debidamente el honorable nombre de mujer.

Sí; en esta época, época de grandeza, cuya aurora ya se inicia con el triunfo del Constitucionalismo, cuán bello me figuro el porvenir de mi patria con la consciente educación de nuestro ser. Yo, tan cansada ya por mi larga vida lodaria, me siento con aliento para bendecir con el entusiasmo que aún vive en el fondo de mi alma, a las generaciones futuras que realicen tal esperanza.

Ilustración sólida, ilustración, para la mujer anhelo. Afortunadamente la índole del sentimiento femenino en nuestro país, no es la de invadir las profesiones masculinas incompatibles con la delicadeza y sencillez del caracter mexicano, pues una mujer con pretensiones masculinas, no es de mi simpatía, no es el bello tipo que yo me forjo de la mujer instruida. No; yo ansío para la mujer mucha ilustración, saber profundo si es posible, para que demuestre al mundo que de la mujer instruida, como más impresionable, como más sencible, como más ferviente, nacerá y se mantendrá por millares de siglos el maravilloso conjunto de verdad y delicadeza, de sensatez y ternura, de razón y poesía ideal supremo de la vida.

¡De poesía! sí, de poesía; pues si ésta es la flor del alma de la mujer; si la poesía es el soplo en la concepción de sus ideas, el ambiente que contorna su grandeza, el amoroso calor de su sentimiento! Si la poesía es tan necesaria a la mujer, como el aire para vivir. Sin poesía a la vista, sin poesía en el pensamiento, sin poesía en el corazón, ¡qué ingrata sería la vida en nuestra condición! no habría felicidad posible, no existiría lo que yo llamo verdadera mujer!

Sigue en la página 11.

10

Figure 1. An inside page banner of Hermila Galindo's newspaper, *La Mujer Moderna*. This newspaper was published in Mexico in 1915 and focused on issues and topics important to Mexican women, such as suffrage, politics, education, women's roles in the public sphere, entertainment, ideas of beauty and fashion, and national and international contemporary events.

call. Decidedly, the phrase "ocupando nuestro puesto," or "occupying our space," serves as this book's thematic thread of women's rhetorical action.

Gutiérrez de Mendoza's rhetoric and actions ushered in the beginning of a feminist movement for Mexican women at the turn of the twentieth century. Her words were an invitation to the oppressed (not only women) to enter a new puesto of resistance. As a campesina (a rural woman) and autodidact from Durango, Mexico, her grassroots background, combined with her self-taught access to literacy, resulted in a critical stance against the governmental injustices unfolding before her. Her published words, symbolically yelled out on paper, functioned as the proverbial foot in the door for women to gain entrance to a puesto that had been denied to them for centuries. Indeed, her tone offended many members of the male power elite and landed her in jail many times. The patriarchal society had a death grip on women's mobility, and so Mexican women were limited in their choices of public puestos. To occupy new, more influential puestos would not come without a struggle.

Wright de Kleinhans also makes reference to occupying a "space." In her writing of *La emancipación de la mujer por medio del estudio*, she uses a variation of *puesto*, employing the word *lugar*. "Conozco el lugar que debo ocupar: yo no soy esclava, sino la conductora de la humanidad" (I know the space that I should occupy: I am not a slave, but rather a guide and leader of humanity).[5] This idea of occupying *un nuevo puesto* resonated with many of the women, and though not overtly stated by all the women, the act of leaving, claiming, or constructing a public puesto was implied. Their writings called women to shed the restrictive positivist ideals and traditions of the nineteenth century and to claim a new self and identity for the next era that included discursive civic participation.

As a Chicana and fluent Spanish speaker, I perceive that the other meaning of *puesto* implies a marginalized position in society. The women's puestos were not imagined. They conjure images of the open air *mercado*, or market posts, where vendors set up shop. These puestos were and still are very much part of the everyday public interaction of Mexican commerce. In the central mercado of nearly every city or pueblo in Mexico, vendors, usually women of the popular class, stand behind colorful wares of fresh fruits, vegetables, candies, or clothing, calling out to shoppers to buy from them. Their discourse is mostly limited to the selling of their wares. These puestos, and the customs surrounding them, date back to the pre-Conquest era and are traditional public puestos where Mexican society intended women to remain.

Indeed, this puesto of commerce did provide many women with public visibility and some economic gains, but it had substantial limitations and negative consequences. Susie Porter's study of Mexican working women during the time of the Porfiriato shows that women's choices for public puestos were expanding beyond the mercados and into factories and small businesses.[6] At the time Gutiérrez de Mendoza published her articles, Mexico's industry and production were expanding and were quickly transforming the spatial organization of the public sphere. Consequently, more women than ever were seen transacting business and working in factories that produced cotton textiles, cigars, and cigarettes. Some of the working-class women in the cigar factories were exposed to a "cultured" and "political" education through the influences of *el lector*, or the person who read newspapers, literature, manifestos, and so forth aloud to the workers.[7] The exposure to these readings later ignited some political and social movements. While women were seen more in public puestos, some were certainly not ideal. The atrocious conditions in these factories prompted women to organize for the first time for their own protection and to prevent exploitation of children. During the workday, they could be found at their puestos, many times hidden by their merchandise, dutifully focusing on the task at hand or tending to their children. However, women's puestos shifted if the women were of the upper class.

Mexican women of the elite class, although seen out in public, simultaneously occupied puestos of limited mobility. Their puesto was the home, and at one time in Mexican Colonial times, women of means were to be seen only through the ornate ironwork of balcony windows. This tradition was beginning to shift toward the end of the nineteenth century, but nonetheless, a wealthy woman was required to reign as queen of the home and serve her nation by raising her children and serving dutifully in a supportive role to her husband. Submission and self-sacrifice to the rules of etiquette and of the ideal *ángel del hogar*, or "angel of the home," were of utmost importance in social settings. Nancy LaGreca notes that this puesto in the home was a "pervasive obstacle" and was meant to keep women from "demanding rights and moving beyond their prescribed place."[8] She says, "It portrayed the perfect women as the Christian, chaste, maternal guardian of the happiness and success of her children, husband, and other family members."[9] To enact this ideal, upper-class women would host parties, attend them around town, and raise money for charities. Toward the end of the century, single women of the petite bourgeoisie were allowed to teach in elementary schools, but like the puestos in the mercado, the schools were extensions of the home. Women were not to veer from occupations of a domestic nature, and if they did, they were seen as betrayers of their family and community.

The public puestos of the mercado, the home, or primary schools were not ones that Gutiérrez de Mendoza was struggling to occupy. She wanted the rhetorical puesto that wields political power and that could have an immediate impact on society. From a rhetorical perspective, the oppressive spatial politics of everyday life are always already entangled with issues of race, sex, class, and domination. The power to speak to the oppressor does not come from occupying the center. It comes from speaking from the margins to the center. The use of the spatial metaphor of puestos aligns with Laura Gillman's idea of gendered experiences of location, which embodies an "interpretive horizon that allows new knowledge to surface."[10] Mexican women's puestos, like those of all women of color, are about the radical politics of locality. Where do they stand? What can be said as they stand in this puesto? Gutiérrez de Mendoza stood at the margins of society, speaking from the puesto of oppositional political, feminine struggle. For me, and through the lens of this study, Gutiérrez de Mendoza is the symbol of Mexican feminine voices emerging at the turn of the century and refusing to follow the tired traditions of silence and abnegation. The power of the socially prescribed puestos was slowly beginning to loosen its grip at the turn of the century through pioneering and revolutionary discursive action combined with radical rhetorical claims of new identities.

Asserting a Rhetorical Puesto

This book is a feminist rhetorical recovery project that attempts to answer the question of which Mexican women journalists and activists were at the forefront of claiming a discursive puesto, or public space, and how they sometimes succeeded and many times failed. Multiple cultural codes and decrees of Mexico through the centuries were carefully crafted to keep women silent, lingering at the margins of society. Societal norms were constructed around these laws and religious sentiments, such as the belief of women's sacred connection to the home, which fed the need for women to remain out of the public sphere. This culture made women's ability to speak out in public a more difficult endeavor. However, in the mid-nineteenth century, with the expansion of literacy, Mexican women began writing and publishing in journals and newspapers, challenging many malecentric positions. Some of these women, who are central to this study, include Laureana

Wright de Kleinhans (1842–96), the religious and political group of Las Mujeres de Zitácuaro (1900), Juana Belén Gutiérrez de Mendoza (1876–1942), and Hermila Galindo (1896–1954). They were among the pioneers and revolutionaries who broke social mores and claimed a discursive space for women's voices, which would gain greater dominance through the twentieth century. Since the Colonial era (1521–1810), intelligent, outspoken women who wrote or attempted to speak in public, such as Sor Juana Inés de la Cruz, were not taken seriously or were silenced, and on some noteworthy occasions, they were even laughed out of political gatherings.

But in the late nineteenth and early twentieth centuries there was an increased fluidity of feminist influences from the United States, Europe, and Latin America, and Mexican women from the elite and middle classes began to use them in order to interrogate their own position within Mexican society. At this time, John Stuart Mill's *The Subjection of Women* (1869) was an important and influential book for women of the elite, and not so elite, classes of Europe, the United States, and Latin America. Mills argued for an equality of the sexes in striving for intellectual freedom as well as suffrage. At the time, these influences spurred the beginnings of feminist sentiments and resistance we see increasingly appearing in newspapers and ladies' journals. The overarching purpose of this study is to document these struggles within a system of feminine denial; to examine the ways in which these women applied their rhetorical skills to negotiate and shift and challenge the prescribed feminine identities; and to look at how they were able to influence emerging national politics of the late nineteenth and early twentieth centuries.

The research surrounding Mexican women in the last thirty years has substantially improved and increased. The acceptance of Mexican women's literary voices, scholarly accomplishments, and public endeavors within the academy in Latin America and the United States has opened many research opportunities. Scholars of Latin American studies focusing on women, such as Anna Macías, Julia and Esperanza Tuñón Pablos, Jean Franco, Jocelyn Olcott, Asunsión Lavrin, Laura Orellana Trinidad, Gabriela Cano, Elvira Hernández Carballido, Mary K. Vaughan, Ana Lau Javien, Joel Bollinger Pouwels, and many others, have conducted extensive archival research and produced works pivotal to uncovering women's lost discursive history. As much work as these scholars have done to highlight Mexican women's voices, researching Mexican women still requires a much greater effort than writing about the Mexican male, mainly because women's works for centuries were not considered worthy of historical preservation or were published under pseudonyms.

Mary K. Vaughan concedes to the fact that it is difficult to recover Mexican women's voices. She writes in the introduction to *Sex in Revolution: Gender, Politics, and Power in Modern Mexico* that "[s]keptics (until recently, the majority of Mexican historians) derided the act of exploring Mexican women's history as one of feminine romantic willfulness: the search for a small group of insignificant actors in obscure places."[11] Equally, Gabriela Cano and Georgette José Valenzuela, in their introduction to the rigorous interdisciplinary historical study *Cuatro estudios de género en el México urbano del siglo XIX* (Four Studies of Gender in Urban Mexico in the Nineteenth Century), trace the many barriers Mexican feminist scholars have faced in gaining an equal ground of study of women in history.[12] More recently, Elvira Hernández Carballido meticulously traces the history of Mexico's press from a gendered perspective.[13] However, the excellent study of *Mujeres insurgentes* (Insurgent Women), an edited collection focusing on women who participated in revolutionary and political upheavals in Mexico and sponsored by a special governmental council on the bicentennial of the Mexican Revolution, reveals that much more work has been done to highlight Mexican women's contributions to public political struggles.[14] Certainly, the tide is shifting. History from a feminine perspective is gaining ground in academic institutions. Not surprisingly, rhetorical feminists who are working to expand the rhetorical canon draw on some of the same language as the scholars of Latin American history who are writing feminist historiographies.

Feminist rhetorical scholars also acknowledge the gaps, the silences, and the unwillingness on the part of male-dominated scholarship to look to women's writing as valued evidence of rhetorical work. Scholars such as Cheryl Glenn, Shirley Wilson Logan, Jacqueline Jones Royster, Carol Mattingly, Jessica Enoch, Dora Ramírez-Dhoore, Hui Wu, and many others have contributed to women's representation in rhetorical history. They have remapped and reorganized the rhetorical collective of voices, opening up previously unavailable spaces for women. However, I agree with Hui Wu, who takes the interpretation of the rhetorical tradition further by stating that "[f]eminist ethno-rhetorical historiography, particularly that of Third World women, remains a largely uncharted territory."[15] I also contend that the field of rhetorical feminist history has developed a dichotomy of African American voices on one end and white Anglo voices on the other, leaving out the richness of diverse voices. In answer to this critique, *Occupying Our Space* charts new rhetorical territory and examines the missing voices of Mexican women in the cultural context of a nation claiming a pioneering cultural identity.

The work of Royster and Kirsch in *Feminist Rhetorical Practices: New Horizons for Rhetoric, Composition, and Literacy Studies* shows us how the field is globalizing its representation of new and different voices.[16] Royster and Kirsch's work provides feminist rhetorical scholars a clear direction in which to proceed in filling historical gaps. Their theoretical work has "centered on the challenges of engaging historical women's lives respectfully and meaningfully—for their day and for our own."[17] In order to do this work, they forward four strategic terms of engagement: *critical contemplation, strategic contemplation, social circulation*, and *globalization*. I cover these terms here because they reflect the ways in which I have approached the study, recovery, and representation of Mexican women journalist's writings. The first approach, critical contemplation, is systemic. This approach looks at the histories and voices that are represented and also at those that are not. It is a "rethinking" and a "speculating about what could be there instead."[18] In looking at the representative feminist scholarship on Mexican people and cultures within rhetoric and composition studies, I saw very little inclusion of their voices, and in an era of growing representation of the Latino population in higher education, this lack of inclusion is problematic. Indeed, as Royster and Kirsch suggest, this method "open[s] the possibility of rescue, recovery, and (re)inscription," which speaks to the goal of this book: to recover Mexican women rhetors. Critical contemplation leads to the second method of strategic contemplation, a quantifiable approach "taking time, space, and resources to think about, through, and around our work."[19] This process requires that we take the time to engage in a dialogue with the women in our studies in order to "understand their words, their visions, [and] their priorities."[20] As a bilingual Chicana, I was able to understand the Mexican women's primary writings in Spanish. This ability to contemplate and dialogue in two languages reflects my own connection with the women and their work. I felt comfortable in approaching their writings and the historical context from which they spoke because of my family connection to the Mexican culture, people, and language.

The last two approaches, social circulation and globalization, focus on the exchange of feminist knowledge within public spaces, which has implications beyond our present settings. Social circulation evokes the "overlapping social circles in which women travel, live, and work," taking into consideration the evolutionary processes of shifting rhetorical practices that occur from one generation to the next.[21] Ultimately, the aim of social circulation is to question the public-private divide that women's voices encounter. It places women's voices in social spaces and makes visible the forms of women's public lives. Lastly, the concept of globalization attends to the shifting territories in which feminist scholars are locating their studies, such as this study into Mexican rhetorics. This feminist revisionary history embodies the focus on transnational rhetorical practices that will, one hopes, not only expand our field's understanding of how to conduct research into non-Western rhetorics, but also alter the ways in which our field perceives Mexicans and women.

Focusing on Diverse Rhetorical Perspectives

Mexican women's writings were pioneering and revolutionary insofar as they wrote about nationalist issues of race, class, and identity and for the very fact that they existed, given the conscious exclusion of women from the discursive public sphere. What the women journalists and activists addressed and how they entered the public sphere pertain not only to the disciplines of Latin American history and women's studies, but also to the field of rhetoric, which seeks to understand the ways women (the speakers) were silenced, how they cleared various puestos from which to communicate their ideas, and how they discussed and grappled with systems of power. A rhetorical perspective of feminist historical writings actively investigates the effect that writing had on the society and the ways it constructed the political reality of the historical moment.

In order to bring the women on the margins of Mexican rhetorical history into clearer view, we must ask focused questions, such as: Which women have been included in the rhetorical tradition, and what has contributed to the difficulty in the recovery of other women? What do the histories of these women who spoke out in public tell us about the rhetorical tradition and the history inscribed within it? How can we create the discursive bridge between Latin American history and rhetoric that would respectfully interrogate and analyze the women's writings? What theoretical lens would respectfully and fully capture their rhetorical stances? These questions and the answers are crucial to expanding rhetorical historiography further into Latin America and recovering new and relevant voices. As these women and their rhetorical actions come into clearer view, their voices will begin to do the work of shifting their rhetorical identities.

When I say that women used rhetoric in order to frame their identities, I think not only of its common Aristotelian definition as the art of persuasion but also of the particular definition from William Covino and David Jolliffe.[22] They define rhetoric as "a primarily verbal, situationally contingent, epistemic art that is both philosophical and practical and gives rise to potentially active texts."[23] By means of the phrase "active texts,"

Covino and Jolliffe suggest that the discourses, whether oral or written, produced by the rhetors and circulated in civic circles have the potential to generate a change in the reality of the historical situation. Rhetoric as an epistemic art, which implies creation of knowledge, also functions as criteria for analysis. Rhetorical analysis is powerful in that it signals the subject's ability to produce and enact knowledge and thereby alter realities. A rhetorical approach enriches historical data by investigating discursive circumstances beyond the exposition of mere "facts." Hence, this stance is powerful in assuming that these women writers were creating and acting upon their knowledge, a concept that exceeds what was deemed possible by or acceptable about women at the time.

Because my scholarship crosses geographic borders by considering Mexican women's writings, I also turn to definitions of rhetoric offered by Mexican rhetorical scholars. Gerardo Ramírez Vidal presents scholars from various disciplines who offer transnational and transcultural perspectives of rhetoric.[24] In "La tradición rétorica" (section I of the collection), Manfred Kraus, Mariateresa Galaz, Lourdes Rojas Álvarez, and others recognize the Greco-Roman "origins" of rhetoric. However, it is important to note that Mexican rhetorical scholars recognize a distinct racial and symbolic division of rhetoric. Various scholars of this collection, including Ramírez Vidal, Rocío Olivares Zorrilla, Ignacio Ramos Beltrán, and others, construct a "retórica mexicana." This ethnic identification is based on the rhetorical practices of indigenous people of Mexico and the shifting nature of these practices throughout history, to include the pre-Conquest to the Colonial eras. This recognition is significant because rhetoric and its studies is "transforming into a hybrid discipline."[25] The concept of a hybrid discipline is rooted in a mixing of racial backgrounds not only biologically but also discursively. This concept will be central to chapter 2 of this book, but for now, Beristáin and Ramírez Vidal in *La palabra florida: La tradición rétorica indígena y novohispana* (The Florid Word: The Indigenous and Novo-Hispanic Rhetorical Tradition) define rhetoric as:

> Así, la retórica está contenida ineludiblemente en toda expresión verbal del ser humano . . . y los estudiosos de retórica tienen como una de sus tareas analizar este carácter natural de las lenguas. En efecto, la teoría retórica no sólo enseña a hablar de modo persuasivo; además, enseña a observar lo persuasivo o los *actos retóricos* en los textos.[26]
>
> Contained inevitably in every verbalization of the human being . . . and scholars of rhetoric have as one of their tasks to analyze this natural aspect

> of language. In effect, rhetorical theory not only teaches to speak persuasively; additionally, it teaches how to observe that which is persuasive, or the *rhetorical acts* in texts.

The distinction that this definition makes in observing "rhetorical acts" in the texts reflects Covino and Jolliffe's understanding of "active texts." In this short comparison of two definitions of rhetoric, one from a Western perspective and the other from a Mexican perspective, we see that both cultures distinguish rhetoric as a persuasive and active practice. "This natural aspect of rhetoric" is the everydayness of language that can function practically as an art of and for the people. From a transnational view, rhetoric emerges as the most powerful tool for change in times of oppression, with the potential to give voice to a silenced group of people, such as the women in this study.

Shifting the purview of the Western rhetorical terrain requires that we transcend the wall, literally and metaphorically, dividing Mexico and the United States. As a Chicana, I cross this border daily in language and thought, giving me the ability to perceive both sides. In this book, I seek to illuminate the rhetorical approaches that the Mexican women journalists and activists were taking in a male-dominated profession through the lens of *mestiza rhetoric*. The word *mestiza*, simultaneously infused with domination and resistance, comes from the Latin American term *mestizaje*, which invokes the racial and cultural blending produced by the Conquest and European domination of the supposed New World. At the time these women were writing, Mexico was in the midst of an identity crisis. Mexicans wanted a measure of strategic separation from their European selves, which they found through a level of acceptance of their indigenous identity, thus producing an alternative third space of identity. But as industrialization extended into Mexico, there was an increase in trade not only of goods but also of ideas in the form of translated works from French, Russian, English, and German scholars, which heavily influenced the societal directions of activists. This crossing and sharing of ideas also was part of the mestizaje.

However, I see mestizaje as a male-dominated frame with which Mexico was constructing its national identity. In the frameworks of Latin American male intellectuals and authors writing about a "mestizo" identity in the nineteenth and twentieth centuries, such as Cuban José Martí, Peruvian José Carlos Mariátegui, and Mexican José Vasconcelos, women were not even an afterthought. Or if they were, the writers conjured images of the Mexican-Indian woman as a mother figure, but never as an intellectual figure. The term *mestiza*, then, recognizes the racial and cultural mixture of nation building, but invokes a powerful reach toward its feminine origins in Malintzin, the Nahua slave turned interpreter, advisor, and lover of Hernán Cortés. The reach toward the original feminine aspect of cultural mixing, which occurred first through discourse, implies that we must consider Malintzin, the mother of the mestizo race, in her intellectual form as rhetor, not sexualized traitor. Mestiza rhetoric, which I interrogate more fully later in this introduction, assumes a feminine approach to expressions of nationhood but also offers a powerful political resistance to the silencing aspects of mestizaje.

Journalistic practices blurred with the literary world of Mexico and served as the main arena in which the concept of mestizaje was promulgated. During the 1880s and 1890s many Mexican intellectuals were contributing to a conversation focused on reshaping and repositioning their nationalist identities through journalistic and literary outlets.[27] Journalism in Mexico concentrated on the *ensayo*, or the essay. Rhetorical historian Cristina Kirklighter notes that the Latin American ensayo was a pivotal element of the epistemological groundings of an author. She states, "The epistemological curious individuals began building their foundations by questioning and understanding their historical location" through careful articulations in the genre of the essay.[28] The Mexican ensayo carried heavy Spanish European influences, but above all, it was considered a male genre that encapsulated logic, a masculine ethos, and rhetorical power.

Mexican newspapers also included a great deal of poetry and pursued topics of local, national, and international politics.[29] Indeed, Celia del Palacio Montiel has noted the important role newspapers played in shaping the history and direction of Mexico.[30] Additionally, Daniel Cosío Villegas, in his edited multivolume collection *Historia moderna de México* (1955–72), touted the late nineteenth century and early twentieth century as the zenith period in Mexican journalism.[31] In these histories, almost all of the journalists mentioned were men, as seen in studies by Diego Arenas Guzmán and Leopoldo Borrás. Yet there were women journalists who also participated in the political and Revolutionary discourse. Hernández Carballido, in her survey of the books written about Mexican journalism, with the first appearing in 1976, corroborates this claim, noting that the participation of women was not even mentioned, which ultimately gives the false impression that women were not part of the journalistic movement.[32] Clearly, historians of Mexico have uncovered many of the writings that contributed to the knowledge of societal and political events of pre- and post-Revolutionary Mexico, and the women who wrote and published their writings, which were numerous, set precedents by contradicting centuries-old social expectations. What these women wrote and did aside from their everyday chores set the stage for women's independence in the future.

Some may ask, Why study Mexican women journalists and activists? What can knowledge of their rhetorical acts provide for us today? First, after various conference presentations, many participants have approached me and stated that they did not even know of Mexican women writers beyond Sor Juana Inés de la Cruz. Further, Mexican women have historically been seen as occupying only the domestic sphere as mothers, housemaids, and servants and the religious realm as nuns. Consequently, the idea that they may have wielded the pen to impact their social conditions and those of others remains an anomalous characterization. Second, the more we know of women's role in the circulation and creation of knowledge, the more we contribute to the changing landscape of the rhetorical tradition. Third, the social framing of Mexican women and Latinas in the field of rhetoric remains a flat, uncomplicated, and uncharted space. Finally, if we believe, also, that discourse shifts realities, then an alternative understanding of Mexican women as knowledge workers can contribute to a broader perspective on Latinas in our present-day society. And so, examining the writings of Mexican women journalists and the language they used to enter the male-dominated sphere of debate is ultimately significant to the study of rhetoric.

Although the women studied in this book came from different sociopolitical backgrounds, they are connected in that they fought against the same silencing patriarchal forces. Could what they practiced and expressed in their writings be called feminist rhetoric? Could it be called feminism? I answer these questions in the affirmative. My definition of feminism aligns with Mary Hawkesworth's concept of feminist rhetoric.[33] She says, "Feminist rhetorics call worlds into being, inscribe new orders of possibility, validate frames of reference and forms of explanation, and reconstitute histories serviceable for present and future projects."[34] Hawkesworth's definition of feminist rhetoric implies that women's discourse is always already political and that it goes beyond the confrontation of prevailing modes of thought. In her article "Feminist Rhetoric: Discourses on the Male Monopoly of Thought," she describes feminism as an active rhetorical project and uses strong active verbs, such as *confront*, *dispel*, *critique*, *illuminate*, *construct*, and *validate*, to convey the dynamic nature of feminism. Hawkesworth's focus on discourse as active relates to the definition of rhetoric by Beristáin and Ramírez Vidal of rhetoric as acts. This frame implies that feminist rhetoric is never a passive activity but is imbued as an inherently political move.

Using the term *feminism* in regard to Mexican women's writings can also be complicated. Feminist scholars of Mexican history have different perspectives on when feminism emerged as a movement in Mexico, but as Anna Macías notes, the roots of feminism in Mexico flourished with women gaining an education.[35] Hence, feminism is not only an active stance against oppressive systems but a strategic critical position emerging from a newly acquired literacy. This position leaves the issue up for some interpretation. For example, Wright de Kleinhans was born in 1846, shortly after the Colonial era (1521–1810), in Taxco, Mexico.[36] She came from an elite background and received a private education appropriate to her status. Her mobility and standing in Mexican society as a poet and literary editor were extremely rare. Therefore, her discourse is notably different in tone, reference, and rhetorical style from that of Gutiérrez de Mendoza, who represents the other end of the class and education spectrum.

Gutiérrez de Mendoza came from an impoverished family and received little formal education, but because she felt the overwhelming desire to understand what was written on the pages of books, she taught herself how to read and write as a young child. Hermila Galindo was born into a wealthy family but lost her mother at a young age. Her father, though, supported her education through her childhood, and she received an education that would sustain her as an adult. But as a young woman, she would always have to work. With an ability to read and write, these women were exceptions to the rule. Male supporters and critics of women's education in the early to mid-nineteenth century heavily debated the issue for years before concrete action was taken. Consequently, the development of feminism in Mexico remained a slow process, but the transformation was indeed in play.

Mexican Women Rhetors: Claiming the Discursive Self

The women chosen for this study, Laureana Wright de Kleinhans, the religious and political group of Las Mujeres de Zitácuaro, Juana Belén Gutiérrez de Mendoza, and Hermila Galindo, are significant because they were among the first to openly challenge the powers that prevented women from sharing their bold ideas in public. These women played various roles—publisher, editor, writer, interviewer—in the publication of their writings. Notably, they were not the only ones writing and active in the public sphere. However, I chose these women for several reasons. From a rhetorical perspective, they produced and published a significant amount of discourse; they utilized and subverted unique genres; they represented a varied range of voices; lastly, their discourse produced the greatest impact in shifting gendered norms. I chose to investigate the period between the mid-nineteenth and early twentieth century because this was the time during which women started to gain more public acceptance within education fields and labor forces. Hence, there were more women inclined to pick up the pen. As we enter the twentieth century, there emerges an early wave of public feminist appeals connected to the struggles leading up to the Mexican Revolution. Prior to this time, women were participating in publication and editing, but only a handful are documented. And lastly, an in-depth look at individual women's civic discursive practices instead of that of many women can provide us with a more nuanced look at rhetorical acts.

Joel Bollinger Pouwels notes that publication of newspapers first appeared in Mexico during the Colonial era, and a few women of means, many of them Spaniards or elite Creoles, had connections to the newspaper culture through their husbands.[37] For example, Juan Pablos, one of the first printers of Mexico, left his printing business to his wife, Jerónima Gutiérrez, after his death in 1560.[38] Several other women in Mexico during the Colonial era, such as Catalina del Valle (printer) and Doña Francisca Flores (publisher), also inherited printing businesses from their husbands.[39] A notable Spaniard, Doña Micaela Benavides de Calderón, also owned a printing press through her husband and was the first female journalist in Mexico, active from 1641 to 1684. Although these women edited and published the newspapers, their editorial focus was not on women's issues. It was not until the early nineteenth century that newspapers or journals tailored their content to women. The majority of these later publications, which will be discussed in depth, were directed and written by men, who perpetuated a male-dominated ideal of womanhood.

Bollinger Pouwels notes that during the Restored Republic (1867–76), liberal reforms offered women a way "to participate more fully in society during this period of intellectual and nationalistic revival."[40] Julia Tuñón Pablos explains that the differences in women's social roles depended a great deal upon their place in the social hierarchy.[41] In this book, I incorporate the contextual circumstances of each woman. Locating them in their material and historical circumstances is of utmost importance because it prevents what Barbara Beisecker calls a modernist affirmative-action approach of merely placing women within the rhetorical canon.[42] While the women are central to this history, "that center can only be understood as an effect of its place in a larger economy of discourse."[43] Intersecting discourses with the hegemonic histories makes palpable the gaps, discontinuities, and fissures of Mexican feminine realties. Like a continuum, each woman in this study represents a different era in Mexican history and a diverse position in society, with different material and cultural realities. Yet all of the woman are connected through the main goal they were working to achieve: recognition as intelligent citizens, not just as mothers of a nation they loved.

Women writers, like Wright de Kleinhans and Gutiérrez de Mendoza, understood that in order to gain access to the male-dominated arena of journalism they would have to narrate their own histories. Many of the women did so through the journalistic genre of the essay. The rhetorical ability to seize the historical moment and locate oneself within an expanse of time is crucial to developing an identity and dismantling that reality that has been preconstructed. Numerous women did write, and their rhetorical intersection with and resistance against the male voices was a public struggle toward nonconformity with the logos of patriarchies past, present, and future. In these women's writings, there is a powerful feminine claim to a nation that had denied them a part in civic action for centuries. Now, by retelling their stories, I am repositioning these women within the Mexican nationalist framework of women bending, challenging, and breaking the gender codes required for them to raise their voices over a century ago.

Wright de Kleinhans and the women within her writing cohort, such as Dolores Correa Zapata, Ignacia Padilla de Piña, Mateana Murguía de Aveleyra, and María del Alba, represent the elite during the dictatorship of Porfirio Díaz, known as the Porfiriato. These women symbolized elite privilege, public order, and high literacy. Their educational and public experiences were far removed from those of the majority of Mexican women. It is important to note that while they were breaking ground, they were also highly constrained under the social constructs of their time. For example, because Wright de Kleinhans's writing skills were extraordinary, she was accepted into the elite literary circles of Mexico City, where writing poetry was a literary practice reserved for the privileged male. Her rare membership in the male puestos of the lyceums was an advantage she was fully aware of and which she used to encourage other women to write. She also invited their submissions to her literary journal, *Las Hijas del Anáhuac* (The Daughters of Anáhuac). The poetry, journalism, essays, and feminine histories she and others wrote represent the beginnings and pioneering movements of Mexican feminist thought. She expressed her emerging feminist ideas in *La emancipación de la mujer por medio del estudio* (The Emancipation of Women by Means of Studying), in which she analyzed the historical and cultural differences between men and women. She argued that women have an equal intellect to move forward, but have been held back by men's self-centered gendered politics. Equally, Gabriela Cano, a contemporary scholar, notes that nineteenth-century women's "intellectual activities were compatible with their domestic chores and family obligations as mothers, wives, daughters, and sisters."[44] Wright de Kleinhans also saw the importance of writing the history of women publishing biographies in *Las Hijas del Anáhuac* and later in *Mujeres notables mexicanas*. With the publication of *Mujeres notables*, we come to know the life stories of women writers who without Wright de Kleinhans's efforts would have otherwise remained unknown.

Wright de Kleinhans's ideas were certainly ahead of their time. Her ideas began to actively emerge in the pre-Revolutionary discourse through works such as the *Manifiesto* of a group of forty women who called themselves Las Mujeres de Zitácuaro. Although their manifesto appeared in a Communist-leaning newspaper, the Zitácuaro women do not make the radical claim of complete feminine independence, claiming instead equal space next to men as their helpmates. However, they condemn the creeping power politics of the Catholic Church, which had been limited under the Constitution of 1857. Their document is also a representation of women using (or strategically appropriating) Mexican political genres, such as the plan, *el grito* (a Mexican cry for action), and the manifesto, to further their ideas. The manifesto of Las Mujeres de Zitácuaro serves as the bridge between the pioneering discourse of Wright de Kleinhans and the revolutionary discourse of Gutiérrez de Mendoza.

At the turn of the nineteenth century, women were becoming more engaged in the polemics of their time, and each of the women's activities reflects this claim. The feminist Zitácuaro document was published in 1901, the same year that Juana Gutiérrez de Mendoza emerged in Mexico City with her small newspaper *Vésper*. With that publication, she began her long career of forty-five years as a radical journalist and activist. Gutiérrez de Mendoza represents a small group of women from the lower classes, including also Dolores Jiménez y Muro and Elisa Acuña y Rosette, who managed to gain access to the male discursive arena. Engaging publicly in the politics of her time would earn Gutiérrez de Mendoza several jail sentences. As an early feminist, her voice would also express the anger of women silenced for centuries. Whereas Gutiérrez de Mendoza, of peasant origins, represents radical politics, Hermila Galindo represents middle-class women, mostly working as teachers and educators during the Revolution, who were also heavily involved in civic discourse and public politics. Galindo emerges during the Revolution as a spokeswoman for the politics of President Venustiano Carranza. Like Wright de Kleinhans, Galindo was accepted into the rare inner circles of intellectuals who felt that women, to some extent, should be allowed in the public domain.

Collectively, these women engaged in a political act of claiming a rhetorical identity and also a unique space, or puesto, in the Mexican public sphere as mestizas. They were a product of Mexican mestizaje: European and indigenous cultural mixing, comprised of a deep history of colonialism, domination, and racial constructions. Díaz's regime offered the elite women access to the European sensibilities through diplomats and their wives who traveled to Mexico during the late nineteenth century. This, in turn, created a particular mestiza who also appealed to the Europeans. Regardless of class, they carried a mestiza consciousness and could not (nor do I believe they wanted to) escape this reality of being Mexican. The ever-present reality of cultural hybridity, of mestizaje, emerges differently in each of the women's writings. We see a surge in the assimilationist politics of the mestizaje in the two eras in which they were writing: 1876 to 1910, the Porfiriato period, and 1920 to 1942, the post-Revolutionary period. The Porfiriato was punctuated by the politics of President Porfirio Díaz, himself a mestizo with indigenous origins but European sensibilities. He celebrated his origins within the festivals and international representations of the country, such as at local celebrations and the world's fairs, making mestizaje an everyday practice. The post-Revolutionary era was dominated by the assimilationist ideas of José Vasconcelos, which Gutiérrez de Mendoza would write against. Hence, the notion of being mestiza was an always already construct in their writings, whether foregrounded or left at the periphery.

The women's rhetorical presence through journalism gendered the historical topography of mestizaje, crafting a mestiza rhetoric, a radical conception of their identity as mexicanas. Here, I strategically draw on Adela Lincona's concept of (b)orderlands rhetorics, which recognizes a both/and also third space conception of being. Ontologically, (b)orderland rhetorics "move[s] beyond binary borders to a named third space of ambiguity and even contradiction."[45] For the purposes of this study, the mestiza rhetoric of Mexican women claims a space of identity in between the conception of mixed race and a masculine ontology. I define mestiza rhetoric as a subversive feminine articulation of a multifaceted existence that invokes multiple histories, subjectivities, and notions of citizenship, functioning as a decolonizing approach to identification outside of the dominant narrative of assimilation. The women's crossing into the new discursive practice of mestiza rhetoric parallels their journey into claiming un nuevo puesto in society. My notion of mestiza rhetoric is grounded in the identity and actions of the mother of the mestizo race, Malintzin. Maligned with the epithet La Malinche, she was intially the slave and later the interpreter, guide, and intermediary of the Spanish *conquistador* Hernán Cortés. She had the gift of tongues, speaking Spanish, Nahuatl, and the Chontal Mayan language. Valued for her intellect, she stood between two empires as interpreter. But masculine history has mostly disparaged her role, calling her a traitor of her people. In fact, she was a skillful rhetor and negotiator. In the next chapter, I build on Damían Baca's framing of Malintzin as "an archetypal border crosser, as a subversive product of conflicting and intertwining worlds."[46] Baca's framing of Malintzin, akin to Mexican historian J. Jesús Figueroa Torres interpretation, places her as a central historical figure as the first subversive rhetor of Mexico.[47]

Mexican women were claiming their past heritage to frame themselves as rightful progenitors of speaking and acting publicly. Shifting the focus, I discuss the historical, educational, and political environments of the mid-nineteenth and early twentieth centuries. These historical constructs explain how Mexican women's voices intersected with patriarchal and nationalistic systems of power and ultimately helped them claim a puesto in the conversation of national politics.

Women's Activism and Education in Nineteenth-Century Mexico

For over three hundred and fifty years, from the time of the Conquest to the end of the Colonial era, and for fifty years after the country achieved independence, educational opportunities for Mexican women were limited. Although there was some recognition that women needed education, they were traditionally kept ignorant to prevent distraction from their domestic duties. Complex politics added to the difficulty of reform. Mexico was dominated by an elitist conservative group that kept the majority of its citizens illiterate and preoccupied with manual labor. It was estimated that four-fifths of Mexicans were illiterate and that four-fifths of the schools were exclusively for men.[48] However, some women, such as the elite and persistent autodidacts, gained an education, but with limited outcomes. Women who entered the convents also received an education and participated in the running of convents and wrote about their mystic experiences in poems and verse, but they engaged only limited audiences, such as their confessors.[49] Not all women entered the religious spaces. Well-known writers and activists, such as Josefa Ortiz de Domínguez (1773–1829) and Leona Vicario de Quintana Roo (1789–1842), were the exceptions to the rule of limited literacy. Ortiz de Domínguez, known as La Corregidora, was a political activist in the Mexican War of Independence of 1810.[50] Her literacy enabled her to play a key role as activist alongside her husband, a local official. Vicario, an autodidact, collaborated with her husband in writing for a variety of journals, but as a writer in her own right, she contributed to political publications. Additionally, scholars Asunción Lavrin and Edith Couturier provide an alternative picture of everyday women who dealt with judicial issues under exceptional circumstances.[51] While there were many other elite women who did receive an education under tutors at home, the majority of women from the lower classes remained illiterate.

Since 1840, liberals in power within the government believed that single women should receive educations that would help them support themselves, but little was done from 1824 to 1855 in terms of advancing women's education.[52] Options for Mexican women during the nineteenth century included marriage, the convent, the hard labor of a lower-class woman, or prostitution.[53] Macías notes that during "the chaotic years that extended from 1810 to 1867, educational opportunities for all Mexicans probably regressed from the levels achieved during the Bourbon Renaissance of 1730 to 1810."[54] The turbulent postindependence period contributed tremendously to the lack of progress in women's education. Even after Mexico gained independence from Spain, the country was in constant turmoil between conservative and liberal factions. Eventually, the opportunities for women to receive an education opened with the period of the Restored Republic (1867–76), which saw the expulsion of the French interlopers and enactment of the liberal Constitution of 1857 under the indigenous president Benito Juárez.

Realizing that women needed education to contribute to the development of the nation-state, positivist reformers began to express the need for women's education.[55] Under Porfirio Díaz, the state apparatus saw the importance of strengthening the family, with women at the center of this vision. The need to educate women, then, was based, not in a feminist vision of liberation from a patriarchal structure, but in one that subordinated them further. Mary K. Vaughan's investigation into women's education provides quotes from a speech given by positivist educator Justo Sierra.[56] His message to the women at the Escuela Miguel Lerdo de Tejada explains why the Mexican government initially wanted to educate women and what was expected of them after they received an education.

> In all Mexican schools we are forming men and women for the home; this is our supreme goal. . . . The educated woman will be truly one for the home; she will be the companion and the collaborator of man in the formation of the family. That is what we want and that is what you are

> being so firmly and morally prepared for. . . . You are called to form [your children's] souls, to sustain the soul of your husband; for this reason we educate you. *Niña querida*, do not turn feminist in our midst. . . . Let the man struggle with political questions and write the laws; you fight the good fight, that of the sentiments and forming souls, which is better than forming laws.[57]

Mexican lawmakers were operating in a contradiction of terms. On the one hand they saw the need to educate women beyond the traditional perspective of the Catholic Church, yet they were replacing one patriarchal system with another. When Sierra addressed the women as "niña querida," a fatherly, gendered phrase meaning "cherished child," we see his patriarchal conviction that grown women were still seen as children. Sierra's ideas were shared by the nation; in fact, many women uncritically accepted this position, but others began to acquire a disapproving stance toward this childish frame.

Educational progress for women had stabilized under the liberal Law of Educational Reform of 1869, which spurred the opening of public secondary schools. Various regions of Mexico were more progressive than others and early on embraced the move to educate women. For example, Yucatán was at the forefront of radical social movements, which included establishing one of the first women's normal schools, called La Siempreviva (The Everlasting). The school was led by a feminist group under the direction of progressive educator and poet Rita Cetina Gutiérrez (1846–1908).[58] In 1870, the women of the school published a newspaper, titled *La Siempreviva*, commemorating the moment with a poem by Cetina Gutiérrez. She invited women to join the movement:

> Listen with attention: *the hour has arrived*
> for woman to ennoble her name!
> Come all [women], come. La Siempreviva
> reclaims your enthusiastic support . . .
> *The hour has arrived*, and today begins
> the regeneration of women![59]

In the latter part of the nineteenth century, the hour had indeed arrived for women—forging inroads into writing and promulgating their voices through publications of their poetry, fiction, essays, histories, and music. But these opportunities were also shrouded in limited access for women.

The Mexican literary arena was an elite puesto. The art of poetry was cultivated in exclusive literary salons (the *veladas literarias*), which were jealously protected by the prominent *literatos*, or literary men, of the time.[60] Like the ensayo, poetry was considered the "genre of genres" and was a popular art form mostly because Mexican culture was an oral culture. Hence, elite oratorical practices, such as the recitation of poetry and florid philosophical essays, flourished at the end of the nineteenth century. Although women like Wright de Kleinhans were encouraged to write and publish poetry, the art form was dominated by men. A writer was not considered a "true poet" unless s/he read her/his work aloud in public. This distinction was important because as Easterling notes, "women did not perform their work" in public forums. "Women writers, for their part, were simply not afforded this opportunity."[61] Consequently, women were presented with impossible obstacles to earn the label of literata. For this reason, the emerging journals for and about women were of ultimate significance in giving women a public forum to practice and advance their literacy.

The first steps for educating women in literacy came in the form of literary and home journals written for women by men. Jane Herrick notes that women readers had few choices in journals.[62] Much like the etiquette manuals of the United States, these early Mexican women's journals avoided polemics and news of society and mostly focused on educating women in their domestic duties. Several of these early journals included *El Semanario de las Señoritas Mejicanas* (The Weekly for Mexican Young Ladies) (1840–42), *Semana de las Señoritas Mejicanas* (Week of the Mexican Young Ladies) (1851–52), *El Álbum Mexicano* (The Mexican Album) (1849), *La Camelia* (The Camellia) (1853), and, later in the century, *El Álbum de la Mujer* (The Album of the Woman) (1884–88) and *El Correo de las Señoras* (The Mail for Ladies) (1883–93).[63] Most of the journals were several pages in length and included such content as dessert recipes, needlework patterns, poetry, and moral lessons on being a mother, along with entertainment and fashion stories. These journals did little to advance women's educational rights, with the exception of *El Semanario*, edited by Isidro Rafael Gondra. Herrick notes that, "[w]hile not denying that there were differences between men and women, *El Semanario* held that they certainly had equal intellectual faculties," and because the woman was of a weaker mind, the editor claimed, this served as all the more reason to give women an education in rational thinking.[64] Herrick's final assessment of the journals considers the falling number of subscribers and the lack of financial assistance to support the publications for women. She concludes that many of them failed because "the creation of such a literate audience [of women] was of little interest to the majority of Mexicans."[65] While this may be partly true, these journals served an important function as the beginnings of literacy and literate practices for women.

Herrick overlooks several journals in her literary historical survey. One of those missed journals, published in 1880 to 1883 by Ramón Manterola and Luis C. Rubín, was *La Mujer: Semanario de la Escuela de Artes y Oficios para Mujeres* (The Woman: Weekly of the School of Arts and Trade for Women).[66] Like many of the other journals written by men, the *Weekly* was directed toward a female audience and was meant to educate and fortify them socially. This publication included the typical essays on women's traditional role in society, along with some content of science and poetry. However, we see a more progressive turn in this journal, which included the writings of Spanish feminist and journalist Concepción Gimeno de Flaquer in a piece titled, "La mujer estudiosa" (The Studious Woman).[67] In this ensayo, she admonished women to become enlightened about the ways of the world. *La Mujer Mexicana* is another overlooked periodical, which emerged in 1901 out of Morelia, Michoacán, under the direction of Mariano de Jesús Torres.[68] Although edited and written mostly by Torres, this monthly journal contained a very different format from the etiquette manuals of the previous century. Torres's journal served as a historiographic forum to recognize Mexican women for their literary and heroic contributions. The introductory issue provides a page-long list of women from history, beginning with biblical women such as Sarah, Rebecca, and Mary Magdalene, then citing women from early history such as Cleopatra, Bernice, Aspasia, Sappho, Corina, and Joan of Arc, followed by more contemporary women from Cuba, Chile, Bolivia, Argentina, and the United States. Finally, he states that "México también tiene sus heroínas, poetas, escritoras y fundadoras" (Mexico also has its heroines, poets, writers, and founders) and provides a list of sixteen additional women.[69] The goal of the journal was to provide biographies of Mexican women who had distinguished themselves through their virtues, intelligence, literary acumen, and any other way that they had brought distinction to their *patria*. The recovery aspect of this journal also serves as a primary source for narratives of Mexican women left out of the pages of history.[70]

With journals like *La Mujer Mexicana*, we begin to see more of an acceptance of women working and distinguishing themselves in public forums. However, Torres could not speak as effectively for them as they could speak for themselves. The women would have to claim their puesto in society through their own voices. They did just that through another monthly journal with the same title of *La Mujer Mexicana*, appearing in 1904 through 1908. This journal was founded by three professional, civic-oriented Mexican women—physician Columba Rivera, lawyer María Dolores Sandoval de Zarco, and professor Dolores Correa Zapata.[71] Their goal was to elevate the Mexican woman to a higher intellectual plane and push for women's rights. Another publication with the same goal, but appearing much earlier, was the literary journal *Las Hijas del Anáhuac: Ensayo Literario* (The Daughters of Anáhuac: Literary Essay), which appeared in Mexico on October 19, 1873, and was organized, written, edited, and published by women.[72] Some of the first contributors included Concepción García y Ontiveros and Guadalupe Ramírez, who supplied poetry and short editorial pieces. These two women gave their real names, while some of the other women used Aztec pseudonyms, such as Xuihtzaltzin, Miahuaxochitl, and Cuatlicue.[73] After hundreds of years of imposed silence, the women's doubt and hesitation about venturing into the public sphere can be seen in the first few lines of the periodical. Their reasons for starting the journal attest to the increased level of education women were beginning to experience. They write:

> Nunca se había publicado un periódico, redactado como el presente por señoritas y esto nos había hecho vacilar desde hace algún tiempo en establecerlo y llevar á cabo nuestra empresa; pero nos hemos animado, viendo que la sociedad moderna se halla á una altura noble y que adelanta de día en día en la vía de la civilización.[74]

> Never before has there been a newspaper such as this one edited by young women, and this fact made us hesitate for some time in establishing it and bringing it forward; but we have been motivated seeing that modern society approaches a higher space and improves day by day on the path to civilization.

Through the rest of the piece, the women pose the question to their readers of why should men be able to publically demonstrate their intelligence while women have to hide theirs. To counter this double standard, they encourage women to read and study so that they may be able to produce "beautiful and correct compositions." They may have encouraged their sisters to write and become literate, but they also warned women that solely studying and writing could cause them to forget their "sublime mission" of being a mother. Women in the late nineteenth century were still heavily bound to the discourse of the home that Sierra had pronounced to the female students. This first attempt at a periodical published by and for women yielded fourteen issues during its run.[75]

A Final Critique and Chapter Reviews

Situating the Mexican women's writings within the rhetorical tradition of the Americas also opens a space of acknowledging the attention, or lack thereof, that has been given to Latinas in the field of rhetoric and composition. *The Rhetorical Tradition*, edited by Patricia Bizzel and Bruce Herzberg, includes Sor Juana Inés de la Cruz, who remains the only Mexican woman in the rhetorical canon. While I do not dispute her importance within the rhetorical tradition, I offer a critique regarding the attention that has been given to her writing. Historically, it has been difficult to include, let alone recognize, other women's voices from Mexico in the canon because of the focus on men. However, from my perspective, so much focus has been placed on Sor Juana's writings that it has created a historical and rhetorical blind spot, leaving other women invisible. While her presence in the tradition is encouraging, the sole inclusion of Sor Juana reinforces the false assumption that other women were not engaged in rhetorical activities. It gives her the unwelcome and erroneous label of literary anomaly. This rhetorical blind spot has led to a silencing and blacking out of other women writers. Sor Juana as a Mexican woman writer is arguably as famous in the literary world as Dante, Shakespeare, or Thomas Aquinas. Conversely, the overanalysis of her writings has served to drown out other voices. From both a broader and focused disciplinary perspective, I suggest that Sor Juana has attracted hyperscholarly attention in the fields of Latin American history, literature, and rhetoric. I am certainly not disputing that her writing was extremely significant, but because of the pressure to include at least one Mexican woman in the annals of history and the canons of literature, Sor Juana's proverbial voice has now reverted to having a silencing effect on other Mexican women.

Gloria Anzaldúa is another woman of color in the rhetorical tradition who serves as a token figure. Although Anzaldúa is of Mexican descent and pulls her theories and histories from Mexico, she situates herself as a Chicana. She is not a mexicana. However, her work has become the central discursive point of theoretical location for anything Chicana (and sometimes Mexican issues), creating a vacuum that has made it difficult to consider other practitioners of mestiza rhetoric. This trend, though, is changing. Most notably, Jessica Enoch has done studies centered on Chicana rhetorical practices that appeared in "*Para la Mujer*: Defining a Chicana Feminist Rhetoric at the Turn of the Century," and her work on pedagogical practices of Latinos, in *Refiguring Rhetorical Education: Women Teaching African American, Native American, and Chicano/a Students, 1865–1911*. In the area of feminist work that crosses the border into Latin America, rhetors count the work of Susan Romano. She looks into pedagogical and rhetorical practices of Tlaltelolco Indians, but neither Enoch's nor Romano's work deals specifically with women writers situated in Mexico as mexicanas. Dora Ramírez-Dhoore contributes to the understanding of the rhetoric of a Chicana identity in her dissertation, "Writing Chicana Identity: Strategies of Resistance and Reformation." Cristina Kirklighter adds to the conversation about crossing national borders with her study in the social influences of the literary essay in *Traversing the Democratic Borders of the Essay*.

To include a literary perspective, there have been some studies from scholars in English departments that have ventured across the southern border to consider the influences of writers from Mexico, Central and South America, and the Caribbean, including Tace Hedrick's *Mestizo Modernism: Race, Nation, and Identity in Latin American Culture, 1900–1940*; Suzanne Bost's *Mulattas and Mestizas: Representing Mixed Identities in the Americas, 1850–2000*; and Nancy LaGreca's *Rewriting Womanhood: Feminism, Subjectivity, and the Angel of the House in the Latin American Novel, 1887–1903*. Yet, despite this positive trend, the fact remains that there has been no rhetorical historiographic research into Mexican women beyond Sor Juana. *Occupying Our Space* marks important steps toward filling this gap.

In chapter 1, "Historical and Theoretical Directions in Mestiza Rhetoric," I expand upon the theoretical lens of mestiza rhetoric from which I examine the women's writing. Mestiza rhetoric goes beyond the conceptual framing of the "new mestiza" that is so widely known through the work of Anzaldúa. Mestiza rhetoric recovers the historical, material, and national conditions of what being mestiza meant for the Mexican women writing from 1875 to 1942. I posit that the women were claiming a feminine national genealogy reaching back to historical accounts of a poised and persuasive Malintzin. Although Malintzin has repeatedly been historicized through a negative, sexualized lens, I join the many Chicana and Mexican scholars who stress the efficacy of her agency and show how she serves as Mexican women's discursive anchor in claiming a national citizenship. In each discursive act of the Mexican women writers, I claim that they are drawing upon the essential Mexican history of Malintzin.

Chapter 2, "*Las Hijas del Anáhuac*: Laureana Wright de Kleinhans and Other Pioneering Women in Journalism in the Late Nineteenth Century," explores the feminist writings and rhetorical methods of the first female journalist in the historical continuum of the feminist discursive emergence in Mexico. Wright de Kleinhans's extensive writings on history, philosophy, and feminist theory represent the vanguard in the feminist movement in Mexico. Her writings and contributions deserve an entire book. This chapter introduces her writings through close readings of her translated writings from *Violetas del Anáhuac*, *La emancipación de la mujer por medio del estudio*, and *Mujeres notables mexicanas*. It investigates Wright de Kleinhans's rhetorical method for establishing a feminine identity on the male-dominated journalist scene. The chapter also examines how her writings and publications in the women's journal *Violetas* [originally *Hijas*] *del Anáhuac* (1887–89), on which she served as literary director, sustained contradictory feminist stances that were simultaneously progressive yet traditional and nationalist and couched in an indigenous understanding of Mexico's history.

Chapter 3, "'Hear Us!': The Feminist Protests of Las Mujeres de Zitácuaro," highlights a rhetorical analysis of a succession of primary documents I call the "protest series." They consist of cultural and feminist protests published in 1900 by a group of women from the liberal club called Josefa Ortiz de Domínguez and Francisca Carrillo, who also referred to themselves as Las Mujeres de Zitácuaro. Examined using the theoretical lens of genre theory, these primary documents reveal the importance of women's evolving public rhetorical expression, identity, and involvement between the time of Wright de Kleinhans's death (1896) and Gutiérrez de Mendoza's more radical writings (1901). More importantly, this chapter will demonstrate that through Las Mujeres de Zitácuaro's immediate reactions to the men's call for formation of liberal clubs, women were able to begin claiming their rhetorical space.

Chapter 4, "*Rompiendo barreras*: Juana Belén Gutiérrez de Mendoza's Revolutionary Rhetoric," provides a historical overview of the early life of Gutiérrez de Mendoza and shows the intersection of her early influences in life, as the daughter of a campesino and wife of a miner, with the philosophies she expressed in her early writings. The broader goal of this chapter is to analyze Gutiérrez de Mendoza's early writings from her newspaper, *Vésper: Justicia y Libertad*, beginning in 1903, and also her writings from this newspaper appearing in early 1910, just months before the start of the Mexican Revolution. In this chapter, I contend that Gutiérrez de Mendoza wrote to assert the political presence of Mexican women in a male-dominated discursive journalistic environment. The newspapers were a new type of imagined community where language, national politics, and cultural consciousness were being created and debated, and Gutiérrez de Mendoza's subjectivity must be considered in this historical process. As a female writer with a mestiza consciousness, speaking and writing in this space reserved for men only, Gutiérrez de Mendoza carved out a discursive space for future mestiza female journalists and writers through her harsh, edgy, and boundary-breaking discourse.

Finally, chapter 5 focuses on Hermila Galindo, one of the more outwardly political feminists of Mexico during the years of the Mexican Revolution. This chapter, "*Mi grano de arena en esa hermosa labor*: Hermila Galindo's Feminationalist Rhetoric," provides background on her life and delves into a rhetorical analysis of her speech "La mujer en el porvenir" (The Woman in the Future) and other extant writings, such as *La doctrina Carranza y el acercamiento indolatino* (The Doctrine of Carranza and the Critical Analysis of the Approaching Indolatino Politics).[76] Galindo's revolutionary discourse introduced an intertextuality of cultures and ideas that she used to resist assimilation into the old governmental and societal regime. The cultural confluence of these writings points to a mestiza rhetoric whose political agenda was feminism in nationalism, a radically new perspective for Mexican women, which gave them a more important role in society, one they had not had before. As an outspoken feminist and proclaimed mestiza, Galindo was at the forefront of blurring the lines between the personal and the political, the intimate and the social. However, her career was short-lived, ending abruptly in 1920 after a violent and sudden change in the political guard. Her agenda found no support with the new president, Adolfo de la Huerta. This chapter will introduce and analyze some of her writings that have yet to be considered by those who study Latin American history, let alone rhetoric.

If a goal of *Occupying Our Space* is to assist Mexican women writers claim a discursive space, it is imperative to present some of their texts in their entirety. At the end of chapters 2 through 5, there appear translations of journal articles, manifestos, or speeches along with the work in Spanish. All of the primary texts originally appeared in Spanish, and in order to give the writing a larger audience, they have been translated into English.[77] I acknowledge that there cannot be a translation that is perfect. The challenge of every translation process is to maintain nuances of tonality, transfer of meaning, rhetorical emphasis, and language fluctuation. But, regardless of what can be lost in translation, a great deal of understanding and bridging between two cultures can also be gained.

Providing access to the Mexican women's writings gives the writers voices anew. Their first struggle was to be heard in an oppressive patriarchal society, and now that they are no longer here to tell their stories, they again struggle to take their puesto in the revolutionary and political history of their day. A translation of a text is more than just a mere transition from one language to another. It is an opening, a rupturing of silences between two cultures. I see the translations of the women's writings bringing about what Audre Lorde calls "the transformation of silence into language and action."[78] The translations here serve as a linguistic bridge that will bring a deeper awareness of another culture of women and their struggles to be heard.

The use of the theoretical lens of mestiza rhetoric, whose underlying objective is a feminist one, clears an open and inclusionary puesto for these women, whose writings would not have been accommodated under a traditional linear feminist lens. Writing from the rhetorical perspective of a mestiza complicates the act of writing merely as a form of protest. A mestiza rhetorical perspective makes concessions for various cultural, social, political, and ethnic stances. It also opens a genre space that looks beyond literary writings. Most importantly, these women's writings are given the respect they deserve through an analysis of how their discourse has been subjected to colonial and neocolonial silencing, rather than merely placing them within the rhetorical landscape. They wrote from multidimensional, complex points of view. They wrote not only as women, but as noncitizen women of color within a colonized territory of mind and body. An exclusively rhetorical feminist perspective would not fully encompass these women's projects as writers.

CHAPTER ONE

Historical and Theoretical Directions in Mestiza Rhetoric

For many feminist critics today, the use of voice by La Malinche, her role as a spokesperson, marks one of her most striking—and positive—disruptions of the patriarchy on both the indigenous and the European sides.
—SANDRA MESSINGER CYPESS, FROM "'MOTHER' MALINCHE AND ALLEGORIES OF GENDER, ETHNICITY, AND NATIONAL IDENTITY IN MEXICO"

Current feminists are becoming sophists in the best sense of the word by describing rhetorical solutions to the crucial problem of defining a theory with the most power for changing women's lives.
—SUSAN JARRATT, FROM *REREADING THE SOPHISTS: CLASSICAL RHETORIC REFIGURED*

The term *mestiza rhetoric* was first coined by Andrea Lunsford in her interview with Gloria Anzaldúa in "Toward a Mestiza Rhetoric," and it was developed further in Damián Baca's book *Mestiz@ Scripts, Digital Migrations, and the Territories of Writing*. Like Anzaldúa, the women considered in my study, Laureana Wright de Kleinhans, Las Mujeres de Zitácuaro, Juana Belén Gutiérrez de Mendoza, and Hermila Galindo, were writing from rhetorical puestos of in-between the borders and peripheries of their gender, race, and culture. Mexican society required that its women best be seen and not heard, a social trait upheld at the turn of the twentieth century by antifeminist writers, such as Andrés Ortega and Julio Sesto. Many women ignored these social boundaries and did write. These women used the generative feminine force of mestiza rhetorics that "are discursive manifestations of continuity and adaptation that comprise . . . survival."[1]

Invoking Royster and Kirsch's strategic imagination, my interpretation of mestiza rhetoric deviates from Anzaldúa's Chicana articulation. I interpret that mestiza rhetoric stems, in part, from the identity theory of mestizaje that emerged in the modernist phase (1880–90) of Latin American literature, history, art, and philosophy. Some of the key male voices of that period include José Martí from Cuba, Manuel González Prada from Peru, and Mexicans such as Ignacio Manuel Altamirano and Guillermo Prieto. These intellectuals embraced their mestizo indigenous roots as a way of understanding their modernist identities.[2]

However, the fact that Mexican women writers from the late nineteenth and early twentieth centuries also understood and articulated this nationalist cultural movement has been largely ignored. They expressed their nationalist sentiments by establishing literary and political journals, writing newspaper essays and articles, appropriating nationalist protest genres, and composing poetry. Similar to Anzaldúa's approach, mestiza rhetoric shifts the focus of the mestizo identity construct to the feminine, rooted in its Mexican mythical past. Instead of Anzaldúa's identification with the archetype of Coatlicue, the Serpent Woman, my research and study connects the women's speaking voices with the female indigenous progenitor Malintzin. In basing mestiza rhetoric theory in the indigenous feminine figure connected with guiding, speaking, and translating, we see her Mexican *sucesoras* claim a historically discursive, not mythical, identity. These women's writings intersected with the national conversation of what it meant to be mexicano and, for the women, mexicana.

The method of historiography plays a central role in envisioning Malintzin and the other Mexican women rhetors at the center of history. Originally, a patriarchal stance of history denied the inclusion of the materials women produced as reason to write them out of history. For this project, I assume a feminist sophistic stance toward historiography, which challenges the exclusion of women in the writing of history. Indeed, feminist rhetorical scholar Susan Jarratt forecasted the expansion of acceptable materials and subject matters of rhetorical history, "resulting in what today would be styled multi-disciplinarity."[3] A sophistic historiography also rejects a foundational logic of continuity and employs the creation of "narratives distinguished by multiple or open causality."[4] Jarratt uses the example of the Greek sophists and the ways in which they challenged the continuity of history through a retelling of stories, such as Gorgias's *Encomium of Helen*. Similarly, I open rhetorical puestos for Mexican women by (1) questioning historical perceptions of the Mexican intellectual tradition and (2) reimagining Malintzin as the female progenitor of mestiza rhetoric.

This repositioning of Malintzin is critical to feminist historiographic correctives. Baca contends, "Expanding [Malintzin's] historical act of translation from its linguistic conception to its present day symbolic and rhetorical potential adds significantly to her role as translator and cultural mediator."[5] Through this same historical repositioning, I show how the Mexican women journalists and activists central to *Occupying Our Space* asserted a rhetorical feminine heritage of the origins of Mexico, which had been labeled as a traitorous and selfish act. Many male critics considered the act of Mexican women claiming the puesto of speaker or writer as a cultural betrayal. For their feminine writing to appear within the public was culturally subversive and resistant. Yet, through a sophistic interpretive stance, the act of ocupando un puesto as speaker, writer, or interpreter redefines and re/visions the negative myth of the mestiza. In this chapter, I unravel the complexities of mestiza rhetoric, which has diverse layers. First, I discuss mestizaje through the history of Malintzin as a primary female rhetor of Mexico. Next, I define mestizaje as a male form of nationalist identification. Then, I encapsulate the theoretical lens of mestiza rhetoric. To close, I situate myself between Latin American studies and rhetoric to articulate how I am listening to, dialoguing with, and representing the voices of Mexican women.

The Indian Mother, Malintzin, as Critical Rhetor

Instead of introducing the concept of mestizaje with the customary examination of new and old theories and theorists, which I will deal with later in the chapter, I begin with the story (*her*story) and life of Malintzin, the Indian mother of the Mexican race.[6] This reversed approach, which I situate as a strategic contemplation of feminist and historical identification, places the feminine aspect of mestizaje at the center of Mexican cultural understanding. For centuries Malintzin has played equally a central and a peripheral role, beginning with the initial moment that the Conquest was historicized. Historically, the male aspect of strength, intelligence, cold logic, and discursive presence, both European and indigenous, has been valued over the feminine, but the tide is slowly shifting. If the process of mestizaje is based upon the coming together of two cultures through the progeny of Spanish conqueror Hernán Cortés and Nahua indigenous woman Malintzin, then the feminine concept of mestiza rhetoric, too, is couched in this "coming together." Mexican feminist scholar Martha Robles casts Malintzin in a positive light in her role as translator in the contact zone of languages, noting that she served as a "verbal bridge, a passageway from words unrelated to her past, remote in all aspects from the names of her experience and without any link with the meaning of the ideas of domination in the European sense."[7] Malintzin, in the initial "coming together" of cultures and people, could not have imagined the future. As a theory of "coming together," mestiza rhetoric critically and respectfully places the Indian mother at the center of this racial and national identity.

Malintzin was born into an influential Nahua family. At a young age, and after the death of her father, she was hastily sold into slavery by her mother.[8] Her place and date of birth are highly contested. J. Jesús Figueroa Torres's analysis shows that a majority of historians locate her birthplace as Xalixco, or Jalisco, and that she could have been born between 1500 and 1510.[9] While these details of her life remain debated, it is fact that Malintzin became the interpreter, mediator, advisor, and lover to Cortés. Mexico's indigenous mother is known by different names. She's known by La Malinche, which carries the most negative connotation, meaning "the mistress of," and refers to her national betrayal of her people. The names Malinal, Marina, and, later, Doña Marina were given to her upon her Christian baptism. Malintzin, the name I call her, is derived from her authentic Nahuatl birth name. Although her existence is verified over and over in ethnographic evidence about the Nahua, Aztec/Mexica, and Spaniards in works by important historians such as Bernal Díaz del Castillo and Fernando de Alva Cortés Ixtlilxochitl, she has passed into the realm of legend, myth, and female archetype, exerting a powerful influence on the perceptions of the Mexican people.[10]

For three years (approximately 1519 to 1521), before she took on the role of mother of a new mestizo race, Malintzin stood and spoke at the center of negotiations and conversations between two empires caught in a contact zone. It is at this apex of power where I locate and theorize this powerful female protagonist. Similar to other important rhetorical figures, like Socrates and Aspasia, Malintzin did not leave writings, letters, or journals as historical documentation. Still, through her act of speaking and translating in three different languages amid powerful men, she can be historicized as one of Mexico's central female rhetors.

Malintzin's perceived role as betrayer of her people (*su raza*) has cast her as a negative, sexualized, mythic Mexican Eve figure, a beguiling and selfish woman who cared only for her survival and personal gain. This argument has been popularized by Mexican writers such as Octavio Paz, who labels her as La Chingada, the Screwed One, and as having taken a "passive" historical role, unable to resist violence and conquest.[11] This longstanding perspective on Malintzin's legacy, he argues, has carried over into the everyday identity of Mexican women and represents "a secret conflict that we have still not resolved."[12] On some level this perception may be true, because, as Paz contends, the Mexican culture is still caught in the double bind of the myth and conquest. Indeed, it is important to note that various contemporary Mexican scholars, such as Nadia L. Orozco and Francisco Xavier Sánchez Hernández, argue that the Mexican identity is much more complex than a historical articulation of Malintzin.[13] Central to the record of Malintzin, many Mexican and Chicana/o writers, such as Norma Alarcón, Alicia Gaspar de Alba, Deena González, Rosario Castellanos, Miguel Ángel Menéndez, Sandra Messinger Cypess, and J. Jesús Figueroa Torres, have rejected her negative persona. Instead, they have re/visited historical narratives to reveal a more courageous and intelligent woman. Entangled in theories of sexuality, class, race, and language, these scholars have tried to undo the centuries of negativity. No doubt, this release is a challenging task. However, undoing the negative perception of her is of utmost importance in order to bring Malintzin's words and actions out of the shadows of history to "sex the colonial imaginary" and track "women's agency on the colonial landscape."[14]

Malintzin's rhetorical acts initiated a stream of narratives for the next five hundred years that would frame and refigure her identity in numerous ways. In fact, the Spaniards gave her the title of La Lengua, literally meaning "the tongue." For centuries, her intellect and linguistic ability have been overlooked, even derided, while the traitor aspect of her actions has played a central role for male historians, such as Octavio Paz and Alfonso Reyes. However, others have taken the opposite perspective. Mexican feminist and literata Rosario Castellanos, in the play *El eterno femenino*, resurrects historical figures through advances in technologies. She engages the pair Cortés and Malintzin in conversations about major historical events.[15] Cortés is portrayed as enacting a "stereotype of feminine behavior," and Malintzin, who speaks her mind in response to Cortés, appears wise and confident. This re/visioning of these events through a theatrical form grants Malintzin speaking agency. More poignantly, it is through Castellanos's poetry that she makes a greater connection between herself as a modern Mexican female writer and the Mexican indigenous mother Malintzin. The last two stanzas of the poem "Malinche" read:

> I advance toward destiny in chains
> leaving behind all that can still hear
> the funeral murmurs with which I am buried.

And the voice of my mother in tears—in tears!
She who decrees my death.[16]

Malintzin reclaims Castellanos's same speaking agency in *Todos los gatos son pardos* by Carlos Fuentes.[17] In this play, Malintzin is tasked with recounting the Conquest and the contact between Cortés and Moctezuma. We see her standing between powerful men speaking her mind. In the connection between her words and soil, we see direct correlation between speaking and geographic identification. She claims, "My tongue is of the land, and nothing can silence it."[18] In one tender moment, couched in philosophical dealings, Cortés speaks openly to Malintzin about reality and how it comes into existence. He recounts that he has been dreaming about words and how everything that happens occurs in language. Calmly and authoritatively, Malintzin answers him, "I had warned you. Only that which has been named exists."[19] Her philosophy here points to Covino and Jolliffe's definition of rhetoric, in that it can create and alter realities. But although Fuentes may endow Malintzin with the knowledge and power of words, in the end, he frames her in the trope of a disgraced figure, one who can no longer claim her land or her people.

If we consider the definition of *rhetoric* as a verbal epistemic art, then the role of speaking for oneself in order to create a divergent reality, outside of a socially prescribed truth, merits the designation of *rhetor*. The interpretations of Malintzin by Castellanos and Fuentes place her in the role of rhetor inscribed with agency and the linguistic knowledge of narrative to call worlds into being. Indeed, this is a complex vision to have of Malintzin. By being endowed with language(s), she was always already using speech at its most fundamental level, to communicate. Walter Ong would assert that in the process of communicating as human beings we constantly make choices of how we will or will not transmit ideas. Words are not merely "impulses," but the recognition of the existence of the other.[20]

Like Castellanos and Fuentes, Norma Alarcón recognizes that the perceived betrayal of Malintzin toward her people was played out, not so much in terms of her sexualized role as a mother, but more so through the use of her intellect and language *outside* of the maternal role.[21] Malintzin spoke the conqueror's language, and she is believed to have betrayed her people by giving Cortés the upper hand. The act of speaking in and with the indigenous and Spanish cultures was connected to intellect and citizenship, both rhetorical appeals of ethos. In order to downplay the role of speaking connected to citizenship for women, the role of motherhood emerged as a powerful feminine trope to create a deep connection to the nation. Mexican writer Andrés Ortega wrote from a feminized perspective to convince his readers that a frame devoid of discourse for Mexican women was best: "Mercy! Unlike you I was not born a man; I was not born for the turbulent arguments of the Parliament . . . neither was I for shameless explanations at the school of Medicine, nor for the brilliant arguments in front of a jury. I was born to wait for you at home, with open arms and modest kisses, in order to be your loving and simple wife, the mother of your children. . . . Educate me according to my nature."[22] These ideas permeated Mexican society.

A form of Mexican feminism, a cultural ideal of women as the family nurturers known as *marianismo*, grew out of a long-standing absence of women's citizenship and served as a reason to deny them a voice for centuries.[23] Motherhood, or the responsibility of raising respectable and contributing members of society, replaced Mexican women's legal claim to "citizenship." This movement or gender typing, a rhetorical move Hawkesworth would label rhetoric of difference, served only to strengthen women's biological position that kept them confined to certain puestos in public life.[24] Speaking outside of this role or to speak for oneself and not in defense of one's children or immediate family, as Malintzin did, caused one to be labeled a heretic or betrayer of one's societal role. In other words, Mexican women who spoke or wrote were claiming the negative historical archetype of Malintzin. Alarcón notes that "because Malintzin the translator is perceived as speaking for herself and not her children and/or the community, she is a woman who has betrayed her primary cultural function—maternity. The figure of the mother is bound to a double reproduction, *stricto sensu* that of her people and her culture."[25] The image of Malintzin speaking to, with, and between the words of powerful men created a misplaced myth that symbolized her as a speaker out of bounds. Historically, other Mexican women who would choose a rhetorical or intellectual puesto were cast in this same masculine light. Grounded in this negative identification for centuries to come, the puesto of speaker, intellectual, and writer was masculinized.

Like Baca's framing of Malintzin, I shift the emphasis from a sexualized ethos of Malintzin to an intellectual and rhetorical identity through mestiza rhetoric. Malintzin's translations and persuasive abilities gained her immediate notoriety among the Spanish and indigenous men.[26] Considering the account of Malintzin's rhetorical intervention, the theory of mestiza rhetoric emerges in the moment Malintzin first spoke as translator, *not* when she gave birth to Cortés's child. Early in the Conquest, Cortés fought battles and skirmishes and made his military strength known to the Native people. After one such severe battle with the Chontal warriors, Malintzin was among the twenty slaves delivered to Cortés as a gesture of peace.[27] They began traveling with Cortés's party aboard his ship. After they had been on the ship for some time, messengers from Moctezuma canoed out and boarded the ship. Townsend recounts the narrative of Cortés's discovery of Malintzin as a valued interpreter.

> With remarkable aplomb, given the circumstances, and apparently very little panic, the messengers demanded to speak to the leader and announced that they bore greetings from Moctezuma. Cortés demanded that Jerónimo de Aguilar tell him what they said. Under pressure, the friar tried to understand; he could not. He spoke a dialect of Maya, but unbeknownst to him, this was Nahuatl. By his own admission, Cortés was irritated. What kind of translator was this? He had gone to a great deal of trouble and expense to ransom him, apparently to no purpose.
>
> Malintzin could have remained silent. No one expected her to step forward and serve as a conduit. By the end of the hour, she had made her value felt. Cortés's secretary and biographer later wrote that afterward he took her aside with Aguilar, asked who she was, and promised her "more than liberty" if she would help him find and speak to Moctezuma. Undoubtedly, he promised her riches; it was what he promised everyone who agreed to aid his cause.[28]

We do not have record of what Malintzin said. However, if we attend to the powerful men's reactions, we can deduce that what she communicated must have been extraordinarily persuasive. Overnight, Malintzin was afforded a much higher level of respect and importance, which would not have been given in any other circumstance. Historian Antonio de Solís wrote, "Doña Marina was a genius with the Mexican and Yucatecan languages, and very quickly learned Castilian because she had a rare natural sharpness of mind that demonstrated her heritage."[29] Her verbal synthesis of the pre- and postcontact worlds demonstrates her superior ability to sustain the tension of dual races and complex rhetorical situations.

The moment she opened her mouth to serve as a conduit, the course of her life and those of the two cultures she stood between were immediately altered, fractured, and split. In stepping into this bordered linguistic puesto, Malintzin simultaneously gained and lost rhetorical agency. She gained agency by making the decision to interpret the words to the conqueror, and she equally lost it because henceforth she was bound to serve as interpreter. In speaking, she put herself under the scrutiny of historians and scribes, where she also lost her agency. There was no turning back. The moment in which she revealed her knowledge of languages is also when she claimed *la facultad* that Anzaldúa describes. "We lose something in this mode of initiation, something is taken from us: our innocence, our unknowing ways, our safe and easy ignorance."[30] Did she speak because she truly wanted to assist in the communication process? Did she speak for self-preservation? Miguel Ángel Menéndez envisions that she spoke with purpose. He says that, "[y]es, she spoke with the conviction and fire of a slave that serves her master when she believes that her master is directing her toward freedom."[31] Regrettably, we will never know Malintzin's true intentions. Regardless of the reason she spoke, it resulted in shifting her puesto from *india esclava* to *india intérprete*. Such a central role as speaker and interpreter was unheard of for a woman. It is this perception of Malintzin that Figueroa Torres considers when he argues her as "Mexico's first citizen, the first Christian, the first Mexican to speak Spanish, and to mix her blood with that of the conquerors."[32]

Figueroa Torres may frame Malintzin as the first subject of various civic and political positions; however, I do not make this same distinction. To say that Malintzin was the "first" or sole indigenous rhetor would be disingenuous, ignoring the history of the codices and accounts by Miguel León-Portilla, expert anthropologist in pre-Conquest history and Nahuatl literature. Josefina Muriel, citing León-Portilla in *Cultura femenina novohispana*, includes several female intellectual notables in her extensive history and anthology of women from pre-Conquest times. One such woman is La Señora de Tula, a poetess and historian in the time of Macuilxochitzin who wrote poetry about the battle of King Axayácatl.[33] Another woman Muriel includes is Xóchitl. The Codex Telleriano-Remensis refers to her as a *tlacuilo*, one who holds a variety of intellectual skills and talents, such as scribe, artist, writer, or sage.[34] She is depicted in the codex annotating information, as would a scribe or historian, and also as the daughter of Hutzilíhuitl.[35] Granted, little is known of these women, yet they served a role as intellectuals in their time. Giving Malintzin and other indigenous women a rhetorical puesto in history, then, dislodges the patriarchal and institutional belief that they played a passive role in times past.

As we've seen, revisionist historians have focused on Malintzin's linguistic abilities, her agency, and her lack of it in making the decisions she carried out. Her unique position of speaking *to*, *from*, *within*, and *for* power created a pivotal feminist intervention in the historical account of the Conquest. Another example of Malintzin's speaking agency focuses on her initial negotiations among the Spaniards and Tlaxcalan people. As with her initial dialogue, her words became the critical cultural and linguistic bridge. Townsend recounts the moment when Cortés had brutally attacked the Tlaxcalan people, and they fought back. However, the indigenous warriors were no match for the force with which the Spaniards came at them with horses and armor. After losing many of their people, the Tlaxcalan chiefs negotiated peace and "attempted to construct a permanent working relationship with the Spaniards—one that would placate the newcomers without tearing asunder the worldview and habits of the people. . . . Malintzin literally stood at the heart of these negotiations."[36] With no one else available to speak between the warring factions, we can deduce that she saved many lives in the Indian villages by allowing a conversation to transpire. The many histories that have survived, such as in the depictions of the codices, show that Malintzin spoke at many different times as the Conquest unfolded. Undoubtedly, she became a crucial player negotiating ideas and pleas within the complexities of two cultures.

It is at these crucial moments of her speaking that we see the subversive feminine rhetor, leader, and authority figure emerge, introducing us to new strategies of intervention. These characteristics of women would later be marginalized by another feminine symbol. Malintzin's words intersected with, and took command of, powerful male discourses of empire, conquest, and combat, creating an altogether different vision of her future and the futures of the races she stood between. This characterization, however, would not prevail. Only ten years after the fall of Tenochtitlán, and after the appearance of La Virgen de Guadalupe to an Aztec Indian, Juan Diego, in 1531, Mexico adopted the vision of Tonantzin/Guadalupe, the abnegating, submissive, and silent figure, as a counternarrative to the figure of the dominant speaking female of Malintzin. Sánchez Hernández contends that the appearance of La Virgen de Guadalupe would serve as the root of the new mestizo nation.[37] She would become the idealized, passive woman for Mexicans and, more recently, Chicanos, and would become the acceptable and traditional silencing myth for women to follow. For many, the feminine character split between Guadalupe and Malintzin depicted the archetypal roles that surround Mexican women: *la madre* (the mother), *la virgen* (the virgin), and *la puta* (the whore). In Mexican and Chicano literature, the Virgen de Guadalupe represents the feminine characteristics that Mexican/Chicana women should mimic because she symbolizes the ideals of marianismo. Tired of the inherent oppression of this patriarchal symbol of conforming, women claiming roles as speakers or leaders were seen as standing in opposition to these ideals by creating a puesto and voice of their own. Hence, the symbol of Malintzin (La Malinche) was synonymous with women stepping away from the submissive role to act as a man in terms of leadership. Many interpretations set up the two female figures as the new dichotomy in a *machista*, or male-dominated, society. In Colonial and independent Mexico, women had little choice but to follow the Guadalupe myth or risk being outcasts. Indeed, Sánchez Hernández complicates this sometimes negative dichotomy, saying that Guadalupe is the universal mother to bring unity to the dual rooted culture.[38] He says that this duality asks the Mexican people to appreciate and embrace the complexity of mestizaje.

Having now examined this multifaceted narrative, we must ask, what are the implications in framing Malintzin as a central female rhetor of Mexico? First, this framing refigures our *nomos*, or "provisional codes (habits or customs) of social and political behavior," of who counts as rhetor.[39] Malintzin's speaking, now and in the past, serves as a point in history that exposes the gap in rhetorical women that extends for more than three hundred years. Currently, there is a substantial gap between the two Latinas in our field, Sor Juana and Anzaldúa, but positioning Malintzin as a Mexican female rhetor exposes another gap of representation between Malintzin and Sor Juana. Works such as Josefina Muriel's *Cultura femenina novohispana* confirm the actions and writings of numerous women, including several indigenous women, writing from civic and monastic puestos. Still, many would be content to keep these women "silenced, gagged, caged, bound into servitude" under the pretext that Malintzin did not produce any writing.[40] My work of radical recovery is similar to Cheryl Glenn's historicizing of Aspasia as a rhetor, which was considered controversial, almost rhetorical heresy.[41] Glenn's historical interpretation, as does mine, "provides an approachable, disruptable ground for engaging and transforming traditional memory or practice."[42]

Secondly, our knowledge of Malintzin as rhetor extends our rhetorical knowledge and challenges us to continuously cross linguistic and cultural borders. Malintzin engaged in a discursive act that placed her in the symbolic puesto of being "in between" two or more cultures and languages. As a fairly new concept for rhetoric, seeing Malintzin as a central rhetor exposes a glaring fault in our discipline, where much more work needs to be done. Lastly, framing Malintzin as a central female rhetor of Mexico forces us to consider the limits of feminist discourse. If Malintzin's act of interpretation and speaking is considered through Mary Hawkesworth's lens of feminist discourses, her interpretative acts qualify as feminist rhetoric. For Hawkesworth "feminist rhetorics call worlds into being, inscribe new orders of possibility, validate frames of reference and forms of explanation, and reconstitute histories serviceable for present and future projects."[43] We can say that the intersection of Malintzin's discourse with two dichotomous worlds triangulates as feminist, mestiza, and rhetorical, creating a new interpretive puesto of mestiza rhetoric. Historically speaking, the myth of Malintzin as translator-speaker has functioned as metonymy when Mexican and Chicana women take a speaking role in society. In becoming public rhetors, Mexican and Chicana women writers, from Malintzin, Sor Juana, Wright de Kleinhans, the forty women of Las Mujeres de Zitácuaro, Gutiérrez de Mendoza, and Hermila Galindo to Anzaldúa, are considered selfish traitors of their people and traditions. "In my culture," Anzaldúa says, "selfishness is condemned, especially in women; humility and selflessness, the absence of selfishness, is considered a virtue."[44] This narrow outlook is inverted when we consider an alternative perspective through a mestiza consciousness. Significantly, the concept of mestizaje offers a clarification of interpretation because when these cultures clash and come together they create a new understanding.

Historical Interpretations of Mestizaje

In the time frame this book examines, from 1875 to 1942, Mexicans were in the historic moment of a modernist reconciliation and were coming to terms with their mixed racial identity, their mestizaje. The term *modernist* relates to the movement in Mexico that began with a need for a "renewal of thought about America and about the rapid changes brought by industrialization."[45] Mexican artists, though, had an understanding that this renewal also should include embracing their ancient indigenous past and connecting it with the industrial and progressive nature of society. This brought many contradictions, but resulted in a modernist mestizaje that would explode after the Revolution. As a result, mestizaje has been one of the most historicized and theorized concepts through centuries of colonial and nationalist times in Latin America and Europe.

Mestizaje can also signify centuries-old prevailing narratives of conquest, rape, slavery, and cultural imperialism, but from a feminist perspective, it also has the power to simultaneously resist and reframe that historical representation. Mestizaje is the product and/or process of the mixing of the European and indigenous races of the supposed New World, invoking and "leaning toward" its Native origins. In its idealized form, mestizaje claims to accept and embrace races on all sides, but underneath the surface, we see mestizaje portending an exclusionary and destructive aspect that further colonizes and assimilates the indigenous. Nonetheless, it has the power to create a strategic third space of identity that resists assimilation to linear identification.

Laureana Wright de Kleinhans, Las Mujeres de Zitácuaro, Juana Belén Gutiérrez de Mendoza, Hermila Galindo, and others were articulating a form of mestizaje rhetoric before José Vasconcelos released his philosophical treatise *La raza cósmica* (1925).[46] The concept already had a long history and a cultural consciousness through Mexican male intellectuals, such as Ignacio Manuel Altamirano and Justo Sierra. In Mexico, the articulation of mestizaje peaked with Vasconcelos's *La raza cósmica*, but the concept has continued to experience popularity even into the twenty-first century. Frida Kahlo and her husband, Diego Rivera, were among the many popular artists during the post-Revolutionary era (1920–40) who embraced mestizaje as a way of "being Mexican." Pinpointing what it means to be Mexican continues to be a struggle. Octavio Paz expresses this challenge best: "Mexicanism is a way of not being ourselves, a way of life that is not our own. Sometimes it is a mask," and sometimes it is a desire to find a true voice. As Mexican writers, men or women are caught within the "ambiguity of [their] tradition."[47] Rhetorical acts serve as an articulation of one's identity, but Laureana Wright de Kleinhans, Las Mujeres de Zitácuaro, Juana Belén Gutiérrez de Mendoza, and Hermila Galindo, as well as many other writers, were seemingly betrayed by their own words. Regardless of which paradigm they chose to embrace—the dichotomous myths of victim versus agent, harlot versus heroine, or the aspect of indigenous versus European—a resolution seemed not to exist. This leaves us asking if there is one true *mexicanidad*. Those for whom it is a lived experience can derive from it multiple, complex interpretations. In order to understand the struggle that can come from living in two worlds, I offer a description of Kahlo's famous painting *Las dos Fridas* (1939).

In her self-portrait, we see two figures of Kahlo seated side by side, holding hands. The figure on the left wears a long, white, European-style dress with elaborate lace covering the bodice and neck. Puffy, layered sleeves cascade down her arms. The Kahlo on the right wears the traditional Mexican attire consisting of a long skirt with a simple blouse. Both figures, with faces that reveal the dark features of a Mexican woman, expose a heart resting outside the bodice. The European Kahlo has the dress fabric torn back, exposing a bleeding heart, while the Mexican Kahlo's heart is whole. A single vein is wrapped around the two figures and links the two hearts. The end of the vein rests bleeding on the lap of the European Kahlo and is held closed by surgical pincers, holding back a stream of life-giving blood. The sharing of blood represents the fluid mixing of ethnic blood of the European and indigenous figures, but also illustrates the traditional side as being whole and complete.

Identifying as a mestiza, Kahlo embraced the feminine face of the identity struggle and re/imaged the masculine concept of colonization. This portrait represents the mestiza accepting the two identities through holding hands and sharing the same blood, but it also shows the European side as suffering, stained, and impure. This artistic interpretation of a dual identity represents different cultural histories and levels of stigma or valorization, which had been ongoing for centuries in Mexico. While Kahlo's representation of mestizaje came late in the modernist movement, it provides a visual representation of the mixed racial representation the women journalists were already speaking to.

In Mexico, mestizaje was and still is an ever-present topos embedded in the discourse. Beginning in the 1870s and 1880s, a radical shift in Mexico's identity was taking hold—not only its identity as a nation, but also its identity at a time when "men and women were experiencing the significance of gender and racial roles in a changing, politicized, and necessarily embodied way."[48] Porfirio Díaz used mestizaje as an assimilationist and historical project that would reconcile the nation's indigenous past with its positivist present and future. Joshua Lund stresses the importance of realizing that mestizaje was "a method for writing the history of Mexico."[49] He says, "Mexican *mestizaje*, then, could be understood as a *necessary fusion* whose assimilating effects held the key to producing a new race, that is . . . a new *national* race."[50] A hybridity of a race and ethnicity emerged.

The rhetoric of the mestizo/a resides in a perpetual space of hybrid paradoxes, resisting assimilation to one or the other half, which can become a complex negotiation when one is articulating it as an identity construct. Mestizaje for the Mexican people was and still is a way of identification. It became part of the efforts of nation building and of establishing a uniquely Mexican identity. Mexico's theoretical understanding of mestizaje is mostly based on the ideas of Vasconcelos, whose theories of unity and acceptance sound promising, but they are couched in contradicting and racist sentiments of eliminating the indigenous population while in the same breath praising them as the root of Mexico's nationhood. On the one hand, he praises the genius of the conquerors, such as Cortés, Francisco Pizarro, Pedro de Alvarado, and Sebastián de Belalcázar, stating that they were "great captains that joined destructive impetus to creative genius."[51] Conversely, in speaking about the creation of a superior history, he states that "it is stupid to initiate our patriotism with Father Hidalgo's cry for independence, or the conspiracy of Quito, or the feats of Bolívar, because if we do not root it in Cuauhtémoc and Atahualpa, it will have no support."[52] Vasconcelos articulates the centuries-long construction of a malecentric strategic assimilation of the Indian, one rooted in recognition of their historical yet peripheral and secondary presence. According to Vasconcelos, women's identity construction was subsumed and forgotten under that of their male counterparts.

The men monopolized the concept of mestizaje. They were speaking of nationhood and the fifth race in purely masculine terms, such as through the histories of Mexico written by Altamirano et al. and published in 1873. These histories left women not just at the periphery of the collective conscious as bearers of the race but completely absent.[53] Ironically, they were the female progenitors of the race, but were not considered as actors in the history. The year 1873 also marks women's early attempts at breaking into the male-dominated puesto of public writing. The women's voices intersected not only with patriarchy and domesticity but also with the greater conversation of national identity taking place in the newspapers, journals, and history books. Their voices were just the beginning of what would be an opening puesto for women to speak and write about their histories.

Continuously at the periphery of society and history, the women were attempting to include themselves within this nationalist conversation of what it meant to be Mexican. As a result of women's exclusion from the political and historical discourse (women did not receive full rights to citizenship, including suffrage and the right to run for office, until 1953), I see mestizaje as a gendered theory that silences women. Many times, overarching systems of societal identification and knowledge, such as the discipline of science, pass under the radar as universally true, neutral, and harmless. Donna Harraway has shown these perspectives to be false.[54] In fact, through reading the early articulations of mestizaje of Latin America (1815–1925), we see the model theorized only by the intellectual men of Latin America, such as Simón Bolívar (Venezuela), José Martí (Cuba), Justo Sierra (Mexico), Ignacio Manuel Altamirano (Mexico), Carlos Octavio Bunge (Argentina), and possibly one of the most famous, José Vasconcelos (Mexico). As we see in Henry Schmidt's 1978 survey of intellectual Mexican thought, women's articulation of nationhood was completely excluded from the literary canon of the nineteenth and the early and mid-twentieth centuries.[55] Schmidt dedicates one paragraph to women's mexicanidad, but he bases his narrow perception upon the pessimistic and sexist lenses of Julio Guerrero and Horacio Barrera, not on the inclusion of any women's literary voices.[56] These exclusions of women's voices from the conversation of mestizaje, from its inception to present times, are at the very core questions of rhetorical power. This reflection illuminates once again how the systematic construction of identity by the intellectuals was denied to women. It is not until the post-Revolutionary era that we see women, such as Frida Kahlo (Mexico), Gabriela Mistral (Chile), Rosario Castellanos (Mexico), and the most renowned contemporary Chicana theorist, Gloria Anzaldúa (United States), enter the picture with artistic, literary, and theoretical conceptualizations of mestizaje.

The end of the nineteenth and into the twentieth century in Mexican history would be the *kairotic* moment that women needed in order to shape their own identities through political and gendered resistance. They constructed their own form of speaking and writing to the nation, which I call mestiza rhetoric. Women at this time strategically sidestepped the potentially masculine and tragic origins of their nation and created an alternative puesto that connected them with the mother of their nation and influential female Mexican rhetor of the Americas, Malintzin. The era of peace in public politics at the turn of the century turned to one of discontent and questioning of the dictatorial regime. In "Feminismo y Revolución," Martha Eva Rocha Islas notes this emerging dissatisfaction that grew among the women, such as Dolores Jiménez y Muro, Juana Belén Gutiérrez de Mendoza, Sara Estela Ramírez, and María Andrea Villarreal González, and recounts the dissenting actions they took against the government.[57] Dissenting voices began questioning Díaz's adherence to the 1857 constitution and his loyalty to the Mexican people. Over the period of a decade, these voices would grow to a crescendo, leading to the Mexican Revolution.

These national politics opened a rare rhetorical puesto for women to speak and act in the public sphere as they never had before. Feminist historian Emma Pérez notes that "[h]istorical events such as the Mexican Revolution show that women's politics may have been subordinated under a nationalist paradigm, but women as agents have always constructed their own puesto interstitially, within nationalism, nationalisms that often miss women's subtle interventions."[58] Pérez uses the term "feminism-in-nationalism" to show how women's voices intersected with nationalism, but she notes that even though women's messages carried a patriotic message, they could speak only from the margins. However, some of the women writing in the pre-Revolutionary era, such as Gutiérrez de Mendoza, contributed to a more central and radical feminine social intervention, which was different from the pioneering voices in that they claimed an identity more separate from the men. Hence, I see the feminine linked more closely to the national aspect than is suggested by Pérez's term, in which the aspects are separated by hyphens. I claim that women were closely engaged in combining the feminized body with national politics, a *feminationalism*.

Within this discourse of feminationalism, the women's writings synthesize sentiments of marianismo and nationalist mestiza identities. The women's historical interpretation shifts the perspective of the masculine project of mestizaje toward an "emphasis on the importance of the maternal to the nation and, most importantly, on the image of the Indian mother as origin of racial and national energies."[59] The dualistic and sometimes contradictory directions in the women's discourse create a mestiza rhetoric.

Mestiza Rhetoric as Theoretical Lens of Analysis

As seen in the previous section's discussion, the concept of mestizaje carries many contradictions. Born out of the enslavement of, violence toward, and colonization of a people, this concept has philosophical underpinnings that have been altered and even appropriated for an expression of national and racial unity. Considering Mexican women journalists as being rooted in the rhetorical acts of Malintzin and mestizaje provides an authentic connection with their nation's past, with which they were grappling in their discourse. To be anchored in the initial rhetorical exchange between two races also brings an understanding that mestiza rhetoric is not only a feminine project but one that is always already steeped in issues of race, class, nation, and sexuality.

Mestiza rhetoric is also a feminist sophistic strategy emerging from a cultural background that recognizes its hybridity, adapts ideas and logics from various cultures, and "creates a symbolic space beyond the mere coming together of two halves."[60] With the re/visioned history and rhetorical actions of Malintzin at its core, mestiza rhetoric can represent this symbolic puesto by calling on indigenous cultural symbols and knowledge, representing an intertextuality of cultures and ideas, while resisting assimilation to a linear articulation of logic, thereby resulting in divergent, subversive texts. Mestiza rhetoric upsets the continuity of the given historical narrative to include an alternative reading of events and perspectives.[61] It emerges from a puesto of suspension between cultural worlds, contributing to a mestiza consciousness in that the Mexican woman writer is able to conceptualize a sophistic reality of herself and her behavior, allowing for an ontological shift. Because mestiza rhetoric is always already a political position, this discourse takes on a Foucauldian component of discourse politics. Readings of Foucault by Steven Best and Douglas Kellner describe discourse politics as ones in which "marginal groups attempt to contest the hegemonic discourses that position individuals within the straitjacket of normal identities to liberate the free play of differences."[62] Hence, as a cultural and political liberating frame, mestiza rhetoric pushes the boundaries of rhetoric and composition's disciplinary understanding and calls for the inclusion of other Mexican and Chicana voices.

The theoretical approach of mestiza rhetoric focuses on what Jan Swearingen calls an emic approach, which examines the documents and the rhetorical strategies the women employed from their own cultural background.[63] A theoretical lens of mestiza rhetoric, which uses Mexico's history as central to its theme, accomplishes two tasks. First, it recognizes the historical situatedness of the female writers who were articulating mestiza rhetoric as a social perspective and their own claim to nationalism. Mestiza rhetoric reflects a Mexican perspective, decolonizing the women's rhetorical actions. While they are already writing from a colonized space, it eliminates a double colonization of their writings. Further, I acknowledge strategically using theories of mestizaje from Mexico and the United States (Chicano/a). Although the theories from scholars in the United States are different from the theories of mestizaje from Mexico because of the authors' geographic and ethnic positions, they articulate valid points about the project of cultural mestizaje and what role it plays in its expression in society.

For example, Chicana theorist Anzaldúa articulates the direction of the new mestiza from a feminist perspective that Mexican women were also experiencing, such as the new consciousness and awakening of a subject separate from old traditions. I find the analysis of Anzaldúa's new mestiza, which places women in the role of historian, to be liberating. Viewed as historians, women are given the power to determine their own rhetorical identity. Anzaldúa's perspective gives the woman an active role: "She communicates that rupture, documents the struggle. She reinterprets history and, using new symbols, she shapes new myths."[64] Baca's definition of mestiza rhetoric also augments the rhetorical process in which many of these women were engaged. "Mestiz@ rhetorical practices create symbolic spaces in which it becomes possible to understand multiple local histories, memories, and rhetorics coexisting, beyond dichotomous assumptions."[65] These points are valid when considering Mexican women's rhetoric.

Secondly, mestiza rhetoric offers a way to filter the complexities and contradictions that arise in the Mexican women's writings. We see each of the women acted and wrote from a different framework within the new mestiza perspective. Wright de Kleinhans took on the role of historian in her essays about past female leaders in *Mujeres notables mexicanas* (Notable Mexican Women) and her articulations of women's rights in *La emancipación de la mujer* (The Emancipation of the Woman). These histories serve as counternarratives and strong patriarchal critiques to those that ignored women. Las Mujeres de Zitácuaro, with their feminist manifesto, altered the purpose of the nation's grito and manifesto for women's independence and, in doing so, articulated a new perspective on women. Gutiérrez de Mendoza rejected the assimilationist rhetoric of Vasconcelos and wrote the creation myth of her people, the Caxcan Indians, while Hermila Galindo included women within the scope of nationalist political writings in "A la mujer latinoamericana." All of these creative rhetorical ways of representing women's identities provided them variable rhetorical stances from within the same lens. The theoretical perspective of mestiza rhetoric and how the women were articulating it in their writing in order to claim a different puesto will be addressed through the subsequent chapters and analysis of Mexican women writers.

Mestiza Rhetoric as Sophistic Strategy

Mestiza rhetoric, as a discourse that encompasses complex notions of being, is also a sophistic strategy of theorizing and historicizing. The Greek sophists taught the antithesis to Plato's concept of immutable truth, which means that there is some eternal truth, whether image or form, that is "discoverable only through negative dialectic."[66] Bringing Plato's static perspective of rhetoric to any study limits the potentiality for change. The sophists, on the other hand, believed that epistemology is based, not on a foundational knowledge, but on a relativistic knowledge that shifts in order to correspond to the historical moment. This perspective is important in considering mestiza rhetoric as a theoretical lens through which to examine the writings of Mexican women journalists, because the study of their rhetorics is rooted in another language and can become problematic regarding issues of translation and representation. However, including Mexican women within the field, along with the various historical artifacts of gritos, manifestos, archived newspaper articles, poems, a baptismal record, and feminist political treatises, redefines rather than affirms preexisting definitions of acceptable texts, languages, or histories.

A sophistic perspective also breaks with the tired trope of well-known Euro- and malecentric stories, such as that of a traitorous Malintzin, and disrupts the acceptance of traditional male historical figures, offering an expanded range of rhetors. The act of standing in at least three different disciplines—rhetoric, Mexican histories/studies, and women's studies—is also part of a sophistic attitude. Indeed, Jarratt's reading of the sophists expands our view of rhetoric, history, and historiography.[67] A specialized reading of a limited number of texts and full knowledge of them all is not the goal, but, rather, the idea is to achieve "an agility in moving between disciplines, standing back from them with the critical perspective characteristic of both history and rhetoric."[68] However, standing between two disciplines or even between two languages is not as easy and clear-cut a matter as Jarratt suggests. The trick is to listen to each perspective and bring in "illuminating meaningful connections, disjunctions, overlaps, or exclusions."[69]

The Rhetoric of Mexican Women: A Method for Listening to Their Voices

How do we go about the process of bringing Latin American histories into conversation with histories of rhetoric in a respectful way, and not merely as tokens within a Western frame? Bringing Mexican women's discourse into the disciplinary realm of rhetoric and introducing rhetorical methods, practices, and theories to Latin American studies, I have engaged in what Krista Ratcliffe calls "rhetorical listening." Part of listening is engaging in critical dialogue, and it is at this juncture of collaboration that I now stand. In *Rhetorical Listening: Identification, Gender, Whiteness*, Ratcliffe sets out a theoretical and practical approach to the identification of cross-cultural and disciplinary differences.[70]

> Rhetorical listening is a trope for interpretive invention, that is, as a stance of openness that a person may choose to assume in relation to any person, text, or culture; its purpose is to cultivate conscious identifications in ways that promote productive communication, especially but not solely cross-culturally. Rhetorical listening requires sitting silently, actively listening to, and critically processing the various cultural discourses being

> articulated and bringing them together to create the groundwork for dynamic communication.[71]

Indeed, Ratcliffe notes the idealistic position of rhetorical listening, but overcomes this by focusing on the fact that there are limitations and possibilities.[72] However, in order for this method to have a realistic effect, Ratcliffe suggests four rhetorical moves that bring a balance to the exchange: (1) promoting an understanding of self and other, (2) proceeding within an accountability logic, (3) locating identifications across commonalities and differences, and (4) analyzing claims as well as the cultural logics within which these claims function.[73] Communications between and among cultures, even when they are mutual, and their rhetorical texts is a process, which is why I add another communicative and narrative-based method of *plática*. This form of dialogue should not to be understood as a Socratic exchange of ideas of reasoned conversation between two people with differences of opinion and backgrounds in order to establish a truth or common ground. I apply the term *plática* as Miguel and Francisco Guajardo set out in their familiar connective pedagogy, which they employ to "nurture and transmit stories to [their] families, [their] students, and to the public at large."[74] Plática is not a combative form of debate but a dialogue based in learning and coming to an understanding of one's own histories and traditions. While rhetorical listening takes place between those from different cultures or backgrounds, pláticas are a more authentic form of listening and speaking to those with whom one shares a culture or language. As a mestiza, I fall between the puesto of action of rhetorical listening and plácticas. In both dialogues, I must be able to grasp the rhetorical negotiations between the various discourses in order to convey an understanding.

This process has the possibility of working if both sides speak the same language. But what if the sides speak different languages? Is this a hindrance to the process of listening? It certainly could be a contributing factor to misunderstanding, unless there is a strong translator with the ability to successfully negotiate the two languages and cultures. Ratcliffe suggests a rhetorical posture of standing under the various discourses in the conversation. "Standing under our own discourses means identifying the various discourses embodied within each of us and then listening to hear and imagine how these discourses might affect not only ourselves but others."[75] Hence, in my dialogue between Mexican women's writings and rhetoric, translation becomes a major part of the exchange. As I noted in the introduction, translation can have a dual effect on the situation or conversation. It can both illuminate and obscure the dialogue. Communication can be complicated by misunderstandings of idioms or nuances. On the other hand, providing translations here has the potential to broaden the limited audience and allow the women's voices to speak anew.

Standing under discourses means listening closely to allow them to permeate us and let them inform our politics and ethics. Standing under these discourses, I have listened carefully to the theoretical calls to include more women of color into the history of rhetoric, and I have also heard the scholars from Latin American studies engaging in conversations about incorporating more women into history. In delving into the archives in Mexico and the United States to recover Mexican women's writings, I have listened with intent to hear the ways in which their words intersect with the history and politics of their time. I have also traveled to places such as Mexico City, the cities of Durango and San Juan del Río in Durango, Mexico, and Zacatecas, Zacatecas, walking the streets, visiting public buildings, and entering the churches the Mexican women may have entered. Seeing their world in conjunction with reading their writings lends a closer understanding of their struggles and daily undertakings.

The key attempt of these writers, such as Wright de Kleinhans, was to provide women with a puesto in which to be recognized as intelligent beings. As we will see, their words and persuasive moves held contradictions and complexities regarding what it meant for them to be mexicana. Most of the women drew from their indigenous past, but not all identified with it. In listening more deeply to their voices, I heard in the circumstance of their discourse and writing style the differences of class as much as I did racial identification. A reader can hear Wright de Kleinhans writing as a Porfirian elite female, who did not have the same understanding of *lo mexicano* as did Gutiérrez de Mendoza, a woman from a background of poverty and an autodidact, writing as a woman who identified more fully with her mother's indigenous past. Yet as mexicanas, they all wrote from a mestiza rhetorical standpoint, fraught with complex messages of race, class, and gender.

The next interpretive move of rhetorical listening is the logic of accountability. Logic of accountability "asks us to recognize our privileges and nonprivileges and then act accordingly."[76] This particular move resonates with James Berlin's insistence that the revisionary historian understand her own situatedness. In other words, historians must provide the present reasons and motivations for writing about particular subjects. This interpretive space allows one to articulate cultural, gendered, and disciplinary identifications and talk back to them. What are my privileges and nonprivileges in this narrative? My motivations to write about Mexican women journalists reach beyond merely seeing a gap in the tradition. I choose to write about Mexican women as a way to share my own dual perception of the world. I lean more toward my mother's Mexican identity than my father's Anglo-French side. As I stand at a juncture of inhabiting multiple cultural puestos, I see my work in the field of rhetoric and composition as a bridge to bring Latin American studies, Mexican women's writings, and rhetoric into conversation.

Further, I identify as a third-generation Chicana with the linguistic ability to read and interpret Mexican women's writings. My parents, especially my mother, cultivated a love for and understanding of the Spanish language and the Mexican culture in and outside our home. In church, I remember laying my head on my mother's warm lap, listening to the congregation sing in English. In one hand she held a hymnal with the Spanish translated lyrics of English and Irish hymns, and with the other hand, her finger would point to the words in Spanish as they were being sung in English. Together, we sang *en español*, and her voice reverberated in my head. Looking back, I understand now that my mother, intelligent and wise, was engaging in a radical language transfer, which to others was an intimate religious moment between mother and daughter. There's a reason it's called your mother tongue. My father, whom many Chicanos and Mexicans call *el mexicano adoptivo*, or "the adopted Mexican," because of his profound understanding of the Mexican culture and people, served a Mormon mission in Mexico in the 1960s during a cultural revolution and later earned his doctorate in Spanish linguistics and literature. Through my father, my family was exposed to a cultural and stylistic range of music. He held a large collection of Mexican and American records. Mariachi music from Vicente Fernández, Beatriz Adriana, and Lola Beltrán played in the evenings, and at times, he switched the records to play Frank Sinatra or Barry Manilow. My father, *el profesor*, also provided the grammatical corrections of "Se dice así" (It is said this way) after our mandatory meal prayer, *always* said in Spanish. I experienced a balance between the indulgent mother tongue and stern grammatical language training.

My grandmother was also a major influence in the direction of my studies. Ramona Rodríguez González was born in 1906 in El Paso, Texas, and grew up in a barrio called Chihuahuita. She was an emerging Chicana voice in the early 1970s, when she published five of her short stories written in Spanish in the El Grito book series of *Chicanas en la Literatura y el Arte* released by Quinto Sol.[77] In the five years living with her in El Paso, we would read the literature of Octavio Paz, Jorge Luis Borges, Gabriela Mistral, Rosario Castellanos, and others. In the moments with my grandmother, either by her bedside or at the dinner table, we engaged in pláticas about the world in which she grew up. She told me about her love of *palabras, dichos y cuentos* and cultivated my love of the Mexican culture that she cherished. I would read to her my bilingual poems, and she would encourage the mestiza writer in me. The pláticas we had, as Guajardo and Guajardo contend, "created the knowledge and allowed for the multiple realities to be (re)represented without being ridiculed."[78] This bilingual and intercultural expression presented my grandmother and me no struggle or misgiving. It was our way of being. With this rich mestiza background, I stand in dual cultural and linguistic puestos that allow my identities to intersect and even bring down discursive borders to put two perspectives into conversation. The multiple puestos of identification I have inherited as an individual and cultivated as a Chicana scholar allow me to talk *back, to,* and *with* both cultures in order to express new disciplinary understandings.

Identification across commonalities and differences is the third move in rhetorical listening. This direction seeks a dialogue between discourses and looks not so much for a consensus but rather for an identification of convergences and divergences.[79] For example, in this rhetorical move I have observed commonalities and differences of history with respect to how Mexican and Anglo women suffered a cultural, societal, and political silencing. I also acknowledge the differences in their historical and cultural situatedness. Mexican and Anglo cultures refused to allow women to speak from the pulpit and wanted to keep them within the roles of domesticity. The women of the United States made progress much more quickly, but both were silenced just the same. From my mestiza cultural identification, it is difficult to ignore the parallels and similarities in both Mexican and United States societies on the silencing not only women of color but of women in general.

Recent work in the comparison of Mexican and Chicana discursive practices has noted that the two have overlapping and similar goals. As observed by Anna Marie Sandoval in *Toward a Latina Feminism of the Americas: Repression and Resistance in Chicana and Mexicana Literature*, the feminine struggle to be recognized as part of society and as a relevant voice within civic and literary discourse transcends the definitions of being Mexicana, Latina, or Chicana.[80] Sandoval recognizes the geographic and social difference, yet "their narratives take on similar experimental forms as well as similar thematics."[81] These shared experiences provide a blurring and sharing of discursive, ethnic, and geographical borders, bringing women who can be seen as firmly situated in one puesto or the other together.

To be colonized as a woman of color brings a double bind of cultural and gendered identity concealment. While women's history of oppression and marginalization has promoted a deep silencing of women in society, we see through studies, such as Jessica Enoch's *Refiguring Rhetorical Education: Women Teaching African American, Native American, and Chicano/a Students, 1865–1911* and Jacqueline Jones Royster's *Traces of a Stream: Literacy and Social Change Among African American Women*, that literacy has been the key to women's social and rhetorical bargaining in becoming part of civic society. Mexican women shared this reality. However, Mexico lagged considerably behind in providing educational opportunities, in giving women the right to vote, and in recognizing women as citizens of their country.[82] Mexican women's historical context from the Conquest to the Mexican Revolution also involves a much different path and way of silencing than those experienced by Anglo and Chicana women. Nonetheless, there does exist an overlap.

The last interpretive move of rhetorical listening requires analyzing the claims and the cultural logics within those claims. This is not to be confused with consensus on the same issue. Different perspectives on similar topics can be polarizing in nature, but rhetorically listening can provide both sides a pause to see that the opposite perspective on an issue arises from differences in lived experiences, culture, race, language, and class. The goal here is to break the endless loop of talking past and over each other, which keeps groups in a static space of disagreement and anger and which perpetuates the status quo. This study introduces women rhetors who did not speak English and brings to light the cultural logics of Mexico's historical moments. In spite of language and cultural differences, we can appreciate their struggle to be heard. Indeed, this study also makes some radical claims, such as positioning Malintzin as a powerful female rhetor of Mexico, endowing her with agency. Some may disagree with this claim. However, if rhetorical listening is practiced, we see the impact she had on Mexico and its people, and even on those now across the border in the United States. Instead of a woman trapped in a fixed historical perspective, she emerges as another rich location of investigation and tradition.

Of course, this method of rhetorical listening sets out an idealized path to follow and offers benefits for both speaker and listener, and so we must be careful to move forward with caution. Rhetorical listening does not solve all the difficulties involved in coming to understand other cultures and perspectives, but it initiates logic of accountability that "invites us to consider how all of us are, at present, culturally implicated in effects of the past."[83] The past includes dysfunctional silencing practices that we may not believe we have contributed to. However, we have looked the other way, wanting to not involve ourselves in the ethical process of righting the wrongs.

I enter into this process of interpretive intervention standing in this puesto as a mestiza and Chicana investigating the voices of mexicanas, with an intention to open up and present new rhetorical puestos of understanding. In a spirit of plática with the Mexican women in this study, I bring a mestiza consciousness to this process of "participating in the creation of yet another culture, a new story to explain the world and our participation in it."[84] Like Anzaldúa, I stand in a puesto in between perspectives, histories, voices, and cultures. My puesto at the margins of rhetoric and in between various disciplines has offered me a greater vantage point from which to listen to rhetorics from both sides. As another voice within the project of *Occupying Our Space*, I offer a theoretical lens that has the potential of generating interest, dialogue, and scholarly pláticas pertaining to the issue of academic representation of Latinas, ultimately blurring the cultural and historical borders that separate our worlds.

CHAPTER TWO

Las Hijas del Anáhuac

Laureana Wright de Kleinhans and Other Pioneering Women in Journalism in the Late Nineteenth Century

Las que abrigamos en el alma el santo afán del engrandecimiento patrio, y atesoramos en el corazón el inefable amor de una hija, no podemos renunciar á la grata esperanza de ver brillar en la frente de México esta nueva conquista de la libertad, y en la frente de nuestras descendientes esta nueva conquista del progreso, llevada á cabo por la emancipación de la mujer.

Those of us who, in our souls, harbor a holy zeal for our nation's greatness, and treasure in our hearts the ineffable love of a daughter, we cannot renounce the pleasant hope of seeing, shining on the brow of Mexico, this new conquest of liberty, and shining on the brow of our [female] descendants, this new conquest of progress carried out by the emancipation of women.

—LAUREANA WRIGHT DE KLEINHANS, *LA EMANCIPACIÓN DE LA MUJER POR MEDIO DEL ESTUDIO* (THE EMANCIPATION OF WOMEN THROUGH EDUCATION)

Laureana Wright de Kleinhans's 1891 declaration did not necessarily echo the political sentiments of the majority of Mexicans in the late nineteenth century. After expelling the Spanish and the French, Mexico had embarked on a postcolonial path to peace and independence. Wright de Kleinhans believed women should reap the rewards of this new liberty and progress, but the social barriers to take part in this emancipation remained in place. She was writing from the historical context of Mexico in a time of perceived peace, order, and intellectual progress. I say "perceived" because this ideal existed primarily for the wealthy and was made possible by the backbreaking labor of the indigenous and poor. Moreover, the national intellectual progress was limited to elite males. Wright de Kleinhans and her cohort of writers were among the few women of their time to take part in various intellectual and literary pursuits. These women, unwavering in their feminine educational commitment, paved the way for their sisters in the next century to take part in more prominent literary professions and vocations. As a member of the literate elite, Wright de Kleinhans recognized that a large majority of Mexican women were entrapped in the domestic puesto. Her writings expressed the conviction that women had a calling to fulfill as leaders and guides in the public sphere.

Wright de Kleinhans's early inroads into Mexican journalism, in the 1870s and into the 1880s, set her on a path toward directing her own journal. Lourdes Alvarado notes that Wright de Kleinhans's early work with *El Monitor Republicano* and *El Bien Público* included contributions to the poetry and literary sections.[1] She also worked under the Spanish author and literary director Concepción Gimeno de Flaquer, who published the popular *El Album de la Mujer*.[2] At one point, after getting married and bearing her first and only child, Margarita, Wright de Kleinhans attempted to retire her literary career. However, the literary friends who surrounded her would not let her relinquish writing.[3] Choosing to continue her career, she was admitted into the rarest of literary circles. In these circles, she would draw attention to her eloquent and confident writing style, which elevated her reputation and even threatened some male writers. Indeed, she would not let her critics silence her opinions on women's rights.

Wright de Kleinhans dedicated a large part of her literary and journalistic writings to highlighting the need for women's emancipation through education. She wrote various papers on the issues of women's rights, most notably *La emancipación de la mujer por medio del estudio* and *Educación errónea de la mujer y medios prácticos para correjirla* (Erroneous Education of Women and Ways to Correct It), published in 1891 and 1892, respectively.[4] Possibly the first theory of female education in Mexico, *La emancipación* stipulates, as its main premise, that women had been kept ignorant of the professions and workings of the world, such as education, medicine, politics, history, and, above all, higher education, which in turn "[las] ha reducido a cero en la gran aritmética del mundo y en la gran familia de la humanidad" (has reduced women to nothing in the grand equation of the world and in the family of humanity).[5] Her treatise, far ahead of its time and not fully agreed upon, argues for substantial change.

The issues Wright de Kleinhans enumerated were extensive and not limited to poetry and progressive ideas about women. A quick examination of her writings clearly demonstrates her intellect. From 1887 to 1889

Figure 2. Image of Laureana Wright de Kleinhans as it appeared in the 1910 publication of her book *Mujeres notables mexicanas.*

she edited the literary journal *Las Hijas del Anáhuac* (The Daughters of Anáhuac), which would change its name after eight issues to *Violetas del Anáhuac: Periódico Literario Redactado por Señoras* (Violets of Anáhuac: Literary Periodical Written by Women) because a journal from 1873 had carried the original name.[6] The writings and weekly edited collections in *Violetas* included poetry, topics of hygiene, science, world travel, world news, philosophical accounts of the Spanish Conquest and Mexican independence, moral philosophy, and, most significantly, biographies of contemporary Mexican women. Having written in a variety of genres, Wright de Kleinhans produced an amazing quantity of work during her life, surpassing many of her American female contemporaries. She published her literary journal every week for two years, and in each volume, her own work generally appeared as a lead piece. Along with the two educational treatises mentioned above, she would also compile a five-hundred-page collection of Mexican women's biographies titled *Mujeres notables mexicanas* (Noteworthy Mexican Women).[7] To provide another perspective, when doing research for this book, I spent three full days and went through two and a half reams of paper copying her works from archival holdings. It would be impossible for this chapter to encompass the entirety of her life's work. This aspiration would require a separate book. In the space of this chapter, then, I attempt to convey the richness of Wright de Kleinhans's extensive works by focusing on her later writings, from 1887 to 1896.

In this chapter, I propose two main concepts to illuminate the complexities of Wright de Kleinhans as an intellectual and as an early feminine activist. First, in keeping with the theme of the text, I suggest that Wright de Kleinhans claimed an elite rhetorical puesto as a mestiza rhetor within a nationalist and intellectual movement that sought to identify la mexicana. Second, I frame her as a Mexican female public intellectual. At the time she was writing, high intellectualism, which Mexican writers expressed through their complex use of language in long, grammatically intricate essays, was in vogue. Rosario Castellanos notes that this style of speech and writing was meant to set a class of people apart from the rest.[8] Many women were deprived of an elite education in the study of literature and oratory, and they remained excluded from the practice of intellectual expression. As a female intellectual, Wright de Kleinhans mastered this florid speech. Of course, this argument of women as public intellectuals is not a new position. My analysis of marginalized Mexican women writers will strengthen the argument made by feminist scholars such as Trinh T. Minh-ha, Audre Lorde, Rosario Castellanos, and Hélèn Cixous. Each of these scholars has highlighted the intellectual quality of women's writings from developing countries. Wright de Kleinhans's writing, and that of the other women in her cohort, opened un puesto nuevo in a masculine public space that would compel men to acknowledge their public presence.

Wright de Kleinhans's significance as a Mexican female writer and intellectual has been overlooked outside of Mexico. Mexican feminine historians and scholars, such as Ana Lau Javien, Lourdes Alvarado, and Lucrecia

Infante Vargas, have recovered and analyzed her works. However, in the United States, little is known about this Mexican female intellectual and the women whose works she published. This feminist historical account, then, seeks not only to illustrate her superior literary and rhetorical accomplishments but also to reveal her intellectual and rhetorical astuteness. This chapter features an analysis of a variety of Mexican women's publications, including the 1873 publication of the first *Las Hijas del Anáhuac* (not the one edited later by Wright de Kleinhans) and also writings by other women Wright de Kleinhans published from 1887 to 1889. After considering the overall goal of the writings from *Violetas*, I position the poetry Wright de Kleinhans wrote, as well as the poetry of the women she published, in the greater tradition of epideictic writing, a form of ceremonial oratory that delivers either praise or blame. Lastly, I analyze the biographies in *Mujeres notables mexicanas* as a rhetorical response to the silencing of women's historical contributions to the nation. In keeping with a sophistic historical stance, my method of analysis is thematic and stylistic, rather than chronological.

Mujeres Intelectuales

In 1865, the Mexican journalist and public intellectual Francisco Zarco defended the freedom and rights of journalists to express their ideas in a speech he gave as a member of the Constitutional Congress.[9] At the time (and even today), Mexican journalists played an important role as public intellectuals. They would enter into the political, literary, or civic spheres of discourse, interacting with the community's literate members in order to enrich a liberal democracy. During the Porfiriato (the dictatorship of Porfirio Díaz), public intellectuals were commonly journalists. They also served as philosophers, poets, historians, and mouthpieces for politicians who were engaged in shaping the national identity. They expressed their ideas in long, complex essays, the preferred genre of the time. The role of the public intellectual in Mexico did not require connection to an academic or state institution. However, many intellectuals were associated with a liberal or positivist mode of thinking. In this light, I define a public intellectual as one with expertise in any given discipline, who expresses these ideas freely in the public domain in order to share knowledge, welcome dialogue, and sustain or challenge political systems. Part of the crucial role of a public intellectual, though, is also taking action in response to one's ideas, and Wright de Kleinhans's active response was to provide the counternarrative to the literary and historical frameworks that devalued women.

Feminist literary critics and theorists, such as Lucrecia Infante Vargas, Emily Hind, and Nancy LaGreca, have re/imagined Mexican and Latin American women writers as intellectuals within a tradition that labeled women's writings as hysterical and illogical. Specifically, Hind uses the term "feminine intellectuality" to reveal the non/space that women occupied as writing subjects.[10] The Mexican male intellectuals known during the Porfiriato as "wizards of progress" would never have conceded the hallowed puesto of the intellectual to women, even if they did write with as much sophistication and confidence as men. Male intellectuals such as Ignacio Gamboa, Félix Palavicini, Julio Sesto, and others argued against educating women for careers beyond the home, warning that it would convert them into ugly, bitter old women.[11] Wright de Kleinhans's belief in women's emancipation and intellectual capacity stood in stark contrast to the men's thought of and control over what they considered worthy of praise. Coming from a public intellectual, Wright de Kleinhans's discourse expressed the knowledge and expertise of a woman living in a suppressive, male-dominated environment.

Regardless of her intellect, during Wright de Kleinhans's time as a female writer in the Porfiriato, her public role was first "angel of the home" and then poet. Early in her career, she became known for her philosophical poems "Dios" (God) and "Huérfana" (Orphan).[12] As discussed in the introduction, the title of poet was rarely given to women. Nevertheless, the recognition of these works and others would gain her entry into exclusive literary lyceums, such as El Liceo Hidalgo, Netzahualcóyotl, and the distinguished Altamirano.[13] Her later works in *Violetas*, *La emancipación*, *La educación errónea*, and *Mujeres notables mexicanas* extended her public puesto beyond her title of poet. The male intellectual hierarchy in Mexico was the ultimate system of power, and because of its negative perspective on women as writers or intellectuals, the title of poet or angel of the home would be impossible for her to lose.[14] Wright de Kleinhans would carry the unfitting and narrow title of poet in her biographical sketch even after she took on the role of literary director and after the publication of her extensive philosophical and historical writings. Her biography in *Violetas* contains a reprint of an editorial by Miguel Bolaños Cacho, quotes by Licenciado Refugio Nicoli, and introductory and final comments by Mateana Murguía de Aveleyra. Before commenting on her writing, Bolaños Cacho positions her in a domestic puesto. "Sentimental y tierna en el hogar, abnegada en las épocas de prueba para la patria, y correcta, fecunda y modesta como escritora, ella personifica la mujer mexicana con todas sus bellezas, contadas sus perfecciones" (Sentimental and tender in the home, self-sacrificing in challenging times of our nation, correct, prolific and modest as writer, she personifies the Mexican woman with all her beauty, with all her perfections).[15] LaGreca notes how accepted this framing of the feminine was at the time. She says, "The Angel of the House was a pervasively consumed model in nineteenth century Latin America; women and men, Positivists and Catholics, liberals and conservatives were counted among its supporters."[16] Compliments of virtue, morality, and motherhood were of the highest regard during the Porfiriato, yet the praises paid tribute to gendered difference and further anchored her in the puesto of the home.

While the commentators do mention her unmatched intellect, they never label her as an intellectual, only as "using her intellect." They continually turn instead to her "virtue," "beauty," and "poetic soul," calling her "la primera poetisa mexicana" (the first female Mexican poet) and comparing her to Victor Hugo in having always defended the rights of the weak.[17] (We can assume that the "weak" were other women and children.) They make the distinction that she uses her intellect, not to prove her rhetorical proficiency, but to fight for the rights of the weaker members of society, as Hugo did through some of his works and politics. In this biography, we see a hesitancy to praise the full force of her intellect. Some of Wright de Kleinhans's male literary contemporaries, though, took her productivity and tone as an affront to their masculinity. For example, Refugio Nicoli, writing from *El Observador de Guanajuato* and quoted by Murguía de Aveleyra as an epithet, claimed that she was a liberal "thinker" who had torn the chains of darkness, but that "el vigor de su intelecto aventaja al de muchos escritores que se juzgan muy varones cuando escriben" (the vigor of her intellect surpasses that of many writers who consider themselves to be very masculine when they write).[18] Neither male critics nor female contemporaries of Wright de Kleinhans crossed the line and labeled her as an intellectual. They negated her intellect to keep within the bounds of the strict gendered rules of the Porfiriato. The denial of her position as an intellectual limited her discourse in its ability to have a larger impact on society in the later part of the nineteenth century.

This caution is consistent with the division of difference in gender at the time. In her study on women during the Porfiriato, Verena Radkau notes that women were defined within a natural existence, a puesto of noncreative neutrality. She says, "El varón hace, la mujer es. El es productivo, puede cambiar las cosas, ella es improductiva, más conservadora que creadora" (The man acts, the woman is. He is productive and can change things, she is unproductive, more conservative than creative).[19] These roles were extremely limiting to women, leaving them only in their procreative puestos. Though the Porfirian perspective greatly neutered the power Wright de Kleinhans's discourse could have, she argued consistently for the equality between men's and women's intellects.[20] However debilitating the Porfirian perspective was to Wright de Kleinhans, I contend that her work *did* play a role in changing the face of journalism for women.

Wright de Kleinhans and the early editorial staff of the first journal with the name of *Las Hijas de Anáhuac* (1873) partially accepted these social puestos and even reinforced them in their writings. Karlyn Kohrs Campbell refers to this rhetorical approach as a "feminine style" women used to "cope with the conflicting demands of the podium."[21] Used by early women's rights advocates, feminine style invited audience participation, promised empowerment, and came across as noncombative so as not to offend the men in the audience. Intellectual women of the time approached their discourse with these strategies to appeal also to their female audiences. However, Concepción García y Ontiveros's journal *Las Hijas del Anáhuac* (1873) and Wright de Kleinahans's journal *Violetas del Anáhuac* (1887–89) reveal a contrast to the nineteenth-century etiquette journals, such as *La Semana de las Señoritas Mexicanas* (The Weekly for Mexican Young Women) (1851), which was dedicated to high literature and art, and also instructing women on how they should live their lives. *La Semana* focused on Eurocentric ways of being for women. This focus both suppressed and silenced the more authentic claim to their culture and cemented women's ways of being. The contributors to this journal were mostly men, such as Manuel Payno and Francisco Zarco, both touted as Mexican intellectuals, important writers of the period, and "experts" in dispensing advice to women.[22] By comparing the two journals edited by women, a reader can distinguish the shift away from the male-dominated discourse (in the first *Las Hijas*) to that of women beginning to rely on their acuity to ascribe intelligence to their own social identity (in *Violetas*).

Early Attempts at Claiming a Voice

During the mid-nineteenth century, Mexican women began searching for a public voice with which to define themselves as citizens of a nation they loved and served—and as humans with the capacity to exercise their intelligence outside the boundaries of the home. LaGreca notes the exchange and value of ideas between Mexico and countries abroad, especially France, which occupied Mexico midcentury.[23] Mexico began participating in the world's fairs in the mid-nineteenth century, many being held in France, and with this contact came the expanse of knowledge and ideas.[24] With this exchange, however, the women of Mexico were exposed to concepts of feminism that were emerging within the United States and Europe. Especially in cultural hubs, such as Mexico City, Guanajuato, Durango, and Yucatán, where a wide variety of ideas were exposed, women from the elite class knew of and read John Stuart Mill's *The Subjection of Women* (1869) in French; it was translated into Spanish in 1892.[25] Progressives also knew of the women's rights efforts led by Susan B. Anthony and others in the United States. With these emerging ideas swirling in the public domain, the young women in the new typesetting program of the Women's School of Arts and Vocations, under the direction of Concepción García y Ontiveros, started a journal in 1873 called *Las Hijas del Anáhuac: Ensayo Literario*.[26] The journal played multiple roles. First, it introduced women to the public sphere of writing and journalism; second, it promoted women's literacy; and third, it initiated Mexican women's early contributions to the identity politics of mestizaje. Although amateur in form and tone, their writings represented a multilayered symbolic act of resistance. On the one hand, the women were participating in a male discursive forum while simultaneously resisting an exclusively European feminine identification. These young student contributors to the journal demonstrated an early example of mestiza consciousness, which Anzaldúa states is a "constant state of *nepantlism*, an Aztec word meaning torn between ways."[27] The young women, learning new skills, were awakened to a new way of expressing their ideas outside the purely oral function.

They were aware of and articulated the emerging discourse that questioned their puesto between European cultural sensitivities and their understandings of pre-Columbian Mexico. At this juncture, I also use the term *nepantlism* to represent the women being torn between breaking the cultural gendered principles forbidding them to speak in public or continuing to follow a societal tradition of silence. While on the one hand there is a "torn between ways" of racial identification, Anzaldúa would also make the claim that there is ambivalence in the cultural aspect of their identity.

First, the title the women selected, *Las Hijas*, represents an early mestiza consciousness, as it articulates an understanding of their indigenous identity. Rubén Medina notes that by the nineteenth century, the concept of mestizaje and its recurring symbols had shifted from being a racial and anthropological term to being a term rooted in the discourse of power and identity formation.[28] The strategic choice of the geographical location of

Anáhuac, the Aztec name for the Valley of Mexico and now the location of Mexico City, locates the women within a dualistic culture in conflict, one of tradition and another of modernization. At the level of heritage and ancestral lineage, by claiming to be *las hijas* (the daughters) of Anáhuac and not *las mujeres* (the women) or *ciudadanas* (citizens) of Anáhuac, they asserted a direct lineage to the kingdom of the Aztecs. The journal's title entangled the women in a rhetorical conundrum of gendered and national identification. On the one hand, Mexican women wanted to be like their French and American sisters, whom they saw taking part in an emerging feminist movement. On the other hand, they wanted their own identification as Mexican citizens, which at the time was still under negotiation.

In order to keep with the pre-Columbian theme of the journal's title, the contributors used pseudonyms from the Aztec Nahuatl language, such as Ilancueitl, Papantzin, Cuatlicue, and Miahuaxochitl.[29] This rhetorical move of identification can illustrate two distinct thought processes. First, it can represent the women's apprehension in making their individual names public. This practice would hold sway for decades to come. It may also suggest that the women tried to represent more writers than were actually contributing.[30] Whatever the reason, their use of these pseudonyms represents a mestiza consciousness expressing resistance to a totalizing European identification through their language. By identifying themselves as early Aztec women, the female writers weaved in and out of the stories of conquest and resistance. Most poignantly, these women assert the historical tradition of Malintzin as women speaking outside the bounds of the home. Further, acting as historical players in their own present time cements the significance of Malintzin's rhetorical acts. The pseudonyms hint at the historical significance related to the era before the European invasion, which acts as a powerful symbolic act of resistance toward European national identification. This claim flew in the face of the belief that women, especially indigenous or Mexican women, should remain silent and hidden. The first issue's editorial, titled "A nuestras lectoras" (To Our Readers) and written by a student using the Nahuatl pseudonym of Ilancueitl, claimed an emergent intellectual puesto for women and illustrates the mental nepantlism they endured.

> Ya no es mal visto que la mujer escriba y exprese sus sentimientos por medio de la pluma, y nada más justo. . . . Además, ¿[p]or qué si el hombre puede manifestar públicamente las galas de su inteligencia, la mujer ha de estar privada de hacerlo, como hay mujeres cuyos talentos igualan á los de los hombres?[31]

> It is no longer frowned upon for the woman to write and express her feelings with the pen, and nothing could be fairer. . . . Besides, why, if a man can show the glories of his intelligence publicly, should the woman be deprived of doing so, since there are women whose talents equal those of men?

Proceeding with caution, the women argue for a rhetorical puesto. However, all too quickly, these paragraphs reveal the women's gendered and social nepantlism, reminding women that they should not choose the pursuit of their intellect over that of their sublime domestic mission. Later in the editorial Ilancueitl writes, "Queremos sí, que la mujer escriba y estudie, pero nunca que por esto, se olvide de sus atenciones domésticas" (Yes, we want women to write and learn, but in doing so, they should never neglect their domestic duties).[32] As early feminine intellectuals, the young girls were choreographing a delicate dance with words. Their audience would have immediately recognized that they were questioning and crossing discursive boundaries that were still firmly implanted within Mexican society.

The first attempt of *Las Hijas* was possibly not well received by the public or other newspapers. The young women's desire to enter the public journalistic scene was present, but the writing style of their amateur publication was unsophisticated. Their style lacked the florid language of the male intellectuals and therefore didn't make a great impact. Bollinger Pouwels states that the women's broadsheet evoked attacks rather than welcomes by three or four newspaper editors.[33] The women hypothesized that their "lack of recognition might be because their articles were boring and contained errors" but that they would "do their best as lowly students to foment the regeneration and emancipation of women."[34] Their readers may have sensed the rhetorical contradictions and dual impulses of domestic versus intellectual identification. Their use of pseudonyms to hide their identities may have conveyed a lack of confidence to the readers. After another decade and with an advanced level of language, these ideas of women speaking in public, claiming ownership of their literacy, and defining la mujer mexicana would hold more credibility.

Another Attempt at Anáhuac

Thirteen years after the last publication of *Las Hijas de Anáhuac*, another women's journal with the same title appeared in Mexico City. This journal was directed by Ignacio Pujol and edited by Laureana Wright de Kleinhans.

Through the writings published in *Violetas del Anáhuac: Periódico Literario Redactado por Señoras* (Violets of Anáhuac: Literary Journal Published by Ladies), Wright de Kleinhans would emerge as a female public intellectual and as one of the most prominent writers and women's rights activists in Mexico. The journal she edited would carry a professional weight that the Women's School of Arts and Vocations student journal could not capture. However, the fluctuation between women's independence to choose an intellectual path or dependence on marriage and domesticity would carry over into this newer journal. There was also the element of racial contradiction presented in the title of *Violetas* that took on the essence and puesto of mestiza rhetoric of contradiction and change. Elvira Hernández Carballido notes that in the nineteenth century in Mexico, the color violet, of the flower, carried "tonos de abnegación y de reivindicación, de dudas y certezas en torno al ser femenino" (overtones of abnegation and grievance, of doubts and certainties of what feminism stood for).[35] This interpretation of the *violetas* parallels with the women's fluctuating discourse in the journal. Carballido goes on to state that it represented questions and warnings to the social changes taking place, but it also represented a level of criticism and irreverence to the status quo.[36] Like the word *hijas* in the title, the use of *violetas* situated women within the ancient Aztec kingdom of Anáhuac. It also added a level of incongruity or dualistic representation of women, signifying an identity in question and in flux. This color fit with Wright de Kleinhans's life and writings, which also carried the essence of mestizaje.

Born in 1846 in Taxco, Mexico, to a wealthy Mexican mother and an American father, Laureana Wright González later married a German, Sebastian Kleinhans. Growing up and living among a myriad of influences, she must have felt the cultural push and pull of diverse ideas. She and the other women writers carried with them the sensibilities of a nation attempting to construct its own identity. Wright de Kleinhans and the female contributors to her journal wrote as traditional Mexican middle- and upper-class women, who positioned themselves as mestizas struggling between conforming to traditional ideologies and pursuing their desire to move away from conventional values. Claiming her and other Mexican women to be of the mestiza social order, Wright de Kleinhans saw Mexican women as the direct beneficiaries of historical racial and cultural mixing. In "Algo sobre la Conquista y la Independencia de México" (Something about the Conquest and Independence of Mexico), she states, "De todas estas castas europeos, criollos, mestizos, zambos, mulatos, et cetera la mestiza predominante hoy, es la que ha venido á recoger los beneficios producidos por los trabajos y sacrificios de los demás"[37] (Of all these colonial castelike constructs, Europeans, Creoles, mestizos, *zambos*, mulattoes, et cetera, the mestizo, which is predominant today, is the one to have emerged to reap the benefits created by the works and sacrifices of the others).[38] Wright de Kleinhans goes on to note that as mestizas, they owe their social comforts to their indigenous side. To the European side, they owe the improvement of the physical nature, their culture, and advancement in arts and science. Most intellectuals of the Porfiriato recognized the indigenous element as an absent presence in their culture of progress and order. Wright de Kleinhans did not express any differing sentiments. This mode of identification would simultaneously intersect with the greater conversation of nationhood and the definition of what it meant to be mexicana.

The opening 1887 editorial of Wright de Kleinhans's journal comes across as direct, confident, and sophisticated, introducing the women writers and their purpose. Most likely authored by Wright de Kleinhans, the writing exemplifies the sophisticated, almost baroque tone and vocabulary used at the time.[39] The presentation of the other women writers is also unwavering. Unlike the women writers from the first journal, most of the writers listed their names on the opening page. Frequent contributors, educated women already in roles as educators or activists—including María del Alba, Dolores Correa y Zapata, Mateana Murguía de Aveleyra, Ignacia Padilla de Piña, María de la Luz Murguía, Emilia Rimbló, Dolores Delahanty, Lugarda Quintero, Concepción Manresa de Pérez, and María del Refugio Argumedo de Ortiz—stood by the three main goals of the magazine: to include women's voices in the world of journalism; to contribute to the construction of a national identity; and to encourage an early form of Mexican feminism. Many of these women, such as Correa y Zapata and Murguía de Aveleyra, held their own as writers, educators, and public activists. However, knowing that they were collectively entering un nuevo puesto, they approached the introduction of women's voices in the public sphere cautiously. The opening lines from the first edition are telling of their prudent rhetorical appeal.

> Saludos: Con el ramo de oliva entre las manos como muestra de la regeneración intelectual de la mujer, vivificadas con las puras enseñanzas de la antigüedad, se presenta hoy al público el modesto Periódico *Las Hijas del Anáhuac* y reverentemente dirige su cordial saludo a todas las clases de la Sociedad, a la Prensa de todos los matices políticos, y a los Hombres del Poder y del Estado; trilogía poderosa que con sus magníficos arneses ha podido evolucionar victoriosamente en beneficio de la paz, el orden y la cultura de la Patria mexicana.[40]

> Greetings: With the olive branch in hand as a token of women's intellectual regeneration, vivified with the pure teachings of classical antiquity the modest Newspaper, *The Daughters of Anáhuac* is presented today to the public and reverently directs its cordial greeting to all classes of Society, to the Press of all political shadings, and to the Men of Power and of the State; powerful trilogy that with its magnificent trappings has been able to evolve victoriously for the sake of peace, order, and culture of the Mexican Homeland.

Rhetorically savvy, the women writers were fully aware that their ideas intersected with the politics of the moment. As a result, they introduced themselves by offering a symbol of peace and used a linguistic flourish in their writing to connect them with the nation's emerging identity.

Such eloquent language was more than a rhetorical accessory. It was "an intrinsic component of the ideals [of] political reconciliation, nationalism, and scientism," writes Tenorio-Trillo of the language use of the time.[41] "For the idea of a modern nation could hardly be conceived without its rhetorical style. In constructing a nationalist ideology, the distinctions between form and content vanished."[42] The Mexican women, who did not have an established voice in society, were forced to talk back, to mimic the high, dominant language popular among the men in order to be heard. Rosario Castellanos writes about the language of the Porfiriato, noting that it was identification beyond "the color of one's skin; one had to add the purity and iniquity of faith and something else: the command of the oral means of expression."[43] Language was not only a means of domination but was also meant to "display signs of distinction . . . to display luxury, to arouse envy, to generate accolades, and the will to compete and to emulate."[44] Here we see language, with its metaphoric and idiomatic flourishes, as a form of domination to silence those who could not conform to the rhetorical style of the time.

As a form of gendered mimicry, Wright de Kleinhans's rhetorical approach reflects present-day theories on histories of rhetoric and marginalized discourses. Berlin notes that rhetorics emerge and are constructed at the intersection of power and are influenced by the material realities of the moment. Berlin states that "rhetorics never answer only to themselves: They reflect and, of equal importance, refract the conditions of their creation and functioning."[45] From a rhetorical observation point, the writings in *Violetas* intersected at the apex of power, "the Press of all political shadings, and to the Men of Power and of the State." They appealed to the Mexican male elite's sense of nation construction, while also encouraging women's involvement in intellectual pursuits. This was, indeed, a difficult puesto to occupy. At this time in Mexico, there was perceived peace and stability throughout the nation. Yet, looking just below the surface of the society, dissident voices such as *Violetas* emerged. The women were beginning to push the boundaries of what was acceptable. By challenging the boundaries, the women occupied the societal margins. bell hooks contends that language is a place of struggle and that "words are not without meaning, they are an action, a resistance."[46] The Mexican women writers, although from the elite classes, occupied the puesto at the margins of their culture, speaking to the male center. However, as bell hooks explains, there is a freedom in this space that doesn't exist in the center.

Ontologically, the journal was fraught with immense ambiguity. Were the women accustomed to their ambiguity? Did they want to occupy the puesto of political power? The articles in *Violetas* emphasized that a woman's highest achievement was that of becoming a mother, yet they also celebrated and encouraged women's intellectual advancement. According to Campbell, this approach of contradictory arguments, motherhood coupled with intellectual pursuits, complemented each other. "Women who argued from expediency did not seek rights for their own sake but only for the good that could be done with them for others."[47] For Wright de Kleinhans, the expectation of mothering in Mexico was one of "abnegation and sacrifice; before the satisfaction of our intimate feelings, we should seek what is beneficial for our children."[48] At the same time, the journal encouraged and praised women who chose pursuits outside the domestic role. Balancing this ambiguity is a significant aspect of living the essence of the mestiza.

The women had their feet in two worlds. They had one in a Mexican patriarchal society that framed them in the trope of domestication and the other in a world of feminine emancipation. In the first published numbers in December 1887, we can see this uncertainty unfold. Indeed, the contributors found it difficult to decide which ideology to embrace. For example, in a column titled "La ilustración y la educación de la mujer" (The Enlightenment and Education of Women), published on December 11, 1887, María de la Luz Murguía warns her readers who "live in the clubs and circles of women that proclaim emancipation of their sex" to understand "that deep down she [the reader] is good and understands that her duties are in the home, where she is the ruling queen."[49]

On the next page, Señora Concepción Manresa de Pérez extols women from around the world who had achieved success in the public realm in a section titled "Mujeres de nuestra época" (Women of Our Era).[50] Manresa de Pérez writes:

> Y México, que marcha con paso firme por la senda progresiva de la civilización, merced al orden y á la paz de que disfruta, nos ofrece como evidente muestra de sus adelantos á nuestra querida redactora, la Srita. Matilde Montoya, que ha recibido últimamente el grado de Doctora en la Escuela de Medicina, después de sustentar un brillante examen.[51]

> And Mexico, which marches with a sure step along civilization's advancing path, thanks to the order and the peace that it enjoys, offers us an obvious example of its advances, our dear columnist, Srita. Matilde Montoya, who has recently received her Doctor's degree from Medical School, after performing brilliantly on her exam.

Evidence of these ideological contradictions can be found in almost every number. The women were caught between keeping tradition and wanting a sense of entitlement by taking part in "civilization's advancing path." They put forward these ideas carefully through acceptable genres, such as poetry. The mixed ideas of women's place in society represent recognition of multiple subjectivities and played a significant part in the mestiza rhetoric they were forging.

Literal and Literary Beginnings

The driving force of *Violetas* focused on providing women a public discursive space in which they could express their ideas and present their writings. In the 1880s the literate community considered the ability to write and perform poetry to a civic audience a determining factor of a person's intellect and a sign of political and literary virility. The focus, though, was on *public* performance, a privilege rarely afforded to women. Stuart Easterling provides a history of Mexican literary and intellectual life, noting that literate males, known as literatos, combined their intellectual prowess with journalism, statecraft, and law.[52] For men, the practices of poetry by literatos served as an important segue into politics. Some of the greatest male poets and essayists in Mexico emerged during this time period, such as Justo Sierra (1848–1912), Manuel Gutiérrez Nájera (1859–95), Guillermo Prieto (1818–97), Vicente Riva Palacio (1832–96), Francisco

Pimentel (1832–93), and Ignacio Manuel Altamirano (1834–93). As was the custom, they published their works and read them aloud in exclusive lyceums, to which Wright de Kleinhans was also admitted.

Having the rare privilege of being included among these literatos, Wright de Kleinhans recognized the need for more women to take part in this display of intellectualism. From the first publication of her journal, she encouraged women to submit their writings, and her efforts were successful. She published a great deal of women's poetry that otherwise would have been lost. The poems can seem oversentimental or flattering to the contemporary reader; however, this style was highly praised in the *veladas literarias* (literary soirées). The literate men "believed these virtues domesticity and sentimentality could be found in the best work produced by Mexican *poetisas*—female poets—and were virtues they often aspired to express themselves."[53] The aesthetic quality of the poems could qualify as overly romantic. However, when these poems are examined through a rhetorical lens, they take on an epideictic rhetorical nature, which features a discourse geared toward ceremony, commemoration, declamation, and demonstration. Though Wright de Kleinhans avoided polemics, she broached current public issues in the form of civic-oriented poetry.

Cynthia Miecznikowski Sheard points out that epideictic rhetoric has been revisited by contemporary scholars but claims that it has been overlooked for its importance as a modern rhetorical approach.[54] Epideictic rhetoric is a form of speech that focuses on open praise or blame in public occasions such as funerals or holidays. It is identified by a florid speech that does not immediately call for action but tends to influence the audiences' values and beliefs.[55] Miecznikowski Sheard claims that epideictic rhetoric has the potential to be "an instrument for addressing private and public 'dis-ease,' discomfort with the status quo," allowing "speakers and audience to envision possible, new, or at least different worlds."[56] If we consider the popular poems in *Violetas* as a form of epideictic rhetoric, then, they are imbued with the power to *shift* the public's beliefs or to "change things," quite the opposite of the Porfirian condition Radkau reported. The topics and themes weaving through the women's writings may have reinforced women in traditional spaces, but because the writings appeared in a public space praising women for their friendship, intellect, and civic engagement, they simultaneously redefined women within a traditionally male culture of intellectualism.

Mexico's discourse framed women as overly sentimental and frivolous but, ironically, also perceived them as superior beings when seen through the domestic lens.[57] This contradictory identity may have discouraged some women from attempting to write. Many had never had a formal education and would have been extremely apprehensive about submitting their work to a literary journal. As literary director, though, Wright de Kleinhans assuaged their fears of appearing unintelligent or foolish, stating that their work "would be thoroughly revised" before it would be presented to an audience.[58] Poetry served as the rhetorical tool that Wright de Kleinhans and her staff used to shape knowledge and affect social beliefs associated with women. Much like epideictic rhetoric, the poetry in Mexican newspapers during the latter part of the nineteenth century, and even before, typically took a tone of flattery or high praise. It was an important part of the political, historical, and societal discursive practices, which included the grandiose adulation of political and church officials, war heroes, writers, artists, and patriotic sentiments and was often infused with deep-seated emotions articulated through complex metaphors and similes.

The women of *Violetas* followed this common rhetorical trope by writing poems that complimented their female friends' accomplishments and lauded courageous women and men from Mexico's past. The women's poetry provided an alternative frame of reference on the nature of women's lives and implicitly asserted that they could express themselves through discursive means. Some verses that achieved these ends were poems such as "La oración matinal" (Morning Prayer) by María del Refugio Argumedo, viuda de Ortiz, dedicated to Presidential First Lady Carmen Romero Rubio de Díaz;[59] "Cuauhtémoc," also by Argumedo, vuida de Ortiz;[60] "Charada" (Charade), dedicated to Wright de Kleinhans by Ignacia Padilla de Piña;[61] and "La mujer," dedicated to Matilde Montoya, the first Mexican female physician, by Dolores Correa y Zapata.[62]

As a common cultural practice, poems were read at public gatherings to commemorate special occasions, and they regularly appeared in Mexican newspapers praising and sometimes criticizing historical and current political figures.[63] For instance, one of the first numbers, from December 4, 1887, dedicated the poem "Poesía" (Poetry) to First Lady Carmen Romero Rubio de Díaz.[64] The author, María del Refugio Argumedo, vuida de Ortiz, read the poem aloud at the inauguration of Casa Amiga de la Obrera (Home of the Friend of the Woman Worker), a day care and health center for women. Part 3, stanza 4 of the poem situates Mexico within the world community of women. It states that if Germany and Spain, as respected nations, had compassion enough for children and working mothers for them to build day care centers, then Mexico was also equal to them because of their First Lady's efforts to procure funding and establish a child care center.

Si la Alemania en su anhelar levanta
Templos á la niñez infortunada,
Y con cariño su dolor quebranta
Besando su cabeza inmaculada;
Si en España una reina pura y santa
Funda un plantel con emoción sagrada,
Aquí tenemos de virtud ejemplo,
Un ángel que amoroso abre este templo.[65]

If Germany in its longing builds
Temples for the unfortunate children,
And with love their sorrow weakens
Kissing their immaculate brows;
If in Spain a queen pure and saintly
Establishes a nursery with a sacred emotion
Here we have a virtuous example,
An angel that lovingly opens this temple.

This poem and its occasion fall under the traditional definition of epideictic rhetoric, but it accomplishes more than merely praising Señora Rubio de Díaz. As Miecznikowski Sheard contends, epideictic rhetoric brings "together images of both the real—what *is* or at least *appears to be*—and the fictive or imaginary—what *might be*," which "allows speaker and audience to envision possible, new, or at least different worlds."[66] Through Porfirio Díaz's political efforts of reconciliation, Mexico began to emerge as a respectable nation on a global scale, and this poem enhanced that view. It placed Mexico on an equal footing with Germany and Spain through the social works of Rubio de Díaz, "an angel that lovingly opens this temple." It commemorated the historic moment of the opening of the first nursery for working women in Mexico. It also created the possibility of a "new world," one that considered Mexico as an admirable nation. Lastly, it included women in Mexican history. This type of laudatory poetry, appearing many times in *Violetas*, contributed to the shifting public values of women and challenged the discourse that women were not in the position to create knowledge. These are only a few of the examples of the poetic accomplishments of a variety of Mexican women appearing in each volume of the journal. The well-preserved pages of *Violetas* serve as an archive rich with Mexican women's writing.

For Mexican women to see their writing published and distributed in public provided them with a rare cultural legitimacy. This marked their first step in challenging the unspoken rules of who was allowed within that sphere.

While we can't definitively claim that collectively these poems or any of the civic writings had a great influence on women's societal acceptance, their writings, nevertheless, were the first steps toward acceptance. *Violetas* boasted a large readership and received praise from some of the most important newspapers and intellects of the time. Newspaper publications and journals in Mexico engaged in the practice of acknowledging one another in print, approving or disapproving of the range of journals' and newspapers' political or social claims. This simple yet powerful rhetorical practice signaled to the public which newspapers were supported by certain political factions or if they were accepted into the sphere of public influence. We also have rich documentation of what the women's audience was saying about them.

In a section titled "Impresiones de la prensa" (Impressions from the Press), *Violetas* published the various reactions of its peers. One of the impressions published came from Manuel Romero in a newspaper titled *El Monitor del Pueblo* (The Instructor of the People).

> Vedlas pasar, son Las hijas del Anáhuac que rompen las cadenas con que en un tiempo estuvo sujeta la inteligencia de la mujer; llaman cariñosamente á sus hermanas y las convidan á tomar parte en ese noble torneo de la inteligencia. . . . ¿Qué diremos de esa publicación? Que le deseamos prosperidad y larga vida.[67]
>
> See them passing by, they are Anáhuac's Daughters who are breaking the chains that at one time had women's intelligence subjugated; they call to their sisters affectionately and they invite them to take part in that noble tournament of intelligence. . . . What can we say about that publication? That we desire prosperity and long life for it.

The Mexican women poets and writers demonstrated an ability to strategically situate themselves linguistically and rhetorically among the intellectual men of the time, where they argued for an identity of their nation and declared the beginning of a new identity for women in the public space as intellectual beings. The literary and journalistic society may have made inclusionary nods toward women writers; however, in the emerging discipline of history, women would have to speak for themselves.

Feminizing Mexican History

During the Porfiriato, one of the focal points in developing an intellectual presence was to provide Mexico with a national identity and international legitimacy by having scholars write the history of Mexico. Historical accounts written during the Porfiriato were controlled by the governmental bureaucratic group of men known as "the wizards of progress."[68] A collection of intellectually elite men that included poets, historians, and scholars, their charge was to create a positive and progressive image of Mexico at the 1889 World's Fair in Paris.[69] The world's fair held in Chicago in 1893 featured a booth of Mexican women's paintings and poetry, but as Tenorio-Trillo notes, "the Mexican government was not truly interested in the modern social concerns with women."[70] The wizards were tasked with writing and distributing propaganda in the form of pamphlets, books, statistics, and speeches. Significant among these authors was the Mexican writer Ireneo Paz, editor and director of Mexico City's *La Patria* (The Nation). He was contracted by the government to write *Los hombres prominentes de México* (The Prominent Men of Mexico). Those who wished to appear in this historical book, mostly men from the Mexican exhibition team and their male acquaintances, could pay fifty pesos for the privilege of being included.[71] This type of insiders' manipulation of history only added to the economic and epistemic control men had over Mexico's discourse. Most distressingly, by offering only elite men the right to pay for their names to be included in the annals of history, the axiological and ontological control was most explicit. It resulted in the total exclusion of women.

Without a doubt, Wright de Kleinhans read and saw this circulation of Mexico's contemporary history as a form of flagrant gendered inequality. The sentiments among Mexican men over women's addition into history was that if they were included, the weaker gender would have liberty to enter into the political realm and lose their place as "the angel of the home" or even risk the loss of their femininity. In response to these circulating sentiments, Wright de Kleinhans published Manresa de Pérez's segment of "Mujeres de nuestra época" as the first effort to historicize women. This segment appeared twice and included short discursive snapshots of women from Mexico and around the world participating in civic and entrepreneurial endeavors. Manresa de Pérez's introduction to the section in the first volume situated the women and men of their newspaper (the director of the paper was male, Señor Ignacio Pujol) and those of their audience in a system of social values that deviated from the norm. Manresa de Pérez writes in the first two paragraphs of the article:

> [N]uestro espíritu se enagena [*sic*] de goces infinitos al considerar que la *mujer material* que ayer vivía oscura y silenciosa al pie de la cuna de sus hijos, que no podía educarse porque solo servía para *nodriza*

> ha despertado hoy para la vida del progreso inspirándose en la cultura moderna. . . .
>
> Ahogada para siempre la estulta preocupación de los hombres de antaño, de que la mujer instruida era nociva á la sociedad, porque su instrucción le hacía perder su carácter de madre cariñosa y de sacerdotisa del hogar; los hombres de la moderna edad, más prácticos y más científicos, más justos y menos egoístas, [están] despreciando los antiguos sistemas.[72]

> [O]ur spirit is infinitely enraptured to consider the physical woman that yesterday lived in darkness and silence at the foot of the crib of her children, that could not gain an education because she lived to serve as a wet nurse, has today awakened to live a progressive life inspired by the modernist culture. . . .
>
> She was eternally drowned in the muffled preoccupation of the men from the past, that the educated woman was harmful to society, because her education made her lose her character of loving mother and priestess of the home; the men of modern times, more practical and more scientific, more fair and less egotistical, [are] rejecting the antiquated systems.

Manresa de Pérez renounced the ontological and axiological stance that educated women would lose their feminine characteristics. Rhetorical appeals such as that of Manresa de Pérez initiated an ontological shift of the way in which women were perceived on a daily basis in Mexican society.

"Mujeres de nuestra época" ran for two issues, listing twelve to twenty different women in each publication. Those who appeared in "Mujeres" were noted for their accomplishments as individuals, not as mothers, wives, or "angels of the home." Another listing from the second number in 1887 includes women such as Mrs. Newton Crosland, who translated *Hernani* by Victor Hugo; Miss Grace Howard, the daughter of a well-known journalist J. Howard, who at the age of twenty-two has set out to establish a school among the Crow Indians; and Mme. Abicot de Ragis, the first woman to have received the Cross of the Legion of Honor from Napoleon III for an act of valor.[73] These were short, one- or two-paragraph biographical sketches of international women of the time that set the tone for women as active participants in the world. They were part of a larger historical frame, but Wright de Kleinhans undertook a much more localized project to include women in the annals of history.

The last seven years of Wright de Kleinhans's life were spent compiling biographies of 124 Mexican women for her book *Mujeres notables mexicanas*, which was not published until 1910, fourteen years after her death.

Many of these biographies had appeared in *Violetas*, but the book includes many more biographies not previously published. She divided the text into four historical periods: "Pre-Columbian/Conquest," "Colonial Era," "Heroines of the Independence," and "Contemporaries." Other women writers, such as Spanish journalist Concepción Gimeno de Flaquer, were also writing histories that dealt with female accomplishments. As noted earlier, Gimeno de Flaquer founded the *El Álbum de la Mujer*, which ran for seven years, between 1883 and 1890.[74] Her influential writings included Spanish and Mexican women, with a clear inclination toward European women.[75] Unlike Gimeno de Flaquer's biographical writings, Wright de Kleinhans's historical accounts focused solely on Mexican women. She highlights relatively unknown women, includes their writings when they could be found, and, most powerfully, re/visions a feminine Mexican history.[76]

For example, the first section of *Mujeres notables* validates Wright de Kleinhans's commitment to the writing of credible history and to the interpretation of a feminized historical account of an indigenous nation. As an intellectual who read and listened to the history of her homeland, she recognized that the greatest injustice leveled against indigenous women was their systematic erasure from history. The women highlighted in the section on the pre-Columbian era were writers, poets, historians, queens, princesses, and heroines, who held various positions of power or who interacted with the influential and powerful—women whose stories heretofore had been buried in the historical archives. As inclusive as this history may seem, she ignored the presence of contemporary indigenous women in the later periods of history. Cano notes that "Indians were a cultural heritage, but not a social component of a modern nation," and because of these beliefs, the Indian women of her time were excluded.[77]

Wright de Kleinhans synthesized bits and pieces of stories from historians such as Bernal Díaz del Castillo, Suárez de Peralta, Carlos de Sigüenza y Góngora, and Manuel Orozco y Berra in order to aggregate the accounts of the indigenous women. The first woman Wright de Kleinhans introduced was La Señora de Tula, the principal wife of the many wives of Netzahualpilli. She quotes an unspecified historical account that said La Señora de Tula was believed to have been "tan sabia que competía con el rey y con los más sabios de su reino, y era en la poesía muy aventajada; que en estas gracias y dones naturales, tenía el rey muy sujeto á su voluntad" (so wise that she competed with the king and the wisest in the kingdom, and was an outstanding poet; through her natural graces and talents she had the king subject to her will).[78] Wright de Kleinhans recounts the narrative in a matter-of-fact tone, with no discussion, commentary, or citation as to who wrote it, other than stating that the era in which La Señora de Tula lived was unknown. Strict historians may not have considered La Señora de Tula a valid historical figure but would have seen her as a legend or myth at best.

In some instances, such as in writing about La Señora de Tula, Wright de Kleinhans applied the same controversial methodology employed by feminist rhetorical historian Cheryl Glenn in the writing of Aspasia. Glenn grants Aspasia great historical and rhetorical credibility based solely on secondary sources that spoke of Aspasia and her works, an approach that has been heavily challenged and debated.[79] Like Glenn, Wright de Kleinhans wrote women like La Señora de Tula into pre-Conquest history, which provides an indication of two ideas she had about history. First, she trusted the accounts given by the historians she quoted, even if some accounts were transcribed from the pictographic codices. Second, she believed that these women played a larger role in society than the historians had acknowledged.

Another indigenous woman's history included was of Malinalxochitl, heroine and sister of Huitizon, great priest and chieftain of the tribes of Aztlán. She would later become ruler of one of the first populated tribes in Mexico.[80] Wright de Kleinhans notes that her story was recounted by Fernando Alvarado Tezozomoc, a colonial Nahua noble and historian, whose history relied heavily on hieroglyphic interpretations. He told of Malinalxochitl's "man like" valor, fighting alongside her brother, Huitziton. After he died in battle, she was next in line to take his place, but "algunos ancianos sacerdotes de la tribu" (some old priests from the tribe) challenged her ascendency to the throne.[81] Instead of fighting for her rightful place, she left the tribe, but not without first persuading the "más sabios y prudentes" (most wise and prudent) members to accompany her to the hills of Texaltepec. The account notes that she established a new settlement through the purchase of land from the inhabitants of Texaltepec, and she was said to have been respected as a wise mother figure.[82]

In the telling of this history, Wright de Kleinhans first presents Tezozomoc's account, but then in the middle of the chronicle, she recounts what other historians interpreted from the codices. "Otros historiadores han interpretado de los jeroglíficos indios que su partida no fue voluntaria y que para deshacerse de ella los sacerdotes dijeron que era una maga, que se había entregado á la hechicería" (Other historians have interpreted from the Indian hieroglyphs that her leaving was not voluntary and in order to get rid of her, the high priests accused her of being a sorceress, and that she had turned to witchcraft).[83] The high priests from her first settlement, intending to taint her credibility, claimed she turned to sorcery. From this other account, it is also believed that Huitziton, her deceased brother, appeared to the high priests speaking against Malinalxochitl and instructed them to abandon her and the other old settlers while they were asleep. Wright de Kleinhans agreed with the critics and historians that these stories and legends about Malinalxochitl eventually elevated her to the level of tradition, then mythology. Among the people of her tribe, she was elevated to the status of goddess.[84] Wright de Kleinhans interpreted Malinalxochitl's mythical and legendary status, not as a discredit to her, as some male historians of her time would be apt to do, but as an indication of her intelligence. Her mythical status, she said, "[l]lama sin embargo la atención que desde tiempos remotos y entre tribus salvajes hubiese ya mujeres que comprobasen con sus hechos igualdad intelectual con el hombre" (calls attention to the fact that even in the distant past among savage tribes there were already women who proved through their actions to be of equal intellect with men).[85]

Through Wright de Kleinhans's feminine representation of history, she created her own methodological approach that contested the cultural boundaries of Mexican women past and present. In her historical dealing with Malintzin, however, Wright de Kleinhans disparaged her actions against her people. Ironically, in a section titled, "Caoniana, Tenepal, o Malinal, (La Malinche)," she takes at face value the interpretations of the historical events by Spanish historians. She does acknowledge her linguistic acuity, but does not seem to forgive or rationalize her actions against her people. Wright de Kleinhans says of Malintzin that she lost sight of her indigenous roots and "rompío toda liga con los pueblos de Anáhuac, desconoció su raza; á mengua debía tener el color bronceado" (she broke all ties with the peoples of Anáhuac, she disowned her race; she must have deemed it a shame to have a bronze colored complexion).[86] This perception of Malintzin was, and remains with some Mexican people, a common sentiment. However, it places full blame of the conquest on the shoulders of Malintzin instead of the invaders, which twists the facts. Regardless of Wright de Kleinhans's feelings toward Malintzin, the historian could not escape the racial contradiction of mestizaje brought on by the colonization of Spain.

Some of the other indigenous women she included were Tecuiloatzin, Tolquequetzaltzin, Zicuetzin, and Zacancozcatl, princesses who were given to Hernán Cortés; Doña Ana Moctezuma, daughter of Moctezuma, given to Hernán Cortés to take as a wife and baptized as a Christian; Tepatl-Xuchitl (1353), princess of Azcapotzalco, celebrated and recognized for having caused, although innocently, a war between the Tepanecas and the Mexicas against the Texcocanos for many years; Tozcuentzin, queen of Texcoc and mother of Ixtlilxochitl "Ome Tochtli," who was known for her valor, intelligence, and high character; Papantzin, a Mexica princess, who is said to have been resurrected and who prophesied the coming of the Spaniards; and Doña María Bartola, from the sixteenth century, the first Mexican female scribe and historian, who according to the histories of Ixtlilxochitl quickly learned Spanish and wrote down the occurrences of battles. Of this last woman, Doña María Bartola, Wright de Kleinhans wrote that it would be only correct to grant her the title of "una estrella de la literatura nacional femenina, por haber sido la primera escritora en la época colonial y la primera mujer historiada" (star of feminine national literature for having been the first writer of the colonial period and the first female historian).[87] These examples from *Mujeres notables* are merely snapshot representations of Wright de Kleinhans's skills as a rhetorician and historian. The history that she includes of indigenous women brings to light a much forgotten realm of social life, the feminine that mainstream male historians from the late nineteenth century were attempting to silence.

Throughout the book, she went beyond the narrative presented and wrote mostly against the grain of the male critics and historians, providing critique and analysis. Wright de Kleinhans critically looked within the interstices of historical accounts and located women who had been overlooked and forgotten, using the established histories of Mexico as her support. She rejected historical narratives and archived works as full, accurate, and unbiased accounts of history, because, as she substantiated in her book by quoting various credible historians, so much of Mexican history had been lost. These findings led her to challenge many viewpoints held by the most respected historians, whom she felt could easily have been misinformed, taken a biased perspective, or used incomplete sources.

Furthermore, she condemns past historians for losing, misplacing, or forgetting historical archives of women's histories and writings. For example, she comments on the loss of a seventeenth-century historical text, *Vidas de religiosas ejemplares* (Exemplary Lives of Nuns of the Religious Order), written by Sor Petronila de San José, abbess of the church Jesús María de México in the seventeenth century.[88] Wright de Kleinhans highlights commentary by Carlos de Sigüenza y Góngora (1645–1700), a respected Colonial author, which stated that Sor Petronila's writings had been cited as one of the "best histories of the time."[89] His remarks on this loss echo Wright de Kleinhans's views regarding the mishandling of historical records written by or about women:

> Si para lograr nuestro objeto de enaltecer por sus obras a nuestro sexo, nos hubiéramos atenido a las crónicas oficiales en éste, como en otros tiempos, nada habríamos obtenido; pues desgraciadamente nuestra historia patria, omisa unas veces, descuidada otras, y más generalmente

> superficial y compendiada, sobre todo tratándose de las proezas cívicas que las mujeres no obstante hallarse privadas del derecho de ciudadanía han llevado a cabo; nuestra historia, decimos, casi por regla general apenas menciona tales proezas si no es que las calla por completo.[90]

> If in order to achieve our objective of honoring our sex for their works, we would have kept to the official chronicles of this time, as in others, we would have obtained nothing at all; because unfortunately the history of our homeland, neglectful sometimes, slighted others, and more generally superficial and truncated, most of all in that which has to do with the civic exploits that women, regardless of their being restricted from the right of citizenship, have carried out; our history, we say, practically as a general rule, barely mentions such exploits if not hushing them up completely.

Wright de Kleinhans was witness to the historical silencing of Mexican women, and most regrettably, this claim rings as relevant today as during Wright de Kleinhans's historical moment.

From the Mexican Colonial period, Wright de Kleinhans also includes many women who had been lost in the archives. For example, Sor Juana Inés de la Cruz at that time may have been considered by many as the only Mexican literary woman. Wright de Kleinhans did recognize Sor Juana's accomplishments and dedicated forty-four pages to her history and literary accomplishments, but she also included twenty-seven other women whom Mexican history did not remember. The first woman highlighted from the Colonial era is a María Guerrero, who was born in Mexico in 1687. Wright de Kleinhans labeled each woman with her expertise or her social title, so we know that Guerrero was a writer and orator. Wright de Kleinhans noted the following about Guerrero from Francisco Sosa's "Efemérides históricas y biográficas," a history of Mexico during the Colonial era first published in 1883.

> Pocos son los detalles que acerca de esta ilustrada oradora y literata se conservan. Notable fue, sin embargo, su mérito, por haberse dedicado á estudios profanos en una época en que las mujeres que saliéndose de la norma común adquirían algunos conocimientos extraordinarios, los sujetaban al cartabón místico, medida que no podían sobrepasar los hombres, y con menos derecho las mujeres.[91]

> Few are the details that are preserved about this educated speaker and literary personality. Her merit was noteworthy, however, in that she

> dedicated herself to nonreligious studies in an age in which women who, breaking free from the ordinary standard, acquired some extraordinary knowledge. They were subjected to the mystic set square, a measure that men could not surpass, and with even less right could women do so.

Wright de Kleinhans notes that rarer than Guerrero becoming a writer and orator was the fact that her father supported her education in Latin and Spanish and also in the study of literature. On October 30, 1731, Guerrero publically recited a panegyric that she authored in Latin in praise of Sor Juana, and in 1747, she published an *elegía latina* for Spanish King Felipe VI. The elegy was also written in Latin, accompanied by the Spanish version, which attested to Guerrero's bilingual abilities. Again to Wright de Kleinhans's deep dismay, these three pieces had been lost, but nonetheless, she continued on with the history. Other Mexican women from the Colonial era whom Wright de Kleinhans resurrected from the archives included Doña Josefa Vergara, philanthropist; Doña María Josefa Yermo de Yermo, philanthropist; Sor Agustina de Santa Teresa, religious teacher and writer, of the Convento de la Purísima Concepción; La Venerable Francisca de San José del Tercer Orden de Santo Domingo, writer; Sor María de la Encarnación, religious teacher and writer, of the Convento del Carmen de Puebla; and Sor María Inés de los Dolores, writer, whose verse "Romance" Wright de Kleinhans published in its entirety. The addition of these women from Colonial history along with their subsequent writings added to women's credibility as writers and thinkers and also implicitly argued that Sor Juana was not an intellectual aberration.

The last two sections of *Mujeres notables* are "Heroínas de la Independencia" (Heroines of the Independence) and "Contemporáneas desde 1820 hasta nuestros días" (Contemporaries from 1820 until the Present Era).[92] In these chapters, Wright de Kleinhans shatters the preconceived notion of the existence of only two women who acted with valor during the era of independence: the figures of María Leona Vicario and Doña Josefa Ortiz de Domínguez, the most recognized and celebrated Mexican women from this era. However, this study includes fifteen other women from the same period. Wright de Kleinhans closes *Mujeres notables* by writing about her contemporaries. There were many accomplished women who gained a level of recognition for their civic valor, education, school directorships, oratory, musical and theatrical skills, philanthropy, and poetry. The biographies, which are accompanied by visual portraits of many of these women, recount their lives in vivid detail. The biographies include the women's paths to receiving an education, their accomplishments in the public sphere, and how they superseded every negative expectation to excel in their endeavors. Again, the critique by Cano that indigenous women of this time were ignored resonates here. This silencing is closely related to the elite attitudes of the time, which rendered the Indian culture an absent presence. As much as she believed in documenting the praises of other women, it is interesting to note that her own biography did not appear in her book. Wright de Kleinhans was a private and equally magnanimous woman. She never brought attention to herself above the accomplishments of other women.

Conclusion

In *La emancipación*, Wright de Kleinhans evokes the feminine rhetorical strategy of declaring un nuevo puesto. She writes, "Conozco el lugar que debo ocupar: yo no soy esclava, sino la conductora de la humanidad" (I know the place that I should occupy: I am not a slave, but rather a guide and leader to humanity).[93] This reallocation of women's "lugar" (place), or puesto, from slave to "conductora de la humanidad" evokes the historical shift of the strong female archetype of Malintzin from india esclava to india intérprete. Just as Malintzin claimed a puesto of knowledge, this mestiza rhetor of the nineteenth century harkens back to Mexico's discursive beginnings and enacts them in her present time.

Caught within the ideologies of positivism, modernism, and Victorian morality, Laureana Wright de Kleinhans's discourse is representative of two historical movements converging in Mexico in the late nineteenth century: one in which scholars, intellectuals, and politicians sought recognition of their country as a respectable nation from the international community; and the other, in which people strove to consider their indigenous roots as part of the national identity. Wright de Kleinhans's rhetoric struck a balance between these two views. She recognized the epistemological barriers that confronted women from every class and race and that were fortified through Mexican society's axiological and ontological beliefs, which conformed to Europe's scientific perspective.

On all levels, women were formally excluded from contributing to a national identity, but Wright de Kleinhans and the other female writing staff and civic contributors of *Violetas* transcended identity boundaries through their weekly publications. Their positions never conformed to one ideology or the other. This challenged the women, as mestizas, to build a tolerance to their ambiguity. As Anzaldúa writes of the nature of the mestiza: "She strengthens her tolerance (and intolerance) for ambiguity. She is willing to share, to make herself vulnerable to foreign ways of seeing and thinking."[94]

Much of Wright de Kleinhans's writing confronted the accepted societal frames by transferring the intellectual expertise from men to women on subjects such as public praise, personal and public morality, history, and poetry. Poetry, a genre traditionally reserved for men, was strategically appropriated by women in *Violetas*. This approach shifted societal constructs that determined who was worthy of being commemorated or eulogized. Her insight into the understanding of racial constructs of the time influenced the history of the indigenous women who had been theorized about but pragmatically forgotten. Wright de Kleinhans claimed un puesto nuevo for hundreds of women who had been erased, and beyond any doubt, many more female Mexican rhetorical figures will emerge as potential subjects for further research.

Saludo y prospecto

Las Hijas [Violetas] del Anáhuac
Año 1, Tomo 1, Numero 1
México, Diciembre 4, 1887

Saludo.

Con el ramo de oliva entre las manos como muestra de la regeneración intelectual de la mujer, vivificadas con las puras enseñanzas de la antigüedad, se presenta hoy al público el modesto Periódico Las Hijas del Anáhuac y reverentemente dirige su cordial saludo á todas la clases de la Sociedad, á la Prensa de todos los matices políticos, y á los Hombres del Poder y del Estado; trilogía poderosa que con sus magníficos arneses ha podido evolucionar victoriosamente en beneficio de la paz, el orden, y la cultura de la Patria mexicana.

Prospecto

A medida que avanza la civilización de los pueblos, va produciendo nuevos elementos de engrandecimiento que crean á su vez nuevas necesidades, las cuales es preciso cubrir, si no se quiere que tales elementos se pierdan ó por lo menos permanezcan estacionarios é inútiles, como permanece la perla en el fondo de los mares, si no va á arrancarla de su escondido lecho la mano laboriosa del buzo.

Entre las necesidades de este género que el adelanto ha hecho surgir del seno de nuestro pueblo, hay una de capital interés que deseamos de preferencia atender, y que consiste en la fundación de un periódico femenil destinado á sostener los intereses, los derechos y las prerrogativas sociales de nuestras compatriotas.

La mujer mexicana, adicta por naturaleza á todo lo bello y á todo lo grande, ha llegado en su mayor parte á un grado bastante elevado de ilustración, y necesita por lo mismo un campo donde pueda ensanchar sus conocimientos y darlos á luz haciéndolos extensivos á su sexo en general, á fin de que se levante á la altura de la sociedad en que vive y de la época que representa.

México, nuestra querida patria, marcha como todos los pueblos americanos á la vanguardia del adelanto intelectual y está llamado á ocupar el lugar que por su ilustración le corresponde en el proscenio de la cultura moderna; pero para ello es necesario que todos y cada uno de sus hijos contribuyamos, siquiera sea con nuestro pequeño grano de arena, al edificio de su futura grandeza.

Poseyendo la conciencia de este grato cuanto sagrado deber, hemos creído que la mejor manera de cumplirlo es mejorar en cuanto nos sea posible la condición actual de la mujer, dedicándole nuestros humildes trabajos, por corta que pueda ser su utilidad; estimulando su amor al arte y á la ciencia; afirmando sus principios morales y cultivando sus bellas dotes literarias; haciéndola tomar parte en el torneo de las letras; proporcionándole el espacio que necesita para explayar sus ideas; animándola para que emprenda la noble campaña del pensamiento contra la apatía, del estudio contra la ignorancia, del progreso contra el atraso, de cuyo choque tiene que desprenderse indefectiblemente la luz.

Esta es la misión que al dar publicada á este semanario nos hemos impuesto, y el objeto que nos proponemos es el de llenar en cuanto nos sea posible esta perentoria exigencia de nuestra cultura, esta apremiante necesidad de nuestro adelanto, poniendo á disposición del bello sexo mexicano en periódico escrito y editado especialmente para fomentar por cuantos medios estén á nuestro alcance, el amplio desarrollo de su instrucción.

Nuestras compatriotas poseen brillantes disposiciones naturales que como los tesoros vírgenes del suelo en que se ha mecido su cuna, aun no han sido explotadas; nosotras queremos ser la *obreras* que descubramos los ricos filones de su inteligencia, las *trabajadoras de la mar* que pongamos á flote las bellas perlas de su talento, y muy felices no conceptuaremos si para lograrlos no bastan á falta de mejores elementos, nuestro acendrado amor patrio, nuestra buena voluntad y nuestro ardiente entusiasmo por la educación completa de la mujer.

Con tal propósito, no sólo ponemos á las órdenes de todas las escritoras de la República las columnas de este semanario, sino que excitamos á las jóvenes que comienzan á hacer sus primeros ensayos literarios, á que nos envíen sin temor alguno sus producciones, en la seguridad de que serán, si lo necesitan, minuciosamente corregidas antes de ver la luz pública.

Ojalá que nuestros trabajos alcancen el loable fin que nos proponemos, pues en él habremos realizado uno de nuestros más bellos ideales: la representación nacional de la mujer en la prensa, con el establecimiento de un periódico femenino mexicano, que tal vez algún día llegue á figurar como uno de los primeros rudimentos de nuestra literatura patria.

La Redacción
[Laureana Wright de Kleinhans]

■ ■ ■

Greetings and Prospectus

The Daughters [Violets] of Anáhuac
Year 1, Volume 1, Number 1
Mexico City, December 4, 1887

Greetings.

With the olive branch in its hands as a token of women's intellectual regeneration, vivified with the pure teachings of times past, the modest Newspaper "The Daughters of Anáhuac" introduces itself today to the public and reverently directs its cordial greeting to all classes of Society, to the Press of all political shadings, and to the Men of Power and to those of the State; powerful trilogy that with its magnificent trappings has been able to evolve victoriously for the sake of peace, order, and culture, of the Mexican Homeland.

Prospectus

While a population's civilization advances, it proceeds to produce new elements of enhancement that, in their turn, create new necessities, which must be satisfied, if such elements are not to be lost or at most remain stagnant and useless, like a pearl in the depths of the seas, if the careful hand of the diver does not pull it from its hidden bed.

Among the necessities of this type that progress has caused to arise from the heart of our people, there is one of crucial interest that we desire to

---

Translation by Joel Bollinger Pouwels

attend to preferentially, and that consists of the establishment of a women's periodical destined to support the interests, rights, and social prerogatives of our female compatriots.

The Mexican woman, naturally drawn to everything beautiful and great, has for the most part reached quite a high level of culture, and therefore she needs a forum where she can broaden her accomplishments and bring them to fruition, applying them to her sex in general, so that woman may be raised to the height of the society in which she lives and the epoch that she represents.

Mexico, our beloved nation, marches like all the American peoples, in the intellectual vanguard and, due to her level of enlightenment, is called upon to occupy her rightful place on the stage of modern culture; but in order to do so, each and every one of her citizens must contribute, even if only with a grain of sand, to the monument of her future greatness.

Possessed of awareness of this duty, as welcome as it is sacred, we believe that the best way to accomplish it is to improve the woman's current condition as soon as we possibly can, dedicating to her our humble labors, no matter how small their utility; stimulating her love of art and science; enabling her to participate in the arena of letters; affirming her moral principles and cultivating her fine literary gifts; affording her the space she needs to elaborate her ideas; encouraging her to undertake the noble combat of thought against apathy, of education against ignorance, of progress against backwardness, so that from the clash, unfailingly, the light of greatness may be released.

This is the mission that we have shouldered as we announce this weekly publication, and the purpose that we have set ourselves is to fill as far as we are able this peremptory requirement of our culture, this urgent necessity of our advancement, putting at the service of the fair Mexican sex a journal written and edited specially to encourage by whatever means are within our reach, the extensive development of her instruction.

Our women compatriots possess brilliant natural potential that, like the untouched treasure of the land that cradled them, has yet to be exploited; we women want to be the *laborers* who discover the rich veins of our sisters' intelligence, we want to be the *workers of the sea* who bring up beautiful pearls of talent, and we will imagine ourselves to be very happy if these achievements can occur, lacking better implements, using our refined love of nation, our good will, and our burning enthusiasm for womankind's complete education.

With this purpose, we not only put this weekly publication's columns at the disposal of all women writers in the Republic, by the same token we also encourage young women who are beginning to write their first literary essays, to send their works to us without any fear, secure in the knowledge that, if needed, their writings will be carefully corrected before appearing in print for all to see.

We hope that our project will reach the praiseworthy goals that we have set for ourselves, since through this publication's success we will have achieved one of our most beautiful ideals: the national representation of the woman in the press, with the establishment of a Mexican feminine periodical, that will perhaps some day earn its place as one of the first rudiments of our national literature.

The Editorial Staff
[Laureana Wright de Kleinhans]

CHAPTER THREE

"Hear Us!"

The Feminist Protests of Las Mujeres de Zitácuaro

Conforme a las luminosas enseñanzas de la moderna sabiduría, la mujer es persona y no cosa; luego derecho tiene y hasta deber, de tomar participio en los movimientos progresistas, y puede y debe iniciarlos.

According to the enlightened teachings of modern wisdom, the woman is a person and not a thing; therefore, she has a right and even a duty, to take part in progressive movements, and she can and should initiate them.
—LAS MUJERES DE ZITÁCUARO (THE WOMEN OF ZITÁCUARO)

At the turn of the century in Zitácuaro, Michoacán, México (1894–1904), there emerged a progressive Presbyterian movement initiated by visiting American missionaries. Three Mexican women, the Colín sisters, Aurora, Guadalupe, and Elvira, led the movement with the help of Benita Amaya de Reyes.[1] These women were activists at the forefront of Mexican civic philosophies, which would later be adopted as secular educational values centered on individual, modernist, and open public education for men and women. Their movement would encourage the ongoing education of women and initiate the opening of a school for girls, Leona Vicario, in February 1902. However, before these changes could take place in the educational system of an already progressive state, the Colín sisters, along with a group of fifty-three other women activists who called themselves Las Mujeres de Zitácuaro (MZ), publicly engaged the anti-Catholic and anti-Díaz politics in the newspapers through a series of articles in 1900. This chapter contends that the MZ's collective political discourse is a social enactment of historical protest genres of the plan, the grito, and the

Tomo IV. Durango, Diciembre 7 de 1900 Núm. 26.

La Bandera Roja.

PERIODICO INDEPENDIENTE, CONSAGRADO Á DEFENDER Y PROPAGAR LOS PRINCIPIOS É IDEAS LIBERALES.

"La enfermedad grave de nuestra época, es la cobardía. No hay el valor de desplegar la bandera, de asumir la responsabilidad de lo que se cree que es la verdad, de poner de acuerdo los actos con las convicciones. Se considera que es prudente y hábil conformarse con los usos, observar las exterioridades, aún cuando en el fuero interno se haya roto completamente con todo esto. No se quiere molestar á nadie ni herir ninguna preocupación. A esto se llama «respetar las convicciones ajenas.»—Esta falta de valor y de sinceridad es lo que prolonga una vida de mentiras y retarda á ojos vistos el triunfo de la verdad.» MAX NORDAU.

Director, propietario y fundador Francisco O. Arce.

La enseñanza laica.—Más sobre el tema de los periódicos clericales como "La Voz de México," "El Tiempo," "El País" y compañeros.

Se atreve á decir la primera que si no se enseña la religión católica en las Escuelas Oficiales, todo va á desmoronarse, fé, verdad, órden, progreso; porque las doctrinas católicas son las únicas que deben formar el corazón del niño.

Esto equivale á pedir al gobierno que sus escuelas dejen de ser laicas y se conviertan en un noviciado de frailes, como son las escuelas clericales; y los preceptores actuales, verdaderos porta-estandartes del progreso sientífico, se truequen en ministros del retroceso.

Por lo demás, estas declamaciones clericales no pueden resistir una discusión, un ligero analisis, pues ya la prensa liberal les ha demostrado mil veces que el gobierno no puede, no debe decidir cual es la verdad religiosa, imponiéndola al pueblo; y esos órganos ultramontanos tienen que callarse persuadidos de la evidencia; no pueden discutir, son incapaces para defender su triste causa, y entonces declamando... pueden, y para eso ocurren á la fé ciega, á la fé que no existe y que dicen se desmoronará, pero no puede desmoronarse lo que ya no existe.

Con relación al progreso, se necesita haber perdido hasta el pudor para darle por fuente, por causa necesaria una religión que lo ha quemado, atormentado y maldecido

Por otra parte, ¿cuál es el fin de la enseñanza? ¿para qué se educa á la humanidad? No puede ser otro que ponerla en posesión de la verdad y del bien. ¿Se encuentra esta finalidad en la religión del Papa? que respondan por nosotros los mil ochocientos y más millones de hombres que no pertenecen á ella; que lo testifiquen todas esas sectas que se apropian exculsivamente la divinidad: que lo digan las naciones más adelantadas del mundo, donde no ha imperado ni impera el credo romanista, y por último que se dirija una mirada á los pueblos donde domina la reli-... bo Clemente, los Borgias, Caserio, los grandes asesinos, los ladrones de la edad media; los escandalosos adúlteros, los envenenadores y anarquistas donde han sido educados sino en esas escuelas donde tanto se habla de Dios?

Desde la conquista de México hasta la página inmortal de la Reforma, en más de tres centurias, no hubo más que esas escuelas donde se enseñaba la inexplicable y menos inteligible teología de Ripalda; y fueron por ventura en esa época menores los asesinatos, los robos, los escándalos, adulterios, la embriaguez y todo género de crímenes? La reciente y contemporánea historia demuestra lo contrario.

La enseñanza laica no puede ser como declaman esos periódicos—la prostitución de las conciencias, toda vez que enseña la moral basada en los eternos principios, los cuales constituyen lo esencial de la conciencia humana, porque si estos principios fueran subversivos, si prostituyeran las conciencias, entonces habría que culpar á ese Dios que los ha esculpido en ellas segú[n] dice la Teodisea. Y si tales principio[s] son santos y morales, ¿cómo pueden se[r] orígen y causa de prostitucion?

La escuela laica no enseña como afirma[n] los eternos declamadores, el materialism[o] pero ni el espiritualismo, porque deja es[as] cuestiones, para que las resuelva la cien[cia], inpenetrable todavía por las inteligen[cias] de la niñez.

Por último, la enseñanza laica no pued[e] predisponer al anarquismo ni á los desór[denes] morales—como se grita desde lo[s] púlpitos y se repite en los periódicos cl[e]ricales—porque la moral natural no pued[e] ser suicida, y lo sería sin duda si lleva[ra] los hombres al mal moral.

Contesten esos periódicos declamador[es] órganos del clericalismo, conteste este no mienta ni engañe en los púlpitos á l[os] cándidos que los escuchan.

I. ZARAGOZA.

La mujer se emancipa de las opresoras cadenas del clericalism[o]

Figure 3. Masthead of the independent newspaper *La Bandera Roja.* It first appeared in 1896.

manifiesto, which connects their circumstances and desired outcomes to a greater political framework of Mexican rhetorical structures.[2]

This chapter centers on four artifacts I call the "protest series." These artifacts include a political plan, a grito, a separate public introduction of women as political subjects, and a manifiesto. All are forms of public protest deeply rooted in Mexico's historical mestizo heritage. Three of these documents, the plan, the grito, and the manifiesto, were written and given voice by the MZ. A fourth document, the introduction to the manifiesto, was written by an anonymous individual, whom I believe could have been one of the women from the activist group. These documents are rhetorical remonstrations in which the women claim their agency as political beings through the nation's sacred calling for women: motherhood. The women did not eschew their maternal role but, rather, embraced it. They used their standing as mothers as their rhetorical platform to condemn the Catholic

Church for establishing illegal convents that denied women their secularly sacrosanct position of motherhood.

The MZ authored and coauthored a series of writings that appeared in *La Bandera Roja* between October and December 1900.[3] The first in the collection of publications presented in this chapter is a short article with an extended title: "Actitud del partido liberal por las revelaciones del Obispo de San Luis.—Movimiento de indignación en toda la República.—Las Mujeres de Zitácuaro" (The Attitude of the Liberal Party Against the Proclamation of the Bishop of San Luis.—Movement of Indignation in All of the Republic.—The Women of Zitácuro), published on October 26, 1900.[4] This article contains the plan and the enunciation of the grito. Another article in the series, "La mujer se emancipa de las opresoras cadenas del clericalismo" (The Woman Frees Herself from the Oppressive Chains of Clericalism), appeared in the December 7, 1900, issue. Written by Ignacio Zaragoza, a pseudonym referring to a famous Mexican general, the short article reads as an introduction and an acceptance of the MZ as active public participants in the emerging political debates.[5] Zaragoza's rhetorical overture speaks of the recent women's grito de Zitácuaro: "!Viva la Libertad!" (Long Live Liberty!), placing it historically among other famous gritos, such as the Independence Day Grito de Dolores. Immediately after Zaragoza's introduction, the full manifiesto appears, which they titled simply as "Manifiesto."[6]

The "protest series" serves as a bridge connecting the nineteenth-century women's epideictic writing to the forceful, politically centered writing that would gradually emerge as Mexico approached the revolution. Indeed, the MZ declared this connection in their main protest document, the manifiesto: "Que el eslabón que junte al siglo XIX con el siglo XX, sea la verdadera emancipación de la mujer" (May the link that joins the nineteenth century with the twentieth century, be the true emancipation of women).[7] Uncovering the "protest series" is an important step in recognizing the early role Mexican women writers played in claiming new public rhetorical puestos as political activists. Very few women at this time in Mexico's history were speaking publicly, let alone declaring themselves independent thinkers and separate from the Catholic Church, an institution that had for centuries held them physically and intellectually imprisoned. Emerging in the midst of the dictatorship under Porfirio Díaz and on the verge of the movement toward revolution, the twelve-point manifiesto, probably the most significant document in the series, was a rhetorical and ideological response against the church's position on the revival of convents and religious servitude. Furthermore, it was a call for women's agency as political beings and members of a nation that had not yet conferred them citizenship.

As part of the greater pre-Revolutionary popular movement of the formation of liberal clubs in Mexico, the MZ group of forty-six women led by Benita Amaya de Reyes, president, and Guadalupe Colín, vice president, formed a liberal club in 1900 called Josefa Ortiz de Domínguez y Francisca Carrillo.[8] Two controversial events sparked the exigency of these women to organize and publicly speak out: the conciliatory policies of President (by then dictator) Porfirio Díaz toward the church, which negated the strong anticlerical laws of 1856 and 1857,[9] and a speech given by Bishop Ignacio Montes de Oca on June 6, 1900, in Paris, France, that highlighted the church's surge in power throughout Mexico.[10] In his speech, Bishop Montes de Oca declared that the renewed success of the church in Mexico was due in part to the support of Mexico's women. After years of struggling to minimize the stranglehold that the church had on Mexico, numerous Mexican women were infuriated by Montes de Oca's claim. To publicize their contempt and disapproval, the MZ group's newly formed liberal club authored a twelve-point manifiesto, published on December 21, 1900, in Durango's nationalist newspaper, *La Bandera Roja*.[11] They contended that women should join the ideological fight initiated months before by the anti–Porfirio Díaz political figures Camilo Arriaga and Juan Sarabia in San Luis Potosí, Mexico.[12]

The MZ's rhetoric emerged within and against strong male discourses of the historical movement leading up to the Mexican Revolution. As the insurrection against the government grew more pronounced at the turn of the century, pockets of civic participation and protest simultaneously opened a greater rhetorical freedom for Mexican women. Significantly, the writings of the MZ in 1900 signaled a new era of discursive practices for Mexican women. In this next century, women would not be socially constrained to a passive, almost conciliatory, approach to politics, as we saw in the writings of Laureana Wright de Kleinhans and her cohort. Indeed, Mexican women would gradually begin to engage in the pre-Revolutionary politics that predominated in protest newspapers, such as Juan Sarabia's *Renacimiento* and the most famous, Ricardo Flores Magón's *Regeneración*.[13] This new rhetorical puesto that Mexican women began to occupy surpassed the romantic sentiments of late-nineteenth-century poetry and embraced the protest genres of revolution and explicit social action.

Indeed, the women's publication of the plan, declaration of the grito, and the presentation of the manifiesto represent Mexican women's early and emerging involvement in civic tradition and action. In order to have written these complex documents in response to the political climate, their discursive actions, such as reading and listening to political discourse, would have formed part of their daily routines. While these women may have been the exceptions to the rule, we see a growing number of Mexican women taking political action. More importantly, the documents of the protest series were at the forefront of a feminist movement that had not yet officially taken shape in Mexico. Consequently, women articulated their feminationalism within a puesto of intervention, such as through the appropriation of nationalist genres.

Genres of Mexican Political Protest

I position the MZ's writings and oral declarations as protest genres within a larger historical context, which helps to illuminate the rhetorical approach they were taking and expands the analysis beyond the text. Carolyn Miller's important work on genre theory in "Genre as Social Action" states that genre is a recurring social form that is grounded in "situated rhetorical action."[14] The three genres the MZ used, the plan, grito, and manifiesto, are culturally grounded and have recurred for centuries in Mexican political discourse. The public application of the genres invokes the "stock knowledge" that accompanies these discursive forms, which in turn brings to bear new understanding of the women's gendered situation "through the recognition of relevant similarities."[15] The lens of genre theory places these texts within a much broader scope of social, cultural, political, and historical context than if viewed as singular compositions. The documents, then, take on a quality of intertextuality, central to rhetoric.

A genre approach is significant because when we look at a singular document that conforms to an identified genre, we can examine within its form a collective end that is expected by the readers. "A genre," Miller contends, "is a rhetorical means for mediating private intentions and social exigence; it motivates by connecting the private with the public, the singular with the recurrent."[16] Instead of viewing a document as an isolated text unconnected to other realities or utterances, a genre approach illuminates the intertextuality within its historical context, its textual and stylistic conventions, and the expected outcomes the authors and audience carry when identifying the use of the genre. Further, the use of the lens of genre theory expands our knowledge of how female rhetors employed genres in order to negotiate social action and reaction.

The women's use of the protest genres—the grito, the plan, and the manifiesto—signaled to their reading public not mere progressive social action, but revolutionary action. In this study, I classify the grito as a Mexican

Revolutionary genre. Each declaration of a grito, marked by a call to and response from an audience, connects that utterance to the historical moment when Mexico sought to break with the Spanish regime on September 16, 1810. On that date, Father Miguel Hidalgo's call to action with the Grito de Dolores initiated the revolt against the Spanish. Since then, Mexicans have used the grito to begin social movements or to commemorate events.[17] Gritos are punctuated with a call to an audience, and the audience repeats the call. Each grito extols the history and patriotism of the people, such as the following cry to celebrate Independence Day: "¡Mexicanos! ¡Viva México! ¡Vivan los héroes de nuestra Independencia!" (Mexicans! Long live Mexico! Long live the heroes of our independence!).[18] Each utterance of the grito is unique to the discursive and historical context. Hence, the group of women from Zitácuaro used a newly minted Mexican grito when they came together in October 1900 to initiate their club's establishment and make known their contempt for the church. Their grito began: "¡Viva la escuela libre y anticlerical de la mujer!" (Long live women's liberal, anticlerical education!)

Two other Mexican genres, the plan and manifiesto, also hold a strong rhetorical heritage in Mexico as civic and pre-Revolutionary documents. The plan, like the manifiesto, is an inherently Mexican political genre that dates back to the revolutionary independence movements of 1821. John Hammerback and Richard Jensen see the Mexican political plan as a precursor to social movements that provide a group's ideology, philosophy, and intentions.[19] Indeed, plans can be seen as the first step to publicly acting upon a grievance. Within the historical context of each plan, clear rhetorical goals were always presented. The goals were "to expand the revolutionaries' circles of followers and gain public support."[20] Hammerback and Jensen note that most plans "vowed support for the Church." However, as we will see, the women turned this aspect of the genre on its head.

Manuel González Ramírez defines the Mexican manifiesto as a political document that emerges at pivotal historical moments with democratic, rebellious, and revolutionary intent and expresses a group's philosophy, principles, future projections, and reasons for action.[21] González Ramírez states that the manifiesto "arises in a particular moment, with the purpose of securing a political, ideological, social, and economic position opposite of those events that are mounting to form part of history."[22] This unique document is a highly charged public rhetorical structure that, according to González Ramírez, became a popular political document for the literate. The MZ saw the use of the plan and the manifiesto not only as a way to situate themselves within the greater patriarchal conversation of nationhood and struggle against the power of the church, but also as a way to assert their female voices and initiate feminist action in the public sphere.

As a set of rhetorical documents written by politically aware and active Mexican women, the "protest series" functions to fill a gap in Mexican discursive history, which has only recognized political documents written by men. Recognition of these primary documents and the women who composed them expands the historical and rhetorical view of Mexican women participating in political discursive projects. The rhetorical canon has been dominated by elite male viewpoints and experiences, and we find a similar situation in the study of Mexican manifiestos. For example, in González's detailed historical work on plans and manifiestos, only documents written by men are recovered and analyzed. Royster's work recognizes the fact that women of color "come to voice amid an environment that is influenced by socio-political constructions of race, gender, and culture, and affected by the implications of power, privilege, authority, and entitlement."[23] Similarly, the MZ claimed a voice through intersecting theirs with the revolutionary rhetoric critiquing the government's conciliatory policies with the church.

Protest Genres as Mestiza Rhetoric

How do the plan, grito, and manifiesto fit into the framework of mestiza rhetoric? Each rhetorical structure is historically positioned in a culture of the emerging mestizo population in Mexico. Countless plans and manifiestos were written during the struggles against the Spanish, the French, and the United States. The original grito signaled strong connections to the caste of *criollos*, individuals of purportedly pure Spanish blood born on Mexican soil, as well as to wealthy mestizos. While the declaration of freedom from Spain was made on the part of the criollos, over time the grito was appropriated by the mestizo mass of Mexican people to signal Mexicans' independence and to spark nationalistic sentiment. More specifically in the MZ's rhetorical situation, a mestiza consciousness of understanding their cultural heritage emerges through their use of the plan, grito, and manifiesto. Their mestiza consciousness is an enunciation grounded in Mexican women's lived experiences that present new societal directions and transcend the hierarchical logic of assimilation.[24]

The women were claiming a history that exalted the mestizo and denied the European construct of the Catholic Church while defining a new feminine political puesto. These rhetorical constructs represent collective expressions that run counter to the prevailing stories of assimilation and colony. As we will see, the women gendered the plan, grito, and manifiesto for their own rhetorical purposes of negating the cultural and gendered assimilationist claims of Bishop Montes de Oca. Before the core analysis of these artifacts, I provide a contextual orientation to the series of primary documents and an explanation of how the women saw themselves within the fabric of society.

Historical and Rhetorical Intersections

In each article, the MZ anticlerical discourse confronted a long-standing historical power structure of the Catholic Church. Since the Council of Trent of 1554, which gave the church power over every aspect of societal life, the church in Mexico had a history of clear hierarchical authority. Marked by the War of Independence in 1810 against Spanish rule, Mexico's liberals had struggled to free the people from the oppression imposed by the church. The long, bloody war for the approval of liberal ideas led to the Constitution of 1857, which established free expression of ideas in public, the freedom of association with groups of one's choice, and limitations on the authority of the church. The passage of these liberal ideas broke with traditional theocracy and infuriated the conservative groups comprised of the ruling class, aristocrats, and clerical officials. The War of the Reform between the conservative and liberal parties quickly erupted after the signing of the constitution and lasted from 1858 to 1861. At the end of the war, the full application of the Laws of Reform completely altered the status of the church. Ecclesiastical properties were nationalized, convents and monasteries were appropriated, and priests were forbidden to wear their sacerdotal garb in public.

For more than three centuries, the church had framed Mexican women strictly as silent subjects, and many devout Catholic Mexicans still clung to those traditional ideologies. The first discursive response of the MZ, then, serves as a rhetorical marker of social action that intersected with two political factions: the authority of the church and the secular patriarchal ideology that suffused Mexican society. The publication of their writings is also significant because Mexican women in general were considered strong supporters of the church, so much so that their support was considered in later congressional meetings as a reason against granting them suffrage.[25] Supplanting this religious connection in the twelve points of their manifiesto, the women claimed their national agency through the secular acts of creating and raising a family. Each point of their manifiesto articulates a belief in the rights of women to be recognized as individual beings, which also reflect the Presbyterian tenets the women infused into their civic understanding. These early feminist claims established women as agents of social and political change that intersected with the laws, ideologies, and politics of the time.

Las Mujeres de Zitácuaro's First Responses

At the turn of the century, leaders of the liberal movement were angry at the Mexican government for numerous reasons: its consolidation of power, corruption in elections, reconciliation with the Catholic Church, and silencing of dissenting voices. The Mexican newspapers echoed calls from liberal groups for a newly elected president and advocated for a movement of renewed strength in the administration of the Laws of Reform. Women's participation in the liberal cause at the end of the nineteenth century was limited, but as early as the turn of the century, many women, such as the Colín sisters, felt compelled to join the liberal cause. Ricardo Flores Magón, director of the newspaper *Regeneración*, which promoted radical anarchist ideas, used many gender-neutral statements that may have encouraged women to join the movement. However, as noted by Emma Pérez, "*Regeneración* printed at least one essay on women, their rights, or their subjugation in almost every issue of the newspaper from its initial publication."[26]

But with politics and society at the turn of the century within the grip of a dictator, women could not wait for a "formal" invitation to join in political activism. So they embraced and acted upon broad statements, such as those issued in August 1900 in San Luis Potosí by Camilo Arriaga's "Invitación al Partido Liberal."

> Que todas las ciudades del país, se organicen y sostengan clubes liberales en constante relación entre sí, que procuren impedir infracciones a las Leyes de Reforma y que por medio de órganos de prensa den a conocer los abusos del clero y propaguen las ideas y los principios liberales.[27]
>
> Let all the cities of the country get organized and support liberal clubs in constant interrelation among themselves, let them try to prevent violations of the Laws of Reform and that by means of entities of the press they might disclose the abuses of the clergy and propagate ideas and liberal principles.

Indeed, the MZ gave an indication in their manifiesto that they saw themselves within these general calls for actions. In the first lines of the manifiesto, the women situate themselves in the larger context of society as "persons" within the republic. The women, confident and secure, assert their reasons for speaking at the beginning of the manifiesto.

> Ese combate tiene la alta significación de la justa defensa de la Nación, y la justa defensa de la personalidad humana, individualmente considerada; por cuanto a la Nación, sabéis ya que es nuestra República, por cuanto a la personalidad, es necesario deciros que somos nosotras: la "mujer."[28]

> That fight has the high significance of the just defense of the Nation, and the just defense of human personhood, considered individually; as for the Nation, you of course know that it is our Republic; when we say "personhood," it is necessary to tell you that we mean ourselves: the "woman."

More generally, *La Bandera Roja* had been energetically writing and publishing feature articles announcing women's separation from the Catholic Church and advocating their educational freedom by an anonymous author using the pseudonym Ignacio Zaragoza. For example, on September 14, 1900, the newspaper published an article titled "Nuestra obra debe ser emancipar a la mujer del clericalismo" (Our Goal Should Be to Emancipate Women from Clericalism), in which Zaragoza posited that women educated within a theocratic system are denied their natural abilities to raise children and become independent thinkers.[29] As a means to full emancipation, this newspaper argued not merely for women's liberation from the church but also for liberation from their ignorance of intellectual topics, such as science.

In a December issue, Zaragoza reported on a school for girls in Durango called El Instituto de Niñas (the Institute for Girls), believed to be the only secondary school for girls in the state.[30] More significantly, the author argues for women's education in the sciences to equal that of their American neighbors. Zaragoza, who in the case of this article I believe was a female author, argues that women should serve in public puestos beyond being schoolteachers, to include medical doctors, lawyers, and journalists. "Adelante con la en[se]ñanza de la mujer mexicana para que pueda igualar á la anglo sajona nuestra vecina de quien se confiese ser la primera del mundo civilizado" (Onward with the education of the Mexican woman so she can be equal to the Anglo Saxon woman who is our neighbor and claims to be the first in the civilized world). In the last paragraph of the article, Zaragoza states:

> ¿Que no estamos viendo que la mujer quiere conquistar un sitio en la sociedad moderna y aceptar todas las penas y los trabajos inherentes á su ambición? Las cortes europeas, norteamericanas ven figurar entre el buen abogado, distinguido médico y notables periodistas á la mujer.[31]

> Are we not seeing that the woman wants to claim a space in modern society and accept all the struggle and work inherent in her ambition? The European and North American courts count among them women as good lawyers, distinguished physicians, and notable journalists.

There was a clear distinction between Mexican women in relation to the international community and the progress they felt needed to be made in society. The argument for women's education and independence was made in the same issue with the women's manifiesto, which shows that women had already been creating an intellectual puesto to make such gendered declarations. Yet again, we see this effort for women to gain a footing in the public realm to be balanced with a claim that they should not lose their modesty or femininity. On the same page as the piece on El Instituto de Niñas claiming a puesto público and in the next column, we see a short, philosophical, almost poetic piece titled "La mujer modesta" (The Modest Woman) and authored anonymously.[32] There is reference to metaphors with nature and philosophical examples of what makes a modest woman, but the short piece does not concretely *define* modesty, such as modesty being that women should not enter the sphere of education. Its definition is vague and left to interpretation.

> La mujer modesta exhala una perfume que penetra suavemente en el corazón: semejante á la violeta, que oculta siempre su corola entre el follaje, no deslumbra cual la arrogante dalia, pero atrae dulcemente y su reinado es más duradero. . . .
>
> El filósofo inglés Joung [*sic*] comprendió perfectamente la necesidad de la modestia en la mujer: exclamaba de continuo [que] "las mujeres no deben tener nada desnudo; hasta los encantos de espíritu deben ser ocultados por el velo de la modestia."[33]

> The modest woman exhales a fragrance that gently penetrates the heart, similar to the violet, which always hides its corolla among the foliage, it

> does not dazzle like the arrogant dahlia, but attracts sweetly and its reign is more lasting. . . .
>
> The English philosopher Joung [*sic*] perfectly understood the need for modesty in women: he exclaimed continuously [that] "women should not leave anything completely exposed; even the charms of the spirit should be hidden by the veil of modesty."

Although the women were coming into a new century of possibilities with schools and literacy, there was this ever-present caution and reminder that women should not lose their air of femininity. But these repeated sentiments did not seem to deter women from responding to the increasing calls to action, such as those found in *Regeneración*.

Certainly, it is difficult, if not impossible, to assess how many women were reading *Regeneración* or any other political newspaper, such as *La Bandera Roja*. However, MZ's quick discursive response to Bishop Montes de Oca's speech represents at least the forty-six women who signed the document as actively listening, reading, and analyzing political discourse. Bishop Montes de Oca's speech—published on August 7, 1900, in a Catholic publication, *El Estandarte*—generated heated protests by such vociferous liberals as Camilo Arriaga. He issued a manifiesto that called for the formation of liberal clubs throughout Mexico to denounce the evils of clericalism.[34] Viewed through González Ramírez's perspective on what inspires people to author public manifiestos, Bishop Montes de Oca's speech served as one of the major events that polarized public opinion and spurred a flurry of anticlerical newspaper articles, the establishment of liberal clubs, and the issuance of manifiestos. With the bishop's speech, the intellectual men of San Luis Potosí announced their political intentions to urge the people, including women, into action.[35] Equally, at a local level, the ideals of the newspaper welcomed women's public intellectual interactions.

The newspaper article beginning with "Actitud del partido liberal," published on October 26, 1900, approximately three months after the bishop's speech was published, marks the first of various artifacts that illustrate the MZ taking a discursive and political stance against Montes de Oca's speech. His speech called for a clear reconciliation between the Catholic Church and the long-standing Porfirian government. It also called for the loosening of Mexican law, which would then turn a blind eye to the unlawful activities of the monasteries and religious schools. Hence, this declaration was deeply troubling to liberals because they feared the gradual gains in power by the church. "Actitud del partido liberal" introduced the MZ group's plan for independence from the clerical teachings, announced the names of the women in the movement, and alluded to the political manifiesto that would be published several months later.

The first several paragraphs of "Actitud del partido liberal," cowritten with members of MZ, announced the participation of other presses around the country in the growing movement.[36] This short, politically confident document reflects the rhetorical astuteness and the agency the MZ were beginning to exercise during the decade leading up to the Mexican Revolution.

> La prensa nacional de todos los Estados ha venido rebosante de artículos más o menos enérgicos, condenando indignada la conducta clerical revelada por el Obispo de San Luis en la Asamblea General de las Obras Católicas que tuvo verificativo en Paris.[37]

> The national press in all the States has been overflowing with articles of varying intensity, indignantly condemning the clerical conduct revealed by the Bishop of San Luis at the General Assembly of Catholic Works, which took place in Paris.

The women's reaction demonstrates not only their discursive rhetorical ability to respond publicly to political issues but also their rhetorical listening abilities. As Díaz and García note, the women of Zitácuaro were on neither the political nor the educational sidelines, many having studied in normal schools sponsored by the Presbyterian Church, where courses in literature, discourse, and grammar were taught.[38] Hence, their reaction to the bishop's speech signifies that they were listening intently to the prevailing political dialogue. Because they were aware of the ongoing debates and references to the other discourses surrounding the speech, they knew that their protests were limited to the Catholic Church and its clergy.

The women were still constrained by the overarching patriarchy of the country but were able to release their frustrations on the church. These passages signaled the emerging indignation of the liberal party, and the women were at the fringes of the movement. In an accusatory tone, they used words and phrases such as "Si es verdad que algunas damas han sido seducidas por el clero y las artimañas de los eternos enemigos de México, esto nada significa ante la historia . . ." (If it be true that many women have been seduced by clerics and the tricks of the eternal enemy of Mexico, this means nothing compared to history . . .) and "la historia, que tiene escrita con letras negras la época pavorosa de la dominación abundante en crímenes y atrocidades . . ." (the history, which has written in black letters of the terrifying domination [of the church] abundant in crimes and atrocities . . .).[39] At this historical moment, women denounced the long-known oppression at the hands of the Catholic Church, but their assertion didn't go as far as to claim freedom from the larger patriarchal system that created the greater power structure of Mexico.

The women's affirmations, by recognition of other newspapers protesting the encroaching dominance of the church, intersected with the larger liberal conversation centered around the speech by Montes de Oca. In "Actitud del partido liberal," the MZ cited the newspaper *El Observador Zacatecano*, saying:

> Amigos y contrarios reconocen la obra siniestra de destrucción, la profunda labor obscura que se dirige a minar cautelosamente el edificio de las leyes. Y en presencia de semejantes acontecimientos, los hombres previsores . . . han dado el grito de alarma . . . y convocan á todos los creyentes á nueva y gloriosa cruzada.[40]
>
> Both friends and opponents all recognize the sinister work of destruction, the deep, dark labor whose purpose is to gradually undermine the edifice of laws. And faced with such events, men of vision . . . have sounded the cry of alarm . . . and summoned all believers to a new and glorious crusade.

The MZ accepted that the writings from *El Observador Zacatecano* "summon[ing] all believers" in the liberal tenets were national exhortations even to women. However, the women were careful to explain that their overt political actions in the founding of a liberal club were in fealty to the call from *El Observador Zacatecano*. They said:

> Allí, después que el sexo masculino protestó de la manera más viril contra los abusos del Obispo de San Luis, la reina del hogar, la mujer, quiso demostrar al prelado instigador que su pon[z]oña no ha llegado por aquel pueblo patriota, ya para demostrarlo de una manera elocuente han publicado la siguiente acta.[41]
>
> There, after the masculine sex in the most virile way protested against the abuses of the Bishop of San Luis, the queen of the home, the woman, wants to demonstrate to the instigative prelate that his poison has not reached to that patriotic people, and to demonstrate it in an eloquent way they have published the following document.

The document the women mention is the plan embedded in the article and set off by quotations. González Ramírez states that a plan "results in a commitment to revolutionary action that justifies or attempts to justify the brutality upon which the insurgent, the rebel, the revolutionary, embarks himself and his followers."[42] Plans and manifiestos, although similar in nature in that they position the author within a certain political and ideological frame for the purpose of protest and governance, contain different discursive cues. Hammerback and Jensen argue that documents, such as the plan, are unique to the Mexican culture and that its significance "become[s] clear only within the context of [its] own rhetorical tradition, a tradition anchored in Mexican history."[43] Davis and Virulegio state that "Mexicans invented the Plan as a political document and no other country, not Spain nor the rest of Latin America, has used the Plan as an instrument of government."[44] They comment on the fervor of the plan, stating that it "arose out of the politics of stagnation . . . it grew out of the Revolution for Independence [of 1810]."[45] The Mexican plan was born out of a grassroots exigency people felt to have their voices heard, originating with the men who were displaced from the cities during the chaos of the War of Independence of 1810 and who were being denied access to everyday channels of communication. They reduced their demands to a one-page document that could be printed off the portable printing press they rolled around on an ox cart.[46] In writing the plan, the MZ embedded their feminine movement within this rich civic rhetorical tradition of grassroots organizing.

Verbal clues would have signaled to their audience that the MZ were emulating the Mexican plan. In a short document set off by quotes embedded in the larger article of "Actitud del partido liberal," the MZ use several key words and phrases that emulate other historic plans. Of the forty plans that González Ramírez published, many of the documents contain the phrase *los que abajo suscribimos* (those below subscribe to the following), which signaled that the undersigned were in agreement with the content of the document. Another familiar discursive pattern found in the historic plans is a declaration marked by *considerando*, meaning "whereas." These phrases draw on formal legal terms to position the proceeding argument. The points in the considerando section make clear to the reader and to the opposition the political and social reasons the group had joined together to present its own solutions to the grievances they outlined.

Each plan commonly listed four or five premises to set out the group's responses to perceived injustices. The MZ begin their plan:

> Las que subscribimos, en representación de la escuela moderna para la mujer, despojada de todo servilismo, y enaltecida por toda exaltación á la libérrima condición de la humanidad:
>
> Considerando: que el clericalismo avasalla hasta degradación, y explota el influjo y ascendiento de la mujer sobre el hombre, explota repetimos este influjo en favor de la fanatización [*sic*] religiosa, en favor

> del desprestigio del excelsas figuras de libertad, del patriotismo y de la civilización, denigrando al gran padre Hidalgo, al gran reformador Melchor Ocampo, al incomparable Benito Juárez.[47]
>
> Those of us who herein under subscribe, in representation of the modern school of women, divested of all servility, and ennobled by every exaltation to the completely free condition of humanity:
>
> Whereas: clericalism enslaves even to degradation, and it exploits the influence and ascendancy of the woman over man, it exploits, we repeat, that influence in favor of religious fanaticism, for the discrediting of sublime figures of liberty, of patriotism and civilization, denigrating the grand Father Hidalgo, the grand reformer Melchor Ocampo, and the incomparable Benito Juárez.

Davis and Virulegio state that the considerando sections elaborate, "often at unconscionable length, upon a dead past yet unburied," but the MZ do not engage in this rhetorical reflection of the past.[48] They include only two more considerando paragraphs claiming that the time had come for women to publicly support their husbands, brothers, neighbors, and sons in the cause of reform. They end the plan with a traditional grito, a common Mexican interactive verbal ritual meant to rally the people to a cause.

El Grito de Zitácuaro

Much like the plan, the symbolic act of the grito is unique to Mexico and the historical context of the time. For almost one hundred years prior to 1900, the grito had become a ritualized event used to incite the people to action. In 1810, at the dawn of September 16, Miguel Hidalgo, a priest in a small town called Dolores, just south of Guanajuato, let out the famous Grito de Independencia, or El Grito de Dolores. Historians vary in their citation of what Hidalgo actually said, and all that remains is a variation of the declaration. Hidalgo's original grito summoned the Mexican people to fight for their independence from Spain and was seen as an overt act of resistance to assimilation within the dominant Spanish culture. Fernando Serrano Migallón's comprehensive history of the grito notes that while ringing the parish bell of Dolores, he could have exclaimed, "¡Mexicanos: Mueran los Gachupines! ¡Mexicanos: Muera el mal gobierno! ¡Viva Fernando VII! ¡Viva América libre! ¡Viva la Virgen de Guadalupe!" (Mexicans: Death to the Gachupines![49] Death to the corrupt government! Long live Fernando VII! Long live America the free! Long live the Virgin of

Guadalupe!).[50] Taking on the form of a male-dominated, military, political, and cultural ritual over the years, the grito evolved into more than a call to arms. It carries within its structure the people's beliefs and ideologies of their cause, holds the epistemological power to mark a moment as historical, memorable, and significant, and stirs the people's patriotism for social change.

The MZ's grito pronounced: "¡Viva la escuela libre y anticlerical de la mujer! ¡Viva la tendencia moderna que la educación es para la patria y no para los conventos! ¡Honor y gloria á Josefa Ortiz de Domínguez! ¡Salud á los iniciadores de San Luis Potosí! H. Zitácuaro Octubre 8, 1900" (Long live the liberal and anticlerical women's school! Long live the modernist trend that education is for the homeland and not the convent! Honor and glory to Josefa Ortiz de Domínguez! Cheers to the initiators of San Luis Potosí! H. Zitácuaro October 6, 1900.) A total of fifty-three women signed their names to the document. This was a bold move for women at that time because of the stigma and ridicule that could accompany such declarations.

The women's grito signaled to their audience that they were claiming membership in the public dominant discourse of protest, which in turn provided them with validity for their cause. More importantly, the women's grito shifted their gendered subjectivity to assert the authority to initiate a feminine movement by marking a moment in history that they could validate as their own. Equally, the use of the grito evokes a mestiza consciousness, which eludes the dichotomous category of the politically active male and female. Here, the strategic use of their discourse enters a symbolic position of inventing in-between gendered and cultural puestos. On the one hand, they were assimilating into their Mexican culture, but on the other, they were breaking from its traditions of feminine abnegation. The men centered in the liberal cause of the nation could not readily deny women's participation in their quest for freedom if the women took part in the men's own ritual of resistance.

While the MZ were drawing from their own cultural rhetorical tradition of declarations, the women were also entering a greater feminine movement of women's affirmations in the United States and Europe. The proliferation and influence of ideas from newspapers, religious missionaries from abroad, recently translated writings (in 1892) of John Stuart Mill's *The Subjection of Women*, and the increased travel between the United States and Mexico brought Mexican women in touch with various feminist activities abroad. Influences on the MZ's rhetorical actions may have also originated from women's declarations and petitions, such as the Seneca Falls

Declaration of Sentiments of 1848 and the Petition for Universal Suffrage of 1866, signed by Elizabeth Cady Stanton, Susan B. Anthony, and other former members of the Women's Loyal National League and presented to the U.S. House of Representatives, as well as the Declaration of Rights of the Women of the United States by the National Women's Suffrage Association, July 4, 1876. Other influences may have been the anarchist writings and sentiments coming from Latin American feminist movements from the Southern Cone.[51] They were joining a larger conversation. A *mezcla*, a mix, of influences contributed to these women's mestiza rhetorical approach. With the MZ assertion, their movement had officially begun.

A Necessary Step: Conferring Ethos onto the Speaker

After the October publication of "Actitud del partido liberal," Zaragoza would write several other fervent articles against the institution of the Catholic Church. But on December 21, 1900, the pseudonymous author would formally introduce the MZ to the public. The newspaper staff of *La Bandera Roja* and the MZ understood the negative public dynamics of women speaking in public and, what is more, the general shock of women taking a political stance. Tuñón Pablos notes that during the Porfiriato women were slowly beginning to attain educations. Yet the implied purpose was to better prepare them for their roles as mothers.[52] She cites Ignacio Ramírez, a liberal reformer from the 1860s, saying that Mexico should not view women as "machines of pleasure" or as "a positive piece of luxury furniture," but at the same time he did not want to consider them "equal to men in teaching posts, in tribunals, at the rostrum, and possibly even in the battlefield."[53] Ramírez continues, "We shall examine women just as today they illuminate our home, shine at banquets and at dances, descend from the altar to form a new family, and are conclusively classified by divine and human laws."[54] Many women felt that if procreation was their predestined duty, then they would claim their personal, public, and political agency through motherhood.

The MZ accepted Ramírez's definition of women as mothers, but at the same time, their manifiesto supports the implied view that they stood against Ramírez's narrow definition of women. From the MZ's perspective, women were also educated and political beings. We see evidence of these ideas expressed in the manifiesto, such as in the first point, where the women claim the "derecho . . . y hasta deber, de tomar participio en los movimientos progresistas, y puede y debe inciarlos" (the right . . . and even a duty to take part in progressive movements, and she can and must initiate them).[55] Their contradictory stances on the issue of women's freedom can be seen as both practical complicity and practical resistance. They wanted to become leaders and initiators of political and social causes, not just followers of great causes. At the dawn of the twentieth century, Mexican women expressed the desire to be heard and considered as individuals with unique thoughts and ideas. However, before they could speak and be taken seriously, society had to confer upon them the public ethos that they lacked.

Historically, marginalized groups have generally lacked the credibility within the dominant culture to speak publicly and be taken seriously. A common trope to confer this ethos onto individuals without the credibility to speak comes from those with greater societal standing. Before the women's manifiesto, a short four-paragraph article introducing them was published with the title "La mujer se emancipa de las opresoras cadenas del clericalismo" (The Woman Frees Herself from the Oppressive Chains of Clericalism). In this prelude article, Zaragoza introduced the women of the liberal club Josefa Ortiz de Domínguez and Francisca Carrillo as a part of the larger nationalist cause of liberalism and anticlericalism, providing the women with rhetorical and historical ethos and thus conferring on them credibility and political clout. Zaragoza gives justification for the women's cause:

> Sí: porque el grito de independencia que resonó en la heroica Zitácuaro el 11 de noviembre último, pasará a las posteridades como ha pasado el grito de Dolores después de haber despedazado las cadenas de nuestra esclavitud; porque el grito brota del inmenso corazón de la mujer oprimida por tantos siglos; porque ese grito proclama los más santos derechos del sexo bello y entre ellos la igualdad con los demás seres racionales.[56]
>
> Yes, because the cry of independence that resounded in heroic Zitácuaro on November 11 last, will continue on to posterities as the cry of Dolores has continued on after having torn into pieces the chains of our slavery; because that cry springs up from the immense heart of women oppressed for so many centuries; because that cry proclaims the most sacred rights of the fair sex and among them equality with other rational beings.

Zaragoza's introduction provided the Mexican women with their own identity and recognized both sexes as having a common ground of the desire to declare freedom from the church.

Several aspects of this short article served to politicize the women even before they pronounced their ideas in the manifiesto. First, using the name of the famous general Ignacio Zaragoza as a pseudonym served as a rhetorical strategy to unite the two causes of national liberalism and the women's position against the church. Further, paralleling the reasons for the women engaging in the ritualized cry for independence with that of the original grito in 1810 functioned as another powerful rhetorical gesture that brought the women into the realm of politics and patriarchy. The final lines of the introduction fully confer upon the MZ their political ethos by inviting them to take part in the public debates and receiving subscriptions to *La Bandera Roja*. "Desde hoy se remitirá nuestro periódico á la heroica Junta 'Josefa Ortiz de Domínguez,' saludándola con el profundo respeto que se merece iniciar tan levantados pensamientos" (Beginning today, our newspaper will be sent to the heroic Assembly "Josefa Ortiz de Domínguez," and we salute those in the Junta with the profound respect that they deserve at the beginning of such lofty thinking).[57] Having been formally accepted into the realm of political action, they were able to advance their cause with their manifiesto.

Nation, Liberty, and Civilization: Las Mujeres de Zitácuaro's Manifiesto

Located at the bottom left of the page, and printed in big, bold type, the liberal women's club announced their political intentions: "Propaganda liberal, MANIFIESTO." Immediately following the title, the introductory phrase of the manifiesto declared in bold capital letters: "OIDNOS" (HEAR US).[58] In a political document written by women that intersects with political and patriarchic powers, the outright expression of what the women wanted from their audience—to be heard—becomes a necessary and significant rhetorical stance. Furthermore, the manifiesto carries stylistic nuances that also become important rhetorical devices, such as the high, formal tone of the Spanish language, the intertextual nature of the manifiesto, the importance of signaling phrases, and gendered uses of the language.

Numerous nuances make the Mexican manifiesto a contextually rich historical genre. González Ramírez presents several important historical and rhetorical features of the manifiesto, and a review of these elements will point to the significance of the MZ's contribution. First, the authors of manifiestos were traditionally military generals, high-ranking officials, or educated public figures. This is true of the noteworthy manifiestos that González Ramírez included in his survey, such as "Manifiesto de Madero al pueblo mexicano, dirigido desde la penitenciaría de Monterrey, N.L." (Manifesto of Madero to the Mexican People, Written from Prison in Monterrey, Nuevo León), written by Francisco Madero, president of Mexico from 1911 to 1913, and "Manifiesto de los Flores Magón sobre su doctrina" (Manifesto of the Flores Magóns Regarding Their Doctrine), written by Ricardo Flores Magón, Librado Rivera, Anselmo Figueroa, and Enrique Flores Magón, all intellectual leaders of the revolutionary movements. Noted by countless histories, these men and their writings kindled dangerous ideas of revolution in the masses.

Second, the language of the documents mirrored the authors' social positions and rang syntactically stiff, which Hammerback and Jensen note is a common tendency in formal documents of the Mexican culture. The high level of education required to participate in the discourse around the manifiesto acted as a boundary that omitted those on the margins of society. The indigenous population and women were among those ultimately excluded from the official revolutionary conversation. The dialogic element of this document would in effect call upon other manifiestos to be written in response. Many times the proposals from those documents found their way into civil codes or laws, as evidenced by the "Manifiesto de Madero." Through the act of authoring a political yet feminist manifiesto, the women positioned themselves as equals to the politicians and intellectuals and, thereby, entered into the realm of political conversation.

The observation that the manifiesto carries elements from previous documents is indicative of a postmodern approach, as opposed to a modernist notion of a text, which views writing as a lone, singular process, distinctive to the individual author. As with many of these documents, the manifiesto can be compared to a patchwork quilt in which each individual involved in the creation of the document contributed her own ideas. The intertextual nature of this document places an emphasis on the social implication of the Mexican women's writing. In "Intertextuality and the Discourse Community," James E. Porter notes that by "identifying and stressing the intertextual nature of discourse . . . , we shift our attention away from the writer as individual and focus more on the sources and social contexts from which the writer's discourse arises."[59] The manifiesto, then, is significant within its social context, pulling concepts from other texts with which to contextualize the meaning of the document. The MZ manifiesto as well recognized that their male counterparts' efforts for the leftist cause were gaining speed at that time in Mexico. The MZ proclaimed:

OIDNOS:

Los hombres de la libertad y del constitucionalismo, se aprestan á una lucha iniciada por las gloriosas postrimerías del siglo XIX y será leal y resueltamente aceptada por la centuria XX.

Ayudémosles en su labor.[60]

HEAR US:

Men of liberty and constitutionalism are preparing themselves for a struggle begun during the glorious last days of the nineteenth century that will be loyally and steadfastly accepted during the twentieth century.

Let us help them in their labor.

Although the group was writing a feminist libratory manifiesto, the women understood the constraints of their cultural puestos. A survey of the forty manifiestos compiled by González Ramírez reveals that the opening expression of the manifiestos seem to identify an audience, and so, for this reason, the women's introductory phrase of "HEAR US" gains rhetorical significance on various levels.[61] Of the manifiestos authored by men, none contain an introduction requesting that their audience lend them a rhetorical puesto. The manifiestos, such as those written by Madero, Díaz, or the Flores Magón brothers, begin with audience appeals such as "Mexicanos," "Conciudadanos" (Fellow Citizens), and "Compatriotas" (Compatriots). Or, more often, no initial address appears, as is observed in "Manifiesto de Pascual Orozco al recibir el mando de fuerzas de Chihuahua" (Manifesto of Pascual Orozco upon Taking Command of the Forces of Chihuahua)[62] and "Manifiesto de Francisco I. Madero acerca del ataque a C. Juárez" (Manifesto of Francisco I. Madero on the Attack of the City of Juárez).[63] With no introductory phrases present, it can be assumed that the male writers wrote with an immediate certainty that they had an attentive audience. On the other hand, when the women proclaimed, "OIDNOS" (HEAR US), they recognized that they were entering into a gendered, public, and social dialogue that negated their voices and limited the scope of their proclamation.

However, the translation of *oídnos*, meaning the imperative command of "hear us," does not provide a full interpretation of what the women were communicating. Instead of the formal *ustedes* form of the verb, *oigan* (hear), they used the *vosotros* form, the familiar plural command of the verb, which is *oíd*. The familiar plural command is used in Spain, but is not typically used in Latin America. Mexicans are inclined to utilize the more formal address of *ustedes*, which comes from the old *vuestra merced*, "your honor." By using the *vosotros*—which is archaic in Spanish America—as a persuasive grammatical device, the women were transforming their readership into an instant brotherhood of Mexican *compañerismo*, signaling their discursive authority and inclusion in the liberal political movement along with the men.

Their manifiesto was the first of many steps taken to gain a feminine discursive identity. The authors identified with liberal men. These men were seen as helpful in achieving an alternative perception of women. The women walked a fine line between a radical rhetorical approach and an approach where they negotiated their contested presence. Much of this document is about ontological paradox, that of writing between the puestos of being. The laws of the land, which kept women from voting or holding office, prevented them from breaking completely free of the prevailing patriarchal ideologies that constrained them. Still, within the rationale of the document the women assert their alliance with the men.

> Ni por qué razón dejar al hombre solo, desastrosamente solo en la lid de la constitucionalidad, cuando nos importan y afectan sus triunfos y derrotas; sus esclavamientos [*sic*] y emancipaciones; su condición digna y viril o cobarde y abyecta, como padre, como esposo, como hijo, como hermano, ó simplemente como prójimo.[64]

> Nor for any reason should men be left alone, disastrously alone, in the struggle for constitutionality, when their triumphs and defeats both matter and affect us; their [periods of] servitude and emancipation; their condition, be it manly and worthy, or cowardly and abject, as father, as husband, as son, as brother, or simply as a fellow human.

Paradoxically, because the women understood their limitations, it contributed to the strength of their message. The group's implied audience included the women of Mexico, but they also needed to educate the men who had the power to accommodate and adjust to their message. Michael Leff argues that "the power of the orator ironically implies humility before the audience. . . . The audience necessarily constrains the orator's intellectual horizons, modes of expression, and even representation of self . . . they must yield to the people they seek to influence."[65] On this occasion, the women's humility served as an ingratiatory strategy because it was a gendered characteristic that had to be used to negotiate different relationships with men and the power they held. The MZ were proclaiming freedom from the orthodox institution of the church while maintaining intact their subjugation to other institutions, those of patriarchy and the nation.

In the tradition of the manifiesto, after the introduction that addressed the women's concerns for their community, a list of numbered statements appeared as the body of the document. (Generally speaking, manifiestos were not textually consistent, though each one was distinguished by the number of proposals it contained.) The MZ included a list of twelve propositions that advanced their cause. The first proposition is the most powerful in its humanistic and feminist position because it implicitly addressed their dehumanization by the male-dominated society.

> 1°. Conforme a l[a]s luminosas enseñanzas de la moderna sabiduría, la mujer es persona y no cosa; luego derecho tiene y hasta deber de tomar participio en los movimientos progresistas, y debe y puede iniciarlos.[66]
>
> First. In accordance with the enlightened teachings of modern wisdom, a woman is a person and not a thing; therefore, she has the right and even the duty to take part in progressive movements, and she can and must initiate them.

This document did not propose the abrogation of the government, nor was it a call to arms. The declaration contained the opinions and societal proposal of women who had been silenced and hidden from the public for centuries.

The MZ claim a dependent independence with the men by also framing them within the context of their same condition. The third statement of the manifiesto makes this clear:

> 3°. Satisfechas como estamos de que no es necesario que hombres nos llamen para asociarnos con ellos, a fin de perseguir los ideales de progreso, porque así como la mujer está incompleta sin el hombre, éste carece de integridad sin la mujer, y por consiguiente sus empresas en el orden de la familia y la sociedad empresas "y de ellos y de ellas" son recíproca y mancomunadamente.[67]
>
> Third. This being recognized, and satisfied such as we are, that it is not necessary for men to call us so we may join with them for the purpose of pursuing the ideals of progress, because even as a woman is incomplete without a man, he also lacks completeness without a woman, and therefore, their undertakings within the order of the family and society, undertakings of "men and women," are reciprocally and are jointly [carried out].

Throughout the manifiesto, there appears to be a play of give and take focused on their claims. The MZ fully rejected the clerical actions, yet they understood that they were bound to the societal duties of motherhood. In the fifth declaration, they labeled those who chose the convents as "verdaderas y conscientes suicidas" (true and conscious suicidal women), and they wrote that by law they should be "persegui[das] con todo el rigor de la inviolabilidad legal" (prosecute[d] with all the rigor of legal inviolability).[68] Going a step further, in the eighth declaration, they criminalized women who "permanec[en] indiferentes, neutrales o enemigas" (remain indifferent, neutral, or enemies) of the convents established throughout the nation.[69]

The manifiesto drew a sharp distinction between the Catholic conservative sects and those who pushed for the adherence to the liberal Laws of Reform. The MZ discourse challenged the traditions and vestiges of the old European "instituciones y doctrinas" (institutions and doctrines) that, as women, they no longer saw relevant in the new century. In their rhetoric, there appeared a hope that the female sex in the coming century will be given her rights of citizenship. They said: "Creemos que en el reloj de la civilización y de la justicia, ha sonado la hora de la emancipación augusta de la mujer, obrada no por 'las armas de hierro' sino por las armas de luz que regeneran" (We believe that the clock of civilization and justice has struck the hour of women's august emancipation, brought about, not by "weapons of steel," but by tools of light that regenerate).[70]

The women continue throughout the text with language that equaled that of the manifiestos being published at the time. The ideas and descriptions regarding Mexico and the future direction of the nation seem elevated and florid, as if to show their ability to use the language. For example, they conclude the manifiesto with the phrase, "esta Patria que nos ampara y ofrenda los efluvios de su luz, las salutíferas corrientes de su atmósfera, las linfas cristalinas de sus ríos . . ." (the Nation that protects us and offers us the effluvia of her light, the salutary currents of her atmosphere, the crystalline streams of her rivers . . .).[71] In the tenth declaration they say, "[D]e la luz esclarece y de fuerza que determina porque la persuasión de que usa el siglo XIX no viene de la costumbre rutinaria sino de una filosofía innovadora" (The argument used by the nineteenth century comes not from daily custom but rather from an innovative philosophy).[72] Much like Wright de Kleinhans's use of the language to gain acceptance into the intellectual community, the MZ used the language of eloquent political protest to become part of the new movement. They close the manifiesto with a traditional salutatory end, inviting other women to join their movement, and ending with "¡Viva la Libertad!" (Long live Liberty!). After the customary ending, the forty-six women sign their names to the document.

Conclusion

Placing the "protest series" within a cultural, political, and gendered context through the lens of genre theory brings the women's rhetorical actions into a clearer view. Mexican plans and manifiestos, like the ones the MZ authored, were not mere ceremonial declarations of ideologies, intentions, and principles written to designate a historical event, nor were they liberating releases of emotions by the authors. These were compelling persuasive documents meant to intersect with the greater history of Mexican discourse. Davis and Virulegio lament that many of the documents they examined for their history on grassroots political documents have all too often been "ignored and now [are] a curiosity to be found only in remote libraries."[73]

These documents are more relevant to our current times than one might first consider. They are rich sources to help us understand the rhetorical strategies of a people and offer an insight into how those of a Latin American background dealt discursively with the hardships of their time. The "protest series" also serves as an example, to Latinas across the Americas, that their literacy and understanding of their culture's discursive practices can serve as a powerful force in gaining a voice in today's society. From a disciplinary perspective, it acknowledges the marked difference of Mexican women's voices in our rhetorical tradition, which has to date been ignored. Bizzell states, "[W]e must hear from rhetoricians who have struggled with culturally complex venues in which they were marginalized, if we are to live and work and function as responsible citizens in the American multicultural democracy."[74] First, these voices must be recovered.

Using mestiza rhetoric as the overarching theoretical lens to examine these women's rhetorical strategies and intersections with the Mexican discursive public illuminates the area of ambiguity from which these women were writing. Mestiza rhetoric starts from a position of resistance to dominant discourses and cultures, whether they be race or gender related. Baca's perspective of mestiza rhetoric reflects a powerful discursive capacity for those who write from this puesto. He states, "Mestiz@ rhetorical practices create symbolic spaces in which it becomes possible to understand multiple local histories, memories, and rhetorics coexisting, beyond dichotomous assumptions."[75] The women writing from the perspective of the mestiza created a new and discursive reality of women as political and public beings. The MZ were at the historical crossroads, garnering influences from at home and abroad. Like Malintzin, they could have stayed silent and allowed the men to shape their reality as religious, submissive women, relegated to the sidelines of history. Instead, they chose to speak for themselves as civic actors and published a plan, pronounced their own grito, and wrote a manifiesto to make their demands heard as a feminine community.

Questions I did not pose in the body of this chapter are: Who read *La Bandera Roja*? Did the words of the women have a lasting effect on their audience? It is certainly possible that Juana Belén Gutiérrez de Mendoza, the woman covered in chapter 4, read their writings. A short time after she published her newspaper, *Vésper*, in Guanajuato in 1901, she sent a letter to the editorial staff of *La Bandera Roja*, which was published on May 19 of the same year. Following the journalistic practice of the time, she sent greetings to the paper and their readers with the following: "*Vésper* saluda a la prensa liberal nacional con las levantadas frases que siguen: ¡Saludos campeones del progreso!" (*Vésper* sends its regards to the liberal national press with the following uplifting words: Greetings champions of progress!).[76] *La Bandera Roja* answered her greetings with just as much enthusiasm.

> *La Bandera Roja* responde a vuestro saludo admirando a la mujer que empuña el glorioso estandarte de la libertad en estos momentos críticos de nuestra historia que se levanta sobre la montaña de preocupaciones y de fanatismo con que el clero tiene oprimida a la mujer Mexicana. . . . ¡Bien venida seáis noble dama![77]

> *La Bandera Roja* answers your greeting by holding in high esteem the woman who brandishes the glorious banner of freedom in these critical moments of our history that is raised above the mountain of worries and of fanaticism with which the clergy has the Mexican woman oppressed. . . . Welcome noble woman!

Discursive exchanges such as these among female and male journalists show that women were gradually being admitted into public discourse. For the women of Mexico, the turn of the century was a time of transition into the era of revolution, which opened doors of opportunity into the public arena and would radically change their discursive identity.

INTERLUDE

Propaganda liberal, Manifiesto.

A las honorables damas liberales de la República; la junta liberal "Josefa Ortiz de Domínguez y Francisca Carrillo"

OIDNOS:

Los hombres de la libertad y del constitucionalismo, se aprestan a una lucha iniciada por las gloriosas postrimerías del siglo XIX y será leal y resueltamente aceptada por la centuria XX.

Ayudémosles en su labor.

Ese combate tiene la alta significación de la justa defensa de la Nación, y la justa defensa de la personalidad humana, individualmente considerada; por cuanto a la Nación, sabéis ya que es nuestra República; por cuanto a la personalidad, es necesario deciros que somos nosotras: la mujer.

Sabéis ya que vivir políticamente, es vivir conforme a la Constitución de '57, que es el gran código mexicano; luego todo lo que sea contra esa constitución, atentado de vida es contra la república; mas como quiera que es un deber de todo mexicano, estorbar, oponerse rechazar todo ataque a la Carta magna que nos gobierna, deber nuestro reputamos levantar la voz para reprobar las infracciones constitucionales; esto es de tan fácil comprensión, que basta enunciarse para admitirse.

Las premisas de todo lo dicho, las forma el avanzado siglo en que vivimos. El patriotismo lo ha sublimado el siglo, por maravilla de su robusta civilización; las tendencias incontrastables, las ha engendrado el siglo en pro de la libertad, por maravilla de su aliento redentor; la prueba de que ha preparado una evolución, es que nosotras hablamos de ella y pretendemos realizarla.

Ni por qué razón dejar al hombre solo, desastrosamente solo en la lid de la constitucionalidad, cuando nos importan y afectan sus triunfos y derrotas; sus esclavizamientos [*sic*] y emancipaciones; su condición digna y viril o cobarde y abyecta, como padre, como esposo, como hijo, como hermano, o simplemente como prójimo. Si cierto es que la mujer puede y

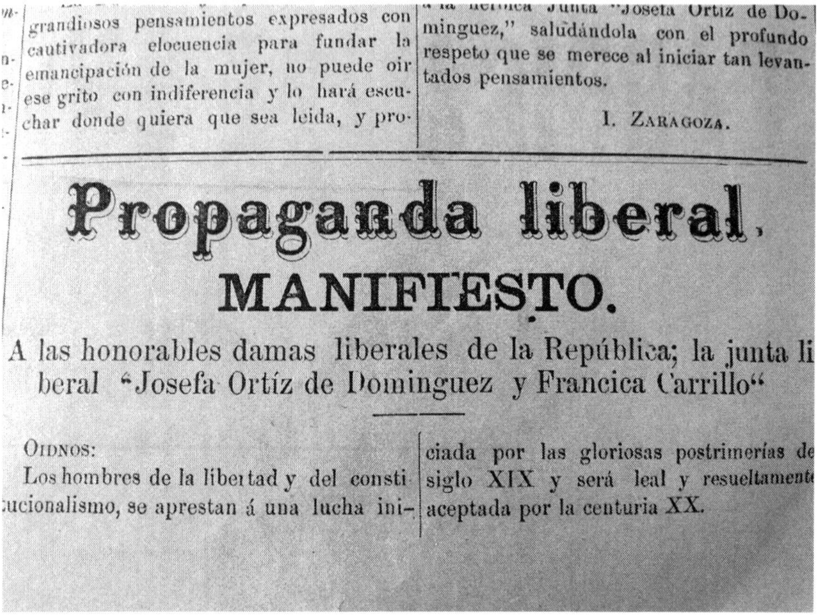

grandiosos pensamientos expresados con cautivadora elocuencia para fundar la emancipación de la mujer, no puede oir ese grito con indiferencia y lo hará escuchar donde quiera que sea leida, y pro-

minguez," saludándola con el profundo respeto que se merece al iniciar tan levantados pensamientos.

I. ZARAGOZA.

Propaganda liberal.

MANIFIESTO.

A las honorables damas liberales de la República; la junta liberal "Josefa Ortíz de Dominguez y Francica Carrillo"

OIDNOS:

Los hombres de la libertad y del constitucionalismo, se aprestan á una lucha iniciada por las gloriosas postrimerías de siglo XIX y será leal y resueltamente aceptada por la centuria XX.

Figure 4. The manifesto of women's rights by Las Mujeres de Zitácuaro appeared in the December 7, 1900, edition of *La Bandera Roja*, a radical liberal independent newspaper published in the city of Durango, Mexico. The manifesto started at the bottom right corner of the front cover page and continued on to fill the next page. The names of all the women who signed the document appear in the translation.

debe tomar participio en el progreso general del mundo, ¿cómo se le podrá prohibir que lo tome en el progreso de la patria? Si la suerte del mundo le interesa, ¿cómo no ha de importarle la condición de su país? Ni nos preguntéis qué resultado práctico tendrá la cooperación nuestra (la de la mujer) porque perfectamente alcanzáis que ayudar a la dignificación de la patria, es ayudar a la dignificación del hogar doméstico. Si el hombre no se avergüenza ante el concurso de todos los progresos modernos, de que le falta dignidad para proclamarse libre él, libre su consorte y libres sus hijos, y libres sus conciudadanos, y libre su patria, la mujer debe advertirle que está él desempeñando papel miserable por cuanto a la opresión.

He aquí, correligionarias nuestras, que no podremos ser libres si nuestros hombres son esclavos; he aquí que el pacto fundamental que garantiza la libertad en todas las circunstancias y fases de la vida mexicana, altamente nos interesa porque envueltas vamos o con su manto de tinieblas por su esclavizamiento [*sic*], o con sus ropajes de luz por su emancipación.

Innumerables ocasiones se ha dicho, y venturosamente es la verdad, como fruto de la plenitud de personalidad en la mujer, no por efecto de exclusión y de mutilaciones del concepto, que la mujer influye casi de manera decisiva en la suerte y destinos del mundo; hagamos, pues, esa influencia feliz y no desastrosa; inclinemos la balanza, pero no al platillo sobre el que ejercen presión los siglos de oscurantismo y de fanatización [*sic*] religiosa; es decir, a las centurias del convento, del confesionario y del santo oficio; pensad en que si la mujer ha de ser de alguien, por razón natural le pertenece mejor a la patria que al clero.

Nosotras creemos que la luz de la filosofía moderna ha demostrado que la misión sublime de la mujer, no es santificar su esterilidad matando la continuidad de la especie humana, devorada esa continuidad por las enormes del monasterio: las sublimes coronas del desposorio y de la maternidad, son sin duda alguna, timbres y señales inequívocas de que la mujer ha cumplido con Dios y con los hombres. Hay una diferencia enorme entre la mujer monja y la mujer civil: la primera podrá ser una flor, pero destinada a morir en sí misma, en tanto que la segunda (la mujer civil), es una flor que se perpetúa por la simiente que riega en los profundos y dilatados surcos de la procreación. De esto puede muy bien deducirse que hemos alcanzado la gran fórmula civil, encerrada en la ley constitucional; socialmente ha de perseguirse a la profesa, como el Código Penal persigue a la suicida; porque la mujer del convento, vivirá para el misticismo, pero nunca para la familia, ni para el hogar, ni para el municipio, ni para el departamento, ni para la patria, ni para la nación, ni para la humanidad. La mujer abrazada única y exclusivamente a los brazos de la cruz, será una resplandeciente visión angélica, pero jamás por jamás constituye el soberbio e inmortal arquetipo de la perpetuidad de las naciones. Esa mujer así, no es ni de la tierra ni del cielo, porque para llegar a Dios no puede ni debe seguir otro camino que no esté tendido en el valle de la humanidad.

Entended y enseñad de una vez por todas, honorables damas de la República, que si el confesionario y el convento pretenden tener derecho alguno sobre la mujer, nunca por siempre será ese derecho ni de más importancia ni de más plenitud que el derecho de la familia, de la patria, de la nación y de la humanidad.

Apliquemos pues todo lo dicho, al movimiento reivindicativo y libertador iniciado en San Luis Potosí.

1°. Conforme a las luminosas enseñanzas de la moderna sabiduría, la mujer es persona y no cosa; luego derecho tiene y hasta deber, de tomar participio en los movimientos progresistas, y puede y debe iniciarlos.

2°. El destino y la misión sublime de la mujer, no es la sustracción de su persona al elemento familiar, social, nacional y humanitario, sino la fundación, el complemento y la perfección de la familia; la integración y perfeccionamiento de la sociedad, del Estado, de la patria y de la Nación.

3°. Reconocido esto, y satisfechas como estamos de que no es necesario que los hombres nos llamen para asociarnos con ellos, a fin de perseguir los ideales de progreso, porque así como la mujer está incompleta sin el hombre, éste carece de integridad sin la mujer, y por consiguiente, sus empresas en el orden de la familia y de la sociedad, empresas de "ellos y de ellas" son recíproca y mancomunadamente.

4°. Deslindado ya por la ilustrada y profunda filosofía actual, que los conventos, no sólo son un calabozo, sino un sepulcro especialísimo y único en su género, porque en él están muertos los vivos, y los muertos que allí están, son los gérmenes de la familia, los gérmenes de la patria y los gérmenes de la procreación humana.

5°. Que las mujeres que a ese sepulcro se entregan, son verdaderas y conscientes suicidas, a quienes la ley civil, derivada de la ley constitucional, debe perseguir con todo el rigor de la inviolabilidad legal.

6°. Que toda doctrina, que toda iniciativa, que toda exigencia, que toda predicación clerical para que la mujer sustraiga a la vida del hogar, de la sociedad, del departamento, del Estado y de la Nación, tiende a paralizar la continuidad de la especie, matando los gérmenes de la reproducción humana.

7°. Que si algunos hombres han comprendido y reconocen estos deberes y otros hombres los desconocen y obscurecen, nosotras debemos estar de parte de los primeros que nos libertan y estrechan hacia ellos, no de parte de los segundos que nos repudian y entregan maniatadas al clericalismo.

8°. Que permanecer indiferentes, neutrales o enemigas a esta reivindicación de la mujer, que se han tragado los conventos establecidos en diferentes lugares de la república, "contra todo derecho y contra toda conveniencia social," es una cooperación delictuosa al triunfo de una aberración y de una indiferencia digna de ser vituperada por los hombres, por las naciones, por la sabiduría y por la justicia.

9°. Que debemos desoír y hasta despreciar toda manifestación é insultos prodigados en contra nuestra, tomándose la maliciosa libertad de pretender mancillar nuestro honor y nuestras intenciones, porque creemos que en el reloj de la civilización y de la justicia, ha sonado la hora de la emancipación augusta de la mujer, obrada no por "las armas de hierro" sino por las armas de luz quemante.

10°. Que el argumento gastado de que se han servido los enemigos de la luz, diciendo que hemos de vivir y morir en las creencias e ideas, instituciones y doctrinas que profesaron nuestros mayores carece en los actuales tiempos, de luz que esclarece y de fuerza que determina, porque la persuasión de que usa el siglo XIX no viene de la costumbre rutinaria sino de una filosofía innovadora.

11°. Que la mejor manera de honrar a nuestros antepasados progenitores no es derramar sobre su tumba las tinieblas del error y de la esclavitud en que vivieron, sino la luz de la verdad de la emancipación que nos alumbra.

12°. Que a los hombres, las instituciones y los gobiernos, familiar, civil y nacional que en lugar de oírnos y juzgarnos conforme a razón y a justicia, nos escarnecen, burlan, vituperan y ultrajan, debemos hacerles ver que si en la profunda noche de los tiempos no han presenciado caer sobre tierra lluvias de estrellas, como expresión de que nuestro planeta se baña también con luz sideral, tampoco habrán presenciado que la ciencia humana se baña por maravilla del perfeccionamiento, con luz providencial. A esos hombres, á esas mujeres, á esas instituciones á esas iglesias, á esa prensa, á esas asociaciones, á esos gobiernos, y en el lugar domestico á nuestros padres, á nuestros esposos, á nuestros hermanos, á nuestros hijos y á nuestros semejantes en general, personifiquémosles en una sola encarnación, en una única persona enferma de podredumbre clerical, para decirle como cuenta San Juan que dijo el Cristo al hermano de la inconsolable Marta: ¡Lázaro, levántate y anda!

En nombre de todo esto y obrando en sentido opuesto a las impudorosas transacciones: en sentido opuesto a las vergonzosas contemporizaciones con que los hombres ni os defienden ni os ayudan siquiera a defenderos del mercenarismo que lleva vuestra virginidad al mercado clerical, para que en lugar de SER MADRES EN LA RESPLANDECIENTE ALCOBA DEL HOGAR, SEÁIS MADRES EN LOS SOMBRIOS SUBTERRÁNEOS DE LA CELDA CONVENTUAL.

En nombre de todo lo grande hasta la excelsitud para reprobar al Obispo Montes de Oca, la vergüenza en que ha pretendido poner a esta Patria mexicana, que nos ampara y ofrenda los efluvios de su luz, las salutíferas corrientes de su atmósfera, las linfas cristalinas de sus ríos, las flores de sus campiñas, las espigas de sus sementeras y el calor de sus hogares. En nombre de todo eso, reasumido en estas palabras: Patria, Libertad y Civilización lanzando rayos de verdad y de viril actitud a quienes intentan arrancaros de los brazos de la sociedad civil, para arrojaros al indecente mesalinismo clerical.

Por todo lo expuesto, HONORABLES DAMAS DE LA REPÚBLICA; os invitamos con la solemnidad que impone una convocación hecha ante Dios y a la faz de las naciones y de nuestra patria, a que SECUNDÉIS NUESTRO MOVIMIENTO, aprovechando la actual oportunidad, que acaso sea la única para tomarla por medida de nuestra alma, de nuestro aprendizaje y de nuestras aspiraciones.

En Dolores Hidalgo tronó el grito de independencia y se hicieron pedazos unas cadenas, las de la exclavitud [*sic*] nacional. En Calpulalpan tronó el grito de independencia y se hicieron pedazos otras cadenas; las del reaccionarismo.

En el Cerro de las Campanas tronó el grito de independencia y se hicieron pedazos otras cadenas, las de la usurpación. En Zitácuaro truena hoy un grito y esperamos que se hagan pedazos otras cadenas, las del clericalismo.

Que el eslabón que junte al siglo XIX con el siglo XX, sea la verdadera emancipación de la mujer.

!Viva la Libertad!

Salón de sesiones de la Junta Liberal Josefa Ortiz de Domínguez y Francisca Carrillo.
H. [Heroica ciudad de] Zitácuaro, Noviembre 11 de 1900
Presidenta, Sra. Benita Anaya de Reyes; Vice-presidenta, Sra. Guadalupe Colín V. de Colín; Secretaria, Srita. Herminia Alcántara; Tesorera,* Srita. Guadalupe Borunda; 1era Vocal,† Aurora Garduño; 2a Vocal, Aurora Colín; 3a Vocal, Elvira Colín; 4a Vocal, Margarita Colín; 5a Vocal, Petra Conto de Rentería; 6a Vocal, Esther Benites; 7a Vocal, Beatriz Benites; 8a Vocal, Concepción López.

Luz U. de Gallegos, Leonor Gallego, Aurelia Iglesias, María Iglesias, Carlota Colín, Teresa García, Florentina López, Natalia Archundia, Margarita Ávila, Francisca Quintana, Emilia M. Vega, Juana Lara, M. Remedios Domínguez, María Rivas, Regina Sanches, Carmen Álvarez, Jacinta Ríos V. de Pérez, Cipriana Pérez, Dolores T. de Rodríguez, Isabel T. Rodríguez, Piedad R. de Rivera, Romana Arroyo, Esther Jimenes, Agripina A. de Solís, Paz Ramírez, Vicenta Telles, Altagracia Domínguez V. de Camacho, Laura

---

* Treasurer.

† *Vocal* means "spokesperson" or "spokeswoman."

Colín, M. Leonor Garduño, Isidora González, Dolores Trejo, Carmen Trejo, Marina López, Rult Hurtado, Juana Hurtado, Adelaida Ávila, Eva Benites, Isabel Miranda, Genoveva Miranda, Felipa Cambrón, Pilar M. Landa y Fernanda Reyna.

■ ■ ■

Liberal propaganda, Manifesto.

To the honorable liberal ladies of the Republic; the liberal committee "Josefa Ortiz de Domínguez y Francisca Carrillo"

HEAR US:
Men of liberty and constitutionalism are preparing for a struggle begun near the glorious end of the nineteenth century and it will be accepted faithfully and with resolve by the twentieth century.

Let us help them in their task.

That fight has the high significance of the just defense of the Nation, and the just defense of human personhood, considered individually; as for the Nation, you of course know that it is our Republic; when we say "personhood," it is necessary to tell you that we mean ourselves: the "woman."

You are already aware that to live politically, is to live according to the Constitution of 1857, which is the great Mexican law code; therefore, everything that be against that constitution, threatens the life of the republic; furthermore that it is a duty of every Mexican, to prevent, oppose, reject every attack on the Magna Carta that governs us, we consider it our duty to raise our voices in order to condemn constitutional infractions; this fact is so easily understood, that stating it is tantamount to accepting it.

The advanced century we live in shapes the premises of what we have said. This century has exalted patriotism, by dint of its robust civilization; the century has engendered incomparable tendencies in favor of liberty, by dint of its redemptive vitality; the proof that this century is prepared for progress, is that we ourselves are speaking of progress and we aim to achieve it.

Translation by Joel Bollinger Pouwels

There is no reason to leave the man alone, disastrously alone in the fight for constitutionality, when his triumphs and defeats are important to us and affect us; his enslavements and emancipations; his situation, be it worthy and virile or cowardly and abject, as father, as husband, as son, as brother, or simply as neighbor. If it is true that the woman can and should participate in the general progress of the world, how can she be prohibited from participating in the country's progress? If she takes interest in the world's destiny, how could the condition of her country not be important to her? Don't even ask us what practical result our cooperation (that of women) might have because you understand perfectly well that helping to dignify the nation, means helping to dignify the domestic sphere. If the man does not feel embarrassed at the accumulation of modern advances, at his lack of self-respect to proclaim freedom for himself, for his spouse and for his children, and freedom for his fellow citizens, and for his nation, then the woman must inform him that, as far as oppression is concerned, he is playing a paltry role.

I put to you, our sister believers, that we cannot be free if our men are slaves; that the fundamental pact that guarantees liberty in all circumstances and aspects of Mexican life, is of great interest to us because we proceed wrapped either in slavery's shadowy mantle, or in freedom's garments of light.

It has been said innumerable times, and fortunately it is true, as fruit of the woman's fullness of personality, not by dint of distorting the concept, that the woman influences, almost in a decisive way, the fortune and destiny of the world; let us ensure, then that her influence is happy and not disastrous; let us tip the scales, but not toward the side weighed down by the pressure of centuries of obscurantism and religious fanaticism; that is to say, toward the centuries of the convent, the confessional and the holy office; instead, reflect that if the woman belongs to anyone, by virtue of natural reason she belongs more preferably to the nation than to the clergy.

We believe that the light of modern philosophy has demonstrated that woman's sublime mission is not to sanctify her sterility, thus killing the perpetuation of the human species, which perpetuation is devoured by the enormous demands of the monastery: the sublime crowns of marriage and motherhood, are without any doubt, the seals and signs that woman has fulfilled her purpose with God and with men. There is an enormous difference between the woman as nun and the woman as secular being: the former can be a flower, but destined to die within herself, while the latter (the secular woman), is a flower that perpetuates herself through the seeds that she sows in the deep and wide furrows of procreation. We can easily deduce from this that we have achieved the great civic formula, enshrined in constitutional law; socially the professed nun must be prosecuted, because the Penal Code prosecutes the suicidal; because the woman of the convent, lives for mysticism, but never for the family, or for the home, or for the municipality, or for the province, or for the native soil, or for the nation, or for humanity. The woman who embraces only the arms of the cross, may be a resplendent angelic vision, but she will never, ever be the serious and immortal archetype of the perpetuity of nations. This latter woman therefore is neither of the Earth nor of Heaven, because to reach God she cannot and must not follow any path except the path that stretches through the valley of humanity.

Understand and teach once and for all "honorable ladies of the Republic," that if the confessional and the convent pretend to have any rights over the woman, these rights will nevermore be more important nor more plentiful than the rights of the family, of the native soil, of the nation, and of humanity.

Let us now apply all of the above, to the restorative and liberating movement that began in San Luis Potosí.

First. According to the enlightened teachings of modern wisdom, the woman is a person and not a thing; therefore, she has a right and even a duty, to take part in progressive movements, and she can and should initiate them.

Second. The destiny and sublime mission of the woman is not the removal of her person from the family, society, or the national and humanitarian scenes, but rather the establishment, the complement and the perfection of the family; the integration and perfection of society, the State, the native soil and the Nation.

Third. Having recognized this, and satisfied as we are that it is not necessary for men to call us to join them, with the objective of pursuing the ideals of progress, because just as the woman is incomplete without the man, the latter lacks integrity without the woman, and therefore, their undertakings and the order of the family and of society, undertakings "both his and hers" are reciprocal and jointly carried out.

Fourth. As defined by the illustrious and profound modern philosophy, the convents, constitute not only a prison, but also a unique and specialized kind of sepulcher, because in the convent "the living are dead" [dead to the world, in the vows], however, what is really dead, are the seeds of the family, of the nation and of human procreation.

Fifth. The women who surrender to this sepulcher, are true and conscious suicidal women, whom civil law, derived from constitutional law, should prosecute with all the rigor of legal inviolability.

Sixth. Every doctrine, every initiative, every exigency, every clergy's sermon whose purpose is to take women from the life of the home, society, province, State and Nation, tends to paralyze the continuity of the species, killing the seeds of human reproduction.

Seventh. If some men have understood and recognize these duties and other men ignore and obfuscate them, we must be on the side of the former, who will free us and draw us closer to them, and not choose the latter, who repudiate us and turn us over in handcuffs to clericalism.

Eighth. For women to remain indifferent, neutral, or enemies to this vindication of women swallowed up by convents established in different parts of the republic, "against all law and against all social suitability," is a criminal conspiracy for the triumph of an aberration and a deficiency worthy of being censured by men, by nations, by wisdom, and by justice.

Ninth. We must ignore and even scorn all expressions and insults heaped up against us, and that take the malicious liberty of aiming to stain our honor and our intentions, because we believe that the clock of civilization and justice has struck the hour of women's august emancipation, brought about not by "weapons of steel" but by tools of blazing light.

Tenth. That the worn-out argument employed by the enemies of the light, saying that we have to live and die with the beliefs and ideas, institutions and doctrines that our elders professed; that this argument leaves the modern times without clarifying light and determined strength, because the argument used by the nineteenth [*sic*; twentieth?] century comes not from daily custom but rather from an innovative philosophy.

Eleventh. That the best way to honor our ancestors and progenitors is to envelop their tombs, not in the shadows of error and bondage in which they lived, but rather in the light of the truth of emancipation that glows within us.

Twelfth. That the men, the institutions, and the governments at all levels—family, civil, and national—instead of listening to us and judging us as reason and justice demand, they mock and make fun of us, vituperate and insult us, we must make them see that if in the deep night of the times, they have not witnessed stars falling like rain to earth, as a message that our planet was bathed in heavenly light, they have also not witnessed human science miraculously bathed in providential light. Let us personify those men, those women, those institutions, those churches, that press, those associations, those governments, and in the home our fathers, our siblings, our spouses, our neighbors in general, let us embody them in one sole person diseased with clerical corruption, in order to tell him what, according to Saint John, Christ told the inconsolable Martha's brother: "Lazarus, arise and walk!"

In the name of all this and contrary to immodest transactions; contrary to the shameful compliance with which men who neither defend you nor help you to defend yourselves against the greediness that carries your virginity to the marketplace, so that instead of BEING MOTHERS IN RESPLENDENT DOMESTIC INTIMACY, YOU BECOME MOTHERS IN THE SHADOWY DEPTHS OF THE CONVENT CELL.

In the name of everything great, even the loftiness of reproaching Bishop Montes de Oca, the shame in which he has attempted to put this Nation— that protects us and offers us the effluvia of her light, the salutary currents of her atmosphere, the crystalline streams of her rivers, the flowers of her countryside, her lands sown with crops, and the warmth of her hearths. In the name of all this, summarized in these words: Nation, Liberty, and Civilization, throwing bolts of truth and virile attitude to those who try to tear women from the arms of civil society, to throw you into indecent clerical abuse.

Based on everything stated, HONORABLE LADIES OF THE REPUBLIC; we invite you with the solemnity imposed by a convocation made before God and the face of the nations and of our country, to SUPPORT OUR MOVEMENT, taking advantage of the present opportunity, which may be the only opportunity to measure our souls, our learning, and our aspirations.

In Dolores Hidalgo the cry of independence rang out and some chains were broken, the chains of national bondage. In Calpulalpan the cry of independence rang out and more chains were broken; those of reactionary bondage.

On the Hill of Bells the cry of independence rang out and more chains were broken, those of [French] usurpation. In Zitácuaro today a cry rings out and we hope that more chains will be broken, those of clericalism.

May the link that joins the nineteenth century with the twentieth century, be the true emancipation of women.

Long live Liberty!

Salon of sessions of the Liberal Committee "Josefa Ortiz de Domínguez y Francisca Carrillo."
H. [Honorable city of] Zitácuaro, November 11th, 1900*

* For the signatories' names, see the Spanish transcription.

CHAPTER FOUR

Rompiendo barreras

Juana Belén Gutiérrez de Mendoza's Revolutionary Rhetoric

Me tiene muy sin cuidado la aprobación o la desaprobación de los demás y me importa bien poco el perjuicio o el beneficio que pueda reportarme lo que hago o lo que digo.

I am not concerned with the approval or disapproval of others, and it matters little to me the prejudicial or beneficial repercussions of what I say and do.

—JUANA BELÉN GUTIÉRREZ DE MENDOZA IN *EL DESMONTE* (CLEARING THE WAY)

The Mexican Revolution opened a myriad of social and political puestos for women that had remained off-limits for centuries. A decade before the Revolution, Juana Belén Gutiérrez de Mendoza (1875–1942), a young, aspiring, and fiery writer and activist, contributed to setting the discursive tone in the political debates in the newspapers. She appeared on the Mexican journalistic scene to claim her own rhetorical puesto of protest with her dissident newspaper *Vésper: Justicia y Libertad*, which was first published in 1901 out of Guanajuato, Mexico. Although a small newspaper, it questioned governmental policies and shattered gendered social conventions, marking the shift from nineteenth-century feminine romanticism to revolutionary discourse. Gutiérrez de Mendoza's mocking, grassroots, and angry tone soared off the page, affecting and arousing the emotions of those who read her newspaper. Her writings gained such a level of attention that they earned her several incarcerations, forced her into exile in the United States, and prompted the seizure of her printing press several times throughout her life. Her writings also garnered the respect of other revolutionary journalists, activists, and generals throughout Mexico. Her writing career spanned forty-five years (1897–1942) and was punctuated by great social upheavals and movements. One intention remained constant with her: to rebel against oppressive forces through public discourse.

Juana Belén Gutiérrez de Mendoza's career as a writer and activist was forged during the years of the precursor movement, a period of social rebellion against the Mexican government, which would eventually lead to revolution.[1] During this era, she claimed a rare discursive puesto within the structures of the male-dominated journalistic scene and antigovernment movement. In 1903, she was named *primera vocal*, first spokesperson, in the radical liberal club of Ponciano Arriaga. Her uncommon position was followed by seven men and two other women, Elisa Acuña y Rosette and María del Refugio Vélez, fifth and seventh spokespersons, respectively.[2] Certainly, there were other women writers involved in this movement, such as Leonor Villegas de Magón, Dolores Jiménez y Muro, and the Colín sisters. However, Gutiérrez de Mendoza was among the most outspoken and active.[3] Despite the dangers brought by such opposition, Gutiérrez de Mendoza continued to write, organize, and speak her mind through various pamphlets, newspapers, articles, and a book on the issues that were most important to her: women, workers, and indigenous people. Her philosophy of life many times deviated sharply from the status quo and the path of least resistance. Indeed, she declared that her name in the official registry in the prisons resonated as "SEDICION-REBELION" (SEDITION-REBELLION).[4]

As a commanding female rhetor, Gutiérrez de Mendoza refused to be swayed by popular ideas, such as the mestizo modernity of racial assimilation espoused and popularized by José Vasconcelos. She also refused to be influenced by the government's renewed alliance with the Catholic Church or the threat of an explosive revolution. She not only articulated her opinions but embodied her rhetoric as a mestiza, acting upon her racial identity in the public sphere and in exile. Her rhetoric emerged through thirty-five years of social movements that operated within a rhetorical form of confrontation and *pleito*.

In this chapter, I contend that Gutiérrez de Mendoza's writing reflected a complex representation of pleito and mestiza rhetoric. The word *pleito* means "argument" or even "lawsuit," but for native Spanish speakers, it is also a word that conjures images of a public disturbance or street fight that draws people's attention. Pleito rhetoric is a form of confrontational rhetoric, a term we will see that Robert Cathcart coins, which does not fully capture the revolutionary discourse under investigation here. But the Spanish expression of the word *pleito* more aptly captures Gutiérrez de Mendoza's rhetorical approach to public protest than the term *confrontational rhetoric*. From a Mexican perspective, pleito rhetoric describes more of an "in-your-face" verbal protest. Equally, her mestiza rhetoric resisted the postcolonial assimilationist projects of the political regime and served as a public feminized form of discourse. For over three decades, her argumentative and defensive form of writing challenged tyrannical political systems. Reading this strong rhetoric that came from a women, politicians and conservatives would label her as an outcast and for a time force her into exile. This exile, however, served as an alternative rhetorical puesto from which she was free to create a new identity as a revolutionary and a mouthpiece for the disenfranchised. Because Gutiérrez de Mendoza's writing spans four decades of dense Mexican history, to cover each significant aspect of her discursive contributions remains difficult.

In this chapter, I divide her writing into three time periods: (1) the pre-Revolutionary era, also known as the precursor movement (1900–1910); (2) the Revolutionary period (1910–1920); and (3) the post-Revolutionary period (1920–1940), which includes the nationalist movement of community reconstruction and which saw the implementation of some of the Revolutionary ideals under President Lázaro Cárdenas (1934–1940). During each period, Gutiérrez de Mendoza took a stand on various issues related to pro-Revolutionary ideals, feminist suffrage, indigenous identities, and worker's rights movements across Mexico. In looking closely at her discourse, we see that Gutiérrez de Mendoza's writing and historical subjectivity directly weave into the political discourses and social movements of each period; therefore, I bring into focus the historical incidents that influenced and opened each puesto from which she spoke.

Conceptualizing Confrontational, Pleito, and Mestiza Rhetorics

Robert Cathcart notes that two distinct types of rhetoric occur within social movements: managerial and confrontational.[5] Managerial rhetoric upholds the existing system and does "not question underlying epistemology and group ethic."[6] Those engaged in managerial rhetoric support slow progressive reform, not full systemic change. Conversely, confrontational rhetoric rejects the prevailing hierarchy and employs the discourse of corrosion and impiety.[7] These distinctions are important to convey; however, revolutions can evolve only from the rhetoric of confrontation. Similarly, pleito rhetoric can be as provoking as confrontational rhetoric, but the Spanish term situates the speakers and their protest in a more contextually authentic puesto of rhetorical action. The Chicano scholar Elías Serna, who coined the expression, uses pleito rhetoric when theorizing the protests of students against the dismantling of the Arizona ethnic studies program and also the strategies used by college students in the 1960s to force universities to create Chicano studies programs on their campuses.[8] The students draw their methods of public dissent from the Mexican Revolutionary protests that emerged during Gutiérrez de Mendoza's era. Hence, Serna's concept of pleito rhetoric moves beyond Cathcart's concept of confrontational rhetoric in that it pushes the boundaries of community knowledge and historical connectivity.

Where confrontational rhetoric challenges the status quo, it can be seen as a universal mode of confronting or analyzing an issue, which doesn't address difference. Conversely, pleito rhetoric includes perceptions of race, class, and ethnicity through a "disruptive epistemological challenge."[9] I present these concepts to show the distinction between managerial and confrontational rhetoric, but I perceive pleito rhetoric to be more authentically in line with the method of discourse Gutiérrez de Mendoza used. Gutiérrez de Mendoza's writing not only exposed the oppressive policies of a dictatorial regime, but it also disrupted the gendered discursive puesto of protest journalism. She joined the precursor movement that began in 1900 with Ricardo and Jesús Flores Magón and other intellectuals. They were speaking against the dictatorial regime through manifestos and protest articles that clearly broke with the existing political system. People had been afraid to challenge Mexico's dictator, Porfirio Díaz, and his policies; yet a small group pressed the subject of unchecked consolidated power. Their public outcry at the turn of the century set the foundation of Mexico's confrontational rhetoric, which exploded in newspapers across the country that a decade later heralded the Mexican Revolution. Their rhetoric could be labeled as pleito rhetoric as well, but Gutiérrez de Mendoza brought her gendered perspective to the scene.

Cathcart explains that confrontational rhetoric occurs in "periods of societal breakdown or when moral underpinnings are called into question," but pleito rhetoric takes the protest to the next level of innovation in a movement.[10] Gutiérrez de Mendoza was among the first women to join the precursor movement, and merely with her public discursive presence she began to question and reframe the puesto women held within the public system of protest. Her discourse pertains to rhetoric of confrontation in that she ceased "to identify with the prevailing hierarchy" and stood "divided from the existing order."[11] Those who confront the system break with the secret order of things and "create a drama or agonistic ritual which forces a response from the establishment commensurate with the moral evil perceived by movement members."[12] Yet her short and scathing articles from 1903 and 1910, such as "¡Ecce homo!," "Al General Díaz," "Protesta," and "Cuando se muera," brought the fight to those in power. Threatened with censure, even death, she pushed against a political system of modernity that marginalized and abused women, the poor working class, and the indigenous people. Indeed, we will see how her rhetoric crossed the boundaries of discursive decorum of Mexican society, which would eventually force her into exile. After the Revolution ran its course, she would argue against José Vasconcelos's racial assimilationist project of mestizaje. Seeing through his utopian narrative as a racist perception, the same as Guillermo Bonfil Batalla has theorized, she believed the promise of unified modernization was a myth, nothing more than another way of promoting European and American ideologies and biological preferences that would lead to a de-Indianization of the culture.[13]

Because of her grassroots lived experiences and knowledge, Gutiérrez de Mendoza understood the epistemological direction of mestizaje. Far removed from the elite mestizo society of Wright de Kleinhans and other Porfirian intellectuals, Gutiérrez de Mendoza closely identified with her mother's Caxcan Indian heritage.[14] Holding up Wright de Kleinhans's mestiza background and discourse to Gutiérrez de Mendoza's, we see two distinct identifications as mexicanas. Wright de Kleinhans's rhetoric served as a managerial discourse regarding the conditions of the Mexican Indian; conversely, Gutiérrez de Mendoza always believed that the indigenous population truly represented "la mexicanidad," and she would later fiercely defend this position.[15] Her racial identification may have complicated her struggle as a woman journalist and activist. Even so, it strengthened her resolve against the social order that ignored the Indian population and silenced women. Nevertheless, she simultaneously carried and rejected the emerging system of mestizo politics. While she identified with the reality of la india, she could not escape the hybridized position of mestiza.

The concept of mestizaje, the mixing of many races as a positive and inevitable process, formed Mexico's future political groundwork, and a majority of the Mexican philosophies, policies, and transformative school curricula were written specifically to integrate indigenous people into the modern world.[16] Gutiérrez de Mendoza recognized that these policies would result in a cultural extinction of her people. Does this ideological separation invalidate her writings from being considered as mestiza rhetoric? On the contrary, I contend that her resistance to Vasconcelos's philos ophies places her writings in a more symbolic light within the mestiza consciousness. The mestiza always already negotiates a puesto of ambiguity, living in two ethnic worlds and multiple ideologies. The praxis of mestiza rhetoric opens a puesto for the development of critical identities, which separates and frees one from the binaries of modernity. Mestiza rhetoric negotiates multiple discursive puestos whereby subjects are able to practice radical identifications of oneself. Gutiérrez de Mendoza's rhetoric and action pedagogies, which assert an active and participatory mode of knowledge distribution and creation, always defended the Mexican indigenous cultures, which became the basis for her revolutionary struggle.

Sowing the Seeds of Rebellion

María Juana Francisca Gutiérrez Chávez was born on January 27, 1875, in San Juan del Río, Durango, to parents of little means.[17] Although she attended school for only a short period of time, this limited exposure provided the crucial introduction to literacy needed for her to recognize her own talents. As an autodidact, she would sharpen her reading and writing skills.[18] She followed the cultural tradition of marrying young and at the age of seventeen married Cirilo Mendoza and moved to Sierra Mojada, Coahuila, where Cirilo found a job as a miner in a mine known as La Esmeralda.[19] During the years that she lived among the miners, she gave birth to three children, Laura, Julia, and Santiago; taught her husband how to read and write; witnessed and lived the miserable, degrading conditions the miners endured; and survived on the menial pay they received.[20] While Gutiérrez de Mendoza was still very young, Cirilo died from complications related to alcohol abuse, leaving her alone to raise three children.[21] Tragedy soon struck the young widow again when her infant son, Santiago, died.

Her struggles in life would have brought many to a breaking point, but it seems her character was only strengthened by these challenges. Her early yet galvanizing experiences as a worker, a wife living in poverty-stricken mining communities, and then a young widowed mother forged her future rhetorical agenda as an activist and journalist. They opened her eyes to the brutal life that hundreds of thousands of Mexicans were living, all in the name of progress and order. The first articles she wrote denounced the treatment of the miners and were anonymously published in three early opposition newspapers, *Diario del Hogar* (México), *El Hijo del Ahuizote* (México), and *Chinaco* (Laredo, Texas).[22] In 1897, authorities from the mines discovered Gutiérrez de Mendoza's connection to the antigovernment publications, and she was sent to prison in Minas Nuevas, Chihuahua.[23] She wrote about her experience as being transformative: "La cárcel, con sus crudas realidades, me advirtió la distancia a que estaba de la verdad" (The jail, with its cruel realities, gave me notice of the distance I was from the truth).[24] The "truth" she discovered was that freedom from tyranny was not solely based in dissolving a single governmental regime. This was the first of many jail sentences she would endure throughout her life. Instead of deterring her activism, each prison sentence only intensified her resolve to live a life of activism and make systemic change.

As difficult as spending time in jail may have been, it afforded Gutiérrez de Mendoza a powerful ethos among the male intellectual revolutionaries in Mexico City. Wearing jail time like a badge of honor, she held a level of credibility proving that she was speaking, not from privilege, but from a puesto of risk taking and willingness to suffer the consequences of speaking truth to power. The Mexican historian Eduardo Arrieta Corral compares her intellectual and social acumen to those of Sor Juana Inés de la Cruz (1651–95), feminist colonial nun, writer, and poet; Francisco Zarco (1829–69), radical journalist and defender of freedom of speech; and José Revueltas (1914–76), protester in the 1968 student-led movement in Mexico City.[25] Corral states that Gutiérrez de Mendoza instinctually knew how to "incorporate her conflictive moment in history" and practice an "indestructible civil courage."[26] At first she published anonymously, a common practice in Mexico to protect the author from backlash, but Gutiérrez de Mendoza began to openly publish her name on the masthead of her newspaper, *Vésper*. This act moved Gutiérrez de Mendoza's discourse closer to the confrontation necessary to reframe her rhetorical puesto as revolutionary.

Confrontational rhetoric is not necessarily an act of violence, states Cathcart, nor a method of warfare. It is "a symbolic enactment which dramatizes the complete alienation of the confronter. As a rhetorical act it is more consummatory than instrumental."[27] Pleito rhetoric, however, takes the fight to the accused, engaging in verbal warfare. In these early years of speaking truth to power, Gutiérrez de Mendoza consummated the path of a revolutionary. She left Durango and headed south to Guanajuato to start her own protest newspaper, *Vésper*,[28] a small paper among the many publications of the time. Like Las Mujeres de Zitácuaro, she wrote anticlerical discourse, catching the attention of the archbishop of Guanajuato, who ordered her press confiscated in 1901.[29] At the turn of the century, a flurry of opposition newspapers emerged that conformed to the elements of pleito rhetoric. Some of these newspapers included *Regeneración* (Regeneration), directed by Enrique Flores Magón in Mexico; *El Demócrata y el Progreso* (The Democrat and Progress), directed by Dionisio Hernández; *El Hijo del Ahuizote* (The Son of the Gadfly), directed by Daniel Cabrera; and *El Clarín* (The Bugle), directed by Alberto M. Alvarado from Durango.[30] Countless newspapers and transitory tabloids, known as *papeles volantes*, literally meaning "flying papers," took issue with the regime and its actions and, most importantly, served as a puesto for a public exchange of ideas. These papers and their antigovernment messages irritated the Mexican government, and as quickly as one newspaper was shut down and the journalists jailed, another, more radical publication would appear. For example, on June 15, 1901, hundreds of copies of the translated version of *The Conquest of Bread*, originally written in French by the anarchist Peter Kropotkin, were printed and distributed from Gutiérrez de Mendoza's printing press.[31] This act could be seen as Gutiérrez de Mendoza's endorsement of or even membership in the anarchist-communist movement, but she never became part of the Communist Party.[32] Kroptkin, as many others at the time, was highly critical of the economic system that was keeping laborers in deep poverty. Publishing this radical text did, however, further expose Gutiérrez de Mendoza's radical sentiments, and her printing press was ultimately confiscated in Guanajuato. She fled Guanajuato with her children and moved to Mexico City early in 1902.

Serving in the puesto as primera vocal, or spokesperson, of the reorganized liberal club Ponciano Arriago, in early 1903 Gutiérrez de Mendoza wrote *Vésper* pieces that were at the forefront of the first serious political opposition to the Díaz regime and led the charge by confronting the people and the government. A series of publications appearing on May 15, 1903, filled with bold, accusatory rhetoric, would prompt the confiscation of her printing press again and her next jail sentence.[33] While the majority of the population was afraid to speak against the government's oppressive regime, Gutiérrez de Mendoza directly confronted the dictator in a piece titled "Al General Díaz."

Gutiérrez de Mendoza regularly spoke directly to her audience in an accusatory tone, hoping to rouse the people to action. In "Al General Díaz," as if wanting to start un pleito, or a fight, she openly addressed the dictator: "Nuestro periódico se ocupa de Ud. continuamente, y hemos llegado, ya ve Ud., hasta tenerle que dirigir nuestra voz directamente, esto haría suponer que venimos a combatirlo a Ud. únicamente" (Our newspaper concerns itself with you continually, and we have come, you see, to have to aim our voice to you directly. This would cause one to suppose that we come to combat only you, that you are our only objective).[34] This approach, also used by other radical newspapers, such as *El Hijo del Ahuizote*, was very different from the mainstream journalistic styles of essay and analysis. It is the sort of speech used to start un pleito. It resembles more the heckling of a politician on the street, the pointing him out in a crowd. On the one hand, this style of direct address could reflect Gutiérrez de Mendoza's lack of formal education. Conversely, it may represent an organic connection to the very people she was defending. Her frequent use of the tactic of pleito rhetoric may have also indicated she saw it as the best rhetorical strategy for this historical situation, which found many citizens blinded by the false peace Mexico was experiencing. She was firm with her sentiments, yet gave people reason to listen to her persuasive appeals. This direct rhetorical approach of pleito rhetoric, stirring the people's emotions toward anger, would become Gutiérrez de Mendoza's trademark.

At the time of the above-mentioned May 15, 1903, issue of *Vésper*, the main intellectual leaders of the liberal movement were imprisoned in the infamous Belén prison.[35] Momentarily, Gutiérrez de Mendoza was one of the few voices of dissent, and the only woman, in the sea of muted publications speaking on behalf of the political dissenters. In another article, published two months later, on July 8, she defended other journalists who had been arrested and threatened with death and continued to target the Mexican people who remained silent in the face of tyranny.

> Pueblo: es tiempo ya de que despiertes y veas a los que te vejan y te encadenan, te roban y te desprecian. Es tiempo ya de que marches al lado de los liberales que luchan por tu redención, guardando con veneración, incólumes a pesar del sacrificio, las obras que nos legaron nuestros héroes y garantizar nuestros derechos y nuestras libertades. Pueblo: Elige entre la Monarquía y la República. Entre los que te encadenan y los que te dan libertades.[36]

> People: right now it is time for you to wake up and see the ones who abuse you and enchain you, who steal from you and look down on you. Right now it is time that you march alongside the liberals who fight for your redemption, watching over with devotion, unscathed in spite of the sacrifice, the works that our heroes bequeathed to us and ensured our rights and our freedoms. People: choose between the Monarchy and the Republic. Between those who enchain you and those who give you freedoms.

Her writings, potent political speeches that reflected the aureate and ostentatious political language, could have been read aloud on street corners or at gatherings. Her journalistic discourse carried, as did many journalists' speech of the time, an oratorical rhythm. This mode of journalistic writing in Mexico was influenced by the speeches and writings of Emilio Castelar (1832–99), the Spanish parliamentary orator, politician, historian, and journalist who asserted an emphasis on linguistic eloquence. Charles Hale uses the term "grandiloquent prose" to describe Castelar's style and says that his "oratorical power, unequalled through the ages . . . was more than political oratory . . . it was also a transmutation into 'oral music' of all of history—philosophy, art, and science."[37] Hale paints Castelar as a supporter of liberal ideals, whose writings appealed to many Mexican readers of *La Libertad* and *El Monitor Republicano*.[38] Mexican writers were influenced by his style and incorporated it into their own public discourse.

Combined with an emotional appeal to the people, many of Gutiérrez de Mendoza's publications read like political oratory suffused with verbal cadences. For example, on May 15, 1903, she wrote a politically chastising piece to the Mexican people titled "A los mexicanos" (To the Mexican People). Throughout the article, there are sections of repeated phrases that create a parallel structure and an emphasis on a key idea or question. In the closing paragraphs of "A los mexicanos," Gutiérrez de Mendoza emphasizes the societal collective's act of having deviated from or forgotten its moral responsibility to freedom of speech.

> ¿A dónde se ha ido la vergüenza de los que así usurpan la representación del pueblo?
>
> ¿A dónde se ha ido el decoro del pueblo que así permite que se le exhiba en grosera caricatura?
>
> ¿A dónde está la dignidad de ciudadanos que así se dejan arrebatar sus derechos?[39]

> What has become of the shame of those who thus usurp representation of the people?
>
> What has become of the honor of the people, who permit themselves to be exhibited thus, in crude caricature?
>
> Where is the dignity of citizens who allow their rights to be taken in this way?

Appearing as distinct paragraphs in the original document, these questions directed at Gutiérrez de Mendoza's audience members produce an emotional appeal, asking them to consider their collective morals. She begins the following line with a poetic interjection, "Oh, México, cuna de los heroísmos, asiento de las libertades, baluarte de los derechos . . ." (Oh, Mexico, cradle of heroism, seat of liberties, bastion of civil rights . . .).[40] Many of Gutiérrez de Mendoza's early writings, such as this, emotionally roused her audience, calling the people to become politically aware and active. It is precisely this type of discourse that drew the attention of not only the Mexican citizenship but also those in political power.

Exile as Rhetorical Puesto

Gutiérrez de Mendoza's writings from 1903, such as in "A los mexicanos" and "¡Ecce homo!," were passionate, infused with emotional appeals.[41] In "¡Ecce homo!" she presents Díaz, the dictator, as a political coward: "¡Aduladores! He allí a vuestro hombre" (Flatterers! Here is your man as he is).[42] In her scornful and sarcastic tone, she declared that Díaz would be "el primer hombre que tiene miedo a las mujeres" (the first man to be afraid of women).[43] Verbal pleitos such as these prompted the regime to confiscate her printing press and once again sentence her to jail. Her multiple imprisonments can be perceived as a forced form of exile that intersects with the broader issues experienced by a woman entering a puesto defined by gender. Most commonly, Mexican women who committed offenses were charged with crimes of sexual deviance and placed in hospitals that functioned essentially as prisons.[44] These practices were enforced to closely monitor the female body in public spaces.[45] Gutiérrez de Mendoza, though, was not charged with any sort of sexual deviance, but rather with discursive deviance. Furthermore, she was not sent to a women's prison, but to the infamous Belén prison along with the male revolutionaries. From this perspective, Gutiérrez de Mendoza's immediate physical and discursive interaction with the most influential revolutionaries in a puesto of exile for political deviants places her at the intersection of social, private, political, and gendered discourses. Her crimes were considered a male infraction, and each circumstance surrounding her various imprisonments served as evidence that her discourse was consistently intersecting with the powerful rhetorics of the politicians.

Gutiérrez de Mendoza's exile would come shortly after her second incarceration. Mexico City courts had prohibited the publication of the revolutionary papers *El Hijo del Ahuizote*, *La Voz de Juárez*, *¡Excelsior!*, and *Vésper*. In order to continue writing and publishing her political dissent, she was invited to Laredo, Texas, by Ricardo Flores Magón, Camilo Arriaga, and other revolutionaries already gathered there. Despite mounting pressure, Gutiérrez de Mendoza found it difficult to leave Mexico, although it became almost impossible to publish her writing. Leaving her homeland would have produced a deeper erasure and silencing beyond the censorship she already endured. She wrote in her autobiography about how the exiled revolutionaries pressured her to join them. "No me resolvía a ir porque sentía pena de ir a luchar al extranjero. . . . Insistieron de tal modo que al fin me fui" (I could not make up my mind to go because I felt sorrow for going to fight in a foreign place. . . . They insisted in such a manner that finally I left).[46] In the end, she chose to join the exiled group in Laredo in 1904.

Typically, exile is perceived as a position in which a person is neither seen nor heard, but strategic rhetors can use the space to their discursive advantage. Kristen Kennedy notes that those who are exiled, whether by force or voluntarily, are those on the margins of society, yet she represents exile as a literal and rhetorical space (puesto) offering the possibility of discursive agency.[47] She states, "They are the minority that is always excluded from creating the very power structures that dominate them."[48] However, exile creates a paradoxical position, which Gutiérrez de Mendoza inhabited as a mestiza crossing borders into foreign lands, providing a puesto from which to speak critically and politically and develop new perspectives. Exile also serves as the consummative act of Gutiérrez de Mendoza's pleito rhetoric. Starting a pleito, as she did, also sets one apart with an aggressive stance, presenting a formal threat to the opposition. Serna points out that this distance, as similarly used by Chicano scholars, creates an "epistemological space . . . created by challenging lies, revealing exclusions, and making successful historical arguments" over past and present injustices.[49] Joining the others in Laredo, Gutiérrez de Mendoza accepted that Texas symbolized the political divide between them and the ruling factions of Mexico.

In Texas, Gutiérrez de Mendoza and the others stayed with Sara Estela Ramírez, an activist and journalist writing from the United States.[50] The group held meetings around Ramírez's kitchen table, and in the course of these meetings, there emerged serious differences regarding the direction of Mexico's politics.[51] Ricardo Flores Magón's solution to Mexico's problems leaned toward an anarchist ideology, whereas Camilo Arriaga's contribution included the support of democracy and of the principles of the 1857 constitution. Their ideological differences eventually led them to a parting of ways. In 1904, Gutiérrez de Mendoza and her companion, Elisa Acuña y Rosette, followed Arriaga to San Antonio, Texas.[52] Acuña y Rosette and Gutiérrez de Mendoza continued to circulate *Vésper*, also publishing a phantom newspaper, *La Protesta Nacional*, which indicated on the masthead that it was being published in Saltillo, Mexico, so as to confuse the Mexican authorities. Sara Estella Ramírez and Gutiérrez de Mendoza, along with other revolutionary women, would later establish Regeneración y Concordia (Regeneration and Concordance), an organization to better the condition of Indians and the proletariat and to improve the education of women.[53] Also, around this time in Texas, California, and the border region other anti-Porfirian radical newspapers were appearing that articulated revolutionary and gendered issues, such as *El Obrero* (The Worker), directed by Teresa Villarreal in San Antonio, Texas (1909); *La Voz de la Mujer* (The Voice of the Woman), published by Isidra T. de Cárdenas in El Paso, Texas (1907); and *Pluma Roja*, edited by Blanca de Moncaleano in Los Angeles, California (1913–15).[54] Gutiérrez de Mendoza was in the company of writers at the cusp of an important emerging Mexican American voice in the United States. However, she never became comfortable with the people and places north of the Mexican border.

> De mi estancia en Texas saqué la convicción de que el fantasma de la intervención con que se nos amenazaba siempre, era eso: un verdadero fantasma, propio para asustar a espíritus pusilánimes. Aunque parezca contradictorio, ese pueblo práctico es pura vanidad. No tiene de formidable más que la apariencia que le da el reclamo.[55]

> From my stay in Texas I took away the conviction that the ghost of the intervention we were always threatened with, was just that: an actual ghost, made to frighten faint-hearted souls. Although it seems contradictory, that practical nation is pure vanity. It does not possess anything more formidable than the appearance that the claim gives to it.

Kennedy states that exile presents an opportunity for those who inhabit that space to engage in social criticism: "the space of exile provides us with another way of thinking through a practice of critique, one that demands an exterior position is taken and a critical space is assumed."[56] Gutiérrez de Mendoza was afforded this opportunity, and her opinions of that puesto reflect a critical stance. While exiled in the United States, she may have felt that she was among the people who were appropriating Mexican indigenous lands openly offered by Porfirio Díaz, and so she may have experienced an inner conflict that would have prevented her from seeing past her colonized perspective. Her negative opinions of the people north of the Río Grande did not change, and they only worsened as she saw their influences permeate throughout Mexican society, such as into the Mexican school curriculum. These ideas would continue to inform her ideological convictions well into the future. However, unlike Ricardo Flores Magón, who stayed in the United States, Gutiérrez de Mendoza could not continue her activism exiled in a foreign land, and she returned to Mexico.[57]

The Road to Revolution

Upon her return in 1905, she wasted no time in organizing her resources and reinitiating the publication of *Vésper*. This newspaper was only a small part of her rhetorical activism, which escalated in the years before the Revolution. For Gutiérrez de Mendoza, the time between 1905 and 1911 was filled with activism and collaboration with other revolutionaries and politicians. In 1907, she collaborated with Sara Estela Ramírez in the reorganization of her newspaper, *La Corregidora*, and helped to establish another political newspaper, titled *El Partido Socialista*, a publication with ties to a group of industrial workers.[58] During this period, she also worked with Dolores Jiménez y Muro and other liberals to organize an association of workers' unions known as Socialismo Mexicano.[59] In keeping with Gutiérrez de Mendoza's character, she utilized the power of discourse to circulate the ideas that represented Socialismo Mexicano and, as a result, cofounded and edited the association's weekly paper, *Anáhuac*.[60]

El Partido Socialista commissioned Gutiérrez de Mendoza to interview Francisco Madero, the candidate who would take Díaz's position of power.[61] As with her other publications, she had a clear understanding that her article about the interview could once again land her in jail and even lead to personal injury. Indeed, after her interview was published in 1907, Gutiérrez de Mendoza was again jailed in the Belén prison.[62] Even though arrests and harassments against the Maderistas continued to increase, in the May 8, 1910, edition of *Vésper*, Gutiérrez de Mendoza continued to fully support Madero. In an editorial titled "Don Francisco I. Madero, candidato a la presidencia de la República" (Don Francisco I. Madero, Candidate for the Presidency of the Republic) she wrote: "Sostenemos la candidatura del Sr. Madero hasta que el triunfo sustituya los esfuerzos, hasta que el himno de victoria sustituya los toques de combate" (We support Señor Madero's candidacy until the victory replaces the efforts, until the victory hymn replaces the calls to war).[63] While this announcement of support may not seem so combative, the mere public support of Madero in this time was a dangerous position. In order to understand the rhetorical temerity of the

1910 publication of *Vésper*, one must also understand the political climate of the period. While other newspapers acquiesced under the pressure of censorship from the dictator, Gutiérrez de Mendoza amplified her rhetorical criticism through verbal pleito.

Evolución, a newspaper published by a group of workers in Mexico City, appeared on May 1, 1910, and fully supported Madero for his candidacy within the Anti-Re-electionist Party.[64] The printer, Rafael Quintero, who later became the leader of the Casa del Obrero Mundial, a major workers' union, urged the workers to "reclaim their rights and fulfill their duties as worthy citizens of a country that . . . celebrates the triumph of democratic institutions."[65] Within the first month of the publication, however, Quintero and the newspaper minimized their use of strong discourse and relied on a less abrasive managerial rhetoric. John Lear states that "[t]he very real possibility of repression forced critics of the government to use rhetorical, elliptical, and abstract arguments and above all to avoid direct attacks on President Díaz."[66] Gutiérrez de Mendoza followed the opposite rhetorical strategy to Quintero's. As the frustration of the people grew to a crescendo, she opted for the more politically dangerous approach of pleito and intensified her rhetorical attacks on activists such as Quintero and his workers for their perceived cowardice; in the same breath, she chastised Díaz for being politically obstinate. Indeed, it was not common for a woman to take the leading puesto in public political criticism.

In the same May 1910 edition of *Vésper*, she published an article titled "Contra todos los tiranos y contra todas las tiranías" (Against all tyrants and against all tyranny). The significance of this article, aside from its use of pleito rhetoric, lies in the fact that she articulated her rhetorical beliefs. From a consubstantial perspective, she replaced her name with that of her newspaper, *Vésper*. By employing the trope of synecdoche, the author became synonymous with the identity of *Vésper*. This feminist representation informed the audience of the author's philosophy and rhetorical strategies, to which she adhered not only in time of revolution but for the rest of her life.

> *Vésper*, altivo siempre, se rebelará eternamente contra todos los tiranos y contra todas las tiranías. . . . *Vésper* no tiene sus energías prestadas de la dureza de la palabra. *Vésper* no tiene sus armas de combate en los arsenales de la injuria. *Vésper* no se yergue ante los magnates para doblegarse ante los idiotas. *Vésper* no fustiga a los tiranos para adular a las multitudes. . . . *Vésper* no se aparta de la prensa que se vende para afiliarse a la prensa que se alquila. *Vésper* no sacrifica nunca la energía

de su perseverancia para la complacencia a las personas. *Vésper* no es la inconsciente arista que sigue el primer impulso que se le imprime. Todo esto no es un exceso de orgullo, sino porque es el único modo que conocemos de entender la independencia.[67]

Vésper, always proud, will rise up forever against all tyrants and against all tyrannies. . . . *Vésper* does not have its energy borrowed from the harshness of the word. *Vésper* does not have its weapons of combat in the arsenals of insults. *Vésper* does not rise up in front of magnates in order to then submit to idiots. *Vésper* does not censure the tyrants in order to cajole the masses. . . . *Vésper* does not separate itself from the press that sells itself to become affiliated with the journalism that gives itself out for hire. *Vésper* does not ever sacrifice the energy of its perseverance for the satisfaction of people. *Vésper* is not a will o' the wisp who thoughtlessly follows the first whim that impresses. All this is not due to an excess of pride, but because it is the only way we know how to understand independence.

Each mention of *Vésper* was followed by an ontological statement, a declaration of one's nature of being. Using a calculated tone, she stated that she would not be bought out or subjected to the passions and fluctuations of the moment, that she would continue to write without fear of retribution. The use of the phrase "la inconsciente arista" proved to be tricky to translate in the enigmatic sentence. A close reading shows that *arista* is derived from the Latin, meaning "edge," and also has Greek roots meaning "excellent, the best." Upon closer analysis, one finds the word *arista* is also a name, which describes the *opposite* of Gutiérrez de Mendoza's character: a continuous state of flux brought about by constantly changing interests. An arista is impatient, restless, and erratic, clever but unreliable. Ultimately, this analysis points to an embodiment of her discourse, which makes clear that she was living what she wrote. Gutiérrez de Mendoza, who held fast to her beliefs, would have the opportunity to prove this philosophy six months after writing this declaration.

In the Revolutionary Ranks

The Mexican Revolution officially began on November 20, 1910, marking the beginning of the long and bloody conflict that would evolve into an extremely complex and wrenching civil war for the people of Mexico.[68] For

Gutiérrez de Mendoza, participation in the Revolution proved to be the true embodiment of her discourse. She understood words to be empty vessels if they were devoid of action. Toward the beginning of the Revolution, she participated with Dolores Jiménez y Muro, Carlos Mújica, and Antonio Navarro in the Complot de Tacubaya, in a conspiracy that was designed to overthrow the Díaz regime in March 1910.[69] The plot was betrayed, and once again she was jailed. She was released when Díaz's presidential replacement, Francisco Madero, came to power. Shortly after her release, the Revolution spiraled out of control, quickly becoming a tumultuous power struggle among political factions. These historical details are significant because Gutiérrez de Mendoza's rhetoric was intimately tied to the ebb and flow of the revolutionary events.

President Madero would not remain in office for long. He, along with Vice President José María Pino Suárez, were kidnapped and assassinated in a coup d'état in 1913 by Victoriano Huerta's followers.[70] Regardless of the death of her chosen candidate, Gutiérrez de Mendoza remained active in the latest revolutionary politics. Along with the all-female group she had organized in 1910, Amigas del Pueblo (Friends of the People), she authored a manifesto in protest of Madero's assassination and printed it in *El Voto* and *Vésper*.[71] In the manifesto, she issued a call for women's involvement in the Revolutionary faction, not as helpmates to men, but as independent women willing to join the cause.

> El Club "Amigas del Pueblo" hace un solemne llamamiento a todas las mujeres mexicanas para que abandonen su proverbial indiferencia, laboren resueltamente en la obra de regeneración humana, desgarrando las viejas tradiciones, despojándose siempre de los prejuicios y dando al mundo el saludable ejemplo de su propia dignificación.[72]

> The Friends of the People Club issues a solemn call to all Mexican women to give up your proverbial indifference, and to resolutely join in the task of human regeneration, ripping away old traditions, forever shedding prejudices, and giving the world the healthy example of your own rise to dignity.

The appeal of leaving behind "old traditions" was consistent with the direction of the Revolution.

Her rhetorical defiance, at times, seems to have been actualized and carried out in isolation from other women. This example shows instead that she brought women together in support of the Revolution. The early activism of many of her peers, such Dolores Jiménez y Muro, Hermila Galindo, and Beatriz González Ortega, at this time was the genesis of a Mexican feminist movement.[73] Women from the popular and middle classes emerged in the ranks of battle as *soldaderas* (female soldiers), nurses, teachers, writers, conference organizers, and activists.[74] During this time, Gutiérrez de Mendoza would become an expert at mobilizing women and other groups.

Her ability to mobilize people can be seen in her willingness to participate in the conflict under Emiliano Zapata, general and leader of the agrarian fight during the first part of the Revolution. With President Huerta now in power, a lack of sympathy prevailed for Zapatistas (supporters of General Zapata). In 1914, Gutiérrez de Mendoza was imprisoned for ten months after being captured while carrying out a mission commissioned by General Zapata.[75] Upon her release, she returned to the rank and file of Zapata's followers, and the general honored her with the title of colonel.[76] While serving under Zapata, Gutiérrez de Mendoza once again faced the deplorable conditions under which the campesinos (peasant farmers) lived and labored. During her time in the field, she published *Vésper* under harsh conditions in makeshift printing spaces and started another journal called *La Reforma* (The Reform) in support of land redistribution among the indigenous peasants.[77]

Her grassroots revolutionary and pleito discourse became a dangerous practice, and through the ten years of the Revolution, the gates of prison became her revolving doors. President Huerta was replaced by the Constitutionalist president, Venustiano Carranza, who also did not support Zapata. Carranza opposed the agrarian revolution and perceived General Zapata and General Pancho Villa as bandits. Being heavily involved in Zapata's revolution, Gutiérrez de Mendoza was once again incarcerated in 1916, along with her seventeen-year-old daughter, Laura, who also became a political activist, for approximately ten months.[78] Carranza brought the Revolution closer to an end by having Zapata assassinated in 1919. Awakening her to the harsh reality of her own idealism, Zapata's death was a turning point for Gutiérrez de Mendoza. The Revolution, which had started out as a movement through which she hoped to bring justice for the campesinos and fair wages for industrial workers, turned into a movement of power grabbing among the elites.

Gutiérrez de Mendoza witnessed the disintegration of a movement that she had once believed would lead to practical solutions.[79] The Revolution did not produce the idyllic outcomes that she, and many others, had expected. True to her character, Gutiérrez de Mendoza altered her course of action, discursively and literally. These sentiments appeared on June 15,

1919, in her new publication, symbolically titled *El Desmonte: Por la Tierra y por la Raza*. The phrase *el desmonte* means "the leveling or clearing away," and the subtitle means "for the land and for the people." The title *El Desmonte* held rhetorical and ontological significance for Gutiérrez de Mendoza, illustrating a shift in her political consciousness. In a piece titled "Desmontado" (Clearing the Way), she openly reflects with her usual sarcasm upon the current situation of Mexican politics. She wrote:

> En mi concepto, la situación en general no es ni mejor ni peor que cuando se inició este movimiento a fines del Siglo pasado, en 1900, cuando por vez primera tomé parte en las protestas populares. Y esto que digo de la situación digo de los hombres; no he visto ninguno mejor ni peor que los demás. . . .
>
> No hay que quedarse a medio camino y perdidos en los escombros; hay que pasar por sobre todas estas mezquindades llegar, vencedores, a la cumbre donde se dan cita todos los que luchan por un ideal.[80]

> In my view, the general situation is neither better nor worse than when this movement started at the end of the last Century, in 1900, when for the first time I participated in the mass protests. And what I say regarding the situation I say of the men; I have not seen one better or worse than the rest. . . .
>
> There must be no stopping in the middle of the path, lost in the ruins; it is necessary to pass over all this wretchedness and arrive, the victors, at the summit, where we will join all those who are fighting for an ideal.

Gutiérrez de Mendoza endeavored to keep the spirit and direction of her revolution alive, promising to clear out the chaos and confusion of the present and to foster a new direction.

More significantly, Gutiérrez de Mendoza filled the pages of this newspaper with her own philosophies about social action and the role discourse plays to bring about change. In the publications of *El Desmonte*, she revealed what she saw as the discursive failings of the Mexican Revolution. In particular, she focused on the politicians' empty words that fell flat and accomplished nothing for the people. Throughout her writing, she displayed the ability to capture a reality regarding a political situation and present it as a philosophy. For example, in an article titled "Hechos, no palabras" (Actions, Not Words), she defined revolutionary discourse as empty talk, stating that only when they are infused with action and change do words become meaningful.

> [L]as revoluciones no se hacen con deseos, ni con discursos, ni con papel impreso; estos no son más que medios de insinuación, de orientación; recursos para llevar a los ánimos la decisión, el convencimiento . . . pero nada más. Medio de preparación muy útiles para ese objeto, pero completamente inútiles, absolutamente ineficaces cuando a eso se reduce todo.[81]
>
> Revolutions are not made with desires, or with speeches, neither with printed paper. These are no more than means of insinuation, of orientation; resources to give decisiveness to the spirit, conviction . . . but nothing else. Very useful means of preparation for that objective, but completely useless, absolutely ineffectual when everything is reduced to that.

In this relatively short piece, Gutiérrez de Mendoza captured simultaneously the essence of rhetoric and the evolutionary nature of social movements. While rhetoric defines and interprets the substance of human activity for those involved in the movement, the movement cannot progress without the action, or praxis, of the discourse. In this critique, she was calling out the revolutionaries who failed to accomplish anything with all their grand public speeches and constitutions. In "Hechos, no palabras," there is a sense of an ideological evolution, of leaving one movement behind and beginning another. Charles Stewart calls this the "evolution of a revolution," where we see "gradual evolutions from one central principle or goal to another, or new social movement."[82] In *El Desmonte*, Gutiérrez de Mendoza articulated this historical movement of leaving behind the Mexican Revolution and moving on to a grander enactment of those beliefs.

Rarely did women so openly critique the men within the political arena, yet Gutiérrez de Mendoza offered a pointed analysis of the men in power. Her tone was in keeping with the pleito rhetoric that had emerged before the Revolution. However, now it took on a tone of deeper frustration with the political situation. Throughout the short-lived newspaper *El Desmonte*, with her unchanged sarcastic tone, she heavily criticized what she saw as ineffectual governmental practices. She wrote, "¿Esperar de los que en la actualidad ocupan los puestos públicos, con Carranza a la cabeza? No sé qué se podrá esperar de un cadáver, como no sean emanaciones malsanas" (Shall we expect anything today from the current officeholders with [President] Carranza in the lead? I do not know what can be expected from a cadaver, other than unhealthy emanations).[83] At the end of the Revolutionary era, she sensed the need to move forward, regardless of the political situation. Indeed, what she saw as a failed revolution, broken promises, and empty praise would have been enough to discourage anyone from seeking an ideal solution for the people, but it only inspired Gutiérrez de Mendoza to continue her work. Her rhetoric would always carry the tone of confrontation, of starting un pleito. In the new era, she would shift her rhetorical agenda to indigenous rural action and women's education.

Challenging and Re/visioning Historical Narratives

The Revolution was over, and while there were other conflicts brewing, such as the implementation of anti-Catholic policies under the new 1917 constitution, the people of Mexico felt a need to move forward as a nation.[84] The post-Revolutionary era (1920–40) would set Mexico on a path seeking an identity rooted in her indigenous past. In response to this new movement, Gutiérrez de Mendoza shifted her discourse and activism in accordance with Mexico's new direction. However, she did not lose sight of her philosophy of fighting for the marginalized communities. In the first months of 1922, she returned to Mexico City and helped organize the groups Acción Femenil (Female Action) and Consejo Nacional de Mujeres Mexicanas (National Council of Mexican Women).[85] This organizational movement on Gutiérrez de Mendoza's behalf signaled a larger societal shift in terms of feminism.

In the early 1920s, a new social revolution emerged, based in a socialist education system led by the philosopher and educator José Vasconcelos, first minister of the Secretaría de Educación Pública (SEP) (Secretariat of Public Education). The SEP's program was infused with ideas of Western eugenics, racial fitness, and domestic science, putting federal teachers on the front lines as promoters of these ideas. Mexico's post-Revolutionary direction looked toward unifying its people through cultural education and communal mobilization. The central conceptual groundwork for cultural unity came from the theories Vasconcelos articulated in his book *La raza cósmica* (The Cosmic Race) (1925).[86] The book's underlying premise included an idealistic, and ultimately racist, view of the nation's future through mestizaje: "What is going to emerge out there is the definitive race . . . made up of the genius and the blood of all peoples . . . more capable of true brotherhood and of a truly universal vision."[87] The idealistic position of creating a multiracial state with a global perspective was the pivotal point of departure for Mexico's new modernist school. Many artists and teachers who accepted Vasconcelos's social call as *maestros rurales*, or rural teachers, hoped it would solve the "Indian problem."

It was believed that the Indian, or the rural peasant population, was "decadent, diseased, and demobilized by backwardness, oppression, and disruption" and was in need of a global perspective.[88] In order to bring about this change, Vasconcelos called the nation's populace to join the movement of educating la raza. Mexico's social engineering movement was a revolution of shifting rhetorics, which can be a subtle yet powerful tool in the process of change. An understanding of this movement is important because as Gutiérrez de Mendoza joined the ranks to become a maestra rural, it framed the subsequent exigency of her discourse from 1920 to 1940. Thousands of the maestros rurales, a majority of them women, were charged with venturing into the indigenous communities in the mountains with the purpose of teaching them about personal thrift and hygiene, but also to cultivate local art, music, and dance, which were tied directly to state progress, modernity, and patriotism.[89] The teachers were more than foot soldiers; they "became explicit political actors" involved in the "redistribution of wealth and power" among the peasants and workers.[90] The SEP's larger educational policy was to modernize the rural patriarchy, remaking the regional family to favor "national, horizontal networks."[91] In other words, the imposed structure would support a capitalist system.

The job of a maestro rural was arduous, lonely, and dangerous. Many teachers lost their lives in the communities they served because of local uprisings against the changes they were proposing. But Gutiérrez de Mendoza flourished in her puesto in Jalisco and Zacatecas because her people, the Caxcan Indians, lived in this region. In 1923, she would become *inspectora de escuelas rurales* (inspector of rural schools).[92] By working as an affiliate of the SEP, Gutiérrez de Mendoza was able to understand the system from within and formulate rhetoric counter to that of the organization and its policies. Vaughan notes that many of the pueblos that were visited by the maestros rurales did struggle "successfully to legitimize their cultures and assert their right to pace the entry of modernity and determine its content and meaning."[93] The actions and discourse of Gutiérrez de Mendoza fit into this historical account.

Gutiérrez de Mendoza used her proficiency as a critical observer to resist what she saw as the destructive history and policies that were being forced upon the indigenous people. From this rhetorical puesto, she was able to reclaim the identity of india intellectual speaking between European and indigenous racial constructs. It is within this role that the very nature of mestiza rhetoric flourishes. Anzaldúa asserts, as Gutiérrez de Mendoza believed, that the dominant culture has "white washed and distorted history," and by taking on the role of a historian infused with a mestiza consciousness, one can reclaim a level of self-determination for one's people.[94] This was Gutiérrez de Mendoza's nuevo puesto as a post-Revolutionary rhetor.

As a historian, Gutiérrez de Mendoza adopted a sophistic method of reworking the dominant culture's reality by rhetorically intervening in the process of intellectual formation. While on one level she adopted a nationalist stance grounded in her indigenous understanding of the world, she rejected the coming together or assimilation of two cultures. Her frustration at the colonizing efforts of the government and school system steadily grew. After teaching from 1922 to 1923 among the indigenous people, she formed a group in Juchipila, Zacatecas, known as the Consejo de los Caxcanes (Council of the Caxcanes).[95] As director, she wrote a lengthy treatise she self-published in 1924 with the same title as her previous newspaper, *¡Por la tierra y por la raza!* (For the Land and for the People!). In the six chapters, Gutiérrez de Mendoza took to task the very organization for which she worked, the SEP, its director, and more generally, the greater population of Mexico.[96]

In chapters 1 and 3, Gutiérrez de Mendoza sets forth the project of myth writing. The writing of myth resides in what Mary E. Hawkesworth calls the rhetoric of vision. This style of rhetoric targets the ideological struggle and "consciously engages in the literary production of reality . . . recoding the dominant cultural symbols" in order to bring about social transformation.[97] With rhetorical flourish and questioning, she makes clear that the return of the Aztec god Quetzalcoatl is just as legitimate as that of the Christian god. The first sentence of chapter 1 reads:

> Ha muchos siglos Tenochtitlán espera que retorne Quetzalcóatl. Esta esperanza, firme como una roca en el alma de los indios, nadie sabe, nadie quiere comprenderla. Es lógico. Sólo un indio comprende el alma de su Raza.
>
> Los extraños han tomado por Mitología lo que es una realidad. . . . Los indios esperan que retorne Aquel que lanzó sus flechas a lo Infinito y del Caos herido por ellas arrancó el Día y la Noche. . . .
>
> ¿Por qué no han de esperar los creyentes al Mesías por la misma razón que los indios esperan a Quetzalcóatl?[98]
>
> For many Centuries Tenochtitlán has waited for Quetzalcoatl to return. This hope, solid as a rock in the soul of the Indians, nobody knows of it, nobody wants to understand it. It makes sense. Only the soul of an Indian understands his own people.

> Strangers have taken for Mythology what is a reality. . . . The Indians hope for the return of the One who threw His arrows into the Infinite and from the Chaos wounded by them created Day and Night. . . .
>
> Why should the believers not wait for the Messiah for the same reason that the Indians await Quetzalcoatl?

Gutiérrez de Mendoza's rhetorical agenda, laid out in the first chapter, was to legitimize the indigenous people's beliefs. The Europeans' encounter with the Mexican people deprived the natives of their cultural reality, and Gutiérrez de Mendoza's rhetorical backlash and questioning turned this modernist denial on its head. With a view of the world not grounded in Eurocentrism, she understood the modernist reasoning to be an extension of the colonizers' perspective that excluded the world of the indigenous from rationality or possible religious validity.

In chapter 2, the treatise sets out to reframe the history of the Conquest and preserve the culture of the Caxcan people. Gutiérrez de Mendoza understood that many false histories had been recorded regarding her people, and she meant to set the record straight. Taking a separatist stance, she stated, "No tenemos ningún interés en que los extraños lean lo que fue escrito solamente para nosotros, puesto que sólo nosotros solamente podemos comprenderlo" (We are not in the least interested in others reading that which was written for us, granted that only we can understand it).[99] She contradicted herself with such statements, because she in turn wrote the history of her people and quoted long historical accounts from *Historia breve de la conquista de los estados independientes del imperio mexicano* (Short History of the Conquest of the Independent States of Imperial Mexico), written by Friar Francisco Frejes in 1839.[100] He presented accounts that "hacían justicia a los indios" (did justice to the Indians).[101] In his writings, Frejes included more than twenty-five pages of historical quotes and narratives regarding battles and encounters. By interweaving citations of this history, Gutiérrez de Mendoza was engaging in a historiography project, looking for more authentic, grounded, and respectful narratives of her people.

At the end of chapter 2, Gutiérrez de Mendoza incorporated into the history a recovery of the festivals celebrated in Juchipila. Part of the SEP's process for a new indigenous cultural transformation included the organization of festivals that celebrated school openings and seasonal changes. Many rural leaders and their people appropriated these festivals as a way to intervene in claiming their own discursive cultural identities, an organic approach to de/colonizing their ways of being. Some of the festivals and rituals the maetros rurales organized involved the learning of *danzas* from different regions of Mexico and the singing of indigenous songs, such as "Los chaparritos," and "Las palmeras."[102] Vaughan notes that female schoolteachers were crucial to the organization of community rituals because they distinguished the festival as a space to enact and reinforce the indigenous people's own identities. As one of these teachers, Gutiérrez de Mendoza reiterated the value of the historical festival of the Caxcan people known as the Danza del Xúchil. This traditional fiesta featured a danza that celebrated the origins of life and was "la fiesta de los Dioses, del Amor y de las Flores."[103] The Teocal-li was the name given to the Caxcan Indian's first cave, where they housed their provisions and memories of Xochiquetzal, goddess of fertility and beauty, and Quetzalcoatl, the feathered serpent deity related to Aztec priesthood and knowledge.[104] Gutiérrez de Mendoza reinforced the importance of the fiesta and danza del Xúchil by documenting their authenticity. She included a musical score corresponding to the danza that she found in the rural community of Juchipila. She recognized the modernist push to eliminate this festival from the pueblo's collective conscience and incorporated the primary document in her history of the people in an attempt to keep the Caxcan cultural memory alive.

Through chapters 4, 5, and 6 of the treatise, Gutiérrez de Mendoza reiterated her argument for the recognition of the Caxcan people through unrepresented historical documents and transcribed sections of other historians' writings. In the epilogue, she forwarded the ultimate insult to the modernist movement—the assurance that the indigenous people, their culture, language, and religious beliefs, would survive. Toward the end of the treatise, Gutiérrez de Mendoza clearly stated the reason for writing about the Caxcan people and affirmed her counterargument against modernism.

> Tenemos un indiscutible derecho a no desaparecer como raza; no queremos formar parte de la especie humana como raza conquistada ni con el pobre carácter de asimilados, y NO RECONOCEMOS A NINGUNA RAZA EL DERECHO DE IMPONERNOS SU CIVILACIÓN. Nuestras aspiraciones y nuestra salvación no están en INCORPORARNOS a otra civilización, sino en RESTAURAR la nuestra.[105]

> We have an indisputable right to not disappear as a people; we do not want to be a part of humankind as a conquered people nor with the poor temperament of an assimilated people. And WE DO NOT RECOGNIZE THE RIGHT OF ANY PEOPLE TO IMPOSE THEIR

> CIVILIZATION ON US. Our aspirations and our salvation are not in BECOMING INCORPORATED INTO another civilization, but in RESTORING OUR OWN.

This quotation clearly positions her discourse within a mestiza consciousness, rejecting the neo-conqueror's position of cultural genocide. With no digressions, Gutiérrez de Mendoza stated plainly that her people did not accept the political and racial definitions articulated in the state-sanctioned curriculum proposed by Vasconcelos. His project, while on the surface seeming inclusive, was not—it was assimilationist.

Mestiza rhetoric seeks a validating vision, exoneration. It looks for "new images of identity, new beliefs about ourselves, our humanity and worth no longer in question."[106] *Por la tierra*'s decolonial historical memory and recovery cleared the way for a new cultural understanding outside of the conviction that the history, as recounted by the colonizers, was the only valid interpretation. As a mestiza, Gutiérrez de Mendoza made the conscious choice of rooting her identity in indigenous people's history as a much more genuine perspective than the popularized movement based in Vasconcelos's theories, which were framed as transitory connections with the indigenous cultures. Anzaldúa calls this authentic path "*El camino de la mestiza*/The Mestiza Way."[107] Taking inventory of one's ancestral inheritance marks the first steps of the mestiza. The next step, a highly rhetorical move, is the decision of what to keep and what to discard. "Luego bota lo que no vale, los desmientos, los desencuentos, el embrutecimiento. Aguarda el juicio, hondo y enraizado, de la gente antigua" (And then she discards what is not valid, the lies, the false stories, the stultification. She awaits the judgment, deep and rooted, in the ancient peoples).[108] Making this subversive rhetorical move of re/visioning, Gutiérrez de Mendoza chose to resurrect the history of her people in the contact zone of modern conquest philosophies. These beliefs clashed with those of the indigenous communities who believed in divergent religious positions, such as the coming of Quetzalcoatl, the practice of ancient rituals and cultures, and the use of indigenous languages.

Gutiérrez de Mendoza's writings certainly did not end with *¡Por la tierra y por la raza!* Tirelessly, she would continue with her activism into the 1930s by writing pamphlets, publishing newspapers, and producing announcements in order to improve upon women's education and puestos within Mexican society. In these writings, she expressed her idea of a radical feminism based in motherhood. Her focus on the indigenous populations as the true identity of Mexico illuminates again a sense of her mestiza rhetoric. Gutiérrez de Mendoza's writing was revolutionary not only because she wrote before, during, and after the Mexican Revolution, but also, and most importantly, because as a public figure she broke all expected notions of women's work. Among the women of this study, she was one of the more prolific writers. She left numerous writings for later generations to study. As Lau Javien shows in her extensive survey on Gutiérrez de Mendoza's writings, she would revive the feminine club of Amigas del Pueblo. Gutiérrez de Mendoza published *Preliminares de Combate* (Preliminary Combat) in February 1935; *Camisas de Colores* (Shirts of Many Colors) in March 1935; and *Toque de Atención al Ejército Nacional* (Warning to the National Army) in April 1935; as well as *La República Femenina* (The Feminine Republic) in 1936.[109] Through these publications, she expressed a radical maternal feminism that critiqued the state, its policies, and the military.[110] For example, *Camisas de Colores* criticized factions on all sides of the political realm, and for her, the maternal instinct was more valued than the talent men believed they had "ya que la mujer era quien tenía una clara visión de la vida en su pureza natural" (since the woman was the one who had a clear vision of life in its natural purity).[111] Gutiérrez de Mendoza's feminism emerged in her later years as a biological one; she proposed in *La República Femenina* a government of and by the women, directed toward women's natural needs.[112]

Her true vocation of teaching would be realized in the years 1937 to 1940, when she was director of the Escuela Industrial Femenina "Josefa Ortiz de Domínguez" (Josefa Ortiz de Domínguez Industrial School for Women), a puesto from which she was later fired.[113] However, she would continue writing and publishing work throughout this time, such as the newspaper *Génesis* (1937), a brochure titled *Más allá de los muros* (Beyond the Walls) (1938), and the biweekly *El Alma Mexicana* (The Mexican Soul) (1935–36 and 1941).[114] As noted with so many of her publications, Gutiérrez de Mendoza had an indomitable desire to communicate her ideas, theories, and political directions. She would remain true to the cultural beliefs she formed in her earlier years when she lived as a young wife among the indigenous miners and as a maestra rural in the mountains among the Indians. She believed the indigenous people of the Mexican race were the true foundation of the nation.

In 1940, two years before her death, in the newspaper *Para Michoacán*, she expressed the basis of her motivations to continue in the struggle for her people: "Sigo creyendo que el elemento aborigen es la única base de la Nación y la familia la única base de la sociedad; de allí que por muy alta que sea la presión que pretendan aplicarme, no habrá humano que logre de mi parte una traición, a la familia ni la raza" (I still believe that the aboriginal element is the only base of the nation and the family the only foundation of society, hence no matter how high the pressure they seek to apply upon me, there is no human power against me that can cause me to betray family or race).[115] It is through these sentiments that her influence as a mestiza rhetor reaches across the many years she practiced her art of rhetoric.

Conclusion

In the post-Revolutionary era, from 1920 to 1940, a Mexican modernist view of the world permeated society as the answer to the so-called Indian problem, and many people accepted its philosophical tenets without question. The articles in *El Desmonte* and the chapters in *¡Por la tierra y por la raza!* disrupt the belief that all of Mexico accepted the myth of modernity forwarded by Vasconcelos. More importantly, they challenge the idea that only men were taking part in shaping the philosophical cultural history of Mexico. The writings of Gutiérrez de Mendoza add to the evidence left by previous scholars that women in Mexico in the early twentieth century did participate in the politics of the Revolution beyond the role of soldadera.

Toward the end of her career, and with the feminist movement in Mexico in motion, Gutiérrez de Mendoza increased her feminist activism, and her ideological convictions shifted toward a radical feminism that elevated motherhood to a superior puesto to take the place of the harsh politics of men. In 1932, after many years of not publishing *Vésper*, Gutiérrez de Mendoza again circulated the revolutionary newspaper in an effort to steer women toward a more active role in post-Revolutionary Mexican politics. She dealt with issues such as women's suffrage and labor. In the final years of her life, she collaborated with artists like Concha Michel and Frida Kahlo to form the radical group República Femenina. Gutiérrez de Mendoza fulfilled the promise she had made in the early writings of *Vésper* when she stated, "*Vésper* siempre ocupará su puesto" (*Vésper* will always occupy its place). She not only occupied this new discursive puesto, she commanded it.

Gutiérrez de Mendoza's rhetorical trademark would be her rhetorical pleito to any concept, person, or organization she felt was politically dysfunctional or was suppressing the people of Mexico. But her efforts didn't always lead to her preferred outcome or solution, and her sentiments are reflected in her last published words. Regardless, she kept writing even when she thought she had a limited audience. Gutiérrez de Mendoza provides us with an example of embodied rhetoric by having entered wittingly and forcefully into puestos that had been closed off to women. After her rhetorical incursions, many more women would begin to take roles in society that pushed the boundaries of centuries-old traditions of female silence.

One of her last publications appeared in 1935 and 1936 in the form of a biweekly titled *El Alma Mexicana*. In this publication, which ran for only four issues, she held to her confrontational character and announced, "¡No callaré! Treinta y cinco años de incesante lucha y sesenta de vida, ponen a cualquiera fuera de combate, o por lo menos sirven para justificar indiferencias o disfrazar cobardías" (I will never be silenced! Thirty-five years of incessant fighting and sixty years of living, can put anyone out of combat, or at least serve to justify indifference or to disguise cowardice)."[116] Her neocolonial understanding of the situation of the disenfranchised people in Mexico kept her writing to the very end of her life. In her older age, she wanted to continue writing, but in the end, she faltered in her belief that her words made a difference. All around her she continued to see the pain and suffering of her people, whom she had tried to help through political, public, and discursive action. This knowledge, she said in *Alma Mexicana*, "no tiene más que esta solución: . . . continuar en la tarea aún teniendo el triste convencimiento de que es inútil" (has only one solution: to continue the work, although bearing the sad conviction that it is all in vain).[117] While she may have believed that her writing was completed in vain, we see that her words in the early part of the twentieth century opened the pathway for women to engage in the public discourse. The importance of her rhetoric and the actions accompanying it historically capture Mexican women's struggle for a superior puesto.

Vésper *siempre ocupará su puesto*

Vésper: Justicia y Libertad
8 May 1910

Una vez más *Vésper* viene a ocupar su puesto en el campo del combate.

Vésper no ha querido luchar sólo por un cambio de personal en la Administración Pública, eso dista mucho de sus grandes anhelos de transformación radical, de su eterna aspiración de justicia y libertad, de sus grandes ideales de suprema redención y si esta vez luchará por los candidatos electos y sostenidos por la convención es porque comprende que sin quitar el primer obstáculo es imposible ir más allá.

Si el Gral. Díaz ha sido un formidable obstáculo para una simple práctica democrática, cuanto más habrá de serlo para una transformación social ante la cual están temblando los tiranos de todo el mundo.

Nosotros podríamos pasar sobre ese obstáculo y seguir la marcha hacia lo inmenso de nuestros ideales; pero, ¿podrían ir como nosotros? Muy pocos ciertamente. Nosotros estamos en plena posesión de nuestra libertad, en pleno uso de nuestro derecho, en pleno ejercicio de nuestra soberanía, para nosotros que hemos despedazado todos los yugos, que nos hemos arrancado todas las cadenas, que hemos arrancado el peso de todas las preocupaciones y de todos los prejuicios, que desconocemos todos los temores y abominamos todas las cobardías, para nosotros no hay tiranía posible y con ser así nos basta para ser inmensamente libres.

Pero ¿cuántos podrán ser libres como nosotros si en este pueblo horriblemente oprimido se ha perdido hasta la noción de libertad?

¿Qué idea de la soberanía se presume tener aquí donde se desconoce la soberanía de todo un pueblo?

Es una locura creer que un pueblo atado al poste de todas las ignorancias, oprimido bajo el peso de todas las tiranías y devorado por todas las miserias, pueda seguir en su marcha a la libertad, que pasa sin detenerse para arrancarle todas sus ligaduras.

No; si queremos que ese pueblo nos siga a ese más allá de la redención, es preciso ayudarlo a que rompa todas sus cadenas; esto es lo que hacemos al combatir la dictadura del Gral. Díaz; esto es lo que hacemos al procurar el triunfo de la candidatura popular.

Por esto al dedicarse a luchar exclusivamente por los candidatos de Convención, *Vésper* no abdica ni hace transacciones de sus principios; se detiene sencillamente a remover el pedrusco interpuesto en el camino.

La nación entera está interesada en esa remoción y bien pudiéramos dejar a los demás esa tarea, en la seguridad de que la llevarán a cabo; pero ni queremos ni debemos hacerlo: no es digno de nosotros esperar a que otros abran el paso para seguir adelante.

No se piense que creemos (como muchos ilusos cuyos nombres podemos citar) que para que el pueblo sea libre basta con que cualquiera sustituya al Gral. Díaz; bien se ha visto a *Vésper* ir solo contra una multitud enloquecida y apasionada, cuando los actos han sido una farsa, las palabras una mentira y los hombres una amenaza para esa misma multitud que por escapar del peligro presente no advertía otro peligro mayor para el futuro; no podrá decirse que nos aturden las palabras, que nos deslumbran las personalidades, que nos hipnotiza la opinión pública, no, ya lo hemos dicho otra vez: "la caída de un tirano no es la caída de la tiranía y si tan resuelta como espontáneamente, venimos a luchar porque el Sr. Madero ocupe la Presidencia de la República, es porque el Sr. Madero nos inspira la más completa confianza respecto a los fines que persigue; es porque tenemos la convicción de que la suerte de este desdichado país mejorará cuando el Sr. Madero esté al frente de sus destinos; y mientras algún hecho no venga a modificar nuestra opinión, *Vésper* siempre ocupará su puesto al lado de los que luchen por el victorioso candidato de la gran Convención.

—Juana B. Gutiérrez de Mendoza

■ ■ ■

Vésper Will Always Occupy Its Space

Vésper: Justice and Liberty
8 May 1910

Once again *Vésper* returns to occupy its post in the field of combat.

Vésper has not wanted to fight for just a change of personnel in the Public Administration; this is a long way from its great desires for radical transformation, from its eternal aspirations for Justice and Liberty, from its

---

Translation by Joel Bollinger Pouwels

great ideals of supreme redemption; and if this time it will fight exclusively for the victory of the candidates chosen and supported by the Convention, it is because it understands that without removing the first obstacle it is impossible to proceed.

If Gen. Díaz has been a formidable obstacle to a simple democratic system, how much more he will be for a social transformation that makes the world's tyrants tremble.

We could surmount that obstacle and follow the march toward the immensity of our ideals; but how many could do the same? Very few, certainly. We are in full possession of our freedom, in full use of our rights, fully exercising our sovereignty; for us who have broken all the yokes, who have torn off all the chains, who have thrown off the weight of all worries and prejudices, who ignore all fears and despise all cowardice, for us there is no possible tyranny; and that is enough for us to be totally free.

However, how many others could be free as we are if in this horribly oppressed country even the notion of liberty has been lost?

What idea of sovereignty over oneself can each one here have where the sovereignty of a whole people is ignored?

It is crazy to believe that a people tied to the post of all ignorance, oppressed beneath the weight of all tyrannies and devoured by all miseries, might continue on its march to join the passing parade of freedom without pausing first to rip off its bonds.

No; if we want these people to follow us to that distant redemption, it is necessary to help them to break their chains: this is what we are doing as we fight the Dictatorship of Gen. Diaz; this is what we are doing to achieve the victory of the popular slate of candidates.

Therefore, upon dedicating itself to fighting exclusively on behalf of the candidates of the Convention, *Vésper* is neither abdicating nor compromising its principles; it is simply pausing to remove the boulder that is blocking the road.

The entire nation is interested in that removal and while we could leave that task to others, assured that it would be carried out; but we neither want nor should do so: it is beneath us to wait for others to open the way forward.

Do not think that we believe (as do many dupes whose names we can cite) that in order for the people to be free it is enough to replace Gen. Diaz with just anyone; it is well known that *Vésper* has been alone in resisting a crazed and excited crowd, when actions were a farce, words a lie and the men a threat to that same crowd that in order to escape from present danger did not perceive another greater danger for the future; no one can say that words confuse us, that personalities dazzle us, that public opinion hypnotizes us; no; we have already said before: “the fall of a tyrant is not the fall of tyranny” and if we come to fight this resolutely and spontaneously so that Mr. Madero will occupy the Presidency of the Republic, it is because Mr. Madero inspires our most complete confidence respecting the objectives that he pursues, it is because we hold the conviction that the fortunes of this unhappy country will improve once Mr. Madero is leading its destiny; and as long as nothing occurs to change our opinion, *Vésper* will always occupy its post beside those who fight for the victorious candidate of the Great Convention.

—Juana B. Gutiérrez de Mendoza

CHAPTER FIVE

Mi grano de arena en esa hermosa labor

Hermila Galindo's Feminationalist Rhetoric

Mujeres latinoamericanas: ¡ojalá mi voz, aunque débil, pero que es respetable porque resuena en defensa de altos principios, halle eco en vuestros corazones!

Women of Latin America: I hope that my voice, although weak, but respectable because it resounds in defense of high principles, resonates within your hearts!

—HERMILA GALINDO, *LA DOCTRINA CARRANZA Y EL ACERCAMIENTO INDOLATINO*

During the Mexican Revolution, Hermila Galindo brought the concept of feminism to a much larger audience in Mexico and Latin America, and, like Gutiérrez de Mendoza, pushed the boundaries of what it meant to be a woman in Mexico.[1] While more women were writing for the public, civic oratory was still strictly reserved for the male bastion of the Mexican intelligentsia. Galindo ignored the antifeminine critiques and claimed a puesto in public speaking, serving on special assignment as spokeswoman for the Constitutionalist president of Mexico, Venustiano Carranza, from 1914 to 1920.[2] As a presidential spokeswoman, she sharpened her oratory skills at conferences she organized, in speeches she presented, and in feminist clubs she managed throughout Mexico. More importantly, because of her political backing, her feminist rhetoric was emboldened on many discursive fronts, such as in her progressive women's magazine, *La Mujer Moderna* (The Modern Woman) (1915). Her rhetorical contributions rest in the

Figure 5. Masthead of Hermila Galindo's newspaper, *La Mujer Moderna*, dedicated to women and women's issues. It first appeared in September 1915 in Mexico City.

intellectual vigor of reasoning, scientific backing, and political relations strategically combined with feminism and nationalism. Until Galindo's appearance as a political speaker, this style had been absent from women's discourse. Her form of feminism was so intertwined with her nationalist politics that the phrase "feminationalist rhetoric" more aptly describes what she was enacting in her discourse.

Surrounded by male politicians in her official puesto, Galindo championed her own ideas about Mexican nationalism, including a radical and controversial feminism that intersected with the Revolution and the formation of a new constitution.[3] Her ideas were highly influenced by European philosophers, such as social feminist August Bebel, feminine progressivist John Stuart Mill, and German phenomenal philosopher Arthur Schopenhauer. Their ideas filtered into her feminationalist initiative of women taking charge of their sexuality and education. The fluidity of these global concepts mixing and integrating into a Mexican feminist view also contributes to Galindo's mestiza rhetoric. As a representative under President Carranza, she was able to deliver her message of gendered nationality on a much grander scale than women writers before her. Considering this influence, we must ask how she tapped into this political power, and also what level of impact did her interventionist discourse have on societal politics?

In this chapter, I first provide the historical background on Galindo's quick ascension into a prominent political puesto—at the podium. In a short period of time, she was able to position herself among leading male political intellectuals and offer a gendered perspective on the emerging masculine nationalist theories of mestizaje. Galindo's strategic feminist project of combining nationalist discourse with a message of women's emancipation was not new, but Galindo used a strict rhetorical logic to counter her opponents. Through the lens of Mary E. Hawkesworth's theory of feminist rhetorics, I contend that Galindo, with her uncommon level of education, political connections, and experience, moved outside the familiar realm of feminist reactionary discourse to one more grounded in political logic, reason, and, most importantly, imagination. Rhetorical strategies of imagination run parallel with mestiza rhetoric. In Galindo's writing, the rhetorical focus is on situating women within the mestizo nationalist discourse, which calls for their unification as citizens of Mexico. We see this imaginative discourse of mestiza rhetoric as a recurring trope in the speeches she gave at the two feminist congresses held in Yucatán in 1916. This discourse became most pronounced in her speeches during a speaking tour in Cuba. Toward the end of her political career, she wrote a book supporting Carranza, titled *La doctrina Carranza y el acercamiento indolatino* (The Carranza Doctrine: An Indolatino Approach), and later another volume, *Un presidenciable: el general don Pablo González* (Presidential Material: General Don Pablo González). From the former text, I examine Galindo's feminist political rhetoric and the historiographic reframing of women.

Claiming a Political Puesto

Galindo's first inroads into politics came through membership in one of the many liberal clubs that backed the Anti-Re-electionist campaign against Porfirio Díaz. These liberal clubs were important in the formation of a feminist movement in that they opened a *puesto público* for women to become involved with the politics of the Revolution. As official members of these clubs, women were able to practice various skills in shorthand, typing, and oratory. In 1908, Galindo joined one of the many political clubs, and from her connections with other politically minded people, she was given her first assignment as an assistant secretary under the political figure Carlos Patoni, who was collaborating as secretary to the governor of Durango.[4] She later moved to Mexico City to work under General Eduardo Hay, who would subsequently be elected as deputy to the Congress of the Union.[5] Through these appointments, her connections among the politically powerful of Mexico, along with her knowledge of the inner workings of the

Mexican political system, increased exponentially. At this time, her politics connected with feminist ideas that were being fomented. Orellana Trinidad notes that Galindo began reading feminist literature such as *Women in the Past, Present, and Future* (1897) by the German socialist August Bebel and *The Subjection of Women* (1878) by the British philosopher John Stuart Mill.[6] By 1914, she became associated with the Constitutionalist movement, which advocated for the resolution of the revolution to come in the form of a new constitution.

On August 20, 1914, Carranza, the Constitutionalist *primer jefe*, first chief, took control of Mexico. The changing of the guard from Huerta to Carranza put Mexico on the path to redesigning the 1857 constitution, so that it included the Revolutionary principles.[7] This was a pivotal moment in Mexican history. Remarkably, a female orator welcomed the leader to his post. When Carranza made his triumphant entry into Mexico City, Galindo was there to receive him. She had been chosen by the political club Abraham González to publicly welcome Carranza with a special speech.[8] In her speech, she made the flattering comparison between Carranza and Benito Juárez.[9] Impressed with the public flattery and Galindo's rhetorical abilities, Carranza appointed her to serve as his secretary and spokeswoman. She would use this appointment to give speeches in support of Carranza and his Constitutionalist policies, while also espousing a strong feminist agenda.

Considering the limiting politics surrounding women at the time, why was Galindo able to affect Mexico and other parts of Latin America with her words? Why was she afforded the podium when so many women were excluded from speaking in public? If Galindo had not received unwavering patronage from President Carranza and his supporters, such as Salvador Alvarado, governor of Yucatán, would she have become as well-known internationally? Helping Galindo's influence were the societal forces—some emerging, others dissolving—that allowed her to be heard at the national level. I am not implying that the circumstances alone gave her full rhetorical agency. It was more of a rhetorical interplay between structural constraints and individual volition that allowed Galindo whirlwind success. She rose to notoriety during a time when women in Latin America, the United States, and Europe were slowly gaining a greater access to the public sphere. She had good timing on her side and was part of this developing movement.

The Mexican Revolution, which was still raging when Galindo took the puesto público, had unquestionably fractured the role of women in society.[10] Women had begun to break out of their confining puestos. At the time, it was not uncommon to see women on the battlefield alongside their men or organizing feminist political clubs. Another significant question regarding the gendered politics of the time includes whether Carranza believed that women could win the vote. I don't believe he truly thought that women could gain suffrage, but his sentiments regarding gender issues were progressive. Indeed, Carranza understood the importance of women gaining a voice and having them speak in favor of the Constitutionalist movement. He knew that Galindo's appointment would garner attention for Mexico from Latin American countries and other international communities that were already publicly discussing women's issues. As the Mexican Revolution was erupting in 1910 and women were evident in the streets and battlefields, two hundred South American women from Peru, Chile, Uruguay, Paraguay, and Argentina gathered in Buenos Aires for the first Congreso Femenino Internacional.[11] Out of the United States there were reports of increased feminist activity in the form of speeches and parades from the National American Woman Suffrage Association, at one time under the direction of Susan B. Anthony. These speeches and parades were directed at pushing for reforms and the vote for women at the state and national levels.[12] From a global perspective, Mexico lagged behind its Latin American and international counterparts in the area of feminine national progress. Galindo's appointment, along with Carranza's policies in favor of women, would bring much-needed positive international attention to Mexico.

As a public rhetor, Galindo did not take her puesto lightly. She not only recognized her social privilege but also considered the possible lack of ethos she projected. Years after her appointment, she publicly reflected on her self-doubts before taking on the position.

> Simpatizadora yo, y no sólo simpatizadora sino defensora de las nuevas ideas sociológicas reveladas al pueblo por el señor Carranza, tuve que seguir naturalmente la ruta marcada por él, es decir abandonar la lucha meramente ideológica para lanzarme a la brega práctica, a la que produce resultados efectivos, a la que de hecho tendrá que traer el mejoramiento político de nuestra patria.
>
> ¿Pero—se preguntará el lector—puede acaso una mujer, por mejor buena voluntad que la anime, por más acendrado que sea su patriotismo, acometer empresa semejante? ¿Puede acaso una mujer, y más si ésta es mexicana inmiscuirse en asuntos trascendentales? ¿Puede tratar problemas que hasta hoy, entre nosotros, sólo han podido ser estudiados por el sexo fuerte? . . .
>
> Pues bien, esas preguntas que de seguro se han hecho los lectores, me las formulé a mí misma antes de acometer tamaña labor, pero una

> sola palabra—la palabra mágica . . . que todo se consigue en la vida: la palabra VOLUNTAD—, grabándose en mi cerebro, me impulsó a no desistir de la resolución que había tomado.[13]

> As a sympathizer, and not only a sympathizer but also a defender of the new sociological ideas made known to the people by Mr. Carranza, I certainly had to follow the path marked by him, that is to say, give up the purely ideological fight in order to undertake practical hard work, which produces effective results, which in fact must bring about the political improvement of our nation.
>
> But—the reader may wonder—can a woman, no matter if the best goodwill may drive her, or how untarnished her patriotism might be, undertake such a mission? Can a woman, and especially if she is Mexican, get involved in transcendental matters? Can she deal with problems among us that, to date, have been only studied by the stronger sex? . . .
>
> Well, those questions that readers have surely asked themselves, I asked them of myself before embarking on such a sizeable undertaking. But a single word—the magic word . . . that achieves everything in life: the word DETERMINATION—, etched in my brain, emboldened me to not give up my commitment.

Galindo was not ignorant of the critics and the antifeminist sentiments in Mexico or abroad, nor was she rhetorically naïve about the implications of her words. In this self-reflective statement, I see her claiming a rhetorical agency that positioned her voluntarily as part of, but separate from, the government puesto she accepted. Galindo's sentiments reflect an awareness of the gendered third space, a feminism-in-nationalism, which Emma Pérez articulates. Pérez theorizes that major historical events like the Mexican Revolution "show that women's politics may have been subordinated under a nationalist paradigm, but women as agents have always constructed their own spaces interstitially."[14] Indeed, Galindo was enacting her own gendered agency in creating a puesto within the structure of the government. I believe, though, that Galindo's projects of nationalism and feminism are far more intertwined than Pérez's feminism-in-nationalism implies.

I propose the term *feminationalism* to represent the strong link between the two "-isms." From the strategic ideological links, Galindo claimed a puesto from which not only to act but also to create a new possibility and reality for women in the social sphere. Galindo's personal and rhetorical agency was not a wellspring of power that came from her being an individual subject, but rather was connected to sociomaterial conditions.

As speaking subjects, we are always already situated within a system of influence at varying levels. Hence, agency is always socially and situationally contingent. Although Galindo was a well-educated Mexican female, without Carranza's governmental support it would have been difficult for her to garner the nationwide audience and ethos she enjoyed.[15]

Beginning in 1914 and extending until 1920, Galindo's career expanded exponentially after her appointment under Carranza. She spoke almost daily to the public and took the position as editor of her own weekly magazine, *La Mujer Moderna* (1915–20). Before the publication appeared, however, Galindo accompanied Carranza to Veracruz, where she delivered her first of many speeches, titled "La reivindicación de la mujer mexicana" (The Redemption of the Mexican Woman), which also appeared in the local paper, *El Dictamen*.[16] This speech, in which she expressed her strong feminist affiliations, launched her speaking tour. In the months ahead, she gave speeches and organized conferences around Mexico. Each time she took to the podium, she defended the Constitutionalist position of Carranza and inflected her own directional feminist discourse into the current national politics. The conferences she organized were held to form feminist organizations whose goal was to "despertar a la mujer para que sea un elemento útil a su Patria, a su pueblo y a ella misma y ayudar a consolidar al gobierno dando un ejemplo al mundo . . . sostenidos por la más noble y más justa de las revoluciones en México" (awaken women to be useful components for their homeland, for their people, and for themselves and to help consolidate the government by setting an example for the world . . . supported by the most noble and most just of the revolutions in Mexico).[17] Another short piece written by Galindo, and published under the title "La mujer como colaboradora en la vida pública" (The Woman as Collaborator in Civic Life), included references to the capacity of women in Mexican society to become educated and move outside their prescribed roles. Galindo's new puesto público as speaker and organizer solidified her nationwide reputation as spokeswoman for a revolutionary feminist ideal.

Political Feminist Rhetoric

Galindo's rhetoric was radically feminist and political, taking on various levels of social and cultural complexity. It was immersed in a nationalist and revolutionary discourse and also included numerous allusions to biblical and religious figures. She strategically tied these allusions and rhetorical tropes in with nationalist and feminist appeals. The ruling faction in

Mexico, which Galindo supported, ardently opposed the Catholic Church. The rhetorical strategy of sanctifying the nationalist movement was used to replace the influence of the church with that of the nation. If we look more deeply into the rhetorical strategies Galindo used to express her national message, two types of feminist rhetoric emerge: one based in reason and one based in vision. These two approaches are the final two levels that political theorist Mary Hawkesworth hypothesizes are political feminist rhetorical strategies.[18] According to Hawkesworth, the four levels of politically charged feminist rhetorics include the rhetorics of oppression, difference, reason, and vision. Hawkesworth's theory provides feminist rhetorics with an epistemological position in which they "call worlds into being, inscribe new orders of possibility, validate frames of reference and forms of explanation, and reconstitute histories."[19] Galindo's rhetoric aptly fits within this frame because her goals were to shift the existing male politics of Mexico. As part of the intellectual class, Galindo used reason and vision as rhetorical tactics to project women into a distinct future where they were politically active citizens instead of subjects defined by the church and the national patriarchy.

Viewing Galindo's discourse through the lens of these strategies is especially helpful to elucidate the complex nature of how Mexican women were engaging the public. Galindo's discourse rose above the reactionary response of anger and victimization, a characterization of the rhetoric of oppression. Gutiérrez de Mendoza's discourse is an example of a rhetoric identified by this characterization. As an entry-level trope to a discussion on feminist rights, the rhetoric of oppression has the potential to disconnect women from valuable dialogue and to locate them within an emotional and impulsive sphere. Women in this position risk distancing and alienating the audience from their cause.

The feminist claims that prevailed in Mexico at the turn of the century and into the second decade functioned within the rhetoric of difference, which separated men and women on the basis of their biology, physiology, and psychology—in other words, as sexed beings. As we saw in chapter 3, the rhetoric of Las Mujeres de Zitácuaro fell under this construct. They believed that a woman's ultimate accomplishment for their nation was through procreation. Framed within the rhetoric of difference, this belief was based in the popular concept of marianismo, a form of feminism that claimed connection to the nation through women's domesticity and motherhood. Hawkesworth notes that "[w]ithin the rhetoric of difference, women are forewarned that in unreflectively attempting to imitate men, they may well destroy the best in themselves."[20] Mexican male journalists and writers of the time also adopted this strategy. Writers such as Horacio Barreda, for example, warned that Protestant feminism would unravel Mexican women's motherly feminine identities in a 1909 series of articles titled "Estudio sobre el feminismo" (A Study on Feminism), published in *La Revista Positiva* (The Positivist Journal).[21]

Within this discourse, the woman's role is predicated on an agency that relies on her biological capacity, not on her ability to act or reason. It can also have the effect of locking women into extenuating cultural circumstances that create dire situations, such as prostitution. The rhetoric of difference was a mechanism for women's survival in a heavily patriarchal society because at the turn of the twentieth century, the societal stage was not yet ready to accept women in any other puesto beyond the domestic space. As we will see in the analysis of the papers and proceedings from the Mexican feminist congresses, many Mexican women were still tied to this cultural framework and would be for some time to come. However, Galindo would attempt to shift the discourse.

Forgoing the rhetoric of oppression and difference, Galindo used the rhetoric of reason, bolstered by scientific fact, to argue for a new position for women in the public sphere. For centuries Mexican women had been kept naïve about the functions of their bodies and sexuality. This practice allowed men to control the social order. Galindo espoused the natural order concept of "scientific morality," which was based on teachings of psychologists, sociologists, and other emerging sciences of the time.[22] Her arguments asked Mexican women to rationally consider their societal positions and imagine a greater future for themselves through education about their own sexuality. We see this reasoning stated many times in her writings. In her response written for the Second Feminist Congress of Yucatán she states:

> No, señores, las ideas cualesquiera que ellas sean, deben pasar por el tamiz del propio criterio, deben de cruzar bajo las horcas caudinas de un razonamiento frío; sólo de este modo puede llegar a poseerse la verdad, así sea en la dosis relativa a que puede aspirar la humanidad imperfecta.[23]

> No, ladies and gentlemen, ideas, whatever they might be, should be sifted through one's own convictions, should be inevitably confronted with cold reasoning; only in this way can truth be possessed, although it might be in the corresponding dose to which imperfect humanity can aspire.

Throughout her speeches, and especially in her writing in *La* doctrina *Carranza y el acercamiento indolatino*, she constantly, overtly, and stylistically references scientific reason. She cites August Bebel, Jacques Novicow, Immanuel Kant, and many others throughout her writings.[24] However, she did not rely merely on reason. Even logic has its limits. One cannot merely reason her way out of a current reality. To make changes requires a vision of the future. The capacity to re/vision reality is the ultimate feminist rhetorical strategy from Hawkesworth's theory. The rhetoric of vision is based on a self-reflective position between thought and language and aims at de/centering the master narrative of patriarchal superiority. Within this strategy, an imagination of the possible, in spite of difficult inscribed realities, prevails. "In targeting the imagination as the primary site of ideological struggle, the rhetoric of vision consciously engages in the literary production of reality . . . recoding the dominant cultural symbols constitutes the key to future social transformation."[25] Invention, myth, allegory, countermyth and narrative, and historiography emerge from this strategy. These elements of the rhetoric of vision are powerful in that they challenge the supposed master narrative. Throughout the twelve years in her puesto, speaking to the public, Galindo wrote of and embodied the counternarrative of women by thinking and working outside the traditional gendered framework. She provided a radical model for women to consider. This is why I position Galindo's discourse between the rhetoric strategies of reason and of vision.

Also a feminist political project, mestiza rhetoric overlaps conceptually with the rhetorics of reason and vision. The scholars of nationalist rhetoric during Galindo's time, such as Ezequiel Chávez, Justo Sierra, and Andrés Molina Enríquez, claimed to base their reason in the hard sciences.[26] They espoused a nationalist and ultimately racist project of mestizaje, which proposed a new national race that was to unify all the Latin American countries. This philosophy was especially relevant during the five years Galindo was writing and speaking, 1915 to 1920. With the Revolution drawing to an end, the concept of national unity became more prevalent, and many believed that mestizaje was the answer to the disjunction among the people.

Philosophers such as Vasconcelos and Sierra recognized the difficulty of a multitude of races assimilating into one people. In opposition, they proposed the mixing of races to prevail as the norm. However, ultimately, their proposal left the indigenous race behind, rendered as an afterthought. This philosophy historicized a variable past of Mexico, based in the indigenous and Spanish races and brought together in a *cosmic*, even sacred, mix in the present. Joshua Lund summarizes the ultimate goal of the mestizaje: "Mexico, or more expansively, Latin America, represents the beginnings of the final phase of humanity's mission . . . [to] enable the emergence of a final race that will include elements of all races."[27] Characterized between the rhetoric of reason and vision, the theory of mestizaje was mostly accepted. It promoted the creation of a hybrid race based on the sciences of the time and was used to legitimize the prophetic dream the scholars had of a unified race. Galindo, like Wright de Kleinhans, embraced this national idealist concept. She wove into the master narrative the participation of both the overarching male mestizo citizen and the mestiza.

Tired of the limiting discourses surrounding women, Galindo came onto the Mexican journalistic scene on September 15, 1915, as editor of *La Mujer Moderna*. The feminism she argued for was just enough outside of mainstream thought to cause serious controversy. The release date of the journal coincided with Mexico's Independence Day. This strategic selection expressed a symbolic connection between the nationalist project and the feminist agenda. Galindo's contributions to mestiza rhetoric heralded a new form of gendering the patriotic experience on the symbolic release date of her feminist publication. In the opening phrases of the journal, in a piece titled "¡Laboremos!" (Let's Get to Work!), Galindo reiterated a crystallization of her message: women wanted to be part of the nation as much as men already were.

> Deseamos honrar este aniversario de redención, inaugurando nuestras tareas periodísticas, con las que deseamos coadyudar [*sic*] a la redención de la patria, la redención de los principios salvadores y la redención de la mujer, levantando el espíritu femenino a la altura de su deber y su derecho, para que no permanezca por más tiempo impacible [*sic*] ante la solución de los más trascendentales problemas sociales y políticos, que afectan tanto al hombre como a la mujer, que es su compañero e igual.[28]

> We wish to honor this anniversary of redemption, by initiating our journalistic undertakings, the ones toward which we desire to work conjointly, toward the redemption of our homeland, the redemption of the saving principles and the redemption of women, by raising the feminine spirit to the same level as her duty and her right, so that she will no longer remain impassive regarding the solution of the most transcendental social and political problems, which affect men as much as women, who are his companions and equals.

This introduction equalizes the relationship between men and women. It also links the salvation of "la Patria" to the salvation of women and vise versa.

Figure 6. Hermila Galindo's goal for *La Mujer Moderna* was to feature Mexican women engaged in activities that were nontraditional for the time, such as writing, law, politics, and entertainment. In this October 31, 1915, edition, the female poet Julia D. Febles Cantón vda. de Palomeque appears on the cover.

Galindo and the contributing women writers of *La Mujer Moderna* focused on reporting and analyzing women from diverse social classes, such as the poet Julia D. Febles Contón vda. de Palomeque, who appeared on one of the covers.[29] Other women who were honored in the pages were Señorita Doctora Sarah Zenil, a professor in Mexico, and Esther López Mora, a teacher of the piano, violin, and mandolin. This approach of offering model professional lives of other women to their audience was similar to the strategy Wright de Kleinhans used in *Las Hijas del Anáhuac*. Where *Las Hijas del Anáhuac* was upholding the ideal of "angel of the home," Olivia Noguez Noguez notes that in *La Mujer Moderna* Galindo's writing from a revolutionary puesto was able to push the boundaries of this feminine construct.[30] The Mexican Revolution radically shifted women's presence in the public puestos, and the shift in possibilities was reflected by Galindo and other contributors' writings. Part of the change in rhetorical puestos came in women entering the public debates and conversations about the ideals, such as suffrage, that they felt should be included in the new constitution.

Women's suffrage seemed attainable for Galindo, her peers, and their supporters because of their unprecedented political and civic participation. She captured a strategic moment in history in the rising feminist movements around the globe. Galindo thought Mexican women capable of mixing their voices with those from the international community. Women were already taking part in the Revolution on and off the battlefield. They were rebuilding and re/imaging Mexico for future generations. They were voicing their opinions as never before in the public arena for several years before the final vote of the new constitution. The date for the Constitutional Convention had not been set, yet factions were building on all sides and vying for the inclusion of their principles in the new constitution. Suffrage movements in Europe and the United States were well publicized, and women felt that the moment was right to ask for the vote. On October 31, 1915, *La Mujer Moderna* included an article titled "Por qué deben votar las mujeres" (Why Women Should Vote), by Clarisa Pacheco de Torres. It reads:

> Las mujeres deben votar: Porque es justo y bueno que las que obedecen las leyes tengan voz para hacerlas. . . . Porque la educación moral y la legislación humanas deseadas por las mujeres se adquirirían más fácilmente si las mujeres votasen. Porque las leyes injustas para la mujeres serían muy pronto reformadas. En Massachusetts y Colorado (Estados Unidos) las madres de familia están consideradas ante la ley, iguales a los padres

> en materia de tutela. . . . Porque la igualdad del sufragio aumentará la proporción de los votantes educados.[31]

> Women should vote: Because it is just and good that those who obey the laws should have a voice in making them. . . . Because unjust laws for women would be very quickly reformed. In Massachusetts and Colorado (United States) housewives are considered to be equal to fathers before the law, on the subject of custodianship. . . . Because equality of suffrage will increase the proportion of educated voters.

In the statements on suffrage that Galindo repeated in various other articles in *La Mujer Moderna*, such as "La cuestión sufragista: para qué quieren el voto las mujeres" (The Suffragist Question: Why Women Want the Vote) and a speech she gave, "Petición hecha por nuestra directora al H. Constituyente sobre el derecho al voto de la mujer" (Petition Made by Our Director to the Honorable Constituent Regarding Women's Right to Vote), she was promoting a public and civic identity for Mexican women not seen before.[32] There was also an interview with her published in *El Universal* in 1917, "La Srita. Galindo opina sobre su candidatura para diputado" (Miss Galindo Gives Her Opinion Regarding Her Candidacy as Representative).[33] In the latter article, Galindo discusses her official announcement of her candidacy for a seat in the Mexican Congress.[34] The appeals in her arguments ranged from the highest humanitarian visions to logic-driven statistics of women who had been given the vote and citizenship in other countries. Equality with their male counterparts in the personal and the public spheres was also a common argument, and Galindo extolled these ideas in her speeches around the country.

Spreading the Word: Political Speeches in Cuba

Galindo was among the first women in Mexico to be given so much freedom and power at the podium both home and abroad. A lengthy tour of Mexico brought her and her speeches before audiences in places such as Motul, Espita, Mérida, Campeche, Tabasco, and Monterrey.[35] In 1916, after this extensive visit in Mexico, Galindo was invited by President Carranza on a special speaking tour in Cuba.[36] Women were not often given the puesto público at the political podium. So speaking to women of her race in distant lands was extremely significant. Her speeches of antiassimilationist nationalism and feminism were delivered to mixed audiences of working-class and military-minded men along with numerous women.[37] Some audiences were solely men. Others were comprised only of women. Galindo adapted and varied her appeals accordingly as she spoke with each audience.

Contextually, each of Galindo's speeches and newspaper articles intersected with the current politics of Mexico.[38] The struggle for power between Revolutionary political and military factions, such with the Villistas in the north and the Zapatistas in the south, continued. A power struggle with the United States over natural resources was also part of the political negotiations. Relations with Mexico's northern neighbor vacillated when Carranza announced a strong nationalist stance, which threatened the petroleum and mining resources the United States had secured under Díaz. In September 1916, while Galindo was delivering speeches in Havana, Cuba, under Carranza's directives, he announced the Constitutional Convention that was to be held in the city of Querétaro in December.

In the moments that she was speaking in Cuba, the power struggle, both political and gendered, was an omnipresent reality that permeated her discourse. As was Galindo's custom, she conveyed her own message of a Mexican and Latin American feminine ideal. Full of emotion and near disbelief that she was in Cuba addressing a group of her compatriots, she opened her speech with the Latin word *adum*, meaning, "I am present; I am here."

> ADUM; sí, heme aquí; heme aquí, por fin, a vuestro lado; heme aquí en medio de vosotras; mi sueño de muchos días háse [*sic*] cumplido, por ventura mía; el instante solemne que tantas veces había previsto en mis horas de gratas y luminosas ensoñaciones, ha llegado a la postre; y yo, la modesta escritora mexicana, la empedernida bohemia de ardiente sangre azteca, encuéntrome [*sic*], al fin, en el seno de un cultísimo grupo de hijas de la encantador Isla, con justa razón apellidada la Perla de la Antillas.[39]

> Truly, I am here; I am here at last, at your side; I am here among you; my long-held dream has come true, because of my good fortune; the solemn moment that I had envisioned so many times in my hours of pleasant and enlightened imaginings, has finally arrived; and I, this humble Mexican writer, the inveterate bohemian of ardent Aztecan blood, I find myself, at last, in the presence of a learned assembly of daughters of this enchanting Island, with just reason called the Pearl of the Antilles.

In her speech, Galindo encapsulated the sense of what it meant for a Mexican woman at that moment in history to be addressing her Latin sisters. Through Galindo's words, at times overly poetic and linguistically antiquated, we can feel the weight of Mexican women's centuries of censure and oppression being lifted, if only momentarily. She was fully aware of the (en)gendered significance of speaking in public, and she used her rhetorical skills to enhance the feminine of her race. With almost excess emotion, she outwardly expressed the essence and vision of what it meant to be mexicana. She mentioned her racial origins in "ardent Aztecan blood," situating her within the greater tradition of mestizaje. With rhetorical ease, Galindo connected mestizaje with the feminine "modesta escritora."

A few days later, in another speech, she declared the unification of the Latin American race in defense against their "common enemy."[40]

> Hoy que me encuentro entre vosotros, ¡oh hijos de Cuba! y que sé que también amáis intensamente las tradiciones, los ensueños, el idioma de la raza a la que felizmente pertenecemos, vengo a deciros aunque sea en mi torpe lenguaje de mujer inculta, que es preciso, si queremos seguir existiendo, que nos agrupemos bajo una misma bandera: nuestros ideales latinos formando así un grupo de naciones, prestas a defenderse mutuamente, cuando en son de combate se presente el enemigo común.[41]

> Today I find myself among you, oh sons and daughters of Cuba, and I know that you also love intensely the traditions, the dreams, the language of the people to whom we fortunately belong, I come to tell you, although it is in the clumsy speech of an uneducated woman, that it is essential, if we want to keep on existing, that we form a group under an identical flag: our Hispanic ideals, in such a way forming a group of nations, quick to mutually defend each other, whenever with intentions of combat our common enemy appears.

In these speeches, we see Galindo use the lofty, almost pompous, Spanish vernacular. Although this was the custom in political speech, she was constrained by her directive under Carranza, even putting herself down by saying she spoke in "the clumsy speech of an uneducated woman." These phrases were used as rhetorical strategies to appeal to those in her audience who may have believed women to be ignorant and incapable of public oratory.

Galindo's purposeful rhetoric directed to the people of Cuba also consistently connected with the ideals of mestiza rhetoric. She made reference to the unifying elements of the mestizo race—traditions, dreams, and language—setting them apart from any Western tradition. The greater call to a renewed Latin American unification was an overt critique of the dominant stories of assimilation. These statements point to the power struggle between U.S. President Wilson and Carranza, with Mexico's president refusing to politically acquiesce to the United States' demands for petroleum and landholding rights.

Galindo's historic visit to Cuba fell in between the First and Second Feminist Congresses of Yucatán. The first was held in January 1916, followed by the next congress in November of that same year. Through Galindo's political connections with Carranza, she was asked to present the main speech at each congressional meeting. Ironically, unknown circumstances kept her from attending these historic gatherings, yet her rhetoric historically remains the center of controversy.

Taking Sides: The Feminist Congresses of Mexico

In October 1915, Salvador Alvarado, Carranza's military governor of Yucatán, initiated the organization of the First Feminist Congress of Yucatán to be held January 1916 and another at the end of the year. The two feminist congresses of Yucatán marked a groundbreaking moment for the feminist movement in Mexico. Many historical accounts paint Alvarado as a progressive and outspoken governor, endorsing education for women and the indigenous plantation workers.[42] He accomplished a great deal to promote education in Yucatán during his time in office.[43] For example, literacy rates soared among men and women from every economic class because schools were opened on the haciendas and in other locations. Along with education reforms, Alvarado made it clear that he was a supporter of women's issues and wanted to put the women on a path of equality before the law. Women were encouraged to take jobs outside of library work, teaching, and needlework. Single women were released from having to stay at home until they were thirty in decree number 167, which came to be called the "Feminist law."[44] Alvarado also held several congresses on education and work between 1915 and 1918, allowing open debates on progressive ideas.[45]

On the one hand, with laws such as decree number 167 and open debates on social issues, it was evident that Alvarado wanted women to be self-sustaining and educated, but he also held a traditionalist concept of the role women's education should play in society.[46] Much of the nation felt that women should be educated, but there was pervasive ambiguity regarding how far women could reach for their independence. The revolutionary rhetoric of individualistic ideals fell short if women truly claimed the ideals. These ambiguities emerged at the First and Second Feminist Congresses, where Galindo promoted women's rights to sex education and suffrage, while others believed that women were educated in order to sustain the home and to remain faithful to the teachings of the Catholic Church. Galindo would express her disdain for those who maintained the latter.

Alvarado invited Galindo to deliver a speech at the First and Second Feminist Congresses, held in January and November 1916, respectively. He allowed the women to organize the conference, and Consuelo Zavala was selected by her peers as the president of the directing body of the event.[47] However, the governor posed these overarching questions to be the thematic focus of the conference.

I. What social means should be employed to release women from the yoke of tradition?
II. What is the role of the primary school in the revindication of women, since the aim of the school is to prepare one for life?
III. What arts and occupations ought the state to promote and maintain whose aim is to prepare women for the dynamic life of progress?
IV. What public functions can and should women undertake, to empower them to be, not simply a guided element, but also a guiding one in society?[48]

Many women who were assigned to prepare resolutions and responses to the questions resigned their puestos. These papers were to be read aloud in public and heavily debated, and women were not accustomed to speak publicly, hence the prospect of having to speak in front of an audience frightened many of the young women. For many women, domestic consequences from fathers or spouses awaited after they followed through with these positions. Nevertheless, the congress afforded women an opportunity to enact civic discourse as had never before been allowed in Mexico.

With Galindo's standing as a government diplomat, she was given time to articulate her feminist ideals among the 620 delegates from around Yucatán. However, she was not able to attend. Galindo's speech, "La mujer en el porvenir" (The Woman in the Future), was read by Señor César A. González to a restricted audience of literate women, mostly middle-class teachers.[49]

> La profecía del Evangelio se ha cumplido. "Los tiempos han llegado." "Bienaventurados los que han hambre y sed de justicia porque ellos serán hartos." Como el minero cava la tierra hasta sus más recónditas

profundidades para extraer de sus entrañas sus codiciados tesoros; . . . así la revolución constitucionalista, una vez obtenido el triunfo de sus armas, comienza a hacer tangibles sus ideales, a convertir en *hechos* sus *promesas*, a transformar la teoría en acción.[50]

The prophecy of the Gospel has come true. "The hour has come." "Blessed are those who hunger and thirst for justice, for they will be satisfied." Just as the miner excavates the most hidden depths of the Earth to extract its coveted treasures . . . in this way the Constitutionalist revolution, having achieved military victory, begins to make its ideals tangible, to convert its promises into deeds, to transform theory into action.

The reference to the national movement as the Gospel was a deliberate rhetorical strategy on the part of the Constitutionalists. This type of identification that connects with, but is separate from, an idea can best be seen through a Burkean lens of consubstantiality. Kenneth Burke states that one object, in this case the Gospel, although separate from the Constitution, is used in order to show an acting together, "and in acting together, men have common sensations, concepts, images, ideas, attitudes that make them consubstantial."[51] Although Galindo espoused antireligious ideas and ontologies, she knew that the majority of the audience was devoutly Catholic. By framing the Constitutionalist message with religious overtones, she may have made the message more easily accepted or considered.

The religious allusions in her speech shift to citations of European social theorists such as Kant and Schopenhauer in support of women's education and sexuality. The radical ideals in this section of the speech drew both extreme criticism and intense approval from conservative and liberal attendees, respectively. Statements such as the following on open sexual understanding for women were part of the reason her speech was voted to be banned.

Cuando Aristóteles consideraba como principio fundamental de educación que el cuerpo debía ser formado primero y el espíritu después, *mens sana in corpore sano*, sabía positivamente que nada existe ni daña tanto el instinto sexual en la mujer, como el cultivo de las funciones espirituales: ante todo, el gran filósofo era un fisiólogo.

Si la mujer en vez de exceso de sensibilidad que preconiza el escritor citado, tuviese una buena dosis de razón sólida y supiese pensar y discurrir justo; si en lugar de ser neurótica y tímida rebosara valor físico y cultivase el músculo y el glóbulo sanguíneo, si poseyese como quiere Stuart Mill, la ciencia del mundo de los hombres y de las fuerzas de la naturaleza, en vez de ignorar completamente cómo se vive y tener sólo la forma y la etiqueta de lo bello, la mujer sería más dichosa y el hombre más honrado.

Generalmente se procura en la mujer el desarrollo de lo que se llama vida del corazón y del alma, mientras se descuida y omite el desarrollo de su razón. Resulta de esto que padece una hipertrofia de vida intelectual y espiritual y es más accesible a todas las creencias religiosas; su cabeza ofrece un terreno fecundo a todas las charlatanerías religiosas y de otro género y es material dispuesta para todas las reacciones.

El vulgo de los hombres quéjase de ello, porque personalmente lo sufre, pero nadie actúa, pues están petrificados en el prejuicio y les asusta un cambio radical en las leyes y una completa modificación en las costumbres.[52]

When Aristotle considered a fundamental principle of education to be that the body should be trained first, before the spirit, *mens sana in corpora sano*, he knew without question that nothing damages the woman's sexual instinct as much as cultivating her spiritual functions: above all, the great philosopher was a physiologist.

If the woman were to have a good dose of solid reason and if she could think and express herself well, instead of having an excess of sensitivity prescribed by the above-cited writer; if instead of being neurotic and timid, she were brimming with physical strength and building muscles and healthy red-blood cells, if she had, as Stuart Mill wants, science from men's world and from nature's forces, instead of being completely ignorant about how one lives and having only the form and manners of beauty, then woman would be more content and man more respected.

Generally, we nurture the development in women of what is called the life of the heart and soul, while we neglect and ignore the development of her reason. The result of this is that she suffers a hypertrophy of intellectual and spiritual life, and she is more vulnerable to all religious beliefs; her head offers fertile ground for all manner of religious and other quackeries, and she is disposed to fickle reactions.

The ordinary man complains about women's lack of reason, because he suffers from it personally, but nobody acts, since all are paralyzed by prejudice and afraid of a radical change in the laws and a complete modification in customs.

Throughout the speech, Galindo made references to philosophers such as Bebel, Novicow, Kant, and Mill, as well as to the educational history of

Sparta. In citing these philosophers, she believed she was keeping within the realm of science and reason, the antithesis of religious thought. Galindo's feminist political rhetoric throughout the speech relied on both reason and vision. Galindo advocated "open-mindedness" and spoke frankly about prostitution and the double standards in the laws that favor men and condemn women. She advised that to solve this problem, young girls should be taught forthrightly about their sexuality. She called for the "revision of the civil and criminal codes" and pulled back the veil of male hypocrisy in Mexican culture.[53] While she loved her country, she understood the culture's duplicity when it came to women's conduct in society.

> Cuando ésta, fascinada, se entrega en brazos del amante, arrastrada por el ineludible instinto sexual, el hombre queda ante la sociedad como un *calavera* agradable, émulo de Don Juan Tenorio . . . y refiere su hazaña con el tono majestuoso con que haría un Jefe revolucionario el relato de la toma de una plaza. Pero la mujer desdichada que no ha hecho otra cosa que cumplir con una de las exigencias de su instinto . . . es relegada . . . al abismo de la desesperación, de la miseria, de la locura o del suicidio. ¡Cuántas veces la gacetilla da cuenta de la infeliz que, para ocultar su *falta* apeló al crimen matando a su propio hijo! Las estadísticas del delito están llenas de casos de infanticidio y aborto provocado, sin contar con los que quedan ocultos, probando cuánta es la pesadumbre de la *vindicta pública*, en el ánimo de la triste mujer que ha delinquido![54]

> When a woman, mesmerized, surrenders herself to her lover, swept away by the ineluctable sexual instinct, the man stands before society as a kind of agreeable daredevil who emulates Don Juan Tenorio . . . he relates his deed in the majestic tone a revolutionary Chief would use to brag about taking a town. But the wretched woman who has done no more than fulfill one of the imperatives of her instinct . . . is cast . . . into the abyss of despair, misery, insanity, or suicide. How often the local newspaper informs us of the wretch who, to hide her *trouble*, resorted to crime, killing her own child! The crime statistics are full of cases of infanticide and induced abortions, leaving aside the unreported cases, proving the deep grief caused by public censure in the soul of the poor woman who has strayed!

At the close of the speech, the audience reacted "a gritos y sombrerazos," an idiomatic phrase meaning "screaming and yelling."[55] Some, however, applauded enthusiastically. The conflicting and impassioned reactions revealed two competing factions regarding the direction feminism should take in Mexico. On the one hand, there were those who wanted to immediately fulfill the promise of the revolutionary cause, to be freed from the yoke of oppression; and on the other, there were those who still held to the traditionalist ideas. A speech by Francisca García Ortiz shows the conservative position of the congress's attendees.

> It is a fact that it is hard for an educated woman to marry. So I think it is a waste for women to be constantly educated farther along. This learning is an obstacle to women's happiness, and it is a pity that minds so beautiful, souls so noble, should not raise progeny who might bring to fulfillment (in the future) our present desires, achieving the pinnacle of civilization. . . . Let us never forget that the woman should always be the delight of the home, the gentle comrade of man.[56]

As a counterargument to Galindo's position, García Ortiz held to the Victorian perspective that women should be the "delight of the home." The conservative group that shared García Ortiz's view of women reacted by demanding that Galindo's speech be expunged from the congressional minutes, calling it "immoral" and "evil." Ultimately, reason prevailed, and the speech remained on the record.

The conference continued with various speeches and concluded with debates on each question posed by Alvarado. Zavala emerged as the unifying voice of the conference. She spoke beyond the ideological premises and brought a practical consensus to the competing factions, who agreed that civil code reforms for property and child rights were needed. Despite the uproar from Galindo's speech, she was invited to speak at the Second Feminist Congress later that year. Again, she was not present to read and respond to her own words. Present or not, she produced a speech that demonstrated her full rhetorical and intellectual skills.

Her second speech, a clear reaction and rebuttal to the congress's attempt to silence her, was read by Elena Torres and titled "Estudio de la Srita. Hermila Galindo con motivo de los temas que han de absolverse en el Segundo Congreso Feminista de Yucatán" (A Study by Miss Hermila Galindo on the Occasion of the Topics to Be Resolved in the Second Feminist Congress of Yucatán). In it Galindo responded indignantly yet rationally to the attempts at the previous congress to silence her first speech.[57] Immediately, in the introduction, Galindo summoned the intellectual mestiza whom all Mexican women admire, Sor Juana Inés de la Cruz. After writing openly for years, Sor Juana finally gave in to the male clergy and was voluntarily silenced, but not until she submitted her rhetorical masterpiece, *Respuesta a Sor Filotea de la Cruz*, which Galindo may have been trying to emulate. She certainly saw the parallels with the church trying to silence her own ideas about liberating and educating women in Mexico. Galindo cited Sor Juana's historical silenc ing by the church and then quoted three stanzas of her poem "Hombres necios que acusáis" (You Foolish and Accusing Men). Instead of accepting defeat, Galindo mounted a defense: "Yo me defenderé, y la opinión pública, que es el Juez, decidirá sobre Nuestra cuestión" (I will defend myself, and public opinion, which is the Judge, will settle this debate).[58]

In this second speech, Galindo refutes every claim that was made against her first speech by using the method of counterpoint presented in the speech's twenty-nine pages.

> No tuve la satisfacción de que se me demostrara con razonamientos sólidos, que mis ideas eran malas, sino que en nombre de una moral que yo no comprendo, y, tras de cánones de conducta que no se citan, ni mucho menos se defienden, se condenó mi trabajo sin analizarlo, se le calificó de peligroso, se evitó que se le prestara atención, y, más aún, con tono pontifical se pidió que se destruyese como indigno de figurar en una sociedad civilizada.[59]

> I did not have the satisfaction to have it demonstrated to me with solid reasoning, that my ideas were bad, but rather in the name of a moral philosophy that I do not understand, and, following rules of conduct that are not quoted, nor are they in any sense defensible, my work was condemned without being analyzed, it was branded as dangerous, it was prohibited that anyone should pay attention to it, and, furthermore, with pontifical tone it was proposed to be destroyed as unworthy to be a part of a civilized society.

Later in her speech, she asks her audience:

> ¿Inmoral mi trabajo porque basada en los principios en que debe descansar un moral científico, perfectamente inteligente, he reclamado en él mucha ilustración para la inteligencia de mi sexo, mucha educación para su voluntad, e igualdad completa de derechos con el hombre . . . ?[60]

> My work is immoral because based on the principles upon which scientific ethics should rest, perfectly intelligent ones, I have claimed in it much erudition for the intelligence of my sex, much education for its will, and complete equality of rights with men . . . ?

She continues in the same rhetorical mode for several paragraphs, asking her audience a question and then, conversely, providing the reasons why her audience would think her writing immoral. Writing in a tone one would use to speak directly to the reader or listener, she clearly communicates the frustration toward her adversaries' epistemological perspective through her intellectual diction. She cites again the European philosophers she quoted in her first speech, while also bringing in the theories of natural selection of Darwin. She discusses at length the civic laws that should be challenged, condemns the teachings of the Catholic Church that keep women shackled in worldly ignorance, brings to light the cultural and social reality of the "fallen woman" as a creation of the hypocrisy of the laws, and, lastly, calls for women's suffrage.

As Nikki Craske contends, there existed an ambiguity surrounding women's rights, which we see clearly within the discourse of the congresses.[61] Regardless of the failed efforts and the conflicting viewpoints on feminism, the First and Second Feminist Congresses were rhetorically significant. They marked the first time that Mexican women organized a state and then national conference on women's issues. The congresses were an antecedent to the struggle women would face on a national level in the decades to come.

The rhetoric used during the congresses fluctuated between rhetoric of difference and rhetoric of reason. Some women, mostly those with strong ties to the Catholic Church, were trapped within the realm of gendered differences, while some were anxious to leave the traditions behind. To keep women from voting, the government would use the excuse that too many women were too closely tied to the church and would have voted conservatively, therefore skewing the vote away from the liberal tenets. The Feminist Congresses represent an expansion of women's puestos as they were slowly "allowed" to publicly express their opinions on women's issues. Although Galindo's discourse was controversial, she was not silenced. It exposed a new direction for women in Mexico. After the congresses, Galindo continued in the puesto of diplomat, which would open many other opportunities for her to expound upon her beliefs.

Galindo's Puesto in International Politics

While Galindo continued in her position as spokeswoman, she was contracted by the government to write *La doctrina Carranza y el acercamiento indolatino*. This book, the author's second intellectual tour de force, is a political and historical manifesto containing two hundred pages divided into twenty-two chapters. With the intent that this book be delivered to and read by all the governments of Latin America, it situates Carranza as a key figure in Latin American racial and economic politics and defends Mexico as the emerging power that has the potential to unite Latin American countries into the great *patria* that confronts the colonizing empires of Europe and the United States. It also discusses issues of World War I and predicts problems that could arise from world capitalism. Most significantly, it places Galindo on the map of international politics of the time.

Toward the end of the Mexican Revolution, a confrontation of power arose between President Woodrow Wilson and Carranza. Carranza's constitutional and revolutionary politics, which emphasized a unified and self-actualizing Mexico, did not correspond to Wilson's ideal of a liberal-capitalist community in the Western hemisphere. In a close analysis of the political relations between Wilson and Carranza, Gilderhus notes that "Wilson presumed a common purpose with Latin Americans and asked that political leaders subordinate selfish goals to the collective good. If they should refuse, he reserved the right to judge."[62] Wilson called upon the Monroe Doctrine to justify intervention if peace and order were not stabilized in neighboring countries.

This policy incensed the Latin American countries, especially Mexico. Carranza was not afraid to voice that he believed the policy to be a hegemonic power on the part of the United States. Galindo reiterated this position throughout the book. Galindo continually alluded to the colonizing forces of the United States, stating that the "weaker" countries should join and protect themselves against the imperial and dominating influences.[63] Drawing on history, economics, sociology, and revolutionary perspectives, both contemporary and historical, Galindo addressed many of these international issues. She cited an array of works, including those of Shakespeare and Tolstoy, Greek history, and Manabendra Nath Roy's history of England as a colonizing occupation in India, as well as economic scholars, such as Norman Angell, among many other scholarly sources. Coupled with her intellectual endeavor, she kept true to her visionary feminist political agenda and spoke of Mexican women in the realm of politics.

Galindo's political puesto under the auspices of Carranza brought her a thorough understanding of international polemics. *La doctrina* reflects that knowledge. However, in this section, I concentrate on how she intersected her feminist rhetoric of vision with national politics. I apply the rhetoric of vision to Galindo's discourse in her writings in *La doctrina* because, as Hawkesworth contends, this level of rhetoric is self-aware and it "consciously engages in the literary production of reality."[64] "For the rhetoric of vision, recoding the dominant cultural symbols constitutes the key to future social transformation."[65] *La doctrina* was an opportunity to interject a feminine realization of Mexico. This vision of national feminism commences on the opening pages of the text. The first page of the book depicts a stern yet paternal full-page portrait of Carranza. On the next page, there appears a paragraph-long dedication to Señorita Angela Galindo, the aunt who had raised Galindo as if she were her own daughter. Galindo dedicated the following:

> Para ti, a quien doy tan dulce nombre, a pesar de no ser tu hija, sino de manera espiritual, . . . para ti, a quien debo todo lo que soy, supuesto que me educaste cuando niña y me guiaste cuando llegué a mujer; para ti éste mi primer libro . . . fruto de tantos y tantos sinsabores como he pasado en mi vida, sobre todo, en mi vida de luchadora por la emancipación de la mujer de mi país, debido al medio hostil en que la educación ancestral de nuestra sociedad me colocaba.[66]

> For you, to whom I give so sweet a name, in spite of not being your daughter, except in a spiritual way, . . . to you, to whom I owe all that I am, since you educated me when I was a little girl and you guided me when I reached womanhood; . . . for you this, my first book, the fruit of so many tribulations that I have gone through in my life, above all, in my life as a fighter for the emancipation of the women of my country, due to the hostile environment in which the patrimonial education of our society placed me.

All the men of power who opened and read the dedication would have known that the political treatise was written by a woman who had struggled to assume this rhetorical puesto. However, this dedication is not an offering of her political reflection to her assumed mother. It is an intimate acknowledgment of her literary abilities to write and expound on a variety of topics.

Much like Wright de Kleinhans, Galindo was not a trained historian, but after careful study of Mexican history, she recognized a patriarchal slant and an obvious gap that left women silenced. Wright de Kleinhans criticized the archivists for losing the writings of women, and Galindo critiqued historians who lacked a philosophical vision of how the past and present are connected.

> A fuerza de observación y de estudio, he llegado a la conclusión de que son muy pocos los verdaderos historiadores. Especialmente en México se consideran como tales a simples cronistas que se concretan a señalar

fechas, a citar hechos más o menos verídicos y a dar los nombres, aureolados por una especie de mitológica fama.

Ha llegado a ser para mí una verdad absoluta, es decir, un axioma sociológico, la idea de que el verdadero historiador es aquel que sabe expresar filosóficamente el por qué del encadenamiento de los movimientos sociales; que sabe, basándose en el pasado y en el presente, inducir lo que en lo futuro deba efectuarse.[67]

As a result of observation and of study, I have come to the conclusion that there are very few true historians. Especially in Mexico, simple chroniclers are considered as such: those who confine themselves to point out dates, to quote more or less actual facts and to cite names, haloed by a kind of mythological fame.

For me an absolute truth has come to exist, in other words, a sociological axiom, this is the idea that the true historian is one who knows how to express philosophically the why and wherefore of the concatenation of social movements; who knows, by basing himself in the past and in the present, how to derive what should take place in the future.

Galindo heeds her own critique and throughout the book follows each historical event with its implications for the present and future of Mexico. For example, in chapter 6, "El imperialismo comercial, supliendo al derecho de conquista" (Commercial Imperialism, Supplanting the Right of Conquest), Galindo presents a re/visioning of Doña Isabel la Católica as one of the forgotten figures among the names of the conquistadores. Galindo reminds her readers of Doña Isabel's benevolent attitude toward the indigenous people and the maltreatment of them by the male conquistadores. The implications of this historical truth were that women served as the foundation of the unification of la raza as one society.

While she may initially take a strong feminist perspective on polemics, in the end, her discourse falls short of framing women beyond their maternal roles. In the final chapter of *La doctrina*, titled "A la mujer latinoamericana" (To the Latin American Woman), she directly addresses the women of her race. This rhetorical turn emphasizes that the political analyses of the previous twenty-one chapters were directed to a male (or mixed male and female) audience, further accentuating the gendered roles in Mexican politics. The first line reads, "Imperdonable me hubiera parecido terminar esta obra sin dirigirme a las mujeres de mi raza" (It would have been unpardonable for me to end this work without speaking to the women of my race).[68] Although Galindo portrayed a grand image of women as "liberated women," in this chapter she connects women to the nation in the traditional civic puesto of marianismo and slips into the feminist rhetoric of difference. She speaks of women's "inexhaustible fountain of compassion," the "priceless lyricism and love," and continues with how "women later become magnificent mothers, self-sacrificing wives, and gentle companions of men."[69] Hawkesworth notes that the rhetoric of difference "seeks to capitalize upon women's strengths," yet the language is wholly essentializing and can have an effect opposite to liberation.[70] This strategy "may mask the social construction of gender and thereby understate the scope of possible social change."[71] As much as Galindo tried to sustain the rhetoric of reason and vision, the power of societal and political tradition pulled her back.

Conclusion

The fact that in the end Galindo surrendered to these traditionalist views does not mean that her discourse was less than revolutionary. She had set a precedent for many feminists to continue the fight into the 1920s and 1930s and until they received the vote in 1947, and later, the right to stand for election in 1953. However, Galindo would not continue in the fight. She would write one more book, titled *Un presidenciable: El general don Pablo González*, and then would disappear from the public stage. The reason for her disappearance is most likely connected with Carranza's ousting from his presidential chair in May 1920. Shortly thereafter, he was assassinated.[72]

These violent political actions around Carranza reveal the risks that Galindo took in supporting a Revolution-era president whose popularity was waning. Galindo was writing in the middle of a Revolution that had brutal outcomes if one supported the wrong faction. Galindo's governmental support immediately disappeared with Carranza's demise.[73] Could it be that Galindo's rhetoric was so closely tied to the ideology of Carranza that she could not continue? Could it be that she saw the fight to give women the vote and a legitimate puesto in Mexican society as so immense that she dropped out of public view? Instead of moving her discourse forward, she married and moved to the United States, where she spent her remaining years with her daughter, Hermila del Rosario, and engaged in intellectual activities such as writing and painting.[74] She eventually returned to Mexico in 1939 to petition the Mexican ministry for her recognition as a veteran of the Revolution.

Galindo's speeches, journal, and books all form an important part of Mexican feminine rhetorical history. Indeed, Valles Ruiz notes that her writings influenced the direction of public policy and international policy.[75]

Her discourse, at the time radical and unconventional, reveals a direction in feminist activities that set the groundwork for future women to eventually win the right to vote and, above all, to break their silence.

> Por mi parte, estoy satisfecha de efectuar este generoso impulso de mi corazón; estoy tranquila de haber obedecido a los mandatos de mi "yo" moral que me obligaban a no permanecer muda e indiferente en momentos en que se ventilan intereses trascendentales y definitivos para MI RAZA, y durante los cuales es necesaria la colaboración de todos los países enamorados del bien.[76]

> For my part, I am satisfied in carrying out this generous impulse of my heart; I am at peace for obeying the mandates of my moral being, that required me to not remain mute and indifferent in moments when transcendental and definitive issues for MY RACE are being aired, moments that necessitate the collaboration of all nations enamored of goodness.

Galindo's discourse ultimately shows that many Mexican women conceptualized themselves as a central part of their nation, not as mestizos, but as mestizas. Much like Galindo, these women saw themselves as capable of providing solutions to societal problems. They set themselves apart from the men with the gendered substitution of the *-a* at the end of the word mestizo. For centuries, that masculine term had blurred and made invisible the women's existence within the fabric of their beloved nation. With this one letter *a*, the women were mestizas—social, political, intellectual, and national subjects—endowed with voices and stories of their own.

A la mujer latinoamericana

POR HERMILA GALINDO

CAPITULO XXII de La doctrina Carranza y el acercamiento indolatino

Imperdonable me hubiera parecido terminar esta obra sin dirigirme a las mujeres de mi raza, yo, que en mi modesta esfera de acción vengo efectuando una constante labor de dignificación y de libramiento de la mujer; yo, que pugno por el ideal de que el sexo femenino ocupe el lugar que en justicia le corresponde en el concierto social; yo, que como nadie, estoy convencida de que las fuentes inagotables de ternura que el corazón de una mujer esconde, los tesoros inapreciables de poesía y de amor que abriga en lo más recóndito de su espíritu, constituirán en lo sucesivo poderosos y eficaces factores de las nobles causas de la humanidad.

La América Latina cuenta con mujeres prodigiosas, con almas heroicas y gigantescas que han hecho de ellas mujeres-símbolos; la historia de nuestras jóvenes nacionalidades nos habla de espíritus femeninos cuyas puertas han estado abiertas al toque de gracia de la bondad y de la grandeza; las mujeres de mi raza por su rara complexidad [*sic*] que las hace ser las más adorables de la tierra, por su temperamento soñador y ardiente; exquisito y apasionado, estoico e impulsivo, tienen que constituir un factor de primer orden en la obra que dejo apuntada en este libro. La emancipación femenina en la América Latina no reviste los caracteres bruscos que la han significado en pueblos de origen sajón; nuestra mujer es la representación del justo equilibrio a que ésta debe llegar en una sociedad más perfectamente organizada que la actual, y ofrece el ejemplo de un espíritu femenino que, sin perder nada de su gracia, de su gentileza, de su tierna sensibilidad, se halle apto para emprender labores que hasta ahora parecían reservadas únicamente para el sexo fuerte.

En México, por ejemplo, se presenta constantemente ante nuestros ojos el espectáculo de mujeres que compiten ventajosamente con el hombre en el desempeño de trabajos rudos; mujeres que luchan denodadamente como el más fuerte varón en las lides del diario vivir; mujeres que saben afrontar serenamente todos los peligros y que se hallan capacitadas para defenderse de todas las asechanzas, y que, sin embargo, no pierden nada de su encanto, de su exquisitez, del perfume con que a Dios le plugo impregnar el alma femenil. Esas mujeres son, más tarde, magníficas madres de familia, abnegadas esposas, dulces compañeras del hombre.

Es indudable que mujeres capacitadas en tal forma, corazones en los cuales la materialidad de la lucha moderna no ha marchitado la fragancia intrínseca, deben ser consideradas como alma y nervio de las acciones trascendentales en la historia de los países y de las razas.

Mi anhelo más entusiasta consiste en que la mujer latinoamericana se interese en la causa que he defendido en este libro; pues mi convicción respecto a que ello indicaría tener adelantado un noventa y nueve por ciento del éxito, es absoluta.

Sí; vosotras, mujeres de mi raza; vosotras que aun sentís palpitar vuestra alma con el recuerdo de nuestras grandezas pretéritas; vosotras que sabéis comprender todo lo que de grande y noble encerraba el alma de la reina Isabel; vosotras que aun lloráis los pecados de amor de doña Marina; vosotras que admiráis el heroísmo de doña Josefa Ortiz de Domínguez y la entereza de doña Leona Vicario; vosotras que aun fijáis vuestros ojos preñados de preguntas en el manto regio con que se cubren nuestras noches americanas; vosotras que aun meditáis sobre el misterio que debe esconderse en los pétalos de nuestras silvestres flores; vosotras que os forjáis leyendas mágicas contemplando la pomposa grandeza de nuestros volcanes y de nuestras serranías; vosotras que aun pretendéis arrancar sus secretos a la limpidez de nuestros lagos; vosotras que sois fuerza y perfume; vosotras que sois huracán y murmullo; vosotras que sois tempestad y quietud; vosotras que parecéis llevar en el fondo misterioso de vuestras pupilas los destinos de pretéritas razas; vosotras que unís al fiero ímpetu de la hembra aborigen el plácido sentimiento de la noble castellana; vosotros, digo tenéis una ALTA, UNA SANTA, UNA IMPRESCINDIBLE MISIÓN QUE CUMPLIR EN EL PORVENIR DE LA RAZA INDOLATINA.

Sois vosotras las encargadas de inculcar en el alma tierna de vuestros hijos los ideales que de broquel han de servirles más tarde contra los embates del utilitarismo y la grosería triunfantes hoy; sois vosotras las que, adormeciéndoles en vuestros regazos, les habéis de relatar los hechos gloriosos de nuestros antepasados; sois vosotras las que habéis de inspirar en sus corazones el santo horror a los atentados y a los atropellos de la fuerza bruta; sois vosotras las que habéis de enseñar que el retintín metálico de una moneda no vale lo que el sonoro desgrane de un verso; sois vosotras las que habéis de infundir en ellos el valor, la energía, la entereza, la alteza de miras, el desinterés idealista, el anhelo de justicia, el amor a lo intangible que los hará más tarde ciudadanos fuertes, nobles y heroicos de la América.

Vosotras podéis, como nadie, enseñar a los niños de hoy el poema grandioso en que actuara el insigne genovés; vosotras sabréis poner calor y pasión en vuestras frases cuando les digáis que aquel hombre surcó los mares, llevado más que al impulso del viento que hinchaba las velas de sus endebles carabelas, en alas del hálito vigoroso de su fe; vosotras sabréis pintarles admirablemente el espectáculo legendario del denodado conquistador que hiciera pavesas sus naves, como para poner el abismo de los mares entre él y sus probables flaquezas; vosotras sabréis describirles vivamente al estoico rey azteca, sonriendo en tanto que las lenguas de fuego mordían sus plantas; vosotras les relataréis inimitablemente la odisea del gran Pizarro; vosotras les hablaréis de las grandezas de los Incas; vosotras sabréis hacerles un retrato fiel de lo que fuera nuestra raza que, desde tiempos inmemorables, contaba con reyes poetas; vosotras conmoveréis sus almas recitándoles leyendas de nuestros lagos y de nuestros níveos volcanes; vosotras, en suma, sabréis empaparlos de un modo tan íntimo en el alma de nuestra raza, que ellos serán paladines entusiastas, apóstoles infatigables de su grandeza y de su libertad.

Relatadles las desgracias que se han abatido sobre nosotros; hacedles saber las injusticias monstruosas que en contra nuestra se han cometido, no les ocultéis que la fuerza bruta se ha abatido más de una vez sobre nosotros; no dejéis de poner ante los ojos de sus espíritus los gestos de heroísmo que nuestros caudillos han tenido cuando la soberbia y la iniquidad de los fuertes han pretendido sojuzgarnos; no lo haréis, estoy segura, con la mira de despertar en ellos mezquinos odios, pero sí con el fin loable de enseñarlos a estar alertas y preparados contra probables infamias.

Enseñadles a amar el Bien y la Libertad; haced que sus almas latan al impulso de los ideales; acrecentad dentro de ellos la llama vigorosa de los santos entusiasmos; apartadlos de las corrientes utilitarias de nuestro siglo; robusteced sus cerebros con la añoranza de las épocas en que se moría por el triunfo de una idea y no por el acaparamiento de un puñado de monedas; demostradles que los fenicios y los cartagineses se hunden en la noche de la historia, sin dejar esa huella de luz que aun se desprende de la vieja Grecia.

Grande e importante es vuestra labor, mujeres de la América Latina; necesitáis, para cumplirla debidamente, estimular las fuerzas vivas de vuestra ternura; reconfortaos pensando en la trascendencia de ella; consolaos con la visión del futuro de nuestra raza.

Por eso yo me dirijo a vosotras, y quiero que os empapéis de la bondad de los ideales que han servido de norma de conducta a los legisladores de mi patria; quiero que os déis cuenta de la nobleza de la causa que en México ha defendido valerosa, estoica, perseverantemente, uno de esos hombres que de cuando en cuando aparecen en la historia de los destinos humanos para trazar nuevos derroteros a las actividades de los pueblos; quiero que hagáis vuestra una causa tan noble y tan justa como la propugnada en los sencillos y trascendentales postulados de la Doctrina Carranza; quiero que os percatéis de que esos postulados constituyen la esencia de los anhelos latinoamericanos, al mismo tiempo que son la más racional y justa sinterización de los medios prácticos para llegar a la obtención definitiva de la paz mundial.

Vuestro sensitivo corazón no puede permanecer indiferente ante el cúmulo de horrores y de dolores que las guerras traen aparejados consigo; sabéis como se han entintado de sangre los campos; habéis tenido noticia de que los cuadros más dantescos que pueda concebir la imaginación humana, se realizaron durante esa cruenta y pavorosa tragedia cuyos rojizos resplandores se contemplaron de polo a polo.

Pues bien; tened presente que los métodos empleados por las naciones del mundo en sus relaciones, han sido la causa de que tanto luto y tanto exterminio se hayan abatido sobre la doliente humanidad; tened en cuenta que esos métodos, lejos de ser radicalmente reformados después de la formidable conflagración, acaban de ser sancionados por todas las potencias fuertes de la tierra, es decir, que la amenaza de la guerra seguirá suspendida sobre todas las colectividades; tened en cuenta que urge un esfuerzo radical para implantar, sobre bases sólidas, la paz universal, y que ese esfuerzo tendrán que realizarlo vuestros hijos, los hijos de la América Latina, ya que las naciones poderosas sólo atienden a la conservación de sus intereses mercantiles y al acrecentamiento de sus riquezas.

Está, pues, en vuestras manos, la más importante y eficaz colaboración en la obra definitiva de la fraternidad humana; está en vuestras manos poner las bases para que el dios monstruoso y feroz de las guerras sea derrocado y ocupe su lugar el blanco cristo del Amor y de la Paz.

Mujeres latinoamericanas: ¡ojalá mi voz, aunque débil, pero que es respetable porque resuena en defensa de altos principios, halle eco en vuestros corazones!

Por mi parte, estoy satisfecha de efectuar este generoso impulso de mi corazón; estoy tranquila de haber obedecido a los mandatos de mi "yo" moral que me obligaban a no permanecer muda e indiferente en momentos en que se ventilan intereses trascendentales y definitivos para MI RAZA, y durante los cuales es necesario la colaboración de todos los países enamorados del bien.

Incansable en mi tarea, espero muy pronto estudiar serena y desapasionadamente cuáles son los principales problemas políticos, sociales, educativos y económicos que es preciso solucionar en la América Latina, pues aun consciente de la poca valía de mis aptitudes, juzgo que la buena intención y el entusiasmo no son ciertamente los más despreciables en toda obra que lleve por objeto remediar los dolores de la humanidad.

Y por hoy, termino esta mala pergeñada obra, rindiendo el más afectuoso, el más sincero, el más entusiasta de mis saludos a las mujeres de mi raza, de quienes hay que esperar fecundos y nobles esfuerzos en pro de las causas justas.

Nadie en mi patria, hasta los momentos en que doy fin a este libro, ha escrito sobre asuntos tan trascendentales como aquellos de que yo, de una manera incidental, he tratado en esta obra. Tal asunto llamado era a ser estudiado por cerebros bien nutridos, por inteligencias acondicionadas a tratar asuntos tan importantes; sólo el inmenso amor que profeso a mi patria, sólo el fanatismo que tengo por mi raza me han impelido a enredarme en problemas tan graves como los que he bosquejado, naturalmente sin pretender solucionarlos en mi pequeña obra. Ya vendrán después de mí escritores de fuste que traten de problemas que tanto interesan a la patria, a dar su autorizada opinión sobre esos asuntos; lo único que me hace sentirme satisfecha, es que nadie puede quitarme la gloria de haber sido la primera en ocuparme de cosas semejantes.

Tras el presente volumen escribiré el segundo, en el cual me ocuparé de los altos problemas sociológicos que están sobre el tapete de la discusión mundial y que serán de hecho el resultado práctico de la última conmoción que ha sufrido la humanidad.

No tengo la ridícula pretensión de que mis aseveraciones sean perfectamente apegadas a la justicia, pero sí digo, enfáticamente, que servirán de causa primordial para discutir los problemas que van a presentarse en un porvenir próximo para el encadenamiento de las agrupaciones humanas, tras el choque que ha sufrido últimamente la progenie humana.

Creo firmemente que no hay esfuerzo, por pequeño que sea, perdido, y por ende, laboraré, dentro de mi insignificancia, primero en pro de la felicidad de mi país y después por la de la humanidad entera, lo que es a mi juicio la única y santa base del socialismo perfectamente racional.

Anuncio, pues, a mis lectores, mi segundo volumen, y espero que lo recibirán con cariño, en vista de la buena intención que lo guiará.

Por lo tanto, en esta postrimera página, no les digo ¡adiós! Sino, ¡hasta luego! . . . .

To the Latin American Woman

BY HERMILA GALINDO

CHAPTER 22 of The Carranza Doctrine: An Indolatino Approach

It would have seemed unpardonable for me to end this work without speaking to the women of my race: I have been laboring faithfully in my modest sphere of action to dignify and liberate women; I am fighting for one ideal, that the female should occupy the place in the social compact that rightly belongs to her; I, more than anybody, am convinced that the inexhaustible fountain of compassion hidden in a woman's heart, the priceless treasures of lyricism and love that she shelters in the depths of her soul, are powerful and effective forces for humanity's future noble causes.

Latin America depends on marvelous women, whose immensely heroic souls have produced extraordinary female exemplars; the history of our young nationalities speaks to us of feminine spirits open to the touch of grace, goodness, and greatness; the women of my race possess a rare complexity that makes them the most loveable on earth, by virtue of temperaments both dreamy and ardent, refined and passionate, stoic and impulsive; these women must join the vanguard in the work that I have noted in this book.

Feminine emancipation in Latin America does not display the harsh characteristics attached to it among peoples of Saxon origin; our woman represents the right balance to be achieved in a more perfectly organized

---

Translation by Joel Bollinger Pouwels

society than the current one; she exemplifies a feminine spirit that, without losing any of her grace, gentility, or tender sensitivity, proves adept at undertaking jobs that before now appeared to be reserved only for the strong sex.

In Mexico, for example, we constantly observe the phenomenon of women who compete advantageously with men in carrying out rough jobs; women who persevere like the strongest men in the daily struggle for survival; women who know how to face all dangers serenely and who are well equipped to defend themselves from all attacks, and who, nevertheless, lose none of their charm, their exquisiteness, the delicate essence that it pleased God to infuse in the feminine soul. These women later become magnificent mothers, self-sacrificing wives, and gentle companions of men.

Undoubtedly, women equipped in such a war, with hearts in which the materiality of the modern struggle has not diminished their intrinsic refinement, must be considered the soul and vital center of transcendental events in the history of nations and of races.

I enthusiastically desire that Latin American women should take up the cause I defend in this book; since I am absolutely convinced that with women's solidarity, we can be ninety-nine percent successful.

Yes; you, women of my race; who still feel your hearts quicken with the memory of our grandmothers' past grandeur; you who can understand the great and noble soul of Queen Isabella; you who weep even for Doña Marina's sins of love; you who admire the heroism of Doña Josefa Ortiz de Domínguez and the integrity of Doña Leona Vicario; you who continue to gaze up at the regal mantle that covers our American nights, your eyes relentlessly questioning the heavens; who still meditate on the mystery hidden in the petals of our wildflowers; who forge magical legends when contemplating the grandeur and pomp of our volcanoes and mountains; who delve into the secrets of our limpid lakes; you are strength and grace; hurricane and breeze; tempest and quietude; you carry the destinies of past races in the depths of your eyes; you combine the untamed impulse of the aboriginal female with the placid sentiment of the noble Castilian race; you, I say, have a HIGH, HOLY, INEVITABLE MISSION TO FULFILL IN THE FUTURE OF THE INDOLATINO RACE.

You are entrusted with instilling in the tender souls of your children the ideals that will serve them later as a shield against the assaults of utilitarianism and vulgarity that are triumphant today; you are the ones who, rocking them to sleep in your laps, will tell them of the glorious deeds of our ancestors; you will inspire in their hearts a saintly horror of past assaults and abuses perpetrated by brute force; you will teach that the metallic clink of coins cannot compare in value with the sonorous recitation of a single poetic line; you will impress on them courage, energy, integrity, high-mindedness, idealistic selflessness, the desire for justice, the love of intangible values, that will later make them strong, noble, and heroic citizens of America.

You are capable, as no one else is, of teaching the children of today the epic story of the renowned Genovese; you will know how to speak with warmth and passion when you tell them that the Admiral who plied the seas was carried along—more than by the wind's power swelling the sails of his fragile caravels—on the wings of the vigorous zephyr of his faith; you will be able to depict commendably the legendary spectacle of the resolute Conquistador who made embers of his ships, as if to put the sea's abysses between him and any future weakness; you will know how to describe vividly to your children the stoic Aztec king, smiling while the tongues of fire licked at his feet; you will relate inimitably the odyssey of the great Pizarro; you will speak to them of the grandeurs of the Incas; you will fashion a true portrait of our race that, since time immemorial, possessed poet kings; you will move your children's very souls by reciting legends of our lakes and snowy volcanoes; you will, in sum, have the wisdom to immerse them so intimately in the soul of our race, that they will grow up to be enthusiastic paladins, indefatigable apostles of its greatness and liberty.

Tell your children about the misfortunes that have disheartened us; let them know of the monstrous injustices committed against us, do not hide from them the fact that brute force has struck us more than once; do not forget to place before the eyes of your children's spirits the feats of heroism that our chieftains have displayed when the arrogance and iniquity of the strong have tried to subjugate us. I am sure that you will do so without trying to awaken in them petty hatred; instead, you will hold to the praiseworthy goal of teaching them to be alert and prepared for possible future infamies.

Teach them to love the common Good and Liberty; make their souls resonate with the pulse of our ideals; cultivate in them the vigorous flame of saintly pursuits; keep them from the utilitarian trends of our century; strengthen their minds with a yearning for the times when one died for the triumph of an idea, and not for the accumulation of fistfuls of money; demonstrate to them that the Phoenicians and the Carthaginians are lost in historical obscurity, without overlooking the beam of light still projected by ancient Greece.

Your task is great and important, women of Latin America; to accomplish it properly, you need to activate the deepest powers of your compassion;

fortify yourselves by thinking about its significance; comfort yourselves with the vision of our race's future.

This is why I am addressing you, and I want you to immerse yourselves in the goodness of the ideals that have served as rules of conduct for the legislators of my country; I want you to realize the nobility of the cause that in Mexico is defended courageously, stoically, tenaciously, by one of those men who appear from time to time in the history of human destiny to design new directions for the people's efforts; I want you to adopt as your own the noble and just cause proposed in the simple yet significant articles of the Carranza Doctrine; I want you to understand that those articles comprise the essence of Latin American desires, at the same time that they are the most rational and balanced synthesis of the practical means of achieving definitive world peace.

Your sensitive hearts cannot remain indifferent to the accumulated horror and suffering brought by the wars; you know that the fields have been stained with blood; you realize that millions of the doomed have enriched the soil with their mortal remains; you have heard that the most infernal episodes conceived by the human imagination, occurred during that bloody, frightful tragedy whose terrifying spectacle was observed from pole to pole.

Therefore, keep in mind that the methods employed by the nations of the world in their relationships, have caused all the mourning and destruction that has rained down on suffering humanity; keep in mind that those methods, far from being radically reformed after the frightening conflagration, have just been approved by all the major powers of the Earth, that is, the threat of war will continue to hang over all peoples; keep in mind that a radical effort is urgently required to implant universal peace upon solid foundations, and that your children, the children of Latin America, will have to carry out that effort, since the powerful nations only attend to preserving their commercial interests and increasing their wealth.

Thus, your charge is to achieve the most important and effective collaboration in the definitive work of humankind; it is in your hands to lay the groundwork for overthrowing the monstrously fierce god of wars and replace him with the just messiah of Love and Peace.

Latin American Women: I hope that my voice, frail but respectable because it resounds in defense of high principles, will echo in your hearts!

For my part, I am satisfied in carrying out this generous impulse of my heart; I am at peace for obeying the mandates of my moral being, that required me to not remain mute and indifferent in moments when transcendental and definitive issues for MY RACE are being aired, moments that necessitate the collaboration of all nations enamored of peace.

Tireless in my work, I hope very soon to undertake an investigation, calmly and dispassionately, into the main problems—of a political, social, educational, and economic nature—that must be solved in Latin America, since, while I comprehend the small value of my skills, I judge that good intentions and enthusiasm are surely not the most negligible talents to bring to the task whose objective is to remedy the suffering of humanity.

And for the present, I end this poor draft of a work, offering the most affectionate, sincere, and enthusiastic of my greetings to the women of my race, from whom we expect fruitful and noble efforts in support of just causes.

No one in my country, even as I finish this book, has written about such significant matters as those that I, in passing, have considered in this work. Such a subject was meant to be studied by well educated minds, by intellects accustomed to treating such important matters; only the immense love that I profess for my country, only the zeal that I have for my race, have driven me to become enmeshed in such serious problems as I have delineated, naturally without aspiring to solve them in my small work. Soon writers of consequence will appear after me to treat the problems of utmost interest in the nation, to give their authoritative opinions about these issues; the only thing that gives me satisfaction is that nobody can deprive me of the glory of being the harbinger of such concerns.

After the present volume I shall write a second one, in which I shall take on the lofty sociological problems that are next on the agenda of world discussion and that will be in fact the practical result of the last upheaval that humanity has suffered.

I do not have the ridiculous pretension that my statements are perfectly aligned with justice, but I do say, emphatically, that what I have put forward will serve as essential motivation for discussing the problems that will present themselves in the near future for the concatenation of human groups, after the shock that the human family has recently suffered.

I firmly believe that there is no effort wasted, no matter how small, and, therefore, I will labor, within my limitations, first for my country's happiness and then for the happiness of all humanity, which is, in my judgment the only pure basis of perfectly rational socialism.

I announce, then, to my readers, my second volume, and I foresee that they will receive it with affection, seeing the good intentions that will guide it.

Therefore, on this last page, I do not say, "Good-bye" to you, but rather, "Until we meet again!" . . . .

Epilogue

In the midst of this circle of presences
I am myself: matter
that burns, diffuses heat and light.
I snap out the reply, rejoicing: "All's well!"
—ROSARIO CASTELLANOS, "CONSCIOUSNESS"

Cheryl Glenn reminds us in *Rhetoric Retold* that our histories must do something. As Glenn contends, feminist rhetorical historiographies challenge the male-dominated stories of rhetoric. Beyond challenging the normative stories, what does this feminist recovery project do? Bringing these women's voices into the conversation of feminist rhetorical historiographies serves as a decolonizing force that is emerging in rhetorical studies. In the years spent charting this rhetorical map of Mexican women journalists and activists, I have come to believe that the act of the author-researcher writing herself into being resides within the interstices of feminist historiography. These histories of Mexican women rhetors are essential because they breathe into form a basis for our Chicana/Latina histories.

I have constructed my own Chicana identity while writing the rhetorical histories of these Mexican women writers. I was raised by my mother, Sandra González, a strong Chicana intellectual, who knew the importance of passing on our family's heritage. She taught me and my siblings Spanish through a rich cultural environment of literature, music, dance, and games in a time when linguistic pedagogy shied away from teaching children two or more languages. Having been a teenager in a racist West Texas town, I unfortunately was afraid and not confident enough to live my Chicana identity. When I moved at the age of nineteen to El Paso, Texas, with my grandmother, Ramona González, she reminded me of the lessons her daughter had taught me. My grandmother, a published Chicana writer, encouraged my interest in discovering writers and language. I began to develop my Chicana identity, and I looked toward Mexican literature and music to cultivate my roots. To my mother and grandmother, who passed on to me the memories, language, and love of our Mexican heritage, I owe a great debt.

The Mexican feminist essayist and poet Rosario Castellanos (1925–74) believed in language as having power to suppress but also to liberate. The words of this feminist historiography not only link to the Mexican women represented on these pages but also "convoke the presence of all the others that are in tune with it."[1] This includes the many women in our lives: *nuestras mamás, abuelas, tías, hermanas y primas* (our mothers, grandmothers, aunts, sisters, and cousins). As young girls, we witnessed these women speak up and out in public or private spaces to defend the rights, inclusion, presence, and puestos of other ladies in our communities. They also form part of this narrative because they come to our minds as we think of the many other women who do not appear in the pages of history. This book's close rhetorical analysis of Mexican women journalists and activists raises the issues of place, space, race, rhetoric, and women's bodies and discourse within public historic puestos of Mexico—from the poetic and intellectual lyceums of the Porfiriato to the protest newspapers of the pre-Revolutionary era and the political podium of the Mexican Revolution. The women of this study, Laureana Wright de Kleinhans, Las Mujeres de Zitácuaro, Juana Belén Gutiérrez de Mendoza, and Hermila Galindo, went public with their feminist discourses of empowerment focused on shifting their realities. In the time period when these women were writing and publishing (1875–1942), their voices in the arena of journalism disrupted and destabilized the traditional rhetorical practice of strictly men speaking in public, thereby setting the groundwork for the many Mexican women journalists who would come after them. Certainly, their feminine embodiment of discourse in various public puestos challenged civic attitudes and perceptions about women, because it forced society to deal with female bodies in environments that had remained masculine domains for centuries.

One of the central goals of this study has been to explore gender as it is connected to the division of power and the ways it unfolds within the many cultural constraints and demands. Recognizing the societal structures that existed at the time, such as the historical patriarchy beginning with Malintzin, was fundamental to enable me to identify and understand the importance of the women's discourse. However, as critical as this first step may be, the women's voices in this history were central to the study. At every turn, I fought the modernist urge to portray these women through a hagiographic lens, as romantic individuals fighting a lone battle against racial, gendered, and political oppression. On the contrary, they were subjects who acted as discursive agents through social structures that were infused with stern, unyielding gendered beliefs and traditions.

The women claimed their public puestos and feminine identities through the same structures that were meant to oppress them. "Power and resistance," Biesecker reminds us, "are two sides of the same coin."[2] The women engaged in practical complicity—by accepting many of the cultural traditions, such as motherhood. They also engaged in practical resistance, which simultaneously challenged the traditions through their discourse. Their discourse then became "a force . . . that establishes a cleft or fissure out of which an unforeseen and undesigned transgression may ensue."[3] Each of these women created a different discursive disposition because their social circumstances and conditions were so diverse. This led each writer to disrupt, fragment, and alter the course of human engagement in different ways.

It is my hope that this study, focused on women's rhetorical contributions and the struggles they endured to have their voices heard, will shake the perception that exists about Mexican women and their intellectual aptitude, past and present. Mexican women journalists' participation in the mid-nineteenth and early twentieth centuries' political and cultural debates further challenges the perception—prevalent on the part of visiting foreigners and Mexican male intellectuals alike—that Mexican women were relatively ignorant of all but religious matters. Visitors such as Pedro Calderón de la Barca and Paula Kolonitz described women as being stuck in difficult social situations. Kolonitz said of the Mexican women that they have a "non-existent" education, concluding that "their ignorance is complete and they have no idea what history and geography are."[4] Mexican men also contributed to the false impressions of women's societal position. In 1903, *El Correo de Durango*, under the direction of Alberto M. Alvarado, published an opinion piece titled "La ilustración de la mujer."[5] The author argued that women *should* receive an education beyond the traditional religious sort, but still viewed women's societal influence as limited to the home. "No es en las asambleas legislativas donde la mujer ha de procurar el bien de los pueblos, sino al pie de la cuna" (It is not in the legislative assemblies where women should enact civic good, but at the foot of the crib).[6] These perceptions, both foreign and local, are difficult to overcome, as seen in the decades of resistance women faced before they finally gained voting rights in 1947. In order to let these narrow views go, we must first listen to their voices.

Listening to Their Voices

This work assumes that rhetoric is epistemic. The discursive actions of these Mexican women can be situated in the realm of those who were empowered to *create* reality rather than to be mere passive participants in history. Furthermore, the histories of these women are divergent yet parallel. They form a pathway in the history of women's writing from the early discourse of Wright de Kleinhans in 1887 to that of Las Mujeres de Zitácuaro in 1900. On this trajectory, the writings of Las Mujeres de Zitácuaro served as a bridge to the more radical voices of Gutiérrez de Mendoza and Galindo, who were writing before and during the Mexican Revolution. Persistent and undaunted, each woman claimed the right to a discursive puesto in the Mexican public sphere, which had yet to recognize them.

So, then, what can the histories of these women *teach* us about engaging a feminist rhetorical space? Laureana Wright de Kleinhans's writings in *Violetas del Anáhuac*, which address the cultural milieu of the time, fall under various categories of philosophical essays, poetry, and history. We see that Wright de Kleinhans, along with other nineteenth-century Mexican women, was indeed contributing to the formation of a national and historical identity from a feminine perspective. Her discourse teaches us that, like many other women throughout history, a Mexican woman writer had to first appropriate the tone, language, and structure of the male Mexican writer. But like all rhetorical women, Wright de Kleinhans and her cohort of writers were much more clever and resourceful in their writing than the men, because they were forced to imbue a hostile power structure with their feminine identity.

Through a genre lens, we see that Las Mujeres de Zitácuaro borrowed traditional rhetorical tropes from the men, but their strategic use of the plan, grito and manifiesto situated them early on within the anticlerical conversation of the nineteenth century. From them we learn that women were fearless discursive actors in the pre-Revolutionary movements of protest. When many males were afraid to connect their identity with their words, Las Mujeres de Zitácuaro signed their names to each of their documents. We also learn that at the turn of the century in Mexico, women were not ready to completely break with the rhetoric of difference, such as the discourse around their fight for motherhood, which defined them as contributing to the building of a nation.

Gutiérrez de Mendoza sustained her rhetorical presence in the public sphere for more than forty years, calling on her courage to continuously voice her opinion in a time when women were not welcome in the public sphere. Her voice, ruthless and intrusive, positively impacted and made it possible for other Mexican women to follow her example and participate in public politics. As much public discourse as she produced, Gutiérrez de Mendoza had, until recently, almost been forgotten in the Mexican Revolutionary histories. Equally, her writings in favor of Mexican indigenous people resisting the assimilationist theories and practices of eugenics have fallen by the wayside. Yet, in recovering her writings from *¡Por la tierra y por la raza!*, we learn that it was a woman who had the rhetorical acumen to counter the racist and silencing writings of José Vasconcelos, one of Mexico's most celebrated philosophers. Women such as Gutiérrez de Mendoza were at the forefront of remembering and writing counternarratives for their own indigenous people. Much ahead of her time, her discourse formed a decolonizing rhetoric resistant to the continuing colonizing European concepts.

Hermila Galindo, the spokeswoman for Carranza, who traveled to Cuba and Colombia in an effort to disseminate and advance his ideas for a Mexican constitution, created a diverse image and reality of Mexican politics. Galindo's public speaking presence set a precedent, although Mexican women's legal admission into politics was still almost forty years in the future. We learn from Galindo's discourse that women were beginning to exert a greater reach into Mexico's political system and that her role as a spokeswoman next to President Carranza helped women across Mexico gain greater public freedom. Through Galindo's rhetorical approach, we also learn that Mexican women, long said to be incapable of political positions, were fully capable of understanding and articulating national and international discourse.

Overall, we discover that the Mexican female journalists in this study were actively participating in civic discourse and were leading the way as agents of social change. These women serve as a beacon to contemporary young Chicana and Latina scholars and also other young female scholars of color. These women's writings point to social possibilities of cultural and gendered identity, even when the strict social structures seem to silence and marginalize their voices. Young writers should learn the rhetorical skill of strategically appropriating genres and conventions that work to critique or intersect with normative beliefs. As women of color, our lives and writings are complex and require a critical new lens to engage in civic discourses.

A modern feminist perspective alone would not have been enough to encompass these women's projects as writers. The use of the additional theoretical lens of mestiza rhetoric creates a postmodern rhetorical puesto for these women. In their modernist settings, they wrote from multidimensional and multisubjective points of view. They wrote not only as women but as women of color within a colonized territory. A mestiza rhetorical perspective recognizes their various cultural, social, and racial stances, eliminating what Chandra Mohanty calls the problematic "assumption of women as an always already constituted group."[7] The most important component of the theoretical lens of mestiza rhetoric is that it takes into account the women's opposition as resisting, not simply the structure of patriarchy, but multiple societal realities, including social, political, religious, and racial. The women were also in a growing industrial setting where they had access to translations of scholars from Europe and the United States, as well as access to books and newspapers from other Latin American countries. The interweaving of ideas and concepts from across the border, overseas, and faraway lands contributed to the element of mestiza rhetoric. They adopted a mestiza consciousness, which takes into consideration the colonized aspect of one's subjectivity. The discourses that are created from this awareness enact another subjectivity that defies modernist binaries. Wright de Kleinhans, Las Mujeres de Zitácuaro, Gutiérrez de Mendoza, and Galindo wrote from the underside of colonial relationships of power, such as from the strong European influences that impacted Mexican history and social politics. The writings of each of the women reflect an understanding of this quandary.

Although I assert that all of the women were contributing to the development of mestiza rhetoric, their level of engagement in racial and gendered understanding varied. Establishing these women's diverse subjectivities was fundamental in this study. For example, Laureana Wright de Kleinhans came from an elite background; she and the cohort of women writers she published, including María del Alba, Ignacia Padilla de Piña, María de la Luz Murguía, Dolores Correa Zapata, and many others, used the elite, grammatically complex, and taxing voice of educated men, reflecting the high, baroque tone of the time meant to keep many others out of the discursive realm. Hermila Galindo also received an elite education at a private school in Chihuahua, ensuring that her writings were published and read by an elite political audience. Her rhetoric originated from a puesto of authority, and although marginalized because of her femininity, it intersected with the power structure of the nation and threatened the status of Mexican politics. Unlike Wright de Kleinhans and Galindo, Gutiérrez de Mendoza received a limited education, yet she taught herself how to read and write. Her background as a daughter of a blacksmith and the experience of living among the indigenous people did not afford her a prestigious position in society. However, it did allow for a perspective and collective credibility that few could claim. She had the authority to speak for and from the indigenous side of the mestizaje. The women who made up Las Mujeres de Zitácuaro came from a religious Presbyterian background. Unlike those from the Catholic tradition, which sought to place women in the convent and teach them only religious educational material, Las Mujeres de Zitácuaro embraced a civic education that included women's participation in cultural education and community edification.

Next Steps in New Directions

The recovery of these socially complex and intellectual voices of Mexican women teaches us that we have many more voices to uncover, analyze, and theorize, and if we are looking correctly, they are not always going to be in English or on the library shelf. We must also ask, what other voices have we not uncovered because of a language boundary? At one time in our discipline, the research trend of studying rhetoric and oratory was primary. In other words, it was grounded in primary research. As Richard Leo Enos reminds us, "[S]cholars would do archival work, field work, translate important primary material, and make theoretical interpretations direct[ed] at explicating primary material, not, as is often now the case, eliciting a reaction to secondary sources."[8] Admittedly, my study does not break any boundaries in research methodologies. I followed this same research process that Enos proposes.

Granted, the writing of the theories and histories I propose were made exponentially more difficult when engaging in two languages. The old, but tried and true, method of translation has the potential to open new and different pathways of knowledge. For me, the exhaustive effort of thinking in two languages while writing this book has been worth the knowledge I am putting forward. At one time, rhetoricians were required to know another language well enough to engage with the primary documents. This would lead to what Enos calls profound and deep understanding of rhetoric. I am suggesting that in order to move forward with our understanding of rhetorics, we must engage with those beyond a Eurocentric way of knowing, beyond our comfort zones of English.

This study uses primary sources from archives in the U.S. Southwest and Central Mexico, fulfilling the call to put archival research at the center of our investigations or risk weakening historical and theoretical accounts. This book also fills a gap in the representation of a large and growing population of Latino/a students across the country. While extensive work has been done in representing African American women in the discipline, the field of rhetoric has a long road to travel in historically representing Latino/a history. This book opens the path for crucial representation of this important population and gives scholars additional role models for writing and theorizing beyond Gloria Anzaldúa and Sor Juana. This book also contributes to our understanding of how women from Mexican backgrounds claimed a discursive space within the repressive power structures, which made it possible for the women to emerge as speaking subjects.

Research on Mexican female journalists from a rhetorical perspective certainly does not end with this current study. On the contrary, this study merely scratches the surface of their writings and the attendant implications. The present collection represents only a sampling of these Mexican women journalists' writings, with English translations. Clearly, a greater effort must be made in order to make more of their writings available to English-speaking audiences. The writings and the ways in which the women made their voices heard reveal the means by which Mexican dominant discourses attempted to silence or diffuse their impact.

In this final call for action to continue researching Mexican women's rhetorics, I quote Castellanos's reason why we must continue the work: "Speak, keep on talking, don't keep quiet, no matter what, because silence frightens; I'm afraid, it seems to me that a long hand in the shadows is going to grab us by the neck and strangle us!"[9] That "hand in the shadows" is the continued domination of women of color's voices and of women's voices in general. Through a clear remembering of those voices, we nourish and cultivate an inclusive future. With these recovered writings by Mexican women in the hands of young Chicanas/Latinas and other women of color today, they will be able to act and learn with courage, knowing that they can change their lives and those of others for the better. They will know of the struggles the women in the past endured, and this may give them valor to evaluate their own circumstances.

These recovered women's voices can have the power to entice young scholars into the archives in search of the many others who have been forgotten. By studying the rhetorical efforts of Mexican women we will be able to reframe our understanding of rhetorical practices south of our border and how those influence our own today. Understanding our rhetorical roots across the Mexican border is crucial not only to give our students historical models of women that reflect their own or different heritages, but also to help us envision a future without linguistic or disciplinary borders.

Notes

Introduction

1. "Las mujeres en el siglo pasado y antepasado y ante-antepasado carecían de educación superior y, cuando alguna por encima de prohibiciones y carencias se atrevía a escribir, lo hacía a escondidas o escudándose tras un seudónimo masculino. . . . ¡Y eso era en Inglaterra! ¿Y en México?"

2. Juana B. Gutiérrez de Mendoza and Elisa Acuña y Rosette, "A los mexicanos," in *Juana Belén Gutiérrez de Mendoza: extraordinaria precursora de la Revolución Mexicana*, ed. Angeles Mendieta Alatorre (México: Copilco Universidad, 1983), 125–30.

3. bell hooks, "Choosing the Margin as a Space of Radical Openness," in *Readings in Contemporary Rhetoric*, ed. Karen A. Foss, Sonja K. Foss, and Robert Trapp (Long Grove, IL: Waveland Press, 2002), 241.

4. Juana B. Gutiérrez de Mendoza, "*Vésper* siempre ocupará su puesto," in *Juana Belén Gutiérrez de Mendoza: extraordinaria precursora de la Revolución Mexicana*, ed. Angeles Mendieta Alatorre (México: Copilco Universidad, 1983), 148–49.

5. Laureana Wright de Kleinhans, *La emancipación de la mujer por medio del estudio*, in *Educación y superación femenina en el siglo XIX: Dos ensayos de Laureana Wright*, ed. Lourdes Alvarado (México: Universidad Nacional Autónoma de México, 2005), 59.

6. Susie S. Porter, *Working Women in Mexico City: Public Discourses and Material Conditions, 1879–1931* (Tucson: University of Arizona Press, 2003), 15.

7. For details on the factory readers, consult Araceli Tinajero, *El Lector: A History of the Cigar Factory Reader*, trans. Judith E. Grasberg (Austin: University of Texas Press, 2007).

8. Nancy LaGreca, *Rewriting Womanhood: Feminism, Subjectivity, and the Angel of the House in the Latin American Novel, 1887–1903* (University Park: Pennsylvania State University Press, 2009), 5.

9. Ibid.

10. Laura Gillman, *Unassimilable Feminisms: Reappraising Feminist, Womanist, and Mestiza Identity Politics* (New York: Palgrave Press, 2010), 146.

11. Mary K. Vaughan, "Pancho Villa, the Daughter of Mary, and the Modern Woman: Gender in the Long Mexican Revolution," in *Sex in Revolution: Gender, Politics, and Power in Modern Mexico* (Durham, NC: Duke University Press, 2006), 23.

12. Gabriela Cano and Georgette José Valenzuela, eds., *Cuatro estudios de género en el México urbano del siglo XIX* (México: Programa Universitario de Estudios de Género, 2001), 10–15.

13. Elvira Hernández Carballido, "La historia de la prensa en México desde la perspectiva de género, " *Informação & Comunicação* 14, no. 2 (2011): 68.

14. Diego Bugeda and Juan Manuel Ramírez Vélez, eds., *Mujeres insurgentes* (México: Siglo XXI Editores, 2010), 9.

15. Hui Wu, "Historical Studies of Rhetorical Women Here and There: Methodological Challenges to Dominant Interpretive Frameworks," *Rhetoric Society Quarterly* 32, no. 1 (2002): 81.

16. Jacqueline Jones Royster and Gesa E. Kirsch, *Feminist Rhetorical Practices: New Horizons for Rhetoric, Composition, and Literacy Studies* (Carbondale: Southern Illinois University Press, 2012), 110–28.

17. Ibid., 7.

18. Ibid., 20.

19. Ibid.

20. Ibid., 21.

21. Ibid., 24.

22. William A. Covino and David Jolliffe, *Rhetoric: Concepts, Definitions, Boundaries* (Boston: Allyn and Bacon, 1995).

23. Ibid., 5.

24. Gerardo Ramírez Vidal, ed., *Conceptos y objetos de la retórica ayer y hoy* (México: Universidad Nacional Autónoma de México, 2008), 9.

25. The original text reads, " . . . se transforma en una disciplina mestiza." In this instance, the literal translation of "a mestiza discipline" would not work. I use the term *hybrid* because, as noted by Rubén Medina in "El mestizaje a través de la frontera: Vasconcelos y Anzaldúa," the terms *mestizaje* and *hybrid* are considered synonymous. It is important to note the original meaning because the term *mestiza* carries with it cultural and academic significance for this study.

26. Helena Beristáin and Gerardo Ramírez Vidal, eds., *La palabra florida: la tradición retórica indígena y novohispana* (México: Universidad Nacional Autónoma de México, 2004), 5.

27. Tace Hedrick, *Mestizo Modernism: Race, Nation, and Identity in Latin American Culture, 1900–1940* (New Brunswick, NJ: Rutgers University Press, 2003), 10.

28. Cristina Kirklighter, *Traversing the Democratic Borders of the Essay* (Albany: State University of New York Press, 2002), 94.

29. See the following sources for a complete masculine history on the newspapers and journalism in Mexico: Rafael Carrasco Puente, *La prensa en México: Datos históricos* (México: Universidad Nacional Autónoma de México, 1962), and Moisés Ochoa Campos, *Reseña histórica del periodismo mexicano* (México: Editorial Porrúa, 1968).

30. Celia del Palacio Montiel, ed. *La prensa como fuente para la historia* (México: Miguel Ángel Porrúa, 2006), 6.

31. Daniel Cosío Villegas et al., *Historia moderna de México*, 10 vols. (México: Editorial Hermes, 1955–72).

32. Hernández Carballido, "La historia," 68

33. Mary K. Hawkesworth, "Feminist Rhetoric: Discourses on the Male Monopoly of Thought," *Political Theory* 16, no. 3 (1988): 444–67.

34. Ibid., 444.

35. Anna Macías, *Against All Odds: The Feminist Movement in Mexico to 1940* (Westport, CT: Greenwood Press, 1982).

36. Lourdes Alvarado, *Educación y superación femenina en al siglo XIX: Dos ensayos de Laureana Wright* (México: Universidad Nacional Autónoma de México, 2005), 14.

37. Joel Bollinger Pouwels, *Political Journalism by Mexican Women During the Age of Revolution, 1876–1940* (Lewiston, NY: Edwin Mellen Press, 2006), 9.

38. Ibid., 10.

39. Ibid.

40. Ibid., 20.

41. Julia Tuñón Pablos, *Women in Mexico: A Past Unveiled*, trans. Alan Hynds (Austin: University of Texas Press, 1987), 48.

42. Barbara Biesecker, "Coming to Terms with Recent Attempts to Write Women into the History of Rhetoric," *Philosophy and Rhetoric* 25, no. 2 (1992): 144.

43. Ibid., 148.

44. Gabriela Cano, "The Porfiriato and the Mexican Revolution," in *Nation, Empire, Colony: Historicizing Gender and Race*, ed. Ruth Roach Pierson and Nupur Chaudhuri (Bloomington: Indiana University Press, 1998), 112.

45. Adela C. Lincona, "Borderlands' Rhetorics and Representations: The Transformative Potential of Feminist Third Space Scholarship and Zines," *NWSA Journal* 17, no. 2 (2005): 105.

46. Damían Baca and Victor Villanueva, eds., *Rhetorics of the Americas: 3114 BCE to 2012 CE* (New York: Palgrave Macmillan, 2010), 146.

47. Ibid.

48. Daniel Levy and Gabriel Szekely, *Mexico, Paradoxes of Stability and Change* (Boulder, CO: Westview Press, 1983), 26–27.

49. Many of these voices of women who entered the convent are being uncovered and translated. See Electa Arenal and Stacy Schlau, eds., *Untold Sisters: Hispanic Nuns in Their Own Works*, trans. Amanda Powell (Albuquerque: University of New Mexico Press, 2010).

50. *Corregidora* is the gendered term of *corregidor*, which implies a local administrative and judicial position.

51. Asunción Lavrin and Edith Couturier, "Las mujeres tienen la palabra: otras voces en la historia colonial de México," *Historia Mexicana* 31, no. 2 (1981): 281.

52. Macias, *Against All Odds*, 9.

53. Ibid., 8.

54. Ibid., 9.

55. Justo Sierra was at the forefront of Mexico's development of a structured educational system. A congressman in the 1880s, he would play a leading role in the educational congresses of 1889 and 1990; in 1901, he took directorship of the education department of the Secretaría de Justicia e Instrucción Pública y Bellas Artes.

56. Mary K. Vaughan, "Women, Class, and Education in Mexico, 1880–1928," *Latin American Perspectives* 4, no. 1/2 (1977), 138–39.

57. Ibid.

58. Macías, *Against All Odds*, 61.

59. Ibid.

60. Stuart Easterling, "Gender and Poetry Writing in the Light of Mexico's Liberal Victory, 1867–ca. 1890," *Mexican Studies/Estudios Mexicanos* 27, no. 1 (2011): 99.

61. Ibid., 103.

62. Jane Herrick, "Periodicals for Women in Mexico During the Nineteenth Century," *The Americas* 14, no. 2 (1957): 135–44.

63. Ibid., 135. These journals can all be located in the digital archives of the Hemeroteca Nacional Digital de México, http://www.hndm.unam.mx.

64. Ibid., 139.

65. Ibid., 144.

66. Ramón Manterola and Luis C. Rubín, *La Mujer: Semanario de la Escuela de Artes y Oficios para Mujeres*, April 15, 1880–August 1, 1883.

67. Concepción Gimeno de Flaquer, "La mujer estudiosa," La Mujer: Semanario de la Escuela de Artes y Oficios para Mujeres 4, no. 158 (1883): 1.

68. Found in the archives of the Latin American Benson Collection, University of Texas, Austin.

69. Ibid.

70. While these journals were about women, there were many others publishing on the emerging pedagogical practices and beliefs of the time. See Morelos Torres Aguilar, "Publicaciones sobre educación en México en el siglo XIX," *Revista Historia de la Educación Latinoamericana* 15, no. 20 (2013): 245–74, accessed September 9, 2014, http://www.scielo.org.co/scielo.

71. Bollinger Pouwels, 31.

72. *Las Hijas del Anáhuac* was also the title that Laureana Wright de Kleinhans chose for her 1887 literary journal. She changed the name several volumes into its publication to *Violetas del Anáhuac*.

73. *Las Hijas del Anáhuac: Ensayo Literario* 1, no. 1 (1873): 1.

74. Ibid.

75. I am assuming that there were only fourteen issues because that is all that was available through the online archives of the Hemeroteca Nacional Digital de México.

76. The translation of this title would be lacking if drawn from only the title. The English title reflects the theoretical approach Galindo takes in the text.

77. Translations completed by Joel Bollinger Pouwels and Neil J. Devereaux. Bollinger Pouwels completed the end of chapter translations, and Neil J. Devereaux completed the in-text translations.

78. Audre Lorde, *Sister Outsider: Essays and Speeches by Audre Lorde* (1984; repr., Berkeley, CA: Crossing Press, 2007), 43.

Chapter One

1. Damian Baca, *Mestiz@ Scripts, Digital Migrations, and the Territories of Writing* (New York: Palgrave Macmillan, 2008), 4.

2. For a detailed examination of these voices, see Tace Hedrick, *Mestizo Modernism: Race, Nation, and Identity in Latin American Culture, 1900–1940* (New Brunswick, NJ:Rutgers University Press, 2003).

3. Susan C. Jarratt, *Rereading the Sophists: Classical Rhetoric Refigured* (Carbondale: Southern Illinois University Press, 1998), 12.

4. Ibid.

5. Damián Baca, "Rhetoric, Interrupted: La Malinche and Nepantlisma," in *Rhetorics of the Americas: 3114 BCE to 2012 CE*, ed. Damián Baca and Victor Villanueva (New York: Palgrave Macmillan, 2010), 147.

6. For an excellent examination of mestizaje, please see Lourdes Martínez-Echazábal, "Mestizaje and the Discourse of National/Cultural Identity in Latin America, 1845–1959," *Latin American Perspectives* 25, no. 3 (1998): 21–42.

7. Martha Robles, *Espiral de voces* (México: Universidad Nacional Autónoma de México, 1993), 18.

8. J. Jesús Figueroa Torres, *Doña Marina, una india ejemplar* (México: B. Costa-Amic, 1975), 48.

9. Ibid., 41.

10. Ibid., 21–22.

11. Octavio Paz, *The Labyrinth of Solitude: Life and Thought in Mexico*, trans. Lysander Kemp, Yara Milos, and Rachel Phillips Belash (New York: Grove Press, 1985), 85.

12. Ibid., 87.

13. Dora Elvira García, Ivón Cepeda, and Shannon Anne Shea, eds., *Visiones de México, 1810–2010: Devenires de una identidad cultural* (México: Editorial Porrúa, 2010), 21, 87.

14. Emma Pérez, *The Decolonial Imaginary: Writing Chicanas into History* (Bloomington: Indiana University Press, 1999), 7.

15. Rosario Castellanos, *El eterno femenino* (México: Fondo de Cultura Económica, 1975).

16. Rosario Castellanos, "Malinche," in *A Rosario Castellanos Reader: An Anthology of Her Poetry, Short Fiction, Essays, and Drama*, ed. and trans. Maureen Ahern (Austin: University of Texas Press, 1988), 96–97.

17. Carlos Fuentes, *Todos los gatos son pardos* (México: Siglo XXI Editores, 1970).

18. Ibid., 82.

19. Ibid., 98–99.

20. Walter Ong, "Voice as Summons for Belief: Literature, Faith, and the Divided Self," in *An Ong Reader: Challenges for Further Inquiry*, ed. Thomas J. Farrell and Paul A. Soukup (Creskill, NJ: Hampton Press, 2002), 262.

21. Norma Alarcón, "*Traddutora, Traditora*: A Paradigmatic Figure of Chicana Feminism," *Cultural Critique*, no. 13 (1989): 63.

22. Gabriela Cano, "The Porfiriato and the Mexican Revolution: Constructions of Feminism and Nationalism," in *Nation, Empire, Colony: Historicizing Gender and Race*, ed. Ruth Roach Pierson and Nupur Chaudhuri (Bloomington: Indiana University Press, 1998), 109.

23. The Mexican root of marianismo is closely connected to marianism, or the European and Roman Catholic's custom of deep devotion to and admiration of the

Virgin Mary. This shows a cultural connection to European customs with a Mexican interpretation.

24. Mary E. Hawkesworth, "Feminist Rhetoric: Discourses on the Male Monopoly of Thought," *Political Theory* 16, no. 3 (1988): 448.

25. Ibid.

26. Camilla Townsend, *Malintzin's Choices: An Indian Woman in the Conquest of Mexico* (Albuquerque: University of New Mexico Press, 2006), 41.

27. Ibid., 40.

28. Ibid., 41.

29. Figueroa Torres, *Doña Marina*, 23.

30. Gloria Anzaldúa, *Borderlands/La Frontera: The New Mestiza* (San Francisco: Aunt Lute Books, 1987), 39.

31. Miguel Angel Menéndez, *Malintzin* (México: La Prensa, 1964), 25.

32. Figueroa Torres, *Doña Marina*, 75.

33. Josefina Muriel, *Cultura femenina novohispana* (México: Universidad Nacional Autónoma de México, 1982), 12. The poem is included on page 13.

34. Ibid.

35. Ibid.

36. Figueroa Torres, *Doña Marina*, 63.

37. Francisco Xavier Sánchez Hernández, "El ícono de la Virgen de Guadalupe: una reflexión sobre la conformación de la identidad nacional," in *Visiones de México, 1810–2010: Devenires de una identidad cultural*, ed. Dora Elvira García, Ivón Cepeda, and Shannon Anne Shea (México: Editorial Porrúa, 2010), 24–25.

38. Ibid., 39.

39. Jarratt, *Rereading the Sophists*, 75.

40. Anzaldúa, *Borderlands/La Frontera*, 22.

41. Cheryl Glenn, "Truth, Lies, and Method: Revisiting Feminist Historiography," *College English* 62, no. 3 (2000): 387–89.

42. Ibid.

43. Hawkesworth, "Feminist Rhetoric," 444.

44. Anzaldúa, *Borderlands/La Frontera*,18.

45. Hedrick, *Mestizo Modernism*, 8.

46. José Vasconcelos, *The Cosmic Race/La raza cósmica*, trans. Didier T. Jaén (Baltimore: Johns Hopkins University Press, 1997).

47. Paz, *Labyrinth of Solitude*, 169.

48. Hedrick, *Mestizo Modernism*, 3.

49. Joshua Lund, *The Impure Imagination: Toward a Critical Hybridity in Latin American Writing* (Minneapolis: University of Minnesota Press, 2006), 71.

50. Ibid., 86–87.

51. Vasconcelos, *La raza cósmica*, 11.

52. Ibid.

53. Eduardo I. Gallo, ed., *Hombres ilustres mexicanos* (México: Imprenta de I. Cumplido, 1873).

54. Donna Harraway, "Situated Knowledges: The Science Question in Feminism and the Privilege of Partial Perspective," *Feminist Studies* 14, no. 3 (1988): 575–99.

55. Henry Schmidt, *The Roots of Lo Mexicano: Self and Society in Mexican Thought, 1900–1934* (College Station: Texas A&M University Press, 1978).

56. Ibid., 56.

57. Martha Eva Rocha Islas, "Feminismo y Revolución," in *Un fantasma recorre el siglo: Luchas feministas en México, 1910–1920*, ed. Gisela Espinosa Damián and Ana Lau Javien (México: Universidad Autónoma Metropolitana Unidad Xochimilco, 2010), 27–60.

58. Peréz, *Decolonial Imaginary*, 33.

59. Hedrick, *Mestizo Modernism*, 16.

60. Baca, *Mestiz@ Scripts*, 5.

61. Ibid., 15.

62. Steven Best and Douglas Kellner, *Postmodern Theory: Critical Interrogations* (New York: Guildford Press, 1991), 57.

63. Jan C. Swearingen, "Song to Speech: The Origins of Early Epitaphia in Ancient Near Eastern Women's Lamentations," in *Rhetoric Before and Beyond the Greeks*, ed. Carol S. Lipson and Roberta A. Binkley (New York: State University of New York Press, 2004), 213.

64. Anzaldúa, *Borderlands/La Frontera*, 82.

65. Baca, *Mestiz@ Scripts*, 5.

66. Bruce McComiskey, *Gorgias and the New Sophistic Rhetoric* (Carbondale: Southern Illinois University Press: 2002), 21.

67. Jarratt, *Rereading the Sophists*, 14.

68. Ibid.

69. Ibid.

70. Krista Ratcliffe, *Rhetorical Listening: Identification, Gender, Whiteness* (Carbondale: Southern Illinois University Press, 2005).

71. Ibid., 25.

72. Ibid.

73. Ibid., 26.

74. Miguel Guajardo and Francisco Guajardo, "Two Brothers in Higher Education: Weaving a Social Fabric for Service in Academia," in *Doing the Public Good: Latino/a Scholars Engage Civic Participation*, ed. Kenneth P. González and Raymond V. Padilla (Sterling, VA: Stylus Publishing, 2008), 62.

75. Ratcliffe, *Rhetorical Listening*, 28.

76. Ibid., 32.

77. Ramona González, "'El Tesoro Enterrado' and Other Stories," in *Chicanas en la Literatura y el Arte*, ed. Herminio Rios, Octavio I. Romano-V, and Estela Portillo (Berkeley, CA: Quinto Sol Publications, 1973), 22–41.

78. Guajardo and Guajardo, "Two Brothers," 66.

79. Ratcliffe, *Rhetorical Listening*, 33.

80. Anna Marie Sandoval, *Toward a Latina Feminism of the Americas: Repression and Resistance in Chicana and Mexicana Literature* (Austin: University of Texas Press, 2008).

81. Ibid., 8.

82. Women in Mexico were not recognized as full citizens or allowed to vote until 1953, while women in the United States were granted suffrage through the Nineteenth Amendment in 1920.

83. Ratcliffe, *Rhetorical Listening*, 34.
84. Anzaldúa, *Borderlands/La Frontera*, 81.

Chapter Two

1. Lourdes Alvarado, *Educación y superación femenina en el siglo XIX: dos ensayos de Laureana Wright* (México: Universidad Nacional Autónoma de México, 2005), 16.
2. Ibid., 17.
3. Elvira Hernández Carballido, *Dos violetas del Anáhuac* (México: DEMAC, 2010), 24.
4. Alvarado, *Educación y superación*, 9.
5. Laureana Wright de Kleinhans, *La emancipación de la mujer por medio del estudio*, in *Educación y superación femenina en el siglo XIX: Dos ensayos de Laureana Wright*, by Lourdes Alvarado (México: Universidad Nacional Autónoma de México, 2005), 41.
6. To eliminate confusion between the two journals, when referencing the earlier 1873 journal of *Las Hijas del Anáhuac*, I will reference it under this original name. When referencing the 1887 journal of *Las Hijas del Anáhuac*, which changed its name to *Violetas de Anáhuac*, I will reference it under the latter title.
7. Many of these biographies had been published in *Violetas* over the period of two years. This work was not published until 1910, fourteen years after her death.
8. Rosario Castellanos, "Language as an Instrument of Domination," in *Women Writing Resistance: Essays on Latin America and the Caribbean*, ed. Jennifer Bowdy de Hernández (Cambridge, MA: South End Press, 2005), 74.
9. Oswaldo Baqueiro López, *La prensa y el estado* (Mérida, Yucatán: ISSTEY, 1992), 98.
10. Emily Hind, *Femmenism and the Mexican Woman Intellectual from Sor Juana to Poniatowska: Boob Lit* (New York: Palgrave Macmillan, 2010), 89.
11. Ana Lau Javien and Carmen Ramos, *Mujeres y revolución, 1900–1917* (México: Instituto Nacional de Estudios Históricos de la Revolución Mexicana, 1993).
12. Mateana Murguía de Aveleyra, "Laureana Wright de Kleinhans," *Violetas del Anáhuac* 1, no. 27 (1888): 315.
13. Ibid., 314.
14. See Lau Javien and Ramos, *Mujeres y revolución* for a detailed study on the male perspective of women's education, emancipation, and societal roles.
15. Murguía de Aveleyra, "Laureana Wright de Kleinhans," 314.
16. Nancy LaGreca, *Rewriting Womanhood: Feminism, Subjectivity, and the Angel of the House in the Latin American Novel, 1887–1903* (University Park: Pennsylvania State University Press, 2009), 11.
17. Murguía de Aveleyra, 315.
18. Ibid.
19. Verena Radkau, *Por la debilidad de nuestro ser: Mujeres "del pueblo" en la paz porfiriana* (México: Centro de Investigaciones y Estudios Superiores en Antropología Social, 1989), 14.
20. Lucrecia Infante Vargas, "Igualdad intelectual y género en *Violetas del Anáhuac: Periódico literario redactado por señoras, 1887–1889*," in *Cuatro estudios de género en*

el México urbano del siglo XIX, ed. Gabriela Cano and Georgette José Valenzuela (México: Universidad Autónoma de México, 2001), 129–56.

21. Karlyn Kohrs Campbell, *Man Cannot Speak for Her: A Critical Study of Early Feminist Rhetoric*, vol. I (New York: Greenwood Press, 1989), 15.

22. Julia Tuñón Pablos, *Women in Mexico: A Past Unveiled*, trans. Alan Hynds (Austin: University of Texas Press, 1987), 49.

23. LaGreca, *Rewriting Womanhood*, 29.

24. Mauricio Tenorio-Trillo, *Mexico at the World's Fairs: Crafting a Modern Nation* (Los Angeles: University of California Press, 1996), 3.

25. Maryellen Bieder, "Women, Literature, and Society: The Essays of Emilia Pardo Bazán," in *Spanish Women Writers and the Essay: Gender, Politics, and the Self*, ed. Kathleen Mary Glenn and Mercedes Mazquiarán de Rodriguez (Columbia: University of Missouri Press, 1998), 29.

26. *Las Hijas del Anáhuac*, October 19, 1873.

27. Gloria Anzaldúa, *Borderlands/La Frontera: The New Mestiza* (San Francisco: Aunt Lute Books, 1987), 78.

28. Rubén Medina, "El mestizaje a través de la frontera: Vasconcelos y Anzaldúa," *Mexican Studies/Estudios Mexicanos* 25, no. 1 (2009): 103.

29. Papantzin was an Aztec princess and sister to Moctezuma; Cuatlicue (or Coatlicue) is the Aztec goddess of birth and death; and Miahuaxochitl was the princess of Tula, the last of the women favored by Moctezuma II. I was unable to locate the identity of Ilancueitl. Information from *Mujeres notables mexicanas* by Laureana Wright de Kleinhans (México: Secretaria de Instrucción Pública y Bellas Artes, 1910).

30. Joel Bollinger Pouwels, *Political Journalism by Mexican Women During the Age of Revolution, 1876–1940* (Lewiston, NY: Edwin Mellon Press, 2006), 24.

31. Ilancueitl, "A nuestras lectoras," *Las Hijas del Anáhuac* 1, no. 1 (1873): 1.

32. Ibid.

33. Bollinger Pouwels, *Political Journalism*, 24.

34. Ibid.

35. Hernández Carballido, *Dos violetas*, 17–18.

36. Ibid.

37. The racial term *zambo* was used in the Spanish and Portuguese empires and refers to peoples in the Americas who were of African and Amerindian heritage. Today, it is considered a racial slur.

38. Laureana Wright de Kleinhans, "Algo sobre la Conquista y la Independencia de México: inconvenientes y ventajas de la dominación española en México," *Violetas del Anáhuac* 1, no. 16 (1888): 218.

39. Hernández Carballido, *Dos violetas*, 24.

40. "Saludos," *Las Hijas del Anáhuac* 1, no. 1 (1887): 1.

41. Tenorio-Trillo, *Mexico at the World's Fairs*, 32.

42. Ibid.

43. Castellanos, "Language as an Instrument," 74.

44. Ibid.

45. James A. Berlin, "Revisionary Histories of Rhetoric: Politics, Power, and Plurality," in *Writing Histories of Rhetoric*, ed. Victor Vitanza (Carbondale: Southern Illinois University Press, 1994), 116–17.

46. bell hooks, "Choosing the Margin as a Space of Radical Openness," in *Readings in Contemporary Rhetoric*, ed. Karen A. Foss, Sonja K. Foss, and Robert Trapp (Long Grove, IL: Waveland Press, 2002), 236.

47. Campbell, *Man Cannot Speak*, 15.

48. Laureana Wright de Kleinhans, "La educación del hogar," *Las Hijas del Anáhuac* 1, no. 2 (1887): 14.

49. María de la Luz Murguía, "La ilustración y la educación de la mujer," *Las Hijas del Anáhuac* 1, no. 1 (1887): 6.

50. This book is not a comparative analysis of American and Mexican women's suffrage; however, it is significant to point out that the neighboring countries' struggles to accept women in the discursive public sphere were very similar. Nan Johnson in *Gender and Rhetorical Space in American Life, 1866–1910* (Carbondale: Southern Illinois University Press, 2002) notes that many women blurred their efforts toward the abolition of slavery by claiming a public voice. In postbellum America, there were mixed feelings about whether women should continue speaking from the podium. See chapter 1, "Parlor Rhetoric and the Performance of Gender."

51. Concepción Manresa de Pérez, "Mujeres de nuestra época," *Las Hijas del Anáhuac* 1, no. 2 (1887): 19.

52. Stuart Easterling, "Gender and Poetry Writing in the Light of Mexico's Liberal Victory, 1867–ca. 1890," *Mexican Studies/Estudios Mexicanos* 27, no. 1 (2011): 97–142.

53. Ibid., 110.

54. Cynthia Miecznikowski Sheard, "The Public Value of Epideictic Rhetoric," *College English* 58, no. 7 (1996): 765–94.

55. Ibid., 768.

56. Ibid., 766, 770.

57. Easterling, "Gender and Poetry Writing," 101.

58. Laureana Wright de Kleinhans, "Prospecto," *Las Hijas del Anáhuac* 1, no. 1 (1887): 1.

59. María del Refugio Argumedo, viuda de Ortiz, "La oración matinal: á la distinguida Sra. Carmen Romero Rubio de Díaz," *Las Hijas del Anáhuac* 1, no. 1 (1888): 10.

60. María del Refugio Argumedo, vuida de Ortiz, "Cuauhtémoc," *Las Hijas del Anáhuac* 1, no. 1 (1888): 21.

61. Ignacia Padilla de Peña, "Charada," *Las Hijas del Anáhuac* 1, no. 4 (1888): 45.

62. Dolores Correa y Zapata, "La mujer," *Las Hijas del Anáhuac* 1, no. 4 (1888): 45.

63. Easterling, "Gender and Poetry Writing," 99.

64. Argumedo, vuida de Ortiz, "Poesía," *Las Hijas del Anáhuac* 1, no. 2 (1887): 23.

65. Ibid., 23.

66. Miecznikowski Sheard, "The Public Value," 770.

67. Manuel Romero, "Impresiones de la prensa," *Las Hijas del Anáhuac* 1, no. 3 (1887): 36.

68. Tenorio-Trillo, *Mexico at the World's Fairs*, 52.

69. Ibid.

70. Ibid., 184.

71. Ibid., 58.

72. Concepción Manresa de Pérez, "Mujeres de nuestra época," *Las Hijas del Anáhuac* 1, nos. 1–2 (1887): 7, 19.

73. Ibid., 19.

74. Bollinger Pouwels, *Political Journalism*, 28.

75. *El Álbum de la Mujer: Ilustración Hispano-Americana* was founded and headed in 1883 by Spanish feminist Concepción Gimeno de Flaquer, an experienced journalist with wealthy patrons. The journal ceased publication when Gimeno de Flaquer returned to Spain in 1890.

76. In *Violetas,* Wright de Kleinhans does include short entries on women from around the world, but foreign women do not receive the attention and space afforded women from Mexico.

77. Gabriela Cano, "The Porfiriato and the Mexican Revolution: Constructions of Feminism and Nationalism," in *Nation, Empire, Colony: Historicizing Gender and Race*, ed. Ruth Roach Pierson and Nupur Chaudhuri (Bloomington: Indiana University Press, 1998), 112.

78. Wright de Kleinhans, *Mujeres notables*, 2.

79. The Greek philosopher Socrates is touted as one of the founders of Western philosophy, and his existence is based solely on secondary sources. His writings do not exist; yet Socrates's validity is not disputed.

80. Wright de Kleinhans, *Mujeres notables*, 2.

81. Ibid.

82. Ibid.

83. Ibid.

84. Ibid.

85. Ibid.

86. Ibid., 25.

87. Ibid., 67.

88. Ibid., 100.

89. Ibid.

90. Ibid., 273.

91. Ibid., 75.

92. Wright de Kleinhans, "Heroínas de la Independencia" and "Contemporáneas desde 1820 hasta nuestros días," in *Mujeres notables*, 233, 313.

93. Wright de Kleinhans, *La emancipación*, 41.

94. Anzaldúa, *Borderlands/La Frontera*, 82.

Chapter Three

1. Eduardo N. Mijangos Díaz and Leticia Mendoza García, "Instrucción cívica y liberal del presbiterianismo en el distrito de Zitácuaro, 1894–1902," *Tzintzún: Revista de Estudios Históricos*, no. 54 (2011), 53–92.

2. The grito is a Mexican leader/response cheer of political solidarity.

3. *La Bandera Roja* first appeared in Durango, Mexico, in 1896 as an independent newspaper to defend and spread the liberal ideas put forward in the 1857 constitution. The authors published anonymously and wrote articles questioning the validity of religion and backing their arguments with scientific data. According to Salomón Meraz, the newspaper's ideas were much ahead of its time, and they could be deemed controversial even by today's standards. Liliana Salomón Meraz, *Historia del*

periodismo en Durango, etapa 1822–1950 (Durango, México: H. Congreso del Estado de Durango, 2010).

4. During this time period in Mexico, newspaper articles did not always distinguish where one author began and the other ended. This article, however, does show a quote included from *El Observador Zacatecano* and then goes on to indicate the declaration of the MZ. Yet it does not indicate who authored the first section of the article. The long title of this piece can offer insight into its different sections. The title is broken into segments, punctuated by periods and hyphens, which could indicate the beginning of one section leading to the next. The first part of the title is "Actitud del partido liberal por las revelaciones del Obispo de San Luis.—" Note the period and dash at the end of the title. The second part of the title after the dash is "Movimiento de indignación en toda la República.—" Note also the period and dash at the end of the title. This section of the title seems to correspond to the section quoted from *El Observador Zacatecano*. The last part of the title, "—Las Mujeres de Zitácuaro." (also ending in a period), could indicate the publication of the women's official declaration or plan, which in the original text is set off by an introduction of the segment and quotes. There is no definitive claim of authorship for this text, and so for the sake of assigning authorship, I will indicate that this article was a joint publication of the MZ and the staff of *La Bandera Roja*.

5. The article "La mujer se emancipa de las opresoras cadenas del clericalismo" was authored by Ignacio Zaragoza, a pseudonym used by one of the writers for *La Bandera Roja*. The newspaper writing staff did not use their personal names on the broadsheet. Instead, they used the names of past generals and leaders of the liberal party as pseudonyms. These names were well known in Mexico, beginning with Francisco O. Arce, the pseudonym used for the director and founder of the newspaper. Other pseudonyms they used, in addition to Zaragoza, were Melchor Ocampo, Miguel Cruz-Aedo, Ignacio Allende, and Ignacio Comonfort.

6. According to the manifiesto, the document was signed on November 11, 1900, in Zitácuaro, Michoacán. The grito, which follows traditional Mexican custom, was officially proclaimed at the signing.

7. Las Mujeres de Zitácuaro, "Propaganda liberal, Manifiesto," *La Bandera Roja*, December 7, 1900, 2.

8. Josefa Ortiz de Domínguez, also known as La Corregidora, wife of the chief magistrate, played a major role in Mexico's independence from Spain in 1810. I was unable to locate information on Francisca Carillo.

9. Karl M. Schmitt, "Catholic Adjustment to the Secular State: The Case of Mexico, 1867–1911," *Catholic Historical Review* 48, no. 2 (1962): 182–204.

10. The complete text of the speech can be found in Manuel González Ramírez, *Manifiestos Políticos, 1892–1912: Fuentes para la historia de la revolución* (México: Fondo de Cultura Económica, 1957), 107–11.

11. In the late nineteenth century and into the twentieth, Communism in Mexico became an attractive political direction for many who saw the situation under the dictator Díaz to be unsupportable. Communism would not take hold in Mexico as a political party, but many revolutionaries used its precepts as formidable directions to critique the power of the church and the government. For a history on Communism in Mexico see Daniela Spenser, *Stumbling Its Way Through Mexico: The Early Years of the Communist International* (Tuscaloosa: University of Alabama Press, 2011).

12. Las Mujeres de Zitácuaro, "Liberal Propaganda," 2.

13. James D. Cockcroft, *Intellectual Precursors of the Mexican Revolution, 1900–1913* (Austin: University of Texas Press, 1968), 94.

14. Carolyn R. Miller, "Genre as Social Action," in *Genre and the New Rhetoric*, ed. Aviva Freedman and Peter Medway (London: Taylor and Francis, 1994), 26.

15. Ibid., 29.

16. Ibid., 37.

17. Fernando Serrano Migallón, *El grito de independencia: historia de una pasión nacional* (México: Miguel Ángel Porrúa, 1981), 201–24.

18. Ibid.

19. John C. Hammerback and Richard J. Jensen, "Ethnic Heritage as Rhetorical Legacy: The Plan of Delano," in *Readings of the Rhetoric of Social Protest*, ed. Charles E. Morris III and Stephen Howard Browne (State College, PA: Strata Publishing, 2006), 305.

20. Ibid., 306.

21. González Ramírez, *Manifiestos políticos*, VII.

22. Ibid., VIII.

23. Jacqueline Jones Royster, "Disciplinary Landscaping, or Contemporary Challenges in the History of Rhetoric," *Philosophy and Rhetoric* 36, no. 2 (2003): 159.

24. Damían Baca, *Mestiz@ Scripts, Digital Migrations, and the Territories of Writing* (New York: Palgrave Macmillan, 2008), 30.

25. Shirlene Soto, *Emergence of the Modern Mexican Woman: Her Participation in Revolution and Struggle for Equality, 1910–1940* (Denver: Arden Press, 1990), 125–33.

26. Emma Pérez, *The Decolonial Imaginary: Writing Chicanas into History* (Bloomington: Indiana University Press, 1999), 63.

27. Camilo Arriaga, "Invitación al Partido Liberal," *La Bandera Roja*, September 14, 1900.

28. Las Mujeres de Zitácuaro, "Propaganda liberal," 2.

29. Ignacio Zaragoza, "Nuestra obra debe ser emancipar a la mujer del clericalismo," *La Bandera Roja*, September 17, 1900.

30. Ignacio Zaragoza, "El Instituto de Niñas," *La Bandera Roja*, December 21, 1900.

31. Ibid.

32. "La mujer modesta," *La Bandera Roja*, December 21, 1900.

33. Ibid. In this quote, there is reference to an English philosopher, Joung. The identity of this philosopher could not be authenticated. The author could be making reference to Carl Jung. However, Jung was Swiss, and his writings would not emerge for several more years.

34. Cockcroft, *Intellectual Precursors*, 92.

35. Ibid., 93.

36. See note 5 for the distinction of authorship.

37. Las Mujeres de Zitácuaro, "Actitud del partido liberal por las revelaciones del Obispo de San Luis.—Movimiento de indignación en toda la República.—Las Mujeres de Zitácuaro," *La Bandera Roja*, October 26, 1900, 2.

38. Díaz and García, "Instrucción cívica," 70–72.

39. Las Mujeres de Zitácuaro, "Actitud del partido liberal," 1.

40. Ibid.

41. Ibid.

42. Manuel González Ramírez, *Planes políticos y otros documentos* (México: Fondo de Cultura Económica, 1954), VIII.

43. Hammerback and Jensen, "Ethnic Heritage," 305.

44. Thomas B. Davis and Amado Ricon Virulegio, *The Political Plans of Mexico* (Lanham, MD: University Press of America, 1987), 13.

45. Ibid., 1.

46. Ibid.

47. Las Mujeres de Zitácuaro, "Actitud del partido liberal," 2.

48. Davis and Virulegio, *Political Plans*, XV.

49. There is no direct translation for the word *Gachupines* in the English language. The term is a derogatory word for Spaniards, specifically those who were born in Spain and who lived in Mexico.

50. Serrano Migallón, *El grito*, 32.

51. Asunción Lavrin, *Women, Feminism, and Social Change in Argentina, Chile, and Uruguay, 1890–1940* (Lincoln: University of Nebraska Press, 1995), 21.

52. Julia Tuñón Pablos, *Women in Mexico: A Past Unveiled*, trans. Alan Hynds (Austin: University of Texas Press, 1999), 60.

53. Ibid., 62.

54. Ibid.

55. Las Mujeres de Zitácuaro, "Propaganda liberal," 1–2.

56. Ignacio Zaragoza, "La mujer se emancipa de las opresoras cadenas del clericalismo," *La Bandera Roja*, December 7, 1900, 1.

57. Ibid.

58. Las Mujeres de Zitácuaro, "Propaganda liberal," 1–2.

59. James E. Porter, "Intertextuality and the Discourse Community," *Rhetoric Review* 5, no. 1 (1986): 35.

60. Las Mujeres de Zitácuaro, "Propaganda liberal," 1–2.

61. González Ramírez, *Manifiestos Políticos*, 3.

62. Ibid., 166.

63. Ibid., 198.

64. Las Mujeres de Zitácuaro, "Propaganda liberal," 2.

65. Michael Leff, "Tradition and Agency in Humanistic Rhetoric," *Philosophy and Rhetoric* 36, no. 2 (2003): 138.

66. Las Mujeres de Zitácuaro, "Propaganda liberal," 2.

67. Ibid.

68. Ibid.

69. Ibid.

70. Ibid.

71. Ibid.

72. Ibid.

73. Davis and Virulegio, *Political Plans*, X.

74. Patricia Bizzel and Bruce Herzberg, eds., *The Rhetorical Tradition: Readings from Classical Times to the Present* (Boston: Bedford/St. Martin's, 2001), 117.

75. Baca, *Mestiz@ Scripts*, 5.

76. "Vésper," *La Bandera Roja*, May 19, 1901, 3.

77. Ibid.

Chapter Four

1. James D. Cockcroft, *Intellectual Precursors of the Mexican Revolution, 1900–1913* (Austin, University of Texas Press, 1968), 4–5.

2. Angeles Mendieta Alatorre, *Juana Belén Gutiérrez de Mendoza (1875–1942): Extraordinaria precursora de la revolución mexicana* (México: Copilco Universidad, 1983), 91–92.

3. For history on other women involved in the Mexican Revolution see Anna Macías, *Against All Odds: The Feminist Movement in Mexico to 1940* (Westport, CT: Greenwood Press, 1982).

4. Mendieta Alatorre, *Extraordinaria precursora*, 16. One of Gutiérrez de Mendoza's common stylistic features was to use all capitals in her writing, as if either to draw emphasis or to mark as shouting.

5. Robert Cathcart, "Movements: Confrontations as Rhetorical Form," *Southern Speech Communication Journal* 43 (1978): 238.

6. Ibid.

7. Ibid., 241.

8. Elias Serna, "Tempest Arizona: Criminal Epistemologies and the Rhetorical Possibilities of Raza Studies," *Urban Rev* 45 (2013), 47.

9. Ibid.

10. Cathcart, "Movements," 238.

11. Ibid.

12. Ibid., 242.

13. Guillermo Bonfil Batalla, *México Profundo: Reclaiming a Civilization*, trans. Philip A. Dennis (Austin: University of Texas Press, 1996), 16–17.

14. Alicia Villaneda, *Juana Belén Gutiérrez de Mendoza, 1875–1942* (México: Documentación y Estudios de Mujeres, 1994), 49, 51, 73.

15. Ibid.

16. Mary K. Vaughan, *Cultural Politics in Revolution: Teachers, Peasants, and Schools in Mexico, 1930–1940* (Tucson: University of Arizona Press, 1997), 26.

17. Certificado de Bautismo, Parroquia de San Francisco de Asís, San Juan del Río, Durango, Mexico.

18. Villaneda, *Juana*, 18.

19. Ibid., 19.

20. Ibid.

21. I could not locate the exact date of Cirilo Mendoza's death.

22. Ana Lau Javien, "Juana Belén Gutiérrez de Mendoza: ¡Me quiebro pero no me doblo!" *Sólo Historia*, Instituto Nacional de Estudios Históricos de la Revolución Mexicana, no. 8 (April–June 2000): 9–14.

23. Mendieta Alatorre, *Extraordinaria precursora*, 63.

24. Ibid., 21.

25. Francisco Zarco and José Revueltas were born in Durango, Mexico, like Gutiérrez de Mendoza.

26. Eduardo Arrieta Corral, "Juana Belén Gutiérrez de Mendoza: olvidada heroína del periodismo político mexicano" (Apuntes Biográficos), in *Tres revolucionarios de México: Tomas Urbina, Orestes Pereyra y Juana Belén Gutiérrez* by Arrieta Corral,

Antonio Arreola, and Javier Guerrero Romero (Durango, México: Comisión de Reinhumación y Homenaje, 1991), 13.

27. Cathcart, "Movements," 245–46.

28. The subtitle of *Justicia y Libertad* was added in 1901, while she wrote and published from Mexico City.

29. Joel Bollinger Pouwels, *Political Journalism by Mexican Women During the Age of Revolution, 1876–1940* (Lewiston, NY: Edwin Mellen Press, 2006), 63.

30. Other newspapers included *El Diablito Bromista* (The Devil Trickster), directed by Antonio de P. Escárcega; *La Democracia Latina*, directed by Adolfo Duclós Salinas in Monterrey; *El Demófilo* (Friend of the People), directed by José Millán in San Luis Potosí; and *El Alacrán* (The Scorpion), directed by Alberto Araus and Mariano Ceballos. See Diego Arenas Guzmán, *El periodismo en la revolución mexicana de 1908 a 1917*, vol. 2 (México: Patronato del Instituto Nacional de Estudios Históricos de la Revolución Mexicana, 1967), 14–20.

31. Cockcroft, *Intellectual Precursors*, 102.

32. Although Gutiérrez de Mendoza expressed radical views, she was not a communist. This philosophical stance is noted when she broke ranks with the Richardo Flores Magón because of his anarchist and communist views.

33. Cockcroft, *Intellectual Precursors*, 114.

34. Villaneda, *Juana*, 132–33.

35. Cockcroft, *Intellectual Precursors*, 114.

36. Mendieta Alatorre, *Extraordinaria precursora*, 136.

37. Charles A. Hale, "Emilio Castelar and Mexico," in *The Political Power of the Word: Press and Oratory in Nineteenth Century Latin America*, ed. Iván Jaksić (London: Institute of Latin American Studies, 2002), 141.

38. Ibid.

39. Mendieta Alatorre, *Extraordinaria precursora*, 129.

40. Ibid.

41. *Ecce homo* is the Latin phrase meaning "Behold the man" used by Pontius Pilate to announce to a crowd of people that Jesus Christ would be crucified.

42. Mendieta Alatorre, *Extraordinaria precursora*, 131.

43. Ibid.

44. Cristina Rivera-Garza, "The Criminalization of the Syphilitic Body: Prostitutes, Health Crimes, and Society in Mexico City, 1867–1930," in *Crime and Punishment in Latin America: Law and Society Since Late Colonial Times*, ed. Ricardo D. Salvatore, Carlos Aguirre, and Gilbert M. Joseph (Durham, NC: Duke University Press, 2001), 157.

45. Emma Pérez, *The Decolonial Imaginary: Writing Chicanas into History* (Bloomington: Indiana University Press, 1999), 37.

46. Mendieta Alatorre, *Extraordinaria precursora*, 22.

47. Kristen Kennedy, "Cynic Rhetoric: The Ethics and Tactics of Resistance," *Rhetoric Review* 18, no. 3 (1999): 42.

48. Ibid.

49. Serna, "Tempest Arizona," 47.

50. Jessica Enoch, "*Para la Mujer*: Defining a Chicana Feminist Rhetoric at the Turn of the Century," *College English* 67 (2004): 20.

51. Mendieta Alatorre, *Extraordinaria precursora*, 23.

52. Villaneda, *Juana*, 34.

53. Nicolás Kanellos and Helvita Martell, *Hispanic Periodicals in the United States, Origins to 1960: A Brief History and Comprehensive Bibliography* (Houston: Arte Público Press, 2000), 23–24.

54. Ibid.

55. Mendieta Alatorre, *Extraordinaria precursora*, 24.

56. Kristen Kennedy, "Hipparchia the Cynic: Feminist Rhetoric and the Ethics of Embodiment," *Hypatia* 14, no. 2 (1999), 59.

57. Ricardo Flores Magón was politically active throughout the years of the Mexican Revolution. He organized protests and was prolific in his writings about social justice. He would die in the Leavenworth, Kansas, prison in 1922. For more on Ricardo Flores Magón, see Chaz Bufe and Mitchell Cowen Verter, eds., *Dreams of Freedom: A Ricardo Flores Magón Reader* (Oakland, CA: AK Press, 2005).

58. Villaneda, *Juana*, 43.

59. Bollinger Pouwels, *Political Journalism*, 69.

60. Bollinger Pouwels notes that the newspaper *Anáhuac* had several connections with other revolutionaries. Gutiérrez de Mendoza cofounded the weekly with José Edilberto Pinelo, who coauthored, with Dolores Jiménez y Muro, the 1911 Political and Social Plan signed by the Tacubaya conspirators. The 1907 editorial board of *Anáhuac* is listed on the front page of the January 1, 1907, issue. The officers included J. Edilberto Pinelo, Juana Gutiérrez, Elisa Acuña y Rosette, and several male representatives.

61. Bollinger Pouwels, *Political Journalism*, 70.

62. Ibid., 71.

63. Mendieta Alatorre, *Extraordinaria precursora*, 147.

64. John Lear, *Workers, Neighbors, and Citizens: The Revolution in Mexico City* (Lincoln: University of Nebraska Press, 2001), 131.

65. Ibid.

66. Ibid.

67. Mendieta Alatorre, *Extraordinaria precursora*, 148–49.

68. For a full account of the Mexican Revolution, see Alan Knight, *The Mexican Revolution*, 4 vols. (New York: Cambridge University Press, 1986).

69. Arrieta Corral, "Olvidada heroina," 15–16.

70. This significant event would be known as La Decena Trágica.

71. Mendieta Alatorre, *Extraordinaria precursora*, 65.

72. Amigas del Pueblo, "El club político femenil 'Amigas del Pueblo' a las mexicanas," *El Voto* (1913): 3.

73. Macías, *Against All Odds*, 49.

74. Women from the lower classes many times had no choice but to follow their men into battle, while women from the upper and middle classes could participate peripherally if they so chose. For more on women's roles in the Revolution see Stephanie Mitchell and Patience A. Schell, eds., *The Women's Revolution in Mexico, 1910–1953* (Lanham, MD: Rowman and Littlefield Publishers, 2007) and Shirlene Soto, *Emergence of the Modern Mexican Woman: Her Participation in Revolution and Struggle for Equality, 1910–1940* (Denver: Arden Press, 1990).

75. Mendieta Alatorre, *Extraordinaria precursora*, 65.

76. Ibid., 64. There is no evidence that Gutiérrez de Mendoza was involved in battle, but while she served as leader of the regiment Victoria, one of the members raped a woman, and upon Gutiérrez de Mendoza's orders, the guilty member was killed as punishment. When the word reached Zapata, many people thought that he would not accept her actions, but he sanctioned her decision and coupled it with a decree that those who engaged in abuse against women should be severely punished.

77. Bollinger Pouwels, *Political Journalism*, 75.

78. Villaneda, *Juana*, 78.

79. Some of the Mexican Revolution's ideals would later be implemented under the policies of President Lázaro Cárdenas between 1934 and 1940. See Mary Kay Vaughan, *Cultural Politics in Revolution: Teachers, Peasants, and Schools in Mexico, 1930–1940* (Tucson: University of Arizona Press, 1997).

80. Juana Belén Gutiérrez de Mendoza, "Desmontando," *El Desmonte: Por la Tierra y por la Raza* 1, no. 1 (June 15, 1919): 1.

81. Juana Belén Gutiérrez de Mendoza, "Hechos, no palabras," *El Desmonte: Por la Tierra y por la Raza* 1, no. 1 (June 15, 1919): 1.

82. Charles J. Stewart, "The Evolution of a Revolution: Stokely Carmichael and the Rhetoric of Black Power," *Quarterly Journal of Speech* 83 (1997): 429–46.

83. Gutiérrez de Mendoza, "Hechos," 1.

84. Alan Knight, "Popular Culture and the Revolutionary State in Mexico, 1910–1940, *Hispanic American Historical Review* 74, no. 3 (1994): 393–443.

85. Villaneda, *Juana*, 82.

86. Henry C. Schmidt, *The Roots of Lo Mexicano: Self and Society in Mexican Thought, 1900–1934* (College Station: Texas A&M University Press, 1978), 117–38. There were other intellectuals at the time who also expressed a *mexicanidad* that shaped the era, such as Antonio Caso, Alfonso Reyes, Samuel Ramos, and Daniel Casío Villegas.

87. José Vasconcelos, *The Cosmic Race/La raza cósmica*, trans. Didier T. Jaén (Baltimore: Johns Hopkins University Press, 1997), 20.

88. Vaughan, *Cultural Politics*, 11.

89. Ibid., 12.

90. Ibid., 6.

91. Ibid., 11.

92. Mendieta Alatorre, *Extraordinaria precursora*, 66.

93. Ibid., 155.

94. Gloria Anzaldúa, *Borderlands/La Frontera: The New Mestiza* (San Francisco: Aunt Lute Books, 1987), 86.

95. Gutiérrez de Mendoza claimed to be descended from the Caxcan people, close descendants to the Mexica people. The Caxcan Indians spoke a language very similar to Mexica.

96. The chapters were not given titles.

97. Mary E. Hawkesworth, "Feminist Rhetoric: Discourses on the Monopoly of Thought," *Political Theory* 16, no. 3 (1988), 457.

98. Juana Belén Gutiérrez de Mendoza, *¡Por la tierra y por la raza!* (México: Consejo de los Caxcanes, 1924), 5.

99. Ibid., 24.
100. Ibid., 25.
101. Ibid.
102. Vaughan, *Cultural Politics*, 60.
103. Gutiérrez de Mendoza, *Por la tierra*, 13–14.
104. Ibid.
105. Ibid., 103.
106. Anzaldúa, *Borderlands/La Frontera*, 87.
107. Ibid., 82.
108. Ibid.
109. Ana Lau Javien, "La participación de las mujeres en la revolución mexicana: Juana Belén Gutiérrez de Mendoza (1875–1942), *Diálogos Revista Electrónica de Historia* 5, nos. 1–2 (2005): 23.
110. Ibid.
111. Ibid., 24.
112. Ibid.
113. Ibid., 28.
114. Ibid. I was not able to locate the actual primary documents of these publications listed by Lau Javien.
115. Ibid., 28.
116. Bollinger Pouwels, *Political Journalism*, 84.
117. Ibid.

Chapter Five

The title of this chapter, *Mi grano de arena en esa hermosa labor*, translates as "My grain of sand in that beautiful work."

1. Hermila Galindo's married name was Hermila Galindo de Topete, which she did not take until 1923, after her work with President Carranza as spokeswoman and journalist. Because her married name postdates her public work, I refer to her as Hermila Galindo.
2. Being the Constitutionalist president meant that he supported the drafting of a new constitution to set Mexico back on the track to prosperity after years of a bloody revolution. For more on Carranza see Mark T. Gilderhus, *Diplomacy and Revolution: U.S.-Mexican Relations Under Wilson and Carranza* (Tucson: University of Arizona Press, 1977).
3. At the time Galindo entered into the political scene, Mexico had been at war for four years and there was a move to write a new constitution to replace the 1857 constitution. Galindo was hopeful that the issue of women's suffrage would be included in the new policies. The new constitution would eventually be signed in 1917.
4. Laura Orellana Trinidad, *Hermila Galindo: Una mujer moderna* (México: Instituto Nacional de Bella Artes, 2001), 30–31.
5. Ibid.
6. Ibid.
7. Revolutionary ideals included the redistribution of lands to indigenous peoples, a strict nationalist stance in terms of land ownership that would limit the influence of

European and U.S. businesses in the national markets of natural resources, a secularization of the country that would further limit the influence of the Catholic Church, and a unification of the people under the racial project of mestizaje.

8. Orellana Trinidad, *Hermila Galindo*, 30–31.

9. Benito Juárez was the president of Mexico from 1858 to 1872 who overthrew Austrian archduke Ferdinand Maximilian, the ruling puppet for the French. This comparison was significant for Carranza because Benito Juárez was the politician he tried to emulate throughout his career.

10. For more on the emergence of women in society during the Mexican Revolution see Shirlene Soto, *Emergence of the Modern Mexican Women: Her Participation in Revolution and Struggle of Equality* (Denver: Arden Press, 1990).

11. Emilie Bergmann et al., *Women, Culture, and Politics in Latin America: Seminar on Feminism and Culture in Latin America* (Berkeley: University of California Press, 1990), 12.

12. Holly J. Maccamon, "Stirring Up Suffrage Sentiment: The Formation of the State Woman Suffrage Organizations, 1866–1914," *Social Forces* 80, no. 2 (2001): 453.

13. Hermila Galindo, *La doctrina Carranza y el acercamiento indolatino* (México, 1919), 160.

14. Emma Pérez, *Decolonial Imaginary: Writing Chicanas into History* (Bloomington: Indiana University Press: 1999), 33.

15. Orellana Trinidad notes that upon the release of Galindo's feminist journal, *La Mujer Moderna*, Carranza urged politicians from around Mexico to order a minimum of fifty subscriptions and distribute them among the teachers. Orellana Trinidad, *Hermila Galindo*, 40.

16. Ibid, 33.

17. Ibid.

18. Mary E. Hawkesworth, "Feminist Rhetoric: Discourses on the Male Monopoly of Thought," *Political Theory* 16, no. 3 (1988), 444.

19. Ibid.

20. Ibid., 449.

21. Orellana Trinidad, *Hermila Galindo*, 18.

22. Ibid., 61.

23. Hermila Galindo, "Estudio de la Srita. Hermila Galindo con motivo de los temas que han de absolverse en el Segundo Congreso Feminista de Yucatán." Segundo Congreso Feminista de Yucatán, El Gobierno Constitutionalista, Merída, Yucatán, November 20, 1916, 7.

24. Ibid.

25. Hawkesworth, "Feminist Rhetoric," 457.

26. Henry C. Schmidt, *The Roots of Lo Mexicano: Self and Society in Mexican Thought, 1900–1934* (College Station: Texas A&M University Press, 1978), 38–65.

27. Joshua Lund, *The Impure: Toward a Critical Hybridity in Latin American Writing* (Minneapolis: University of Minnesota Press, 2006), 87.

28. Hermila Galindo, "¡Laboremos!," in *Sol de libertad: Hermila Galindo: feminista, constitucionalista y primera censora legislativa en México*, by Rosa María Valles Ruiz (México: Instituto de Cultura del Estado de Durango, 2010), 226.

29. A sample list of the contributors to the journal included: Señoras (married women) María Luisa de la Torre de Otero, Clarisa P. de Torres, Beatriz M. de Santa María, Micaela Rosado de P.; Señoritas (single women) Candelaria Ruz Patrón, Salomé Carranza G., María de Jesús Carranza, Lucía Bustamante, Rosario Rivas Hernández, María Pachecho, and Bolivia M. de Rivas. These names are cited from the director's column published October 31, 1919.

30. Olivia Noguez Noguez, "Hermila Galindo y 'La Mujer Moderna' (1915–1916): abriendo espacios; entre la domesticidad y los derechos por la igualdad," Revista Historia 2.0, Conocimiento histórico en clave digital 4 (2012), accessed September 16, 2014, http://historia2.0.historiaabierta.org/.

31. Pacheco de Torres, "Por qué deben votar las mujeres," *La Mujer Moderna*, no. 1 (October 31, 1915): 14.

32. Hermila Galindo, "La cuestión sufragista: para qué quieren el voto las mujeres" and "Petición hecha por nuestra directora al H. Constituyente sobre el derecho al voto de la mujer," in *Sol de Libertad: Hermila Galindo, feminista, constitucionalista y primera censora legislativa en México*, by Rosa María Valles Ruiz (México: Instituto de Cultura del Estado de Durango, 2010), 228–29, 243–47.

33. "La Srita. Galindo opina sobre su candidatura para diputado," in Valles Ruiz, *Sol de libertad*, 24–47.

34. The results of the election showed that Galindo had won the vote; however, her win was denied by the government because women had not been given citizenship in the Constitution of 1917.

35. Orellana Trinidad, *Hermila Galindo*, 33.

36. Ibid.

37. The antiassimilationist position was aimed at the political dispute between the United States and Mexico. The nationalist belief was based on the nations of Latin America coming together to fight economic, cultural, and territorial colonialism.

38. For complete texts of speeches, letters, and articles published outside of *La Mujer Moderna*, such as in *El Pueblo*, see Valles Ruiz, *Sol de libertad*, 173–301.

39. Galindo, *La doctrina*, 162.

40. The "common enemy" she makes reference to is the United States. Mexico saw the United States as making advances on the sovereignty of their nation. President Woodrow Wilson, holding a liberal capitalist stance toward Latin American nations, had intervened in Mexico's business and held port in Veracruz for months. As Carranza came into power, there was a growing distrust against the United States, which wanted to protect its interests in oil and mining in Mexico. Carranza was on a path contrary to U.S. capitalist ideas, and that was to protect Mexico's right to self-determination.

41. Galindo, *La doctrina*, 164.

42. Ramón D. Chacón, "Rural Educational Reform in Yucatán: From the Porfiriato to the Era of Salvador Alvarado, 1910–1918," *The Americas* 42, no. 2 (1985): 214.

43. Ibid.

44. Macías, *Against All Odds*, 67.

45. Orellana Trinidad, *Hermila Galindo*, 71.

46. Pérez, *Decolonial Imaginary*, 40.

47. Orellana Trinidad, *Hermila Galindo*, 76.

48. Alaide Foppa and Helene F. de Aguilar, "The First Feminist Congress in Mexico," *Signs* 5, no. 1 (1979): 194.

49. Orellana Trinidad, *Hermila Galindo*, 69.

50. Hermila Galindo, "La mujer en el porvenir," First Feminist Congress, Government of Yucatán, Merída, Yucatán, November 29, 1915, 1.

51. Kenneth Burke, *A Rhetoric of Motives* (Berkeley: University of California Press, 1969), 21.

52. Galindo, "La mujer," 5.

53. The arguments she makes here reflect the ideas that Laureana Wright de Kleinhans made two decades before in *La emancipación de la mujer por medio del estudio*.

54. Galindo, "La mujer," 8.

55. Orellana Trinidad, *Hermila Galindo*, 83.

56. Foppa and Aguilar, "First Feminist Congress," 199.

57. Galindo, "Estudio de la Srita. Hermila Galindo." In this section, I can provide only a short and insufficient analysis of what she truly accomplished in the response, but allow me to say that this speech needs a deep rhetorical analysis to uncover its rhetorical treasures. I believe this piece to be her first tour de force.

58. Ibid., 4.

59. Ibid., 7.

60. Ibid., 8.

61. Nikki Craske, "Ambiguities and Ambivalences in Making the Nation: Women and Politics in 20th-Century Mexico," *Feminist Review* 79 (2005), 118.

62. Gilderhus, *Diplomacy and Revolution*, 3.

63. Galindo, *La doctrina*, 124–25.

64. Hawkesworth, "Feminist Rhetoric," 457.

65. Ibid.

66. Galindo, *La doctrina*, 1.

67. Ibid., 8.

68. Ibid., 187.

69. Ibid., 187–88.

70. Hawkesworth, "Feminist Rhetoric," 452.

71. Ibid.

72. Gilderhus, *Diplomacy and Revolution*, 110.

73. When Galindo backed the losing presidential candidate, she would have been blacklisted (it's called being "burned," *quemado/a*) by the winning candidate and his administration. In Galindo's case, the winning candidate, Álvaro Obregón, probably had Carranza assassinated. As a result, Galindo would have been unable to occupy any public puesto under Obregón or his successor, Plutarco Elías Calles.

74. Martha Eva Rocha, "The Faces of Rebellion: From Revolutionaries to Veterans in Nationalist Mexico," in *The Women's Revolution in Mexico, 1910–1953*, ed. Stephanie Mitchell and Patience A. Schell (Lanham, MD: Rowman and Littlefield Publishers, Inc., 2007), 26.

75. Rosa María Valles Ruiz, "Hermila Galindo, un caso de feminismo ilustrado en los albores del siglo XX," *Revista de Historia de América* 142 (2010): 49.

76. Galindo, *La doctrina*, 191.

Epilogue

1. Maureen Ahern, ed., *A Rosario Castellanos Reader: An Anthology of Her Poetry, Short Fiction, Essays, and Drama* (Austin: University of Texas Press, 1988), 250–53.

2. Barbara Biesecker, "Coming to Terms with Recent Attempts to Write Women into the History of Rhetoric," *Philosophy and Rhetoric* 25, no. 2 (1992): 152.

3. Ibid., 155.

4. Julia Tuñón Pablos, *Women in Mexico: A Past Unveiled*, trans. Alan Hynds (Austin: University of Texas Press, 1987), 53.

5. "La ilustración de la mujer," *El Correo de Durango* 1, no. 4 (November 15, 1903). The piece was published anonymously, but it could have originated from the desk of the director or the other two contributors named on the masthead, Ernesto Galarza or Pedro S. Díaz.

6. Ibid.

7. Chandra Talpade Mohanty, *Feminism Without Borders: Decolonizing Theory, Practicing Solidarity* (Durham, NC: Duke University Press, 2003), 23.

8. Richard Leo Enos, *Greek Rhetoric Before Aristotle* (Anderson, SC: Parlor Press, 2012), 8–9.

9. Rosario Castellanos, "Language as an Instrument of Domination," trans. Maureen Ahern, in *A Rosario Castellanos Reader: An Anthology of Her Poetry, Short Fiction, Essays, and Drama*, ed. Maureen Ahern (Austin: University of Texas Press, 1988), 251.

Bibliography

Primary Sources

Amigas del Pueblo. "El club político femenil 'Amigas del Pueblo' a las mexicanas." *El Voto* (1913): 3.

Argumedo, viuda de Ortiz, María del Refugio. "Cuauhtémoc." *Las Hijas del Anáhuac* 1, no. 1 (1888): 21.

———. "La oración matinal: á la distinguida Sra. Carmen Romero Rubio de Díaz." *Las Hijas del Anáhuac* 1, no. 1 (1888): 10.

Arriaga, Camilo. "Invitación al Partido Liberal." *La Bandera Roja*, September 14, 1900.

Correa y Zapata, Dolores. "La mujer." *Las Hijas del Anáhuac* 1, no. 4 (1888): 45.

Galindo, Hermila. *La doctrina Carranza y el acercamiento indolatino*. México, 1919.

———. "Estudio de la Srita. Hermila Galindo con motivo de los temas que han de absolverse en el Segundo Congreso Feminista de Yucatán." Segundo Congreso Feminista de Yucatán, El Gobierno Constitutionalista, Merída, Yucatán, November 20, 1916.

Gimeno de Flaquer, Concepción. *El Album de la Mujer: Ilustración Hispano-Americana*, 1883–90.

———. "La mujer estudiosa." *La Mujer: Semanario de la Escuela de Artes y Oficios para Mujeres* 4, no. 158 (1883).

Gutiérrez de Mendoza, Juana Belén. "Desmontando." *El Desmonte*, June 15, 1919.

———. *¡Por la tierra y por la raza!* México: Consejo de los Caxcanes, 1924.

Ilancueitl [pseud.]. "A nuestras lectoras." *Las Hijas del Anáhuac* 1, no. 1 (1873): 1.

"La mujer modesta." *La Bandera Roja*, December 21, 1900.

Las Mujeres de Zitácuaro. "Actitud del partido liberal por las revelaciones del Obispo de San Luis.—Movimiento de indignación en toda la República." *La Bandera Roja*, October 26, 1900.

———. "Propaganda liberal, Manifiesto." *La Bandera Roja*, December 7, 1900.

Manresa de Pérez, Concepción. "Mujeres de nuestra época." *Las Hijas del Anáhuac* 1, nos. 1–2 (1887): 7, 19.

Murguía, María de la Luz. "La ilustración y la educación de la mujer." *Las Hijas del Anáhuac* 1, no. 1 (1887): 6–7.

Murguía de Aveleyra, Mateana. "Laureana Wright de Kleinhans." *Violetas del Anáhuac* 1, no. 27 (1888): 314–17.

Pacheco de Torres, Clarisa. "Por qué deben votar las mujeres." *La Mujer Moderna*, October 31, 1915.

Padilla de Peña, Ignacia. "Charada." *Las Hijas del Anáhuac* 1, no. 4 (1888): 45.

Romero, Manuel. "Impresiones de la prensa." *Las Hijas del Anáhuac* 1, no. 3 (1887): 36.

Torres, Mariano de Jesus. "Introduction." *La Mujer Mexicana*, February 1901.

Wright de Kleinhans, Laureana. "Algo sobre la Conquista y la Independencia de México: inconvenientes y ventajas de la dominación española en México." *Violetas del Anáhuac* 1, no. 16 (1888): 217–18.

———. "La educación del hogar." *Las Hijas del Anáhuac* 1, no. 2 (1887): 15.

———. *Mujeres notables mexicanas*. México: Secretaría de Instrucción Pública y Bellas Artes, 1910.

———. "Prospecto." *Las Hijas del Anáhuac* 1, no. 1 (1887): 1.

Zaragoza, Ignacio [pseud.]. "La mujer se emancipa de las opresoras cadenas del clericalismo." *La Bandera Roja*, December 7, 1900.

———. "El Instituto de Niñas." *La Bandera Roja*, December 21, 1900.

Secondary Sources

Ahern, Maureen, ed. *A Rosario Castellanos Reader: An Anthology of Her Poetry, Short Fiction, Essays, and Drama*. Austin: University of Texas Press, 1988.

Alarcón, Norma. "Traddutora, Traditora: A Paradigmatic Figure of Chicana Feminism." *Cultural Critique*, no. 13 (1989): 57–87.

Alvarado, Lourdes. *Educación y superación femenina en el siglo XIX: dos ensayos de Laureana Wright*. México: Universidad Nacional Autónoma de México, 2005.

Anderson, Benedict. *Imagined Communities: Reflections on the Origin and Spread of Nationalism*. New York: Verso, 1983.

Anderson, Rodney D. "Mexican Workers and the Politics of Revolution, 1906–1911." *The Hispanic American Historical Review* 54, no.1 (1974): 94–113.

Anzaldúa, Gloria. *Borderlands/La Frontera: The New Mestiza*. San Francisco: Aunt Lute Books, 1987.

Arenal, Electa, and Stacy Schlau, eds. *Untold Sisters: Hispanic Nuns in Their Own Works*. Translated by Amanda Powell. Albuquerque: University of New Mexico Press, 2010.

Arenas Guzmán, Diego. *El periodismo en la revolución mexicana (de 1908–1917)*. Vol. 2. México: Patronato del Instituto Nacional de Estudios Históricos de la Revolución Mexicana, 1967.

Arrieta Corral, Eduardo, Antonio Arreola, and Javier Guerrero Romero. *Tres revolucionarios de México: Tomás Urbina, Orestes Pereyra, Juana Belén Gutiérrez*. Durango, México: Comisión de Reinhumación y Homenaje, 1991.

Arrom, Silvia Marina. *The Women of Mexico City, 1790–1857*. Stanford, CA: Stanford University Press, 1985.

Baca, Damían. *Mestiz@ Scripts, Digital Migrations, and the Territories of Writing*. New York: Palgrave Macmillan, 2008.

Baca, Damían, and Victor Villanueva, eds. *Rhetorics of the Americas: 3114 BC to 2012 CE*. New York: Palgrave Macmillan, 2010.

Baqueiro López, Oswaldo. *La prensa y el estado*. Mérida, Yucatán: ISSTEY, 1992.

Barrón, Luis. *Carranza: el último reformista porfiriano*. México: Tusquets Editores México, 2009.

Bergmann, Emilie, Janet Greenberg, Gwen Kirkpatrick, Francine Masiello, Francesca Miller, Marta Morello-Frosch, Kathleen Newman, and Mary Louise Pratt. *Women, Culture, and Politics in Latin America: Seminar on Feminism and Culture in Latin America*. Berkeley: University of California Press, 1990.

Beristáin, Helena, and Gerardo Ramírez Vidal, eds. *La palabra florida: la tradición retórica indígena y novohispana*. México: Universidad Nacional Autónoma de México, 2004.

Berlin, James A. "Revisionary Histories of Rhetoric: Politics, Power, and Plurality." In *Writing Histories of Rhetoric*, edited by Victor Vitanza, 112–27. Carbondale: Southern Illinois University Press, 1994.

Best, Steven, and Douglas Kellner. *Postmodern Theory: Critical Interrogations*. New York: Guildford Press, 1991.

Bieder, Maryellen. "Women, Literature, and Society: The Essays of Emilia Pardo Bazán." In *Spanish Women Writers and the Essay: Gender, Politics, and the Self*, edited by Kathleen Mary Glenn and Mercedes Mazquiarán de Rodriguez, 25–54. Columbia: University of Missouri Press, 1998.

Biesecker, Barbara. "Coming to Terms with Recent Attempts to Write Women into the History of Rhetoric." *Philosophy and Rhetoric* 25, no. 2 (1992): 140–61.

Bizzel, Patricia. "Feminist Methods of Research in the History of Rhetoric: What Difference Do They Make?" *Rhetoric Society Quarterly* 30, no. 4 (2000): 5–17.

Bizzel, Patricia, and Bruce Herzberg, eds. *The Rhetorical Tradition: Readings from Classical Times to the Present*. Boston: Bedford/St. Martin's, 2001.

Bollinger Pouwels, Joel. *Political Journalism by Mexican Women During the Age of Revolution, 1876–1940*. Lewiston, NY: Edwin Mellen Press, 2006.

Bonfil Batalla, Guillermo. *México Profundo: Reclaiming a Civilization*. Translated by Philip A. Dennis. Austin: University of Texas Press, 1996.

Borrás, Leopoldo. *Historia del periodismo mexicano: del ocaso porfirista al derecho a la información*. México: Universidad Nacional Autónoma de México, 1983.

Bost, Suzanne. *Mulattas and Mestizas: Representing Mixed Identities in the Americas, 1850–2000*. Athens: University of Georgia Press, 2003.

Bufe, Chaz, and Mitchell Cowen Verter, eds. *Dreams of Freedom: A Ricardo Flores Magón Reader*. Oakland, CA: AK Press, 2005.

Bugeda, Diego, and Juan Manuel Ramírez Vélez, eds. *Mujeres insurgentes*. México: Siglo XXI Editores, 2010.

Burke, Kenneth. *A Rhetoric of Motives*. Berkeley: University of California Press, 1969.

Campbell, Karlyn Kohrs. *Man Cannot Speak for Her: A Critical Study of Early Feminist Rhetoric*. Vol. 1. New York: Greenwood Press, 1989.

Cano, Gabriela. "Más de un siglo de feminismo en México." *Debate Feminista* 7, no. 14 (1996): 345–60.

———. "The Porfiriato and the Mexican Revolution: Constructions of Feminism and Nationalism." In *Nation, Empire, Colony: Historicizing Gender and Race*, edited by Ruth Roach Pierson and Nupur Chaudhuri, 106–20. Bloomington: Indiana University Press, 1998.

Carrasco Puente, Rafael. *La prensa en México: datos históricos*. México: Universidad Nacional Autónoma de México, 1962.

Castellanos, Rosario. "Language as an Instrument of Domination." In *Women Writing Resistance: Essays on Latin America and the Caribbean*, edited by Jennifer Browdy de Hernández, 73–77. Cambridge, MA: South End Press, 2005.

———. *El eterno femenino*. México: Fondo de Cultura Económica, 1975.

Cathcart, Robert S. "Movements: Confrontation as Rhetorical Form." *Southern Speech Communication Journal* 43 (1978): 233–47.

Chacón, Ramón D. "Rural Educational Reform in Yucatán: From the Porfiriato to the Era of Salvador Alvarado, 1910–1918." *The Americas* 42, no. 2 (1985): 207–28.

Clark de Lara, Belem, and Elisa Guerra Speckman. *La república de letras: asomos a la cultura escrita del México decimonónico*. 3 vols. México: Universidad Nacional Autónoma de México, 2005.

Cockcroft, James D. *Intellectual Precursors of the Mexican Revolution, 1900–1913*. Austin: University of Texas Press, 1968.

Cosío Villegas, Daniel, et al. *Historia moderna de México*. 10 vols. México: Editorial Hermes, 1955–72.

Covino, William A., and David Jolliffe. *Rhetoric: Concepts, Definitions, Boundaries*. Boston: Allyn and Bacon, 1995.

Craske, Nikki. "Ambiguities and Ambivalences in Making the Nation: Women and Politics in 20th-Century Mexico." *Feminist Review* 79 (2005): 116–33.

Cypess, Sandra Messinger. *La Malinche in Mexican Literature: From History to Myth*. Austin: University of Texas Press, 1991.

———. "'Mother' Malinche and Allegories of Gender, Ethnicity, and National Identity in Mexico." In *Feminism, Nation, and Myth: La Malinche*, edited by Rolando Rombero and Amanda Molacea Harris, 14–27. Houston: Arte Público Press, 2005.

Davis, Thomas B., and Amado Ricon Virulegio. *The Political Plans of Mexico*. Lanham, MD: University Press of America, 1987.

Domecq, Brianda. *Mujer que publica . . . mujer pública: ensayos sobre literatura femenina*. México: Editorial Diana, 1994.

Easterling, Stuart. "Gender and Poetry Writing in the Light of Mexico's Liberal Victory, 1867–ca. 1890." *Mexican Studies/Estudios Mexicanos* 27, no. 1 (2011): 91–142.

Enoch, Jessica. "*Para la Mujer*: Defining a Chicana Feminist Rhetoric at the Turn of the Century." *College English* 67 (2004): 20–37.

———. *Refiguring Rhetorical Education: Women Teaching African American, Native American, and Chicano/a Students, 1865–1911*. Carbondale: Southern Illinois University Press, 2008.

Fernández Aceves, María Teresa, Carmen Ramos Escandón, and Susie Porter, eds. *Orden social e identidad de género México, siglos XIX y XX*. Guadalajara: CIESAS, 2006.

Figueroa Torres, J. Jesús. *Doña Marina, una india ejemplar*. México: B. Costa-Amic, 1975.

Foppa, Alaide, and Helene F. de Aguilar. "The First Feminist Congress in Mexico." *Signs* 5, no. 1 (1979): 192–99.

Franco, Jean. *Plotting Women: Gender and Representation in Mexico*. New York: Columbia University Press, 1989.

Fuentes, Carlos. *Todos los gatos son pardos*. México: Siglo XXI Editores, 1970.

Gallo, Eduardo I., ed. *Hombres ilustres mexicanos*. México: Imprenta de I. Cumplido, 1873.

García, Dora Elvira, Ivón Cepeda, and Shannon Anne Shea, eds. *Visiones de México, 1810–2010: devenires de una identidad cultural*. México: Editorial Porrúa, 2010.

Garner, Paul. *Porfirio Díaz: Profile in Power*. New York: Longman, 2001.

Gilderhus, Mark T. *Diplomacy and Revolution: U.S.-Mexican Relations Under Wilson and Carranza*. Tucson: University of Arizona Press, 1977.

Cillman, Laura. *Unassimilable Feminisms: Reappraising Feminist, Womanist, and Mestiza Identity Politics*. New York: Palgrave Press, 2010.

Glenn, Cheryl. *Rhetoric Retold: Regendering the Tradition from Antiquity Through the Renaissance*. Carbondale: Southern Illinois University Press, 1997.

———. "Truth, Lies, and Method: Revisiting Feminist Historiography." *College English* 62, no. 3 (2000): 387–89.

González Ramírez, Manuel. *Manifiestos Políticos, 1892–1912: Fuentes para la historia de la revolución*. 4 vols. México: Fondo de Cultura Económica, 1957.

———. *Planes políticos y otros documentos*. México: Fondo de Cultura Económica, 1954.

González, Ramona. "El Tesoro Enterrado" and Other Stories. In *Chicanas en la Literatura y el Arte*, edited by Herminio Rios, Octavio I. Romano-V, and Estela Portillo, 22–41. Berkeley, CA: Quinto Sol Publications, 1973.

Guajardo, Miguel, and Francisco Guajardo. "Two Brothers in Higher Education: Weaving a Social Fabric for Service in Academia." In *Doing the Public Good: Latino/a Scholars Engage Civic Participation*, edited by Kenneth P. González and Raymond V. Padilla, 61–82. Sterling, VA: Stylus Publishing, 2008.

Guerra, Lucía. *Mujer y escritura: fundamentos teóricos de la crítica feminista*. Santiago de Chile: Editorial Cuarto Propio, 2008.

Hale, Charles A. "Emilio Castelar and Mexico." In *The Political Power of the Word: Press and Oratory in Nineteenth Century Latin America*, edited by Iván Jaksić, 128–41. London: Institute of Latin American Studies, 2002.

Hammerback, John C., and Richard J. Jensen. "Ethnic Heritage as Rhetorical Legacy: The Plan of Delano." In *Readings of the Rhetoric of Social Protest*, edited by Charles E. Morris III and Stephen Howard Browne, 304–19. State College, PA: Strata Publishing, 2006.

Harraway, Donna. "Situated Knowledges: The Science Question in Feminism and the Privilege of Partial Perspective." *Feminist Studies* 14, no. 3 (1988): 575–99.

Hart, John Mason. *Revolutionary Mexico: The Coming and Process of the Mexican Revolution*. Berkeley: University of California Press, 1987.

Hawkesworth, Mary E. "Feminist Rhetoric: Discourses on the Male Monopoly of Thought." *Political Theory* 16, no. 3 (1988): 444–67.

Hedrick, Tace. *Mestizo Modernism: Race, Nation, and Identity in Latin American Culture, 1900–1940*. New Brunswick, NJ: Rutgers University Press, 2003.

Hernández Carballido, Elvira. *Dos violetas del Anáhuac*. México: DEMAC, 2010.

———. "La historia de la prensa en México desde la perspectiva de género." *Informação & Comunicação* 14, no. 2 (2011): 66–95.

Herrick, Jane. "Periodicals for Women in Mexico During the Nineteenth Century." *The Americas* 14, no. 2 (1957): 135–44.

Hind, Emily. *Femmenism and the Mexican Woman Intellectual from Sor Juana to Poniatowska: Boob Lit*. New York: Palgrave Macmillan, 2010.

hooks, bell. "Choosing the Margin as a Space of Radical Openness." In *Readings in Contemporary Rhetoric*, edited by Karen A. Foss, Sonja K. Foss, and Robert Trapp, 235–42. Long Grove, IL: Waveland Press, 2002.

Infante Vargas, Lucrecia. "Igualdad intelectual y género en *Violetas del Anáhuac: Periódico Literario Redactado por Señoras, 1887–1889*." In *Cuatro estudios de género en el México urbano del siglo XIX*, edited by Gabriela Cano and Georgette José Valenzuela, 129–56. México: Universidad Autónoma de México, 2001.

Jarratt, Susan C. *Rereading the Sophists: Classical Rhetoric Refigured*. Carbondale: Southern Illinois University Press, 1998.

Johnson, Nan. *Gender and Rhetorical Space in American Life, 1866–1910*. Carbondale: Southern Illinois University Press, 2002.

Kanellos, Nicolás, and Helvita Martell. *Hispanic Periodicals in the United States, Origins to 1960: A Brief History and Comprehensive Bibliography*. Houston: Arte Público Press, 2000.

Keller, Hans. "After the Fall: Reflections on Histories of Rhetoric." In *Writing Histories of Rhetoric*, edited by Victor Vitanza, 20–37. Carbondale: Southern Illinois University Press, 1994.

Kennedy, Kristen. "Cynic Rhetoric: The Ethics and Tactics of Resistance." *Rhetoric Review* 18, no. 1 (1999): 26–45.

———. "Hipparchia the Cynic: Feminist Rhetoric and the Ethics of Embodiment." *Hypatia* 14, no. 2 (1999): 48–71.

Kirklighter, Cristina. *Traversing the Democratic Borders of the Essay*. Albany: State University of New York Press, 2002.

Knight, Alan. *The Mexican Revolution*. 4 vols. New York: Cambridge University Press, 1986.

———. "Popular Culture and the Revolutionary State in Mexico, 1910–1940." *Hispanic American Historical Review* 74, no. 3 (1994): 393–443.

Krauze, Enrique. *Mexico, Biography of Power: A History of Modern Mexico, 1810–1996*. Translated by Hank Heifetz. New York: Harper Perennial, 1998.

LaGreca, Nancy. *Rewriting Womanhood: Feminism, Subjectivity, and the Angel of the House in the Latin American Novel, 1887–1903*. University Park: Pennsylvania State University Press, 2009.

Lau Jaiven, Ana. "La participación de las mujeres en la revolución mexicana: Juana Belén Gutiérrez de Mendoza (1875–1942)." *Diálogos Revista Electrónica de Historia* 5, nos. 1–2 (2005): 1–32.

Lau Jaiven, Ana, and Carmen Ramos. *Mujeres y revolución, 1900–1917*. México: Instituto Nacional de Estudios Históricos de la Revolución Mexicana, 1993.

Lavrin, Asunción. *Women, Feminism, and Social Change in Argentina, Chile, and Uruguay, 1890–1940*. Lincoln: University of Nebraska Press, 1995.

Lavrin, Asunción, and Edith Couturier. "Las mujeres tienen la palabra: otras voces en la historia colonial de México." *Historia Mexicana* 31, no. 2 (1981): 278–313.

Lear, John. *Workers, Neighbors, and Citizens: The Revolution in Mexico City*. Lincoln: University of Nebraska Press, 2001.

Leff, Michael. "Tradition and Agency in Humanistic Rhetoric." *Philosophy and Rhetoric* 36, no. 2 (2003): 135–47.

Levy, Daniel, and Gabriel Szekely. *Mexico, Paradoxes of Stability and Change*. Boulder, CO: Westview Press, 1983.

Lincona, Adela C. "Borderlands' Rhetorics and Representations: The Transformative Potential of Feminist Third Space Scholarship and Zines." *NWSA Journal* 17, no. 2 (2005): 104–29.

Logan, Shirley. *"We Are Coming": The Persuasive Discourse of Nineteenth Century Black Women*. Carbondale: Southern Illinois University Press, 1999.

Lorde, Audre. *Sister Outsider: Essays and Speeches by Audre Lorde*. 1984. Reprint, Berkeley, CA: Crossing Press, 2007.

Lund, Joshua. *The Impure Imagination: Toward a Critical Hybridity in Latin American Writing*. Minneapolis: University of Minnesota Press, 2006.

Maccamon, Holly J. "Stirring Up Suffrage Sentiment: The Formation of the State Woman Suffrage Organizations, 1866–1914." *Social Forces* 80, no. 2 (2001): 449–80.

Macias, Anna. *Against All Odds: The Feminist Movement in Mexico to 1940*. Westport, CT: Greenwood Press, 1982.

Martí, José. *The America of José Martí: Selected Writings*. Translated by Juan de Onís. New York: Noonday Press, 1953.

Martínez-Echazábal, Lourdes. "Mestizaje and the Discourse of National/Cultural Identity in Latin America, 1845–1959." *Latin American Perspectives* 25, no. 3 (1998): 21–42.

Mattingly, Carol. "Telling Evidence: Rethinking What Counts in Rhetoric." *Rhetoric Society Quarterly* 32, no. 1 (2002): 99–108.

McComiskey, Bruce. *Gorgias and the New Sophistic Rhetoric*. Carbondale: Southern Illinois University Press: 2002.

Medina, Rubén. "El mestizaje a través de la frontera: Vasconcelos y Anzaldúa." *Mexican Studies/Estudios Mexicanos* 25, no. 1 (2009): 101–23.

Mendieta Alatorre, Angeles. *Juana Belén Gutiérrez de Mendoza: extraordinaria precursora de la Revolución mexicana*. México: Copilco Universidad, 1983.

Menéndez, Miguel Angel. *Malintzin*. México: La Prensa, 1964.

Miecznikowski Sheard, Cynthia. "The Public Value of Epideictic Rhetoric." *College English* 58, no. 7 (1996): 765–94.

Mijangos Díaz, Eduardo N., and Leticia Mendoza García. "Instrucción cívica y liberal del presbiterianismo en el distrito de Zitácuaro, 1894–1902." *Tzintzun: Revista de Estudios Históricos*, no. 54 (2011): 53–92.

Miller, Beth. *Rosario Castellanos: una conciencia feminista en México*. Chiapas: Universidad Autónoma de Chiapas, 1983.

Miller, Carolyn R. "Genre as Social Action." In *Genre and the New Rhetoric*, edited by Aviva Freedman and Peter Medway, 23–42. London: Taylor and Francis, 1994.

Miller, Marilyn Grace. *Rise and Fall of the Cosmic Race: The Cult of Mestizaje in Latin America*. Austin: University of Texas Press, 2004.

Miller, Thomas P., and Melody Bowdon. "Archivists with an Attitude: A Rhetorical Stance on the Archives of Civic Action." *College English* 61, no. 5 (1999): 591–97.

Mohanty, Chandra Talpade. *Feminism Without Borders: Decolonizing Theory, Practicing Solidarity*. Durham, NC: Duke University Press, 2003.

Montiel, Celia del Palacio, ed. *La prensa como fuente para la historia*. México: Miguel Ángel Porrúa, 2006.

Muriel, Josefina. *Cultura femenina novohispana*. México: Universidad Nacional Autónoma de México, 1982.

Noguez Noguez, Olivia. "Hermila Galindo y 'La Mujer Moderna' (1915–1916): abriendo espacios; entre la domesticidad y los derechos por la igualdad." *Revista Historia 2.0, Conocimiento histórico en clave digital* 4 (2012), accessed September 16, 2014, http://historia2.0.historiaabierta.org/.

Ochoa Campos, Moisés. *Reseña histórica del periodismo mexicano*. México: Editorial Porrúa, 1968.
Octalog. "Octalog II: The (Continuing) Politics of Historiography." *Rhetoric Review* 16, no. 1 (1997): 22–44.
Ong, Walter. "Voice as Summons for Belief: Literature, Faith, and the Divided Self." In *An Ong Reader: Challenges for Further Inquiry*, edited by Thomas J. Farrell and Paul A. Soukup, 259–75. Creskill, NJ: Hampton Press, 2002.
Orellana Trinidad, Laura. *Hermila Galindo: Una mujer moderna*. México: Instituto Nacional de Bellas Artes, 2001.
Paz, Octavio. *The Labyrinth of Solitude and Other Writings*. Translated by Lysander Kemp, Yara Milos, and Rachel Phillips Belash. New York: Grove Press, 1985.
Pérez, Emma. *The Decolonial Imaginary: Writing Chicanas into History*. Bloomington: Indiana University Press, 1999.
Porter, James E. "Intertextuality and the Discourse Community." *Rhetoric Review* 5, no. 1 (1986): 34–47.
Porter, Susie S. *Working Women in Mexico City: Public Discourses and Material Conditions, 1879–1931*. Tucson: University of Arizona Press, 2003.
Radkau, Verena. *Por la debilidad de nuestro ser: Mujeres "del pueblo" en la paz porfiriana*. México: Centro de Investigaciones y Estudios Superiores en Antropología Social, 1989.
Ramirez-Dhoore, Dora. "Writing Chicana Identity: Strategies of Resistance and Reformulation." PhD diss., University of Nebraska–Lincoln, 2003. Order no. 3092585.
Ramírez Vidal, Gerardo, ed. *Conceptos y objetos de la retórica ayer y hoy*. México: Universidad Nacional Autónoma de México, 2008.
Ratcliffe, Krista. *Rhetorical Listening: Identification, Gender, Whiteness*. Carbondale: Southern Illinois University Press, 2005.
Riva Palacio, Vicente, Juan de Dios Arias, Alfredo Chavero, José María Vigil, and Julio Zárate. *México a través de los siglos: Historia general y completa del desenvolvimiento social, político, religioso, militar, artístico, científico y literario de México desde la antigüedad más remota hasta la época actual*. 6th ed. 5 vols. México: Editorial Cumbre, 1967.
Rivera-Garza, Cristina. "The Criminalization of the Syphilitic Body: Prostitutes, Health Crimes, and Society in Mexico City, 1867–1930." In *Crime and Punishment in Latin America: Law and Society Since Late Colonial Times*, edited by Ricardo D. Salvatore, Carlos Aguirre, and Gilbert M. Joseph, 147–80. Durham, NC: Duke University Press, 2001.
Robles, Martha. *La sombra fugitiva: Escritoras en la cultura nacional*. 2 vols. México: Imprenta Universitaria Nacional Autónoma de México, 1985.
Rocha, Martha Eva. "The Faces of Rebellion: From Revolutionaries to Veterans in Nationalist Mexico." In *The Women's Revolution in Mexico, 1910–1953*, edited by Stephanie Mitchell and Patience A. Schell, 15–35. Lanham, MD: Rowman and Littlefield Publishers, 2007.
Rocha Islas, Martha Eva. "Feminismo y Revolución." In *Un fantasma recorre el siglo: Luchas feministas en México, 1910–1920*, edited by Gisela Espinosa Damián and Ana Lau Jaiven, 27–60. México: Universidad Autónoma Metropolitana Unidad Xochimilco, 2010.

Romano, Susan. "The Historical Catalina Hernández: Inhabiting the Topoi of Feminist Historiography." *Rhetoric Society Quarterly* 37, no. 4 (2007): 453–80.

Royster, Jacqueline Jones. "Disciplinary Landscaping, or Contemporary Challenges in the History of Rhetoric." *Philosophy and Rhetoric* 36, no. 2 (2003): 148–66.

———. *Traces of a Stream: Literacy and Social Change Among African American Women*. Pittsburgh: University of Pittsburgh Press, 2000.

Royster, Jacqueline Jones, and Gesa E. Kirsch. *Feminist Rhetorical Practices: New Horizons for Rhetoric, Composition, and Literacy Studies*. Carbondale: Southern Illinois University Press, 2012.

Salomón Meraz, Liliana. *Historia del periodismo en Durango, etapa 1822–1950*. Durango, México: H. Congreso del Estado de Durango, 2010.

Sandoval, Anna Marie. *Toward a Latina Feminism of the Americas: Repression and Resistance in Chicana and Mexicana Literature*. Austin: University of Texas Press, 2008.

Schmidt, Henry C. *The Roots of Lo Mexicano: Self and Society in Mexican Thought, 1900–1934*. College Station: Texas A&M University Press, 1978.

Schmitt, Karl M. "Catholic Adjustment to the Secular State: The Case of Mexico, 1867–1911." *Catholic Historical Review* 48, no. 2 (1962): 182–204.

———. "The Díaz Conciliation Policy on State and Local Levels, 1876–1911." *Hispanic American Historical Review* 40, no. 4 (1960): 513–32.

Serna, Elias. "Tempest Arizona: Criminal Epistemologies and the Rhetorical Possibilities of Raza Studies," *Urban Rev* 45 (2013): 41–57.

Serrano Migallón, Fernando. *El grito de independencia: Historia de una pasión nacional*. México: Miguel Ángel Porrúa, 1981.

Soto, Shirlene. *Emergence of the Modern Mexican Woman: Her Participation in Revolution and Struggle for Equality, 1910–1940*. Denver: Arden Press, 1990.

Spenser, Daniela. *Stumbling Its Way Through Mexico: The Early Years of the Communist International*. Tuscaloosa: University of Alabama Press, 2011.

Stewart, Charles J. "The Evolution of a Revolution: Stokely Carmichael and the Rhetoric of Black Power." *Quarterly Journal of Speech* 83 (1997): 429–46.

Sutherland, Christine Mason. "Feminist Historiography: Research Methods in Rhetoric." *Rhetoric Society Quarterly* 32, no. 1 (2002): 109–22.

Swearingen, Jan C. "Song to Speech: The Origins of Early Epitaphia in Ancient Near Eastern Women's Lamentations." In *Rhetoric Before and After the Greeks*, edited by Carol S. Lipson and Roberta A. Binkley, 213–26. New York: State University of New York Press, 2004.

Tenorio-Trillo, Mauricio. *Mexico at the World's Fairs: Crafting a Modern Nation*. Los Angeles: University of California Press, 1996.

Tinajero, Araceli. *El Lector: A History of the Cigar Factory Reader*. Translated by Judith E. Grasberg. Austin: University of Texas Press, 2007.

Torres Aguilar, Morelos. "Publicaciones sobre educación en México en el siglo XIX." *Revista Historia de la Educación Latinoamericana* 15, no. 20 (2013): 245–74. Accessed September 9, 2014, http://www.scielo.org.co/scielo.

Townsend, Camilla. *Malintzin's Choices: An Indian Woman in the Conquest of Mexico*. Albuquerque: University of New Mexico Press, 2006.

Tuñón Pablos, Julia. *Women in Mexico: A Past Unveiled*. Translated by Alan Hynds. Austin: University of Texas Press, 1999.

Valle, José del. "Spanish, Spain, and the Hispanic Community: Science and Rhetoric in the History of Spanish Linguistics." In *Interpreting Spanish Colonialism: Empires, Nations, and Legends*, edited by Christopher Schmidt Nowara and John Nieto Philips, 139–62. Albuquerque: University of New Mexico Press, 2005.

Valles Ruiz, Rosa María. "Hermila Galindo, un caso de feminismo ilustrado en los albores del siglo XX." *Revista de Historia de América* 142 (2010): 37–56.

———. *Sol de libertad: Hermila Galindo, feminista, constitucionalista y primera censora legislativa México*. México: Instituto de Cultura del Estado de Durango, 2010.

Vasconcelos, José. *The Cosmic Race/La raza cósmica*. Translated by Didier T. Jaén. Baltimore: Johns Hopkins University Press, 1997.

Vaughan, Mary K. *Cultural Politics in Revolution: Teachers, Peasants, and Schools in Mexico, 1930–1940*. Tucson: University of Arizona Press, 1997.

———. "Pancho Villa, the Daughters of Mary, and the Modern Woman: Gender in the Long Mexican Revolution." In *Sex in Revolution: Gender, Politics, and Power in Modern Mexico*, edited by Jocelyn Olcott, Mary K. Vaughan, and Gabriela Cano, 21–35. Durham, NC: Duke University Press.

———. "Women, Class, and Education in Mexico, 1880–1928." *Latin American Perspectives* 4, nos. 1/2 (1977): 135–52.

Velasco Valdés, Miguel. *Historia del periodismo mexicano (apuntes)*. México: Librería de Manual Porrúa, 1955.

Villaneda, Alicia. *Justicia y libertad: Juana Belén Gutiérrez de Mendoza (1875–1942)*. México: Documentación y Estudios de Mujeres, 1994.

Villanueva, Victor. "On the Rhetoric and Precedents of Racism." *CCC* 50, no. 4 (1999): 645–61.

Vitanza, Victor J., ed. *Writing Histories of Rhetoric*. Carbondale: Southern Illinois University Press, 1994.

Weigand, Phil C., and Acelia de Weigand. *Los orígenes de los caxcanes y su relación con la guerra de los nayarits: Un hipótesis*. Zapopan, México: Colegio de Jalisco, 1995.

Wertheimer, Molly Meijer. *Listening to Their Voices: The Rhetorical Activities of Historical Women*. Columbia: University of South Carolina Press, 1997.

Wu, Hui. "Historical Studies of Rhetorical Women Here and There: Methodological Challenges to Dominant Interpretive Frameworks." *Rhetoric Society Quarterly* 32, no. 1 (2002): 81–97.

Yeager, Gertrude M., ed. *Confronting Change, Challenging Tradition: Women in Latin America History*. Wilmington, DE: Scholarly Resources, 1994.

Index

Page numbers followed by *f* indicate figures. Numbers followed by n indicate notes.

Abraham González Club, 168
Acción Femenil, 152
"Actitud del partido liberal por las revelaciones del Obispo de San Luis.—Movimiento de indignación en toda la República.—Las Mujeres de Zitácuaro," 96, 105–7, 224n4. See also *La Bandera Roja*
Acuña y Rosette, Elisa, 3–4, 20, 133, 143–44, 229n60
Agustina de Santa Teresa, Sor, 86
Alarcón, Norma, 37–39
El Álbum de la Mujer, 25, 60, 81
El Álbum de la Mujer: ilustración Hispano-Americana, 223n75
El Álbum Mexicano, 25
"Al General Díaz," 136, 139–40
El Alma Mexicana, 158, 161
"A los mexicanos," 141–42
Altamirano, Ignacio Manuel, 34, 44, 47, 64, 75
Alvarado, Alberto M., 139, 180, 186, 206
Alvarado, Lourdes, 60, 62
Alvarado, Salvador, 168
Amaya de Reyes, Benita, 93, 97, 126
Amigas del Pueblo, 148, 158
Anáhuac, 67–68, 145
ángel del hogar, 7–8, 64–65, 177
Anthony, Susan B., 67, 111, 169
anti-clerical discourse, 138–39
Anti-Re-electionist Party, 146
Anzaldúa, Gloria, 28–29, 33, 43–44, 48, 50–51, 67, 87–88, 153–54
archetypal roles, 42–43
Argumedo de Ortiz, María del Refugio, 71; "Cuauhtémoc," 76; "La oración matinal", 76; "Poesia," 76–77
Arriaga, Camilo, 97, 102, 142–43
Aspasia, 43, 82
Azteca, 179

Baca, Damían, 22, 33, 50–51
La Bandera Roja, 95*f*, 96–97, 103, 105, 111, 113, 223n3; audience, 120; greetings to *Vésper*, 120; "La mujer modesta," 104–5; "Nuestra obra debe ser emancipar a la mujer del clericalismo," 103
Barrera, Horacio, 48, 173
Bebel, August, 166, 168, 174, 184–85
Beisecker, Barbara, 18
Beltrán, Lola, 55
Benavides de Calderón, Micaela, 18
Berlin, James, 54
El Bien Público, 60
Bizzel, Patricia, 28, 119
Bolívar, Simón, 47
Bollinger Pouwels, Joel, 9, 18, 69, 91–93, 127–31, 162–64, 199–203, 216n77
Bonfil Batalla, Guillermo, 136
Borges, Jorge Luis, 55
Bourbon Renaissance, 23
Bunge, Carlos Octavio, 47
Burke, Kenneth, 183

Cabrera, Daniel, 139
Calderón de la Barca, Pedro, 206
La Camelia, 25
Camisas de Colores, 158
Campbell, Karlyn Kohrs, 66

Cano, Gabriela, 9–10, 19–20, 81, 87
Cárdenas, Lázaro, 134, 230n79
Carranza, Venustiano, 20, 149, 165, 168–69, 179–80, 189–90, 192, 208, 231n2, 232n15
Casa Amiga de la Obrera, 76–77
Casa del Obrero Mundial, 146
Castelar, Emilio, 141
Castellanos, Rosario, 37–38, 48, 55, 62, 72, 204–5, 211
Cathcart, Robert, 134
Catholic Church, 24, 96, 101–2, 105–7, 188
Caxcan Indians, 51, 136, 153, 156, 230n95
Cetina Gutiérrez, Rita, 24
"Los chaparritos," 155–56
"Charada," 76
Chicanas en la Literatura y el Arte, 55
Chinaco, 138
citizenship, 39, 47, 233n34
Cixous, Hélèn, 62
El Clarín, 139
Coatlicue, 34. *See also* Cuatlicue
Codex Telleriano-Remensis, 41
Colín, Aurora, 93, 102, 126
Colín, Carlota, 126
Colín, Elvira, 93, 102, 126
Colín, Guadalupe, 93, 97, 102, 126
Colín, Laura, 126–27
Colín, Margarita, 126
Colín sisters, 93, 133
Colonial era, 7–9, 18
compañerismo, 115–16
Complot de Tacubaya, 148
Congreso Femenino Internacional (1910), 169, 173
Congreso Feminista de Yucatán (January 1916), 180–86
Congreso Feminista de Yucatán (November 1916), 180, 186–88, 234n57
The Conquest of Bread (Kropotkin), 139
Consejo de los Caxcanes, 154
Consejo Nacional de Mujeres Mexicanas, 152
Constitutionalist movement, 169
"Contra todos los tiranos y contra todas las tiranías," 146–47
Correa y Zapata, Dolores, 19, 27, 71, 209–10; "La mujer," 76
La Corregidora, 145
El Correo de Durango, 206, 235n5
El Correo de las Señoras, 25
Cortés, Hernán, 15, 21, 35–37, 39–40, 42, 83
Cosío Villegas, Daniel, 15
Covino, William, 12–13
Creoles, 18
"Cuando se muera," 136
Cuatlicue, 27, 68, 221n29
"Cuauhtémoc," 76
Cuba, 178–81
"La cuestión sufragista: para qué quieren el voto las mujeres," 178
Cypess, Sandra Messinger, 33, 37

danza del Xúchil, 156
Declaration of Rights of the Women of the United States, 111
de Gallegos, Luz U., 126
del Alba, María, 19, 71, 209–10
de la Luz Murguía, María, 71, 209–10; "La ilustración y la educación de la mujer," 73
El Demócrata y el Progreso, 139
El Demófilo (, 228n30
de Sigüenza y Góngora, Carlos, 81, 84–85
"Desmontado," 150
El Desmonte: por la Tierra y por la Raza, 150–51, 159; "Desmontado," 150; "Hechos, no palabras, 150–51
Devereaux, Neil J., 216n77
El Diablito Bromista (, 228n30
Diario del Hogar, 138
Díaz, Porfirio (Porfiriato), 19–23, 45, 48, 63–64, 77–79, 97, 135; and anti-Porfirian newspapers, 144; opposition to, 139, 146, 148
Díaz del Castillo, Bernal, 36, 81
El Dictamen, 171
"Dios" (God), 64
discourse politics, 50, 114; anti-clerical discourse, 138–39; public discourse, 120
La doctrina Carranza y el acercamiento indolatino (Galindo), 167, 173–74, 188–90; dedication, 190; excerpts, 165, 190–91, 194–203; *A la mujer latinoamericana*, 194–203
Domecq, Brianda, 3
"Don Francisco I. Madero, candidato a la presidencia de la República", 145–46

Las dos Fridas, 44–45
Durango, México, 67; *El Correo de Durango*, 206, 235n5; El Instituto de Niñas, 103

"¡Ecce homo!", 136, 142
La Educación errónea de la mujer y medios prácticos para correjirla, 60, 64
education: Law of Educational Reform of 1869, 24; in nineteenth-century Mexico, 22–28; and *puesto* of school, 7–8; SEP and, 152–53, 155–56; La Siempreviva school, 24; women's, 22–28, 60, 64, 111
El Grito series, 55
La emancipación de la mujer por medio del estudio, 19, 51, 60, 87, 234n53
Enoch, Jessica, 10, 29, 57
Enos, Richard Leo, 210
Escuela Industrial Femenina "Josefa Ortiz de Domínguez" (, 158
Escuela Miguel Lerdo de Tejada, 23–24
El Estandarte, 105
"Estudio de la Srita. Hermila Galindo con motivo de los temas que han de absolverse en el Segundo Congreso Feminista de Yucatán", 186–88, 234n57
"Estudio sobre el feminismo", 173
El eterno femenino, 37
ethos, 111–13
Evolución, 146
¡Excelsior!, 142

Febles Cantón, Julia D., 176*f*, 177
Felipe VI, 86
feminationalism, 49, 170–71
feminine intellectuality, 64
feminine style, 66
feminism: based in motherhood, 157–58; definition of, 16; Mexican, 17, 39, 149; Protestant, 173; radical, 157–58; term, 16–17
feminism-in-nationalism, 48–49, 170
"Feminismo y Revolución," 48
feminist congresses: international, 169, 173; of Yucatán, 180–88, 234n57
feminization, of Mexican history, 78–87
Fernández, Vicente, 55
festivals or fiestas, 156
Figueroa Torres, J. Jesús, 22, 36–37, 41
Foucault, Michel, 50
Fuentes, Carlos, 38

Galindo, Angela, 190
Galindo, Hermila, 8–9, 17–18, 20, 31, 33, 44, 51, 149; *A la mujer latinoamericana*, 194–203; background and education, 209–10; in Cuba, 178–81; "La cuestión sufragista: para qué quieren el voto las mujeres," 178; *La doctrina Carranza y el acercamiento indolatino*, 165, 167, 173–74, 188–91, 194–203; "Estudio de la Srita. Hermila Galindo con motivo de los temas que han de absolverse en el Segundo Congreso Feminista de Yucatán," 186–88, 234n57; at Feminist Congresses of Yucatán (1916), 180–88; in international politics, 188–92; "¡Laboremos!," 175; "La mujer como colaboradora en la vida pública," 171; "La mujer en el porvenir," 182–86; *La Mujer Moderna*, 5*f*; "Petición hecha por nuestra directora al H. Constituyente sobre el derecho al voto de la mujer," 178; *Un presidenciable: el general don Pablo González*, (167, 192; as presidential spokeswoman, 165–66, 168–71, 208; "La reivindicación de la mujer mexicana," 171; rhetorical approach, 165–93, 208–10; "La Srita. Galindo opina sobre su candidatura para diputado," 178; time period, 205, 207; as veteran, 192
Galindo de Topete, Hermila, 231n1. *See also* Galindo, Hermila
Gamboa, Ignacio, 64
García y Ontiveros, Concepción, 27, 66–67
Gaspar de Alba, Alicia, 37
gender issues, 169, 205–6
Génesis, 158
genres, protest, 98–101
Gimeno de Flaquer, Concepción, 26, 60, 81, 223n75
Glenn, Cheryl, 10, 43, 82, 204
globalization, 11–12
González, César A., 182–83
González, Deena, 37, 100
González, Ramona, 204–5
González, Sandra, 204–5
González Ortega, Beatriz, 149

González Prada, Manuel, 34
González Ramírez, Manuel, 99–100, 105, 107–8, 113–15
Gorgias, 34
el grito, 20, 223n2; as genre, 98–101; El Grito de Dolores, 99, 109; El Grito de Independencia, 109; *el grito* de Zitácuaro, 109–11
Guadalupe, La Virgen de, 42–43
Guanajuato, Mexico, 67
Guerrero, María, 85–86
Gutiérrez de Mendoza, Juana Belén, 3–9, 17–21, 31–33, 44, 48–51, 120, 132–60, 229n60; as activist, 133, 145–47, 152, 157–59; "Al General Díaz," 136, 139–40; "A los mexicanos", 141–42; background and education, 17, 54, 209–10; in battle, 230n76; birth, 137; *Camisas de Colores*, 158; as colonel, 149; "Contra todos los tiranos y contra todas las tiranías," (146–47; "Cuando se muera," 136; "Desmontado," 150; "Don Francisco I. Madero, candidato a la presidencia de la República," 145–46; early writings and first articles, 137–38, 141–42; "¡Ecce homo!," 136, 142; exile, 142–45; "Hechos, no palabras," 150–51; heritage, 230n95; incarceration, 137, 142, 145–46, 148–49; as *inspectora de escuelas rurales*, 153; as *maestra rurale*, 153; as *mestiza*, 157; more radical writings of, 30; political views, 228n32; *¡Por la tierra y por la raza!*, 154–57, 159, 208; *Preliminares de Combate*, 158; printing press, 139; "Protesta," 136; *La República Femenina*, 158; in Revolutionary ranks, 147–52; rhetorical agenda, 155; rhetorical approach, 136–37, 140, 153–54, 160, 172, 207–8, 227n4; as social critic, 144–45, 153–54; stylistic features, 227n4; as teacher, 158; time period, 205, 207; *Toque de Atención al Ejército Nacional*, 158; "*Vésper* Siempre Ocupará Su Puesto", 4–6, 161–64; as writer, 133
Gutiérrez de Mendoza, Laura, 149

Hammerback, John, 99, 108, 114
Harraway, Donna, 47
Hawkesworth, Mary E., 16, 44, 167, 172, 174
Hay, Eduardo, 167
"Hechos, no palabras," 150–51
Hedrick, Tace, 29
Hernández Carballido, Elvira, 9–10, 15, 70
Herrick, Jane, 25–26
herstory, 35–36
Hidalgo, Miguel, 99, 109
Las Hijas del Anahúac, (1887), 19–20, 60–61, 69–74, 177. See also *Violetas del Anáhuac: periódico Literario Redactado por Señoras*
Las Hijas del Anáhuac: ensayo Literario (1873), 27, 63, 66–68; "A nuestras lectoras," 68–69
El Hijo del Ahuizote, 138–40, 142
Historia breve de la conquista de los estados independientes del imperio mexicano, 155
historical directions, 33–58; challenging and re/visioning, 152–59; herstory, 35–36; interpretations of *mestizaje*, 44–49; Mexican history, 78–87; pre-Conquest, 82; revisionist, 41–42, 152–59; rhetorical intersections, 101–2
historiography, 155
Los hombres prominentes de México, 79
"Huérfana," 64
Huerta, Victoriano, 148–49
Hugo, Victor, 65
Huitizon, 82–83

identity: *mestizo*, 14–15, 34; racial, 136
Ilancueitl, 68, 221n29; "A nuestras lectoras," 68–69
"La ilustración y la educación de la mujer," 73
Indian problem, 152
indigenous songs, 155–56
El Instituto de Niñas, 103
intellectuals: high, 62; public, 63–64; wizards of progress, 64, 79. See also *mujeres intelectuales*
international politics, 188–92
"Invitación al Partido Liberal," 102
Ixtlilxochitl, Fernando de Alva Cortés, 36
Ixtlilxochitl "Ome Tochtli," 83–84

Jarratt, Susan, 33–34, 52
Javien, Ana Lau, 9, 62, 158
Jensen, Richard, 99, 108, 114

Jiménez y Muro, Dolores, 20, 48, 133, 145, 148–49, 229n60
Jolliffe, David, 12–13
journalists, 15, 59–88. *See also specific journalists*
journals, 25–27. *See also specific journals*
Juana Inés de la Cruz, Sor, 16, 28, 43–44, 85, 138, 186–87; *Respuesta a Sor Filotea de la Cruz*, 186–87
Juárez, Benito, 23, 168, 232n9
Junta Liberal Josefa Ortiz de Domínguez y Francisca Carrillo, 30, 97, 112–13. *See also* Las Mujeres de Zitácuaro

Kahlo, Frida, 44–45, 48, 159
Kant, Immanuel, 174, 183–85
Kennedy, Kristen, 143–45
Kirklighter, Cristina, 15, 29
Kleinhans, Sebastián, 70
Kropotkin, Peter, 139

"¡Laboremos!," 175
LaGreca, Nancy, 7–8, 29, 64, 65–67
La Malinche (Malintzin), 21–22
Lavrin, Asunsión, 9, 23
laws (Mexico): decree number 167 ("Feminist law") (Mexico), 180; Law of Educational Reform, 24; Laws of Reform, 101–2, 118
Leona Vicario school, 93–94
León-Portilla, Miguel, 41
La Libertad, 141
El Liceo Hidalgo, 64
Lincona, Adela, 21
listening, rhetorical, 52–53, 57
literacy, 22–23
literary soirées (*veladas literarias*), 25
literatos, 25
Logan, Shirley Wilson, 10
López Mora, Esther, 177
Lorde, Audre, 3, 62
Lund, Joshua, 45, 174–75
Lunsford, Andrea, 33
lyceums, 75

Macías, Anna, 9, 17
Maderistas, 145–46
Madero, Francisco I., 114, 145–46, 148; "Manifiesto de Francisco I. Madero acerca del ataque a C. Juárez," 115; "Manifiesto de Madero al pueblo mexicano, dirigido desde la penitenciaría de Monterrey, N.L.," 114
la madre, 42–43
maestros rurales (rural teachers), 152–53
Magón, Enrique Flores, 114, 139
Magón, Jesús Flores, 135
Magón, Ricardo Flores, 97, 102, 135, 142–43, 145, 228n32, 229n57; "Manifiesto de los Flores Magón sobre su doctrina," 114
Malinalxochitl, 82–83
"Malinche," 37–38
Malintzin, 15, 29–30, 34–44, 57, 205–6; as La Chingada, 36–37; as Doña Marina, 36, 40; as La Lengua, 37; as Malinal, 36; as La Malinche, 21–22, 36, 43; as Marina, 36; as slave, 36, 40–41; as translator and interpreter, 35–36, 39–41, 44; Wright de Kleinhans on, 83
"Manifiesto de Francisco I. Madero acerca del ataque a C. Juárez," 115
"Manifiesto de los Flores Magón sobre su doctrina," 114
"Manifiesto de Madero al pueblo mexicano, dirigido desde la penitenciaría de Monterrey, N.L.," 114
"Manifiesto de Pascual Orozco al recibir el mando de fuerzas de Chihuahua," 115
manifiestos, 99–101, 115, 117
Manresa de Pérez, Concepción, 71; "Mujeres de nuestra época," 73–74, 79–80
María de la Encarnación, Sor, 86
María Inés de los Dolores, Sor, 86
marianismo, 39, 42–43, 217n23
Mariátegui, José Carlos, 14–15
Martí, José, 34, 47
Más allá de los muros, 158
Mattingly, Carol, 10
Medina, Rubén, 67, 214n25
Mendoza, Cirilo, 137
Menéndez, Miguel Ángel, 37, 41
mestiza (term), 14–15, 214n25
mestizaje, 34–36, 136–37, 214n25; goal of, 174–75; historical interpretations of, 44–49
mestiza rhetoric, 14, 21–22, 31, 119–20, 134–37, 153–54, 157–58, 208–9;

definition of, 50–51; historical directions in, 33–58; protest genres as, 100–101; theoretical directions in, 33–58
Mexicanism, 44
Mexicas, 83, 230n95
Mexico: Colonial era, 7–8, 18; Constitution, 23, 101, 177, 233n34; Constitutional Convention, 179; feminism in, 17, 39, 149; history of, 78–87; Independence Day, 175; journalism in, 15; nineteenth-century, 22–28, 59–88; political protest in, 98–100; Porfiriato period, 21; post-Revolutionary period, 21, 134, 152–59; pre-Revolutionary era (precursor movement), 134–36; Restored Republic, 18–19, 23; Revolution, 10, 48, 134, 147–52, 168–69, 177, 229n74, 231n7; SEP of, 152–53, 155–56; War of Independence, 22–23; War of the Reform, 101. *See also* laws (Mexico)
Mexico City, Mexico, 67–68
Miahuaxochitl, 27, 68, 221n29
Miecznikowski Sheard, Cynthia, 75
Mill, John Stuart, 166, 184–85; *The Subjection of Women*, 9, 67, 110, 168
Miller, Carolyn, 98
Minha-ha, Trinh T., 62
Mistral, Gabriela, 48, 55
Moctezuma, Ana, 83
modernism, 44, 87
modernization, 136
modesty, 104–5
Mohanty, Chandra, 209
Molina Enríquez, Andrés, 174
El Monitor del Pueblo, 78
El Monitor Republicano, 60, 141
Monroe Doctrine, 189
Montes de Oca, Ignacio, 97, 101, 105
Montoya, Matilda, 76
morality, 87, 173, 186; scientific, 173; Victorian, 87, 186
motherhood, 39, 42–43, 111; expectation of, 73; feminism based in, 157–58
"La mujer," 76
La Mujer: semanario de la Escuela de Artes y Oficios para Mujeres, 26
"La mujer como colaboradora en la vida pública," 171
"La mujer en el porvenir," 182–86
"Mujeres de nuestra época," 73–74, 79–80
Las Mujeres de Zitácuaro (MZ), 8–9, 17–18, 30, 33, 44, 51; "Actitud del partido liberal por las revelaciones del Obispo de San Luis.—Movimiento de indignación en toda la República.—Las Mujeres de Zitácuaro," 96, 105–7, 224n4; background and education, 210; feminist protests of, 94–120; first responses, 102–9; *el grito*, 109–11; plan, 108–9; *Propaganda liberal, Manifiesto*, 20, 96–97, 111–19, 121–31; rhetorical approach, 172–73, 207; time period, 205, 207
Mujeres insurgentes (Insurgent Women), 10
mujeres intelectuales (intellectual women), 63–66
Mujeres notables mexicanas, 20, 51, 61*f*, 62, 64, 80–87; examples of, 80–84
"La mujer estudiosa" 26
La Mujer Mexicana (1901), 26
La Mujer Mexicana (1904–1908), 27
La Mujer Moderna 5*f*, 165–66, 166*f*, 171, 175–77, 176*f*, 232n15; "La cuestión sufragista: para qué quieren el voto las mujeres," 178; "¡Laboremos!," 175; "Por qué deben votar las mujeres," 177–78
"La mujer modesta," 104–5
"La mujer se emancipa de las opresoras cadenas de clericalismo," 96, 112, 224n5
Mujica, Carlos, 148
Murguía de Aveleyra, Mateana, 19, 64–65, 71
myth writing, 154

National American Woman Suffrage Association, 169
nationalism, 134, 174–75, 233n37; feminationalism, 49, 170–71; feminism-in-nationalism, 48–49, 170
National Women's Suffrage Association, 111
Navarro, Antonio, 148
nepantlism, 67
Netzahualcóyotl, 64
Netzahualpilli, 81
newspapers, 15–16, 18; anti-Porfirian, 144; opposition, 139; *papeles volantes*, 139. *See also specific newspapers*
Novicow, Jacques, 174, 184–85
"Nuestra obra debe ser emancipar a la mujer del clericalismo," 103

Obregón, Álvaro, 234n73
El Obrero, 144
El Observador de Guanajuato, 65
El Observador Zacatecano, 107, 224n4
oídnos (hear us), 115–16
"La oración matinal," 76
Orellana Trinidad, Laura, 9
Ortiz de Domínguez, Josefa (La Corregidora), 22–23, 86–87, 110, 224n8

Pablos, Juan, 18
Pacheco de Torres, Clarisa, 177–78
Padilla de Piña, Ignacia, 19, 71; background, 209–10; "Charada," 76
"Las palmeras," 155–56
Papantzin, 68, 84, 221n29
papeles volantes, 139
Para Michoacán, 158–59
El Partido Socialista, 145–46
La Patria, 79
patriarchial systems: opposition to, 24
Paz, Octavio, 36–37, 44, 55
Pérez, Emma, 48–49, 102, 170
"Petición hecha por nuestra directora al H. Constituyente sobre el derecho al voto de la mujer," 178
Petition for Universal Suffrage, 110–11
Petronila de San Jose, Sor, 84–85
Pimentel, Francisco, 74–75
Pino Suárez, José María, 148
plan, 99–101, 108
plática, 53, 55–56
Plato, 51
Pluma Roja, 144
"Poesía," 76–77
poetry, 25, 76–77, 88
political speeches, 178–81
Porfiriato. *See* Díaz, Porfirio
¡Por la tierra y por la raza!, 154–57, 159, 208
"Por qué deben votar las mujeres," 177–78
positivism, 87
post-Revolutionary period, 21, 134, 152–59
precursor movement (pre-Revolutionary era), 134–36
Preliminares de Combate, 158
Presbyterian Church, 106
Presbyterian movement, 93, 102
Un presidenciable: El general don Pablo González, 167, 192
Prieto, Guillermo, 34, 74
Propaganda liberal, Manifiesto, 20, 96, 121–31; ending, 118–19; excerpts, 115–18; text, 121–27, 122*f*; translation, 127–31
protest: feminist, 94–120; genres, 98–101; political, 98–100; series, 30, 95–96, 100, 119–20; verbal, 134
"Protesta" 136
La Protesta Nacional, 144
pseudonyms, 27, 68–69
public: discourse, 120, 222n50; readings, 76–77
puesto, 4–6; of commerce, 6–7; definition of, 4; domestic, 7–8, 64–65, 177; of home, 7–8, 64–65, 177; political, 167–71; of public school, 7–8; *público*, 167–68, 173, 178–79, 206, 222n50; revolutionary, 177; rhetorical, 8–12, 142–45; of school, 7–8
Pujol, Ignacio, 69, 79

Quetzalcóatl, 154, 156–57
Quinto Sol Publications, 55

racial assimilationism, 136, 179–80, 233n37
Ramírez, Sara Estela, 48, 143–45
Ramírez-Dhoore, Dora, 10, 29
Ramírez Vidal, Gerardo, 13–14
Ratcliffe, Krista, 52–53
La raza cósmica 44, 46–47, 152
La Reforma, 149
Refugio Nicoli, Licenciado, 64–65
Regeneración, 97, 102, 105, 139
"La reivindicación de la mujer mexicana," 171
La República Femenina, 158
Respuesta a Sor Filotea de la Cruz, 186–87
Restored Republic, 18–19, 23
retórica mexicana, 13
La Revista Positiva, 173
Revolutionary period, 10, 48, 134, 147–52, 168–69, 177; ideals of, 231n7; women's roles in, 229n74
Revueltas, José, 138
rhetoric: (b)orderlands, 21; Chicana, 28–29; confrontational, 134–39; definition of, 12–14; as epistemic art, 13, 207; feminationalist, 165–93; feminist, 11,

16, 44; historical intersections, 101–2; managerial, 134–36; *mestiza*, 14, 21–22, 31, 49–51, 100–101, 119–20, 134–37, 153–54, 157–58, 208–9; of Mexican women, 52–58; nationalist, 174; of oppression, 172; *pleito*, 133–39; political feminist, 171–78; of reason, 173; revolutionary, 132–60; rhetorical acts, 13–14; rhetorical listening, 52–53, 57; types in social movements, 134–35; of vision, 174. See also *mestiza* rhetoric
Riva Palacio, Vicente, 74
Rivera, Diego, 44
Robles, Martha, 35–36
Rodríguez González, Ramona, 55–56
Rojas Álvarez, Lourdes, 13
"Romance," 86
Romano, Susan, 29
Royster, Jacqueline Jones, 10, 57, 100
Rubin, Luis C., 26
Rubio de Díaz, Carmen Romero, 76–77

Salomón Meraz, Liliana, 223n3
Sanches, Regina, 126
Sánchez Hernández, Francisco Xavier, 37, 42–43
Sarabia, Juan, 97
Schopenhauer, Arthur, 166, 183
Secretaría de Educación Pública (SEP), 152–53, 155–56
La Semana de las Señoritas Mejicanas, 25, 66
Seneca Falls Declaration of Sentiments, 110–11
La Señora de Tula, 41, 81–82
SEP. *See* Secretaría de Educación Pública
Serrano Migallón, Fernando, 109–10
Sesto, Julio, 33, 64
La Siempreviva, 24
Sierra, Justo, 23–24, 44, 47, 74, 174–75, 215n55
Socialismo Mexicano, 145
soldaderas, 149
Sosa, Francisco, 85–86
Spaniards, 18
"La Srita. Galindo opina sobre su candidatura para diputado," 178
Stanton, Elizabeth Cady, 111
strategic terms of engagement, 11
Swearingen, Jan, 50

Tecuiloatzin, 83
Teocal-li, 156
Tepanecas, 83
Tepatl-Xuchitl, 83
Texcoc, 83–84
Texcocanos, 83
Tezozomoc, Fernando Alvarado, 82
theoretical directions, 33–58
Tlaltelolco Indians, 29
Tlaxcala Indians, 42
Todos los gatos son pardos, 38
Tolquequetzaltzin, 83
Tonantzin/Guadalupe, 42
Toque de Atención al Ejército Nacional, 158
Torres, Mariano de Jesus, 26
Tozcuentzin, 83–84
Tuñón Pablos, Esperanza, 9, 111
Tuñón Pablos, Julia, 9, 18

El Universal, 178

Vasconcelos, José, 14–15, 21, 133, 136, 152, 174–75, 208; *La raza cósmica*, 44, 46–47, 152
Vaughan, Mary K., 9–10, 23
La Venerable Francisca de San José del Tercer Orden de Santo Domingo, 86
verbal protest, 134
Vésper: Justicia y Libertad, 3–6, 20, 132, 138–39, 142–49, 159, 228n28; "Contra todos los tiranos y contra todas las tiranías," 146–47; "Don Francisco I. Madero, candidato a la presidencia de la República," 145–46; greetings to *La Bandera Roja*, 120; prohibition against, 142; reinitiation of, 145–47; "*Vésper* Siempre Ocupará Su Puesto," 4–6, 161–64
"*Vésper* Siempre Ocupará Su Puesto," 4–6, 161–64
Vicario, María Leona, 86–87
Vicario de Quintana Roo, Leona, 22–23
Vidas de religiosas ejemplares, 84–85
Villa, Pancho, 149
Villistas, 179
Violetas del Anáhuac: periódico Literario Redactado por Señoras, 30, 60–66, 69–74, 87–88, 207, 220n7, 223n76; "Charada," 76; "Cuauhtémoc," 76; "La ilustración y la educación de la mujer," 73; "Impresiones

de la prensa" section, 78; literal and literary beginnings, 74–78; "La mujer," 76; "Mujeres de nuestra época," 73–74, 79–80; "La oración matinal," 76; "Poesía," 76–77; "Saludo y prospecto," 89–93
la virgin, 42–43
vision: revisionist history, 41–42; rhetoric of, 174
voting rights, 110–11, 148, 169, 177–78, 219n82
El Voto, 148
La Voz de Juárez, 142
La Voz de la Mujer 144

wars (Mexico): War of Independence, 22–23; War of the Reform, 101
Wilson, Woodrow, 180, 189, 233n40
wizards of progress, 64
women: abuse against, 230n76; activism, 22–28; as *ángel del hogar*, 7–8, 64–65, 177; citizenship of, 39, 47, 233n34; definition of, 65–66, 111; early attempts at claiming a voice, 66–69; education of, 22–28, 111; future directions for, 210–11; as journalists, 15, 59–88; Mexican, 17–22, 52–58, 66–69; in Mexican Revolution, 229n74; as mothers, 111; in nineteenth-century Mexico, 22–28; *puesto público* for, 167–68; rhetoric of, 52–58; rhetors, 17–22; sexual understanding for, 183–84; and suffrage, 110–11, 148, 169, 177–78, 219n82; writers, 25. See also *mujeres intelectuales*; *soldaderas*
Women in the Past, Present, and Future (Bebel), 168
Women's Loyal National League, 111
Women's School of Arts and Vocations, 67
World's Fair: Chicago (1883), 79; Paris (1889), 79
Wright de Kleinhans, Laureana, 6–9, 17–19, 30, 33, 44, 59–88, 61*f*, 190; background and education, 17, 70–71, 209–10; death, 30; "Dios" (God), 64; *Educación errónea de la mujer y medios prácticos para correjirla*, 60; *La emancipación de la mujer por medio del estudio*, 19, 51, 60, 87, 234n53; "Huérfana", 64; key attempt, 54; *Mujeres notables mexicanas*, 20, 51, 61*f*, 62, 64, 80–87; poetry, 64; as "la primera poetisa mexicana", 65; as public intellectual, 62, 64–65, 69–70; rhetorical approach, 62, 70–73, 87–88, 136, 207, 209–10; "Saludo y prospecto", 89–93; time period, 205, 207
Wright de Kleinhans, Margarita, 60

Xochiquetzal, 156
Xóchitl, 41
Xuihtzaltzin, 27

Yermo de Yermo, María Josefa, 86
Yucatán, 24, 67; Feminist Congresses (1916), 180–88

Zacancozcatl, 83
zambo (term), 221n37
Zapata, Emiliano, 149, 230n76
Zapatistas, 149, 179
Zaragoza, Ignacio (pseudonym), 103–4, 111; "La mujer se emancipa de las opresoras cadenas de clericalismo," 96, 112, 224n5; "Nuestra obra debe ser emancipar a la mujer del clericalismo," 103
Zarco, Francisco, 63–64, 66, 138
Zavala, Consuelo, 182, 186
Zicuetzin, 83
Zitácuaro women. *See* Las Mujeres de Zitácuaro

About the Author

Cristina Devereaux Ramírez is an assistant professor at the University of Arizona and has traveled extensively throughout Mexico conducting in-depth studies in various archives. Her investigative interests include feminist rhetorics, archival research, and Mexican culture.